# Conflict Management in Divided Societies

This exciting and innovative new textbook takes a multi-perspective approach to the study of conflict management in divided societies.

Offering a wide range of perspectives from leading experts in the field, the book examines the philosophies underpinning constitutional design, the actors and processes involved and the practicalities of the settlement process, combining conceptual and theoretical contributions with empirical case studies. In so doing, the contributors provide a comprehensive introduction to the study of conflict management in divided societies.

Features and benefits of the textbook:

- clearly explains the theories underpinning constitutional design, including power sharing, centripetalism, power dividing and territorial self-governance;
- surveys the key actors and processes involved in designing and implementing peace settlements, including the evolution of diplomacy in peacemaking, with separate chapters on crafting solutions for divided societies from the perspectives of the UN, EU, AU and NGOs;
- explores the realities on the ground, with chapters written by specialists drawing on their experience of working in conflict zones.

Written in a clear and engaging style, this book is essential reading for all students of conflict management.

**Stefan Wolff** is Professor of International Security at the University of Birmingham, UK.

**Christalla Yakinthou** is Country Manager of the International Center for Transitional Justice's Cyprus Program and Honorary Research Fellow in the department of Political Science, University of Western Australia.

# Conflict Management in Divided Societies

Theories and practice

Edited by
Stefan Wolff and Christalla Yakinthou

Routledge
Taylor & Francis Group

LONDON AND NEW YORK

First published 2012 by Routledge
2 Park Square, Milton Park, Abingdon, Oxon, OX14 4RN

Simultaneously published in the USA and Canada
by Routledge
711 Third Avenue, New York, NY 10017

*Routledge is an imprint of the Taylor & Francis Group, an informa business*

*British Library Cataloguing in Publication Data*
A catalogue record for this book is available from the British Library

*Library of Congress Cataloging in Publication Data*
Conflict management in divided societies : theories and practice / edited by Stefan Wolff & Christalla Yakinthou.
    p. cm.
Includes bibliographical references and index.
1. Conflict management – Philosophy. 2. Conflict management – Methodology. 3. Conflict management – Case studies. 4. Ethnic conflict – Prevention – Case studies. 5. Divided government. I. Wolff, Stefan, 1969– II. Yakinthou, Christalla, 1980–
JZ6368.C65 2011
303.6'9 – dc22                                                              2011013052

ISBN: 978-0-415-56373-4 (hbk)
ISBN: 978-0-415-56374-1 (pbk)
ISBN: 978-0-203-80300-4 (ebk)

Typeset in Sabon by Taylor & Francis

# Contents

# Tables

# Contributors

**John Akokpari** holds a doctorate from Dalhousie University, Nova Scotia, Canada. He has taught and researched in Dalhousie University, St. Mary's University (both in Canada), the University of Lesotho and is currently Senior Lecturer in the Department of Political Studies at the University of Cape Town, South Africa. He was a Visiting Research Fellow at the Institute of Developing Economies at Chiba, Japan, between January and June 2007. Akokpari has published widely on a variety of topics on African politics, including civil society, democratisation, development, foreign policy, globalisation, international migration, conflicts, regionalism, conflict management and the environment.

**Janine Natalya Clark** is a lecturer in International Politics and Ethnic Conflict in the Politics Department at the University of Sheffield. She received her PhD in 2006 from the University of Nottingham and was subsequently a Postdoctoral Research Fellow in the International Politics Department at Aberystwyth University (2006–2009). Before joining the University of Sheffield, she held lecturing posts at the University of York and Queen's University of Belfast. Her research interests include post-conflict societies, particularly in the former Yugoslavia and the African Great Lakes; conflict resolution; war crimes; transitional justice and the relationship between criminal trials and inter-ethnic reconciliation. Clark is the author of *Serbia in the Shadow of Milošević: The Legacy of Conflict in the Balkans* (I.B. Tauris, 2008), and recent work includes: 'Justice, Peace and the International Criminal Court: Limitations and Possibilities', *Journal of International Criminal Justice* (2011); 'UN Peacekeeping in the Democratic Republic of Congo: Reflections on MONUSCO and Its Contradictory Mandate', *Journal of International Peacekeeping* (2011); 'Transitional Justice, Truth and Reconciliation: An Under-Explored Relationship', *International Criminal Law Review* (2011) and 'Missing Persons, Reconciliation and the View from Below: A Case-Study of Bosnia-Herzegovina', *Southeast European and Black Sea Studies* (2010).

**Craig Collins** is Coordinator of the Initiative on Quiet Diplomacy (IQd), which seeks to address the causes of conflict by developing institutions within inter-governmental organizations, by providing key actors with tools and techniques to address recurring issues, and supporting and facilitating dialogue and mediation processes. In his work with IQd since its inception in 2004, Collins has engaged representatives of governments, regional and other IGOs, and conflict parties to build effective inter-governmental conflict prevention mechanisms, effectively employ a quiet, problem-solving approach to working with parties, and promote the meaningful participation of women and marginalized groups. Among other experience in this field, Collins has contributed to official and non-official processes in the Middle East, South Asia and the Pacific Islands; advised IGOs, governments and NGOs; and advocated policy change and early action. He has also worked for the UNDP to develop Pacific regional capacities for preventive diplomacy. Collins has specialized in the structures, mandates and conflict prevention practice of IGOs, and in the relationship between human rights protection, good governance and conflict management. He holds a Master's of Law and Diplomacy from The Fletcher School of Law and Diplomacy.

**Adrian Guelke** is Professor of Comparative Politics and Director of the Centre for the Study of Ethnic Conflict in the School of Politics, International Studies and Philosophy at Queen's University, Belfast. Recent publications include *The New Age of Terrorism and the International Political System* (IB Tauris, 2009), *Terrorism and Global Disorder* (IB Tauris, 2006) and *Rethinking the Rise and Fall of Apartheid* (Palgrave Macmillan, 2005), as well as the co-edited second edition of *A Farewell to Arms?* (Manchester University Press, 2006) on the Northern Ireland peace process. Studies he has edited in the field of politics and ethnicity include *The Challenges of Ethno-Nationalism* (Palgrave Macmillan, 2010) and *Democracy and Ethnic Conflict* (Palgrave Macmillan, 2004). He is the chair of the International Political Science Association's research committee on politics and ethnicity, as well as the editor of the journal *Nationalism and Ethnic Politics*.

**Anoulak Kittikhoun** is a political affairs officer at the UN Department of Political Affairs in New York. Previously, he was Research Associate at the Ralph Bunche Institute for International Studies, Adjunct Professor at Brooklyn College, and Adviser at the Permanent Mission of Laos to the UN. He received his PhD in political science from The City University of New York Graduate Center. He was the co-editor, with Thomas G. Weiss, of the March 2011 special issue of the International Studies Review on 'Theory vs. Practice', bringing together leading scholars and practitioners to explore issues such as regionalism, rising powers, disarmament, fragile states, responsibility to protect, sanctions, human rights, development, environment and financial governance.

**Virginie Ladisch** leads the International Center for Transitional Justice's work on children and transitional justice, as well as the country program in Cyprus. From the time she joined ICTJ in 2006 until 2009, Ladisch worked as part of the Reparative Justice Unit, and with the Canada and Turkey country programs. Prior to joining ICTJ, she conducted research on reconciliation in Cyprus, was the Project Coordinator at the Crimes of War Education Project and served as an election monitor in Guatemala. In 2000, Ladisch was awarded a Thomas J. Watson Fellowship for independent research, during which she carried out extensive fieldwork on truth commissions and reconciliation in South Africa and Guatemala. The results of her research on the challenges of reconciliation in Cyprus have been published in the Journal of Public and International Affairs and the Cyprus Review. Ladisch holds an MA in International Affairs from the School of International and Public Affairs (SIPA) at Columbia University and a BA in Political Science from Haverford College.

**John Packer** is Professor of International Law and the Director of the Human Rights Centre at the University of Essex. Before taking up this post in 2007, he was the project coordinator and principal investigator for the Initiative on Quiet Diplomacy, as well as acting as a consultant to several international organizations, governments and NGOs. He was Director of the Office of the OSCE High Commissioner on National Minorities from 2000 to 2004, where he previously served as legal advisor (1995–2000). From 1991 to 1995 he was a human rights officer at the United Nations, where he investigated serious violations of human rights in Iraq, Burma and Afghanistan. He has also worked for the International Labour Organisation and the UN High Commissioner for Refugees. Packer has an extensive publication record and is an internationally recognized expert in the field of minority rights and conflict prevention. He is a member of a number of editorial boards of scholarly journals, including the *Human Rights Law Journal*, the *International Journal on Minority and Group Rights*, the *European Yearbook of Minority Issues* and *Ethnopolitics*. He also sits on the Boards of a number of NGOs and is an Advisor to the Club de Madrid.

**Katia Papagianni** heads the Mediation Support Programme at the Geneva-based Centre for Humanitarian Dialogue. Before joining the Centre, she worked for the Office of the UN High Commissioner for Human Rights and UNDP. Her work has focused on political transitions, power-sharing in mediation efforts and constitution-making processes. Her experience includes work for the National Democratic Institute in Russia, the OSCE in Bosnia and Herzegovina and the UN in Iraq. She holds a doctorate in political science from Columbia University, New York; a Master's degree in Public Administration from Princeton University; and a Bachelor's degree from Brown University. She has taught on peace- and state-building at Columbia University and the Geneva Graduate Institute for International Studies. She has published extensively on mediation and peacebuilding.

**Benjamin Reilly** is Professor of Political Science in the Crawford School of Economics and Government at the Australian National University. He is the author of six books and over 60 journal articles and book chapters on issues of democratization, constitutional reform, party politics, electoral system design and conflict management, and has advised numerous governments and international organizations on these subjects. His latest books are a study of democratization and political reform in Asia and the Pacific, *Democracy and Diversity: Political Engineering in the Asia-Pacific* (Oxford University Press, 2006), and an edited volume, *Political Parties in Conflict-Prone Societies* (United Nations University Press, 2008). He is currently a Visiting Professor at Johns Hopkins University's School of Advanced International Studies (SAIS) in Washington, DC.

**Philip G. Roeder** is Professor of Political Science at the University of California, San Diego. He received his PhD from Harvard University. A specialist on the politics of the Soviet successor states and on nationalism, Roeder is the author of *Where Nation-States Come From: Institutional Change in the Age of Nationalism* (Princeton University Press) and *Red Sunset: The Failure of Soviet Politics* (Princeton University Press). He is the co-author of *Postcommunism and the Theory of Democracy* (Princeton University Press) and co-editor of *Sustainable Peace: Power and Democracy After Civil Wars* (Cornell University Press). His articles have appeared in such journals as the *American Political Science Review*, *World Politics* and *International Studies Quarterly*. He is currently working on two longer-term projects on 'Nationalist Secessionism and Independence' (i.e., when is granting secessionists independence the best policy option) and on 'Alternatives to Independence' (i.e., what are the consequences of various institutional arrangements designed to avoid granting independence to secessionists).

**Álvaro de Soto,** a Peruvian diplomat, participated in a number of conflict management efforts in his 25-year career as a senior United Nations official. Among these he mediated the 1990–1 negotiations that brought an end of the war in El Salvador, led the comprehensive attempt from late 1999 to April 2004 to solve the Cyprus problem and was the chief envoy for the Arab–Israeli conflict from 2005 to 2007. He is a member of the Global Leadership Foundation, a Senior Fellow at the Ralph Bunche Institute, an Associate Fellow at the Geneva Centre for Security Policy and a visiting professor at the Paris School of International Affairs at Sciences Po.

**Nathalie Tocci** is Deputy Director of the Istituto Affari Internazionali and Associate Editor of *The International Spectator*. She received her PhD in International Relations from the LSE in 2003. She was a Research Fellow at the Centre for European Policy Studies in Brussels (1999–2003), a Jean Monnet and Marie Curie Fellow at the European University Institute in Florence (2003–7) and a Senior Fellow at the Transatlantic Academy in Washington (2009–10). Her research interests include European foreign policy, conflict resolution and the European neighbourhood, with a particular focus on Turkey, Cyprus, the Mediterranean, the Middle East and the South Caucasus. Tocci is the winner of the 2008 Anna Lindh award for the study of European foreign policy. Her major publications include *Turkey's European Future: Behind the Scenes of America's Influence on EU–Turkey Relations* (2011); *The European Union, Civil Society and Conflict* (2011); *Cyprus: A Conflict at the Crossroads* (2009); *The EU and Conflict Resolution: Promoting Peace in the Backyard* (2008); and *EU Accession Dynamics and Conflict Resolution: Catalyzing Peace or Consolidating Partition in Cyprus?* (2004).

**Thomas G. Weiss** is Presidential Professor of Political Science at The CUNY Graduate Center and Director of the Ralph Bunche Institute for International Studies. He directed the United Nations Intellectual History Project (1999–2010) and was President of the International Studies Association (2009–10), Chair of the Academic Council on the UN System (2006–9), editor of Global Governance, Research Director of the International Commission on Intervention and State Sovereignty, Research Professor at Brown University's Watson Institute for International Studies, Executive Director of the Academic Council on the UN System and of the International Peace Academy, a member of the UN secretariat and a consultant to several public and private agencies. He has authored or edited some 40 books and 175 articles and book chapters about multilateral approaches to international peace and security, humanitarian action and sustainable development. His latest authored volumes are: *What's Wrong with the United Nations and How to Fix It* (2009); *UN Ideas That Changed the World* (2009); *Global Governance and the UN: An Unfinished Journey* (2010); and *Humanitarianism Contested: Where Angels Fear to Tread* (2011).

**Marc Weller** is Professor of International Law and International Constitutional Studies at the University of Cambridge, Director of the Lauterpacht Centre for International Law and a Fellow of Hughes Hall. He has authored, edited or co-edited some 20 books, including most recently *Iraq and the Use of Force in International Law* (OUP 2010), *Political Participation of Minorities* (Oxford University Press, 2010), *Contested Statehood* (Oxford University Press, 2009), *Escaping the Self-determination*

*Trap* (Nijhoff, 2008), *Peace Lost* (Nijhoff 2008), *Settling Self-determination Disputes through Complex Power-sharing* (Nijhoff 2008), and *Universal Minority Rights* (OUP, 2007). In addition to his academic interests, Professor Weller has been active as legal advisor to governments and international organizations and as counsel in international litigation. He has also been involved in a number of international peace negotiations and has advised in many instances on post-conflict constitution-making and state-building. He has served as consultant to the United Nations, as legal expert to the African Union and as expert consultant for the Council of Europe.

**Stefan Wolff** is Professor of International Security at the University of Birmingham. He is a specialist in contemporary security challenges and has extensively written on ethnic conflict, international conflict management and state-building. Among his 15 books to date are *Ethnic Conflict: A Global Perspective* (Oxford University Press 2006, 2nd ed. 2007) and the *Routledge Handbook of Ethnic Conflict* (2010, with Karl Cordell). Wolff is the founding editor of the journal *Ethnopolitics* and an associate editor of *Civil Wars*. Wolff is a graduate of the University of Leipzig, the University of Cambridge and the London School of Economics and Political Science.

**Christalla Yakinthou** is Country Manager (Cyprus) at the International Center for Transitional Justice, co-founder of the Bluestocking Institute for Global Peace and Justice and a Senior Honorary Research Fellow at the University of Western Australia. Prior to joining ICTJ, she taught at Notre Dame University and the University of Western Australia and consulted for a number of government and non-government organisations. Her areas of research interest include the protection of human rights in Europe, political design for conflict societies, power-sharing, and the role of ethnic conflict and historical memory in political architecture. She holds a PhD in Political Science and International Relations from the University of Western Australia and a Masters-equivalent diploma in European Public Law from the National and Kapodistrian University of Athens (Academy of European Public Law).

**I. William Zartman** has served as the Jacob Blaustein Professor of International Organizations and Conflict Resolution at the School of Advanced International Studies at Johns Hopkins University for nearly 20 years, during which he also directed the School's Conflict Management and African Studies programs. Previously, Zartman was Olin Professor at the U.S. Naval Academy, Halevy Professor at the Institute of Political Studies in Paris and a visiting professor at the American University in Cairo. Among his numerous publications are *International Cooperation: The Extents and Limits of Multilateralism* (2010); *Peacemaking in International Conflict: Methods and Techniques* (2007); *Cowardly Lions: Missed Opportunities to Prevent Deadly Conflict and State Collapse* (2005); *Peace Versus Justice: Negotiating Forward- and Backward-Looking Outcomes* (2005); *Rethinking the Economics of War: The Intersection of Need, Creed and Greed* (2005); *Preventive Negotiation: Avoiding Conflict Escalation* (2001); *Power and Negotiation* (2000); *Collapsed States* (1995); *Elusive Peace* (1995) and *Ripe for Resolution: Conflict and Intervention in Africa* (1985). Zartman is a frequent consultant to governments and international organizations. He holds a PhD in international relations from Yale University and received an honorary doctorate from the Catholic University of Louvain.

# Foreword

*Álvaro de Soto*

Javier Pérez de Cuéllar, the fifth UN Secretary-General, told me – more than once – that every morning before leaving his house he would place a bag of ice on his head as a prophylactic measure to ward off intrusive emotions. Assuming this was a metaphor, what I found most revealing was the tacit admission, by a world-class master of unflappability, that keeping his emotions in check required discipline and self-control. He could have fooled me.

No matter how disciplined they are, those who work to solve conflicts or manage crises do not operate in laboratory conditions, but in a human context of confrontation and violence, actual or contained. In the fast-moving heat of on-the-run policy formulation, adrenalin flows, passions develop and emotions are formed. Their recollections will be shaped by personal experience and perspective that is unavoidably coloured by those passions and emotions.

In my quarter-century at the UN under three secretaries-general, much of it dealing with conflict, I have worked on a number of crises. I was sometimes in charge, in other cases I was a supervisor, in yet others I was part of a policymaking team. Three of the five cases discussed in *Conflict Management in Divided Societies: Theories and Practice* were among them.

This has proved to be something of a trial in the current circumstances: as a practitioner, I was involved in how those crises were handled. The editors of this book knew full well that this internalized turmoil was part and parcel of my work. And yet they asked me to write this Foreword. Other readers, however, may not know this, and I do not wish to mislead them.

Reader, therefore, please note: in penning this, I have had to exercise some significant restraint. My version of Pérez de Cuéllar's prophylactic bag of ice has consisted of staying away from most of the book, reading only the – I hasten to say – lucid and pithy Introduction written by the editors Christalla Yakinthou and Stefan Wolff. I studiously avoided taking up the offer to read the rest of the book in either draft or final form. I therefore find myself in the position of being both writer of this Foreword and prospective reader of the book; albeit a reader who looks forward to the publication of the book with unusual anticipation.

Thus I find myself in the odd predicament of writing without having read, for example, Chapter 13 on Cyprus, in which Christalla Yakinthou considers the 'Annan plan' for Cyprus. That document – all five versions of it – was one in which I am proud to have played a role. Yakinthou contends that the document 'significantly increased [inter- and intra-communal] tension'. Since the very purpose of the 'Annan plan' was to help to bring to an end that kind of tension, my reaction to this was somewhat reserved. If one day I must take issue with Yakinthou's (perhaps unintended) conclusion – which I doubt, knowing her to be extremely persuasive – it will be in another forum.

My quarter-century at the UN witnessed much: from the depths of the Cold War to the fall of the Berlin Wall – with the vast opportunities, breakthroughs and achievements that accompanied and followed it; the horrors of what occurred in the first half of the 1990s in the former Yugoslavia, Somalia and Rwanda; the attacks of 9/11 at the dawn of the new millennium and the 'global war on terror' in its aftermath. The Introduction to this book thus resonates with piercing clarity. It transports me back in time, first to the giddy early weeks of 1992, when the UN seemed at last to be coming into its own.

The heads of government at the Security Council's first summit on 31 January 1992 – a kind of policymakers' Olympus one might say – met on the heels of the unparalleled flurry of diplomatic achievements of the last three and a half years of Pérez de Cuéllar's decade in office. With Pérez de Cuéllar in the lead, or the UN as a framework, long-standing thorny issues had been successfully tackled: Soviet troops had left Afghanistan; the wars in Cambodia, Angola, Mozambique, El Salvador and between Iran and Iraq had ended; the long-postponed independence of Namibia had been achieved; a promising ceasefire had been established and a self-determination process been launched in Western Sahara; the Contra War in Nicaragua had come to an end; and negotiations had started to end the violence in Guatemala. It was a time of great hope; the 15 leaders can be forgiven for having issued a statement that bordered on hubris.

They asked Boutros Boutros-Ghali, the new Secretary-General, for his recommendations on how to improve the capacity of the UN for preventive diplomacy, peacemaking and peacekeeping. *An Agenda for Peace*, the resulting report, contained an array of ideas, some new, some mined from the past, others repackaged. But there was a recurring theme: in coming years the UN's agenda would be dominated by internal conflict. This was a sobering thought given that this was not what the founders had anticipated when they designed the UN at the end of the Second World War.

Boutros-Ghali's insight led him to a corollary: whereas after interstate war, armies return to their territories, following internal conflict, former combatants must find ways to coexist in the same geographical space. As I. William Zartman puts it (in Chapter 4): 'when the parties end an internal conflict, they are under deep internal strains and have to construct new relations within the political system'. 'Essentially', the editors tell us (in their Introduction), 'the question that emerges is then how to build sustainable peace and democratic governance in divided societies ravaged by conflict'.

Thus, in addition to preventive diplomacy, peacemaking and peacekeeping, on which he had been asked to make recommendations, Boutros-Ghali added an issue of his own, which he placed at the same level. He called it 'post-conflict peace-building'. No one can accuse him of having coined a term designed to trip lightly off the tongue. But it was clear enough to launch a thousand international civil servants – at the UN, its programmes and specialized agencies, as well as the Bretton Woods institutions – into an epic, take-no-prisoners turf war which, notwithstanding the creation of the UN Peace-building Commission at the 2005 World Summit, in some ways rages to this day. Boutros-Ghali was not wrong in his assessment: making sure that peace is sustainable is proving to be a major challenge of our time – one with which the organized international community has yet to come to terms in a coherent way.

In managing conflict within states, Yakinthou and Wolff note 'the challenges inherent in creating a plan that is workable in the long term, rather than one that is just immediately acceptable to the parties'. It follows that such planning must take place as an integral part of negotiating a peace agreement, rather than await the silencing of the guns.

The need to create, reinforce or reform institutions so that future disputes can be addressed peacefully must be stressed. As Philip Roeder puts it (in Chapter 3): 'institutional design should not only address the issue of ending a current conflict that may have already become intense, but should seek to shape politics in future years in ways that avoid escalation or re-escalation of conflict to such intensity'. Virginie Ladisch, author of the Guatemala case study (Chapter 11), raises an apposite warning in relation to 'overly vague accords that do not include a firm implementation schedule and verification structure'. Often, however, international involvement in the aftermath of internal conflict is more intrusive and prolonged than is politically acceptable – both to the international community and the country concerned – over time.

Despite the narrowing of mediation space brought about by the 'global war on terror' that followed the 9/11 attacks, and which has resulted in the quarantining of groups and organizations whose cooperation is indispensable to ending certain conflicts, we are witnessing, in recent years, what appears to be an inexhaustible supply of actors attracted to conflict management in far-flung corners of the globe. Not long ago an envoy of the Secretary-General in an African conflict counted a dozen simultaneous such efforts that immensely complicated his task. It is hard to see how this can contribute positively to the search for peace.

The proliferation of would-be mediators may perhaps be explained, at least in part, by the widespread misapprehension – notwithstanding the challenges that I have referred to above – that peacemaking is essentially low-tech work. Some politicians may be drawn by the glamour of peacemaking. The fact that it entails painstaking, open-ended work with frequently elusive and reluctant warring parties, and that it rarely leads to Hollywood-like happy endings, takes a while to digest in the comfort of distant capitals.

Yakinthou and Wolff clearly see the limitations inherent in this trend, observing that 'international actors in conflict management remain constrained … because they frequently compete over, rather than share information [and] mistrust each other's motivations and long-term strategic interests'. I remain deeply sceptical that even a coherent and well-coordinated multi-actor conflict management effort can be positive. Rather, my inclinations are less tolerant and I continue to adhere to the key principle of the Pérez de Cuéllar school of peacemaking: the unity and integrity of the mediation effort are crucial to its success. Parties to conflict invariably excel at playing one would-be mediator off against another. Cross-cutting traffic of well-meaning peacemakers is not self-organizing; the magic hand of the market can't work miracles; indeed it can discourage them. I am particularly wary of collective efforts where actors of different types attempt to work together: on balance, my view is that, in the field of conflict management, additions subtract, and collective diplomacy is by and large a contradiction in terms.

This is a growing challenge for the organization of human affairs, rendered more complex by the shift from state-centred to human-centred approaches to conflict management and resolution – and the consequent increase in the levels and types of actors involved.

*Conflict Management in Divided Societies* reminds us of many of these challenges and sets out the options clearly and systematically. At the same time, it refrains from insisting that the choice is easy or indeed that there is only one way to go. In fact, the editors are scrupulously modest about what they seek. It is 'to provide the space for the engagement among different experts' regarding different approaches to conflict management in divided societies. They go out of their way to emphasize – though it should go without saying – that they do *not* seek to establish a one-size-fits-all approach.

They are equally restrained and understated about what they have achieved. They confess that their empirical basis for generalization is too small to be authoritative, so they 'can only draw some tentative conclusions at this stage, pending further more sustained comparative research'. What they can confidently do, they tell the reader, 'is point to, and illustrate the conditions under which conflict management can achieve and sustain peace in divided societies'.

Policymakers, of course, view academics as hopelessly ivory-tower-bound creatures with little experience or understanding of the real world or, more to the point, of the work of practitioners such as themselves. Surely a practitioner dreamed up the well-worn joke in which a political scientist, in reaction to a practitioner's successful achievement, responds, 'that's all very well, but will it work in *theory?*' Academics, for their part, are intellectually contemptuous of policymakers and other practitioners, whom they see as ignorant bunglers who should seek advice from properly educated people.

Are these caricatures? Unquestionably. But the point about caricatures, in fact what amuses us about them (or hurts, as the case may be), is that they highlight a kernel of truth or a salient feature out of context, and exaggerate or distort it so as to produce a portrait that is instantly recognizable.

Political scientists and conflict management policymakers and brokers are, of course, distinct communities. Each has its discrete methods, standards and jargon. They may be forever fated to find it difficult to communicate. This is a pity, because academics such as the contributors to this volume can help practitioners to understand where they went wrong, what they could do better, whether a correct course is still possible or, if not, how they might proceed from there. There will always be an acute need for this because the ability to draw lessons on his or her own is rarely part of a practitioner's skill set.

In this regard I have a final announcement to make: if the refreshingly readable Introduction to *Conflict Management in Divided Societies* is any indication of the quality of the book's subsequent chapters, and the harbinger of a new trend, let the word go out that the communication gap may be narrowing. As a practitioner with an ear attuned to changes in context, I sense the possibility, clear and imminent, that this book may indeed be read, and actually used, not only by policymakers, but also by genuine flesh-and-blood practitioners of the conflict management and resolution trade. Would that it were so: I commend it to them.

Looking back at a 25-year career at the UN dealing with a variety of conflict management and conflict resolution challenges, involving a significant degree of improvisation, including in divided societies, I don't mind saying that such a book would have been of considerable help. May it assist those who follow, be they international civil servants or envoys, governmental representatives or NGOs (but, please, not all at the same time or, God forbid, collectively).

Istanbul
June 2011

# Acknowledgements

There are many people to whom we are indebted for having helped to bring this project to fruition. Starting from a merely notional idea that there has been for too long something of a disconnect between theories and practice of conflict management in divided societies, we were exceptionally privileged to have as contributors to this book a collection of remarkable scholars who shared this perception and our aspiration to begin to bridge this gap. Not only have our contributors presented us with reflective chapters that are valuable as individual pieces of analysis, but they have also been willing to engage with each other's work to help us to build this volume, which as a whole transcends the sum of all individual contributions. Above all, we want to thank our colleagues – their goodwill and enthusiasm for this project has made it a pleasure to develop.

While most edited volumes are the result of conference proceedings, our project has profited from the reverse. We had the opportunity to discuss first drafts of most of the chapters at a workshop at the 2010 annual conference of the International Studies Association in New Orleans. We are grateful to the ISA for supporting us with a Catalytic Research Workshop Grant and to the Economic and Social Research Council of the UK. This workshop was instrumental in facilitating a comprehensive exchange of ideas among the participants and played a critical role in the book's evolution. Our contributors took time out of their busy schedules, and sacrificed a New Orleans Mardi Gras to share their chapters, and we believe that the book is a much better product for it.

Last but by no means least, we would also like to express our thanks and appreciation to Craig Fowlie, Nicola Parkin and Lindsey Hall at Routledge for facilitating the publication process with such grace and professionalism.

Stefan Wolff and Christalla Yakinthou
Birmingham and Nicosia
July 2011

# Abbreviations

| | |
|---|---|
| AA | association agreement |
| ACP | African, Caribbean and Pacific Group of States |
| AMIB | AU Mission in Burundi |
| AMIS | AU Mission in Sudan |
| AMISOM | AU Mission in Somalia |
| AMU | Arab–Maghreb Union |
| ANC | African National Congress |
| AP | action plan |
| ARF | ASEAN Regional Forum |
| ARS | Alliance for the Re-Liberation of Somalia |
| ASEAN | Association of Southeast Asian Nations |
| ASF | African Standby Force |
| AU | African Union |
| AV | alternative vote |
| BBTG | broad-based transitional government |
| CARDS | Community Assistance for Reconstruction, Development and Stabilization |
| CDG | Chicken Dilemma Game |
| CDR | Comité pour la Défense de la République |
| CEH | Comisión para el Esclarecimiento Histórico |
| CEWS | Continental Early Warning System |
| CFSP | Common Foreign and Security Policy |
| CMCA | Commission of Mediation, Conciliation and Arbitration |
| CMI | conflict management initiative |
| CNDD–FDD | Conseil National pour la Défense de la Démocratie–Forces de la Démocratie |
| CSDP | Common Security and Defence Policy |
| DDRRR | demobilization, disarmament, repatriation, resettlement and reintegration |
| DFS | Department of Field Support |
| DOP | Declaration of Principles |
| DPA | Department of Political Affairs |
| DPKO | Department of Peacekeeping Operations |
| DRC | Democratic Republic of the Congo |
| DUP | Democratic Unionist Party |
| EAC | East African Community |
| EC | European Commission; European Community |
| ECCAS | Economic Community of Central African States |

| | |
|---|---|
| ECOMOG | Economic Community of West African States Monitoring Group |
| ECOWAS | Economic Community of West African States |
| EDF | European Development Fund |
| EEC | European Economic Community |
| EIDHR | European Initiative for Democracy and Human Rights |
| ENP | European Neighbourhood Policy |
| ENPI | European Neighbourhood and Partnership Instrument |
| EU | European Union |
| FNL | Forces for National Liberation |
| FRG | Frente Republicano Guatemalteco |
| GA | General Assembly |
| GDP | gross domestic product |
| HCNM | High Commissioner on National Minorities |
| HSG | heads of states and government |
| ICC | International Criminal Court |
| ICISS | International Commission on Intervention and State Sovereignty |
| ICTR | International Criminal Tribunal for Rwanda |
| ICTY | International Criminal Tribunal for the former Yugoslavia |
| ICU | Islamic Courts Union |
| IDP | internally displaced person |
| IEC | Independent Electoral Commission |
| IFI | international financial institution |
| IfS | Instrument for Stability |
| IGAD | Intergovernmental Authority on Development |
| IGO | intergovernmental organization |
| IRA | Irish Republican Army |
| JEM | Justice and Equality Movement |
| KLA | Kosovo Liberation Army |
| MAD | mutual assured destruction |
| MDR | Mouvement Démocratique Républicain |
| MILF | Moro Islamic Liberation Front |
| MINUGUA | UN Verification Mission in Guatemala |
| MONUC | Mission of the UN in Congo |
| MPCI | Patriotic Movement of the Ivory Coast |
| MPIGO | Popular Movement of Ivory Coast's Far West |
| MRND | Mouvement Révolutionnaire National pour le Développement |
| MSC | Military Staff Committee |
| NATO | North Atlantic Treaty Organization |
| NF | New Force |
| NGO | non-governmental organization |
| NI | Northern Ireland |
| NURC | National Unity and Reconciliation Commission |
| OAU | Organisation of African Unity |
| OCHA | Office for the Coordination of Humanitarian Affairs |
| OFMDFM | Office of First Minister and Deputy First Minister MP |
| ONUC | UN Operation in the Congo |
| ORPA | Organización del Pueblo en Armas |
| OSCE | Organization for Security and Cooperation in Europe |

| | |
|---|---|
| PBSO | Peacebuilding Support Office |
| PCA | partnership and cooperation agreement |
| PCTA | Provisional Cypriot Turkish Administration |
| PDC | Parti Démocrate-Chrétien |
| PDG | Prisoners' Dilemma Game |
| PKF | peacekeeping force |
| PKO | peacekeeping operation |
| PL | Parti Libéral |
| PLO | Palestine Liberation Organization |
| PR | proportional representation |
| PSD | Parti Social Démocrate |
| R2P | responsibility to protect |
| RoC | Republic of Cyprus |
| RPF | Rwandan Patriotic Front |
| SAA | Stabilization and Association Agreement |
| SADC | Southern African Development Community |
| SAP | Stabilization and Association Process |
| SG | secretary-general |
| SLM/A | Sudan Liberation Movement Army |
| SRSG | Special Representative of the Secretary-General |
| STV | single transferable vote |
| TACIS | Technical Assistance for the Commonwealth of Independent States |
| TFA | transitional federal assembly |
| TFG | transitional federal government |
| TFSC | Turkish Federated State of Cyprus |
| TMT | Türk Mukavemet Teşkilatı [Turkish Resistance Organization] |
| TNA | transitional national assembly |
| TRNC | Turkish Republic of Northern Cyprus |
| TSG | territorial self-governance |
| TUV | Traditional Unionist Voice |
| UCR | United Cyprus Republic |
| UDA | Ulster Defence Association |
| UG | unity government |
| UN | United Nations |
| UNAMIR | UN Assistance Mission in Rwanda |
| UNDOF | UN Disengagement Observer Force |
| UNDPKO | UN Department of Peacekeeping Operations |
| UNEF | UN Emergency Force |
| UNFICYP | UN Peacekeeping Force in Cyprus |
| UNGOMAP | UN Good Offices Mission in Afghanistan and Pakistan |
| UNIFIL | UN Interim Force in Lebanon |
| UNMIK | UN Interim Administration Mission in Kosovo |
| UNOMUR | UN Observer Mission Uganda–Rwanda |
| UNTSO | UN's Truce Supervision Organization |
| URNG | Unidad Revolucionaria Nacional Guatemalteca [Guatemalan National Revolutionary Unity] |
| USIP | United States Institute of Peace |
| UUP | Ulster Unionist Party |

# Introduction

*Christalla Yakinthou and Stefan Wolff*

Conflict management is a process that aims at channelling the violent manifestation of an incompatibility of goals between two or more parties into a political process where their disputes can be addressed by non-violent means. While conflict management, over time, may lead to conflict resolution, i.e., when the incompatibility between the parties ceases to exist or loses its political salience, its main objective, in our view, is to find and sustain an institutional arrangement in which conflict parties have greater incentives to abide by political rules of dealing with their dispute than to use, or revert to, violence in pursuit of their incompatible objectives. This is clearly a significant challenge at the best of times, but one that has been confronted with varying success, by academics and policymakers alike, leading to the emergence of significant bodies of conflict management theories and practice.

From an academic perspective, there are several, not always well-integrated strands of literature that deal with conflict management in divided societies, offering theories on the origins and causes of such conflicts, their evolution and consequences over time, and how different actors, including in the broader regional and international environment (should) respond to them. These literatures cut across different disciplines from history, anthropology and sociology, to political science and international relations, and to constitutional and international law and development studies, as well as all their relevant sub-fields. Contributors to the respective debates utilize a wide range of approaches to studying conflict and conflict management in divided societies, offering insights based on statistical analysis, as well as single and comparative case studies, increasingly combining different approaches to generate more robust findings. In terms of conflict management practice, too, the diversity of actors, and with them of goals, approaches and agendas has increased. More knowledge and more activity, however, has not simultaneously increased either shared understanding of, or success in, conflict management in divided societies. This is not to say that there is no common ground among academics or no track record of success, but in both areas significant room for improvement remains for more integration and coherence.

This book does not seek to establish a one-size-fits-all approach to conflict management in divided societies. Rather, it sets itself the aim to provide the space for the engagement among different experts and to offer an opportunity to present, but not necessarily pass judgement on, different approaches. Most of the contributors to this volume have had the opportunity to present draft versions of their chapters at a workshop co-sponsored by the International Studies Association and by the UK's Economic and Social Research Council, with additional support from the British Academy. Workshop interaction and an often laborious editing process have not produced wholesale agreement among the contributors on how, when, where and by whom conflict in divided societies is best managed, nor were they meant to achieve this. What has been accomplished, though, is a more coherent view on how we can improve our general understanding of the conditions under which conflict management can succeed: by engaging thoroughly with theories of institutional design and examining their strengths and weaknesses; by analysing the opportunities and constraints of key conflict management processes and actors in the broader international system; and by studying and comparing in depth individual cases of success and failure of conflict management and drawing the necessary lessons to inform future conflict management efforts. This introductory chapter systematizes and synthesizes these different elements and offers a number of conclusions that are relevant for the field of conflict management in divided societies beyond what is discussed in this volume.

Thus, this book asks a number of questions: on what principles should a political solution be designed? Who is engaged in 'designing' such a solution and why? What are the implications of favouring a particular solution or entrusting a certain actor with designing it? What is their record of success and where are the main challenges? What happens in the actual cases? What if the actors managing the conflicts are compromised, or if their structures are ineffective? How can we reliably measure and explain success and failure? Conversations and knowledge exchange among and between academics, activists and policymakers on these issues are not new, nor have they diminished in importance. To the contrary, as more and more knowledge is produced, conflicting evidence emerges, and actual understanding may not be improved. Bringing together contributors with academically informed expertise and first-hand knowledge of conflict management in divided societies offers a unique opportunity for reflection and creates space for enhancing theories and practice of conflict management.

The difficulties of engaging across the academic–policy divide are clearly understood. Benjamin Reilly raises an important point when he notes that the centripetal model should be seen as 'an ideal type rather than a coherent, all-encompassing prescription'. In applying models to situations of conflict, the actors involved in managing conflict infrequently take from only one model; most often, power-sharing mechanisms are combined with some centripetal recommendations. If the groups are territorially concentrated, then elements of self-governance, too, are often incorporated, and sometimes, though not frequently, power is also divided along liberal principles of political theory. This touches on a central theme of the book: managing conflict in divided societies is not a straightforward process where problems and solutions are neatly delineated along an 'if, then' basis. The models themselves are contested, and it is not always clear when a particular model or mechanism should be recommended. Actors, especially international actors, often have a preference for one or another type of model, as well as varying understandings of the conditions of their successful application. The UN, for example, leans towards power-sharing governments and proportional representation in post-conflict societies. In fact, its mediation support team consists of experts on security, constitutions, gender, natural resources, mediation and dialogue, and power sharing. Power sharing is the only specific constitutional model for which they have sought a specialist within this initiative. In addition, internal dynamics are often such that what may be best might not be possible; the interlocutors simply may not accept particular mechanisms or reforms. Internal and external pressures may lead parties to agree on institutions, but without corresponding will or capability for their implementation and operation.

An important question within this broader dilemma is how to manage conflict, and especially conflicts in which the players are not equal in terms of their power and legitimacy. How does a state, essentially a super-bureaucracy, engage with a single-issue guerrilla group that demands a share of the state's resources? What is the process of engagement with one-dimensional actors who are not familiar with the diplomatic 'rules'? In the post-9/11 age, how do international organizations such as the UN, ostensibly specialized in managing conflict, negotiate minefields of recognition while dealing with the consequences of asymmetric power relations? What is the role that unofficial diplomacy can and has played to manage conflicts that are difficult for official diplomacy to deal with without support? Has there been a real contribution by non-governmental organizations (NGOs) and other actors in the conflict management process? How can conflict managers deal with the emergence of an unholy trinity of civil war, transnational organized crime, and international terrorism that require distinct responses but are often close to impossible to disentangle? Is it possible to dismantle the power structures that privilege, and reinforce the roles of, criminal gangs, militias and ethnic entrepreneurs without allowing them to destroy a fledgling peace process?

Managing conflict between states, or making peace between states, is not the same as trying to achieve the same *within* states. As William Zartman puts it (Chapter 4 in this volume), 'when states make peace among themselves, the signing units generally remain intact and continue operations; when the parties end an internal conflict, they are under deep internal strains and have to construct new relations within the political system'. Essentially, the question that emerges is then how to build sustainable peace and democratic governance in divided societies ravaged by conflict; in fact is it possible to accomplish these two aims simultaneously?[1] The challenges inherent to creating a plan that is workable in the long term, rather than one that is just immediately acceptable to the parties, is highlighted by Marc Weller's comment on Kosovo, emphasizing that 'generating a settlement that might be acceptable to Belgrade was the principal objective. Making peace prevailed over the attempt to achieve a workable constitutional design' (see Chapter 12).

In Chapter 3 on power dividing, Philip Roeder argues that 'institutional design should not only address the issue of ending a current conflict that may have already become intense, but should seek to shape politics in future years in ways that avoid escalation or re-escalation of conflict to such intensity'. Janine Clark's analysis of conflict management in Rwanda would suggest that this warning was not sufficiently heeded there: she argues that the Arusha Accords were 'a major contributing factor to the genocide' (see Chapter 10). This resonates, but with far less grave consequences, in Christalla Yakinthou's conclusion in Chapter 13 that the Annan plan for Cyprus also significantly increased inter- and intra-communal tension. In cases where the agreements themselves lead to increased violence, or harm the prospects for sustainable peace, what are the ethical responsibilities on the part of those managing the conflict?

Extending beyond Cyprus, moreover, the lack of elite support for peace veils a deeper and more problematic challenge: public readiness to end the conflict. Another fundamental question, therefore, is whether conflict management is possible in cases where there is a complete lack of inter-group trust, because then the principal challenges to adopting and implementing solutions are not only overcoming the usual zero-sum interlocutor mentality and harnessing international support but also bringing, and keeping, the broader public on board. Here the role of civil society and NGOs is critical. As Katia Papagianni points out in Chapter 9, they can fill gaps and bridge divides, but their effectiveness is limited if they are not seen as equal partners in the complex and often long-term *process* of conflict management.

These initial observations set the context in which we have conceptualized and structured this volume. In taking a multi-perspective approach, the different contributions examine the philosophies that underpin constitutional design, the actors that are involved in the process of conflict management, their agendas and capabilities and the processes through which they engage with conflict parties with a view to bringing about sustainable peace. Combining conceptual–theoretical contributions with empirical case studies, this volume encourages both its authors and its readers to reflect on the state of the field in its entirety. What relationships exist between the theorists, the practitioners and the activists? How do these outsiders relate to the conflict parties? What impact do they have on their decisions to continue fighting or settle for a compromise? Where are the gaps between theory and practice, and how has this affected peacemaking? Consequently, the book is set out in three parts: discussing theories, actors and processes, and cases, respectively. Part I provides an exposition of the three primary models underpinning constitutional design, consociationalism, centripetalism and power dividing. Part II assesses the role of processes and actors in the conflict management process, discussing traditional and quiet diplomacy; as well as the contributions made by the UN, the EU, the AU and NGOs. Part III examines how these theories, processes and actors pan out in the real world of conflict management, illustrated by case studies of Rwanda, Guatemala, Kosovo, Cyprus and Northern Ireland.

## Conflict management as institutional design

Focused essentially on the *outcome* of negotiations, the institutional design approach is about finding the right 'formula' acceptable to the conflict parties (see Zartman 1989). The institutional bargain achieved in negotiations is determined by a wide range of factors and in turn influences the likelihood of the success of the conflict regulation process as a whole. This relationship, however, is not linear, and the quality of leadership[2] of the immediate conflict parties, including their ability to 'deliver' to their constituents, and of external diplomatic efforts to assist local leaders throughout the negotiation, implementation and operation phases of the conflict management process co-determine eventual success or failure.

Existing theories of conflict management generally acknowledge the importance and usefulness of institutional design in conflict management, but offer rather different prescriptions about what the most appropriate models are to achieve stable conflict settlements. From an institutional design perspective, three theoretical approaches have dominated the conflict management literature: consociationalism, centripetalism and power dividing. This is not to say that they are the only approaches, but they have generated, among themselves and by engaging with each other, a vast amount of academic and policy debate.[3]

An examination and synthesis of the existing literature on ethnic conflict management[4] suggests three different areas in which institutions can have an impact on conflict management in divided societies: (a) state construction, related particularly to questions of territorial structure; (b) the institutions of government, concerning among others the composition and powers of the executive, legislative and judicial branches of government and the relationship between them; and (c) rights and identities of individual citizens and groups, i.e., the question if, and to what extent, individuals or groups are privileged.

Each of the three theories that are discussed in Part I of the book offers different prescriptions and emphasizes distinct institutions in its approach.

Consociationalism is the most widely applied and contested model of managing (especially ethnic) conflict in divided societies. Thus, the book begins with an examination of this theory. In Chapter 1, Stefan Wolff discusses consociational theory by focusing on what he considers to be its two main institutional design dimensions: power sharing and territorial self-governance (TSG). He argues that the complementarity of power sharing and TSG is such that, when repositioned as the two core components of consociationalism, they have the potential to evolve the consociational approach to conflict management. While not frequently written about in this way, Wolff points out that TSG arrangements and power-sharing mechanisms occurring together has developed into what is becoming increasingly known as 'complex power sharing' or 'complex consociation', thus also facilitating the theory's movement away from its corporate consociational origins, towards a now more common, albeit not necessarily more widely adopted, liberal consociational prescription. Power sharing and TSG complement each other by giving potentially separatist groups a stake in politics at the centre, while lowering the contentiousness of politics at the centre by allowing groups to govern themselves, especially in relation to policy areas that they consider essential for their self-preservation as groups. In its liberal consociational form, this approach emphasizes the importance of privileging identities that emerge as predominant as a result of democratic electoral contests, regardless of whether they are based on ethnicity, religion, language, ideology, class, etc., rather than prescribing the holders of which identities should be the beneficiaries of power-sharing and TSG arrangements.

For some time now, Reilly has been developing the theory of centripetalism. In Chapter 2, he argues that centripetalism's strength is its emphasis on nudging 'the basis of representative democracy in divided societies away from the politics of ethnic solidarity and towards greater interethnicity'. Centripetalism is based on the idea that managing conflict in ethnically divided societies is best done by creating institutional incentives which encourage cross-ethnic alliances and create multiple identifications. It is opposed to one of power-sharing theorists' core claims that designing political institutions which create space for hardened identities to coexist is the basis of stabilizing divided societies. In cases of conflict which are more stable, Reilly claims that there is a growing trend towards centripetal approaches to conflict management, especially in parts of the developing world.

In Chapter 3, Roeder focuses on power dividing, also known as the multiple-majorities approach. Unlike Reilly, who describes centripetalism as an ideal type, Roeder emphasizes that power dividing 'describes not a philosophical ideal type, but a prudential strategy of institution building'. In a nutshell, it is designed to 'lower the stakes in politics'. Essentially, the approach focuses on limiting the influence of cultural communities in policymaking, while encouraging civil society and private interests to provide for the needs of citizens. It places heavy emphasis on political, cultural, and economic pluralism to undermine the development of pillarization. Power diving is firmly placed within the liberal political philosophy of minimizing government involvement, extending this vision to societies in conflict. In direct opposition to power sharing, the model is based on the belief that the cultural needs of citizens are constantly changing, and so institutions should facilitate a strong civil society and avoid entrenching structures which privilege one or another group.

Unlike power-sharing approaches, power-dividing theorists recommend different institutional approaches between organs and types of jurisdiction, in order to strengthen the development of competing interest groups in each field of interest. It centres on a 'strategy that avoids the monopolism of any single mode of representation'. In this approach, it also differs from consociationalism and centripetalism, which all place emphasis on the design of specific institutions and rules. Roeder also acknowledges that this essentially means that power dividing is unlikely to become the solution of choice in divided societies where there are a limited number of parties which have escalated conflict to the level of violence and which demand a share in power in order to end the conflict. Instead, he argues that power-dividing strategies become more salient when both the conflict and the negotiating parties represent multiple groups and interests that are not just cultural, and where external powers continue to exercise considerable authority over institutional design.

Clearly, the underlying assumptions about the drivers of conflict in divided societies and the dynamics they give rise to are fundamentally different among the three theories of consociationalism, centripetalism, and power dividing, and so are their core institutional design prescriptions – despite the fact that all three theories of conflict management share a common goal: to craft institutions which facilitate the (re)building of trust between groups and in the institutions by which they govern themselves and which consolidate democracy and stability within a divided society. The different answers, in part, have their roots in different perspectives on the nature of identities, especially how malleable they are, and on the importance and impact of elites, groups and individuals in the conflict management process.

The approach of consociationalists is to create or preserve political stability in a context in which cooperation among groups is difficult, if not impossible, thus relying on elites to stabilize a volatile political process. Centripetalism, in contrast, aims to create the conditions through which groups can begin to grow tendrils of cooperative behaviour. By using self-interest to reduce the incentives for combative elite behaviour, groups and their leaders learn to view one another through a different lens. Yet more focused on the importance of individuals over elites, power dividers pursue a strategy that seeks to ensure that power is not concentrated in too few sets of hands by creating or reinforcing fully integrated societies in which power is already fractured along multiple lines.

The shift from a focus on elites to groups and to individuals is mirrored when conflict management is considered as a process over time: from immediate post-civil war stabilization through conflict reduction and its eventual transformation. Neither empirically nor conceptually is the value of consociational institutions in the early post-violence phase much contested.

The strength of consociationalism is that it does not require communities to cooperate; only cooperative elites who represent, and hold the trust of, their respective groups. Thus, it can be implemented more quickly than other models, because it does not require a conflict to be transformed, merely halted. Its weakness is that it is a model accused of freezing societies in such a way that they are eternally in the 'conflict management' stage: structures based on the concept of keeping groups separate means that there is little institutional capacity to encourage transformation of the situation. Consociationalism's attempt to overcome this weakness by moving from rigid structures to flexible design is illustrated in some of the case studies. In his chapter on Kosovo, Weller argues that the UN had learned to soften consociationalism by learning from 'the experiences with excessive consociationalism under the Dayton Accord for Bosnia and Herzegovina, there were no hard vetoes or blocking powers'. Cyprus also wavered between liberal and corporate consociational characteristics, and in an observation of how conservative interlocutors can block creative mediators, we see how identity in the first versions of Cyprus's Annan plan began as fluid and self-defining, and was whittled down by interlocutor demands until the provisions governing identity became rigidly predetermined.

However, the long-term success of complex consociational designs is difficult to measure, primarily because they are recent phenomena. Power sharing and TSG face a common dilemma. That is, it is often claimed that TSG is a 'slippery slope towards the break-up of existing states', and that power sharing sharpens antagonisms between already dangerously opposed groups. On the other hand, not offering a high degree of self-governance to territorially concentrated groups is unlikely to prevent or settle conflict. Wolff argues that liberal consociationalism is so valuable because it ensures effective representation of self-determined identity groups in decision making, and that TSG 'allows self-governing territories ... to be defined from the bottom-up, rather than be prescribed top-down'. Wolff closes his chapter with the bold statement that this makes liberal consociationalism 'a truly, rather than deficient democratic strategy of conflict management in divided societies'. What these assertions point us to are several simple, but important points which are sometimes forgotten in the battles over model supremacy.

The question of how to build or maintain democratic structures in conflict societies is an important one. The principle of power sharing is so valuable because, as Reilly points out in his chapter, the political effects of ethnic or other divisions must be constructively managed. At the same time, there is also growing agreement that centripetal principles help to develop long-term political stability. Thus, institutional structures which build in electoral incentives for groups which appeal to the 'other' also encourage a reshaping of narratives, a moving out of zero-sum politics into self-interested cooperation. Eventually, the theory goes, this builds a new political culture where groups that compromise and seek power based on goals that appeal to groups in discord become stronger, while ethnic or conflict entrepreneurs lose traction because they are electorally marginalized.

Thus, it is becoming more usual for a combination of both approaches to be used. In both Cyprus and Northern Ireland (proposed) institutional designs are based broadly on principles of power sharing and self-governance, while also adopting preferential voting systems as a means of encouraging cross-communal cooperation. Similarly, aggregative parties which transcend regional bases of support were encouraged in a number of Latin American countries, including Guatemala, as shown by Ladisch in Chapter 11.

Like Reilly, Roeder argues that power sharing is a 'quick fix' solution, and that other methods are needed to moderate, rather than deepen, the conflict-causing divisions. One of Roeder's most important points about power dividing in the context of this book is that, unlike power sharing and centripetalism, power diving 'seeks to give greatest opportunity for individuals to develop multiple, situation-specific, cross-cutting identities'. However, he also acknowledges that identity-group leaders have significant incentives to oppose the development of structures which are designed to directly undermine their power base. Crucially, thus, all three theories recognize that there are limits to what institutional design alone can achieve – without elite buy-in agreements, they are unlikely to be fully implemented or to be operated in a way in which they can live up to their original promise.

## Processes and actors

Looking at three different international governmental organizations – the UN, the EU and the AU – and one NGO – the Humanitarian Dialogue Centre – as well as the evolution of traditional and quiet diplomacy, Part II examines the way in which key actors in the international arena conduct the 'business' of conflict management, what their strengths and weaknesses are and how successes and failures can be explained. Similarly to the preceding discussion on institutional design, a significant body of literature exists here, detailing both processes and actors and the conditions under which they can succeed.[5] Our and our contributors' purpose is less to retell stories already told, but to examine what processes and actors contribute to conflict management, how they link theories of institutional design to the concerns, skills and visions of local leaders in actual conflict situations over time.

In the opening chapter of Part II, Zartman assesses four major shifts that have contributed to a more pronounced role for diplomacy in conflict management. He argues that the notion of *security* has expanded not only covering states but also, and independently of them, populations; that there is now more emphasis on *prevention*, with reaction a more distant second when it comes to conflict management; that the *scope* of state interests has been reconceptualized and reaches beyond narrow views of power and military security to include 'strategic, enlightened national and humanitarian interest'; and that, finally, the *arena* of conflict management has undergone a geographic and conceptual redefinition.

Within the framework of human security, Zartman explains the reorientation towards the responsibility to protect (R2P) and universal jurisdiction. He highlights that the legal and political implications of these two emerging axes of diplomacy are still evolving. Subsequent chapters illustrate their still-contested nature, and illustrate Zartman's point that both R2P and universal jurisdiction 'carry the issue of human security directly into the offending state, with incontrovertible effect'. The UN, for example, was compelled to mediate in Guatemala in the 1990s, in part, out of this increasing prioritization of human security; a point that Ladisch explores in Chapter 11 on Guatemala. Kittikhoun and Weiss join Zartman in his position on R2P, maintaining that 'R2P's relevance to conflict management is that it sees sovereignty to include a state's responsibility to protect its populations as the foundation for enduring peace' (see Chapter 6).

Zartman reminds us that managing intrastate conflict is complex, and often involves rebuilding political systems as well as social group dynamics between former conflict parties. On top of that, those who are managing the conflict frequently fight their own battles to remain engaged in what is often a long-term process. Subsequent chapters in Part II point to the challenges of sustained commitment to the management of a conflict. The chapter also emphasizes that conflict management has a number of dimensions that are not immediately obvious: rebels are not natural negotiators; they must be trained. In addition, rebel groups tend to fracture and proliferate; a significant challenge to managing a conflict. And, of course, there are unforeseen consequences of training rebels to become negotiators. In addition, the role of the military is key, be it international or local, because it is the military that will train a police or local security force, or from the numbers of the military that these institutions will be formed.

Craig Collins and John Packer (Chapter 5) show how important the role of quiet diplomacy is, and examine the impact of it in cases where official diplomacy is an impractical option. Quiet diplomacy is 'employed to prevent or resolve violent conflicts which may arise *within* states as a result of tensions between state authorities and one or more of the communities of which the state is comprised, or between communities'. Collins and Packer outline the range of techniques used in quiet diplomacy, including 'confidential bilateral exchanges, multiparty discussions or round-tables, technical consulting, and facilitating access to other sources of advice and/or the financial and material resources necessary for policy implementation'. They characterize it as primarily a 'problem-solving' role. But the diplomat also functions as a conduit between their institutions and the actors in the conflict, and sometimes between the international community and the conflict. Collins and Packer's timely suggestions work both ways and ideally should also have the ability to quietly galvanize international financial or structural resources and the relevant expertise in order to progress towards peace, and sometimes to help to prevent the recurrence of conflict.

Quiet diplomacy is based on developing enduring relationships with actors at all levels of the conflict in order to create space for dialogue and to find or build commonalities between groups. Working quietly, the third-party actor needs credibility, experience and skill. All of this must be supported by adequate resources. Because of its nature, quiet diplomatic involvement has the ability to keep stakes lower by avoiding public scrutiny of interlocutors' every action, and so creating a space for more creative engagement by the actors.

However, quiet diplomacy remains a method of engagement yet to be fully developed. It is still an ad hoc process dominated by a few eminent persons, who have limited resources and support, and a narrow range of skills. The institutions supporting them do not always have the experience and credibility necessary to encourage parties to seek their advice. Despite this, there are a number of contexts in which 'the demand for effective facilitation and mediation far outstrips supply'. The authors note that for these situations 'even good *enough* offices would be notable progress'.

Anoulak Kittikhoun and Thomas Weiss assess the UN's historical role in conflict management, labelling the work of the organization 'imperfect but indispensable'. The UN's profile as a conflict manager has also increased post-Cold War. Formally, the UN encourages parties to resolve their conflicts internally, and view the UN as a last resort. In their chapter they outline the roles each of the UN bodies play in conflict management broadly. For our purposes, the UN Security Council and the UN Secretary-General are the two most interesting UN bodies. The authors also point out that the UN Secretary-General plays a dual role; and that much of the UN's work revolves around quiet diplomacy. In addition, the work of the Department of Political Affairs in the Secretariat plays an important role in analysis, peacemaking and preventive diplomacy. As the UN has evolved, it has also developed the understanding of how conflict management is perceived; making it clearer that 'conflict management not only requires reacting to immediate threats to individuals but the structural prevention of armed conflicts by addressing their socio-economic root causes' an expansive understanding of the term.

They also note the important innovation of peacekeeping, and underline the critical role played by UN peacekeepers on the practical level: managing the outbreak or recurrence of violence so that peacemakers can continue their work in a more stable political environment. So-called post-Cold War 'second-generation peacekeeping' further developed the role of UN conflict management. Many of the missions, including Kosovo, 'aimed to help previously divided societies move towards consolidation and legitimate governance after civil wars'. As Weller also explains in his chapter, in Kosovo, the UN led and coordinated a large civil and security presence which included NATO, the UN High Commissioner for Refugees, the Organization for Security and Cooperation in Europe and the European Union.

Nathalie Tocci's contribution on the EU as an emerging actor in this field in Chapter 7 begins with the reflection that the EU's history and reason for existence is closely intertwined with the principles of conflict resolution and management. The EU is a self-perceived peace project. Its approach to managing conflicts is based on the dual goals of advancing peace externally and within its own borders. Supporting claims made in earlier chapters, Tocci argues that 'the Union has typically prioritized the territorial integrity of states alongside the respect for group and individual rights within them'. It is partial to power-sharing and territorial models of conflict management. It rarely supports changing international boundaries, with two notable exceptions: the Balkans and the Middle East. While the Union's philosophy has been fairly consistent, Tocci points out that in practice its application of those principles has been less so. It was too ineffective to react to the tragedies in the Balkans throughout the 1990s. Its inability to share sovereignty internally, and to act in unison regarding foreign policy considerably undermines the EU's claims to being a serious actor in conflict management.

Tocci's chapter explains the different approaches of the EU's policy of conflict management over the short, medium and long term. In the latter, it operates mainly within the Common Foreign and Security Policy. In the former, the Union tends to focus on building structural capacity in conflict societies by providing significant amounts of EU aid and technical assistance programmes. In addition, the European Development Fund is increasingly directed towards building democracy, human rights and good governance. A number of geographic and thematic policy instruments focus on building economic and second-generation human rights.

The African Union (AU) evolved out of the Organization of African Unity in July 2002. John Akokpari in Chapter 8 reviews the strengths and weaknesses of the AU over its eight years of life. He explains that its limited resources and structural weaknesses have seen it emphasizes military intervention and peacekeeping as primary strategies of conflict management. He uses the relative success of the AU in Burundi and the Ivory Coast, and its failures in Somalia and Darfur to explain why the organization's conflict management record has been 'remarkably unimpressive' despite good intentions. Most significantly, Akokpari argues that the AU's failure to establish itself as a credible actor in the region is due to its habit of addressing symptoms of conflict, rather than root causes. This is due in part to inadequate financing, the reluctance of member states to provide resources, and the AU's reliance on external actors. However, it has also strengthened its hand by enabling itself to impose sanctions, economic and other embargoes on violating states, though this has had limited success.

While the AU has adopted a philosophy of 'African solutions for African problems', limited financial and structural capacity means that it depends heavily on external actors, which undermines the Africa-centred approach it emphasizes. The AU also faces severe internal division, especially on the International Criminal Court (ICC) front. Deep division over the indictment of Sudanese president Omar al-Bashir by the ICC on the charges of war crimes, crimes against humanity and genocide is affecting the AU's ability to manage the conflict in Darfur. The chapter emphasizes that, as is also the case with the EU and UN, there remains a large gap between the organization's key principles and their translation into action.

The final chapter in Part II examines the emerging role of NGOs as actors contributing to conflict management. Katia Papagianni begins Chapter 9 by asking why NGOs have moved into a field which has been traditionally dominated by states and state sovereignty. She argues that unlike the other actors examined, NGOs are most adept and useful in the context of intrastate conflict. This is directly linked to the development of a gap created by the limited ability of the actors examined in the previous chapters to deal effectively with sovereignty-related complexities of intra-state conflicts. The chapter explains how the need for NGOs in conflict management arose because 'especially governments of strong states facing armed oppositions, tend to refuse the interference of prominent outsiders in their internal affairs and may prefer the assistance of quiet private third parties who can ensure confidentiality'. These parties are primarily useful because they can sidestep the problem of bestowing legitimacy upon unrecognized groups, though increasingly restrictive recent extensions to US counter-terrorism laws are also restricting the ability of American NGOs to have any contact with organizations on blacklists.

Papagianni also raises an important point: that NGOs in this field are criticized for 'crowding already crowded mediation processes'. As she points out, the field of conflict management has become quite populated, especially over the last decade. The truth of this is underlined in both the Rwandan and Guatemalan case studies. However, there are a number of dangers in this, first among which is the potential for belligerents to 'mediator shop'; that is, to give different messages to different mediators, and play them against each other while continuing the conflict. This raises questions about who is really managing a given conflict, if everyone is involved in it. Conflicts such as Afghanistan, which houses special envoys from twenty-seven different countries, run the risk of becoming circus sideshows with bombs attached.

The processes and actors focused on in Part II are central to managing conflict in divided societies, albeit not exclusively so. In some cases such as the work of NGOs in the field, or in quiet diplomacy, their role is primarily facilitative. In large intergovernmental organizations such as the UN and in regional originations with global reach such as the EU they contribute more directly to crafting, implementing and maintaining peace settlements, while organizations such as the AU struggle to live up to their aspiration of successful conflict management and are highly dependent on outside support. Though often portrayed as impartial actors, the internal workings and pressures of all these actors affect the process of conflict management and its outcomes: how actors engage, with what agenda, which resources they commit and for how long changes from case to case and over time.

Both Zartman, in his chapter on the evolution of diplomacy, and Papagianni, in her chapter on the role of NGOs, note the evolving role of vertical multilateralism in diplomacy; that is, the formal and informal, official and unofficial cooperation of governmental and non-governmental international organizations in conflict management. This is happening against the background of the UN only gradually acquiring the capabilities to rise to the challenges that its expanded role in conflict management in the post-Cold War world has generated. As Kittikhoun and Weiss point out, the primary strengths of the UN remain its legitimacy and moral authority and the formative role it has played in the field of preventive diplomacy and the development of R2P. Yet, these cannot mask its weaknesses and failures. Its embarrassing drawdown of UNAMIR on the eve of the Rwandan genocide in 1994 is linked to both the organization's habit of stalling and its flawed decision-making processes. Its lack of an overarching central authority, and the difficulty of establishing priorities are also highlighted, as is interdepartmental competition and ineffective coordination within the organization. Perhaps most importantly, the UN walks a very thin line to protect its neutrality, and has not yet learned how to overcome the particular challenges of working in conflicts where 'sovereignty issues are pronounced'. Here, then, there is scope for closer harmonization of efforts between the roles of diplomacy and quiet diplomacy, using the strengths of each to overcome their weaknesses.

One of the most important advantages the EU holds is its ability to generate incentives for peace, especially to third countries that seek to become EU member states. However, to become a more credible actor outside this sphere of immediate influence, the EU will need to develop its capacity to offer incentives beyond those of enlargement. Its extensive economic reach is one such avenue of influence. And where the UN's legitimacy is its strength, the EU's lack of credibility in conflict management is a serious weakness for the organization.

In Akokpari's examination of the AU, he emphasizes a point which is also applicable to the EU and UN – that there remains a large gap between the organization's key principles and their translation into action. What is most obvious from the case of the AU is the fact that international organizations can only be as good as their member states allow them to be. Where state interests and security trump those of populations, to use Zartman's terminology, international organizations will lack opportunities to manage conflicts effectively and to develop long-term capabilities to do so. This is as much true for the UN, where the process of institutional reform has achieved relatively little since the end of the Cold War, as it is for the EU, where progress has been made, but at a pace that is hardly commensurate with the organization's economic wealth and political aspiration. Nonetheless, the EU is making important contributions to conflict management in divided societies beyond its own borders and its immediate neighbourhood, including in terms of its commitment to 'effective multilateralism' as a foreign policy goal. Its prioritization of working together with other states and international organizations could have the effect of promoting a greater degree of cooperation among actors, and a more efficient division of responsibilities and thus more effective development and deployment of global capacities for successful conflict management.

That said, the role played by NGOs so far has been important because they have been able to create and sustain a dialogue with all conflict parties, thereby continuing the information chain. They add to building trust and sustainable peace. However, the strength of NGOs in this field is also their weakness. Because they are independent they are relatively free to sustain dialogue with all parties, even during particularly tense periods. But the long-term success of conflict management requires follow-up by parties with tangible power, and so NGOs have limited capacity to contribute to the final settlement of conflicts. They are necessarily a link in the conflict management chain, and often a valuable one, because they have little actual power of their own. With its deeper reach, it is perhaps in this space that quiet diplomacy can strengthen the work begun by (and sometimes side by side with) NGOs; in the creation and sustaining of dialogue in sensitive contexts. But equally risky is the possibility that having NGOs participate in conflict management could allow states and international organizations to sidestep their responsibility to intervene in conflicts. A coherent, multi-actor, multitrack conflict management strategy in which individual efforts are sufficiently coordinated is one of the primary prerequisites for successful conflict management in divided societies. This is widely recognized, yet difficult to attain, not least because conflict management is rarely the singular goal of any of the actors involved. States have a broad set of strategic interests, international organizations are dependent on state consent and available resources, NGOs have funding requirements, the individuals acting as mediators or facilitators have their own preferences, allegiances and capabilities. However necessary diplomacy (in the broad sense of international involvement) is for successful conflict management, it is not a panacea or limitless resource to be drawn upon until conflict parties are ready to make peace. International actors in conflict management remain constrained not only by the will of the parties on the ground, but also because they frequently compete over, rather than share information, because they mistrust each other's motivations and long-term strategic interests, and because they suffer from limitations on human and financial resources. Understanding the sources of these constraints is an important first step in overcoming them, but it would be foolish to assume that this can be accomplished quickly and comprehensively against the background of a narrowing political reality defined by the 'war on terrorism' and its corollary effects, as well as ever-tighter financial resources available to relevant actors.

## Conflict management in practice: the empirical evidence from case studies

Part III of this volume examines the key issues brought out in the preceding two parts in a series of case studies, drawing on successes and failures from around the world. The cases were selected because they each illustrate a key issue in the development or implementation of processes that are designed to manage or end conflict. They cannot cover all such issues, but they are therefore purposefully diverse to illustrate that, for all necessary context sensitivity, there are recurring issues of conflict management across different divided societies and that there are important lessons that can be drawn. Analysing conflict management in Rwanda, Guatemala, Kosovo, Cyprus and Northern Ireland, each of the authors has reflected on whether the design being applied was the most appropriate, on the motivations and capacities of the core actors and on the current situation.

As Clark illustrates in chapter 10, Rwanda is a key case study for this volume primarily because it illustrates in very stark terms what can often be an enormous and repeated gap between the theory and practice of conflict management. Very little attention has been paid in the literature to the development and implications of the Arusha Accords, signed in August 1993, which preceded the Rwandan genocide. On paper, Rwanda should have been a success. It had inclusive talks, the conflict parties expressed commitment to the process, international support was evident. But illustrating the tragedy of the *realpolitik* element of conflict management, international appetite for implementing the Accords waned at the most crucial period, and in a now sombrely repeated story, the international community withdrew almost all of its military and logistical presence from the country on the eve of the genocide, despite repeated warnings from many quarters. The day after the genocide ended, the RPF established a power-sharing government that implemented the Accords, and it appeared that stability might return to Rwanda. However, the reform-oriented government soon collapsed, and now tension continues to rise alongside the Kagame regime's attempts to build unity and reconciliation through suppression and exploitation of ethnicity.

Clark outlines how the conflict management process was inclusive in Rwanda while drawing up the Arusha Accords. Zaire and Tanzania played key roles at different points, both independently and under the OAU. Underlining Papagianni's point about engagement overkill, the OAU, the UN, Zimbabwe, Zaire, Uganda, Senegal, Nigeria, Burundi, Belgium, France and Germany were all involved or present in the negotiations. Indeed, Rwanda is referred to as a 'laboratory' where the conflict management capacity of regional and subregional organizations was tested; and goodwill was not always the basis of engagement.

Both Rwanda and Guatemala were cases where agreements were signed, but serious tension remains. While Rwanda's peace plan was very detailed, Virginie Ladisch emphasizes in Chapter 11 that Guatemala's accords were far-reaching but lacking guidance on how to attain the broad vision of a reformed society outlined in the peace agreement. The accords left 'too much up to future political negotiations without factoring in the lack of political will or fierce opposition those reforms would face'. Part of the Guatemalan accords' interest to this volume lies in how unique they were, at least in concept. The reforms presented 'a blueprint for transforming Guatemala into a politically, socially, economically and culturally more inclusive state'. This vision of transformation was rooted in the belief that to overcome the conflict, the accords needed to understand both the causes and consequences of the violence, and how to address them. The accords, then, were an ambitious example of conflict transformation, without a map of how to move society towards this vision. Ladisch warns 'be wary of overly vague accords that do not include a firm implementation schedule and verification structure'.

In Guatemala, the military's support for the peace process was crucial to its success, and indeed, the military is an institution whose role in conflict management is often empirically significant, yet analytically overlooked. Also important in the Guatemalan process was the involvement of civil society in the peace process. Despite the fact that their mandate was limited, the inclusion of civil society at the negotiating table was a 'unique innovation'. Ladisch also points to another important area in the conflict management process, though this time by virtue of its absence: in Guatemala, as in many processes, the voices of victims as a genuine partner in the negotiations were ignored. While the international community contributed a variety of actors to the mediation process, an interesting development was also the coordination of the efforts of international financial institutions under the UN; in an unusual development, the financial institutions regarded the country's sharp socio-economic disparities as a key contributor to conflict which needed to be removed in order to secure lasting peace. The UN, as the primary mediator, suffered from a 'leverage problem': with only a General Assembly resolution as its basis, it 'lacked the credibility that would have come with a Security Council resolution'. This affected negatively the UN's ability to ensure compliance during implementation, when the accords faced significant internal resistance.

The Cypriot case of conflict management is somewhat more straightforward. Yakinthou points out in Chapter 13 that the UN has been the primary mediator for almost four decades, and has overseen periods of apparent progress, retraction and most of all stalemate during that period. In the lead-up to the Republic of Cyprus's accession to the EU in 2004, the EU also took an increasing role in managing the conflict. In many ways, Cyprus illustrates Tocci's arguments that the EU's perspective on conflict management is long term and structural, focusing on building capacity over time. Cyprus also shows us that in an environment that has been highly nationalistic for half a century, even moderate elites have very little room to manoeuvre: history, and the way it continues to be lived, can become a problem.

Cyprus also demonstrates the difficulties faced by mediators with limited leverage: the UN could almost be viewed as a third victim of the Cyprus conflict. But the UN seems to have also evolved in response to contexts such as Cyprus: the failure of traditional mediation in drawn-out disputes such as Cyprus has changed its approach to peacemaking, making it more assertive. Certainly the Annan plan is exemplar of this point, though post-Annan the organization has withdrawn very quietly into a more reactive role.

Kosovo illustrates many of Zartman's points about recent changes in diplomacy and their consequences. In Chapter 12, Weller explains that Kosovo was such a complex issue because 'it touched on a number of important structural aspects of international order' at exactly the period when the post-Cold War world was searching for new principles to guide diplomacy. Both the principle of non-intervention and the doctrine of territorial integrity became inhibiting factors for a peaceful settlement of the Kosovo conflict. At the same time, NATO and the EU were reshaping themselves. Weller also highlights that Kosovo revealed an important shortcoming of the international community: its ability to deal with only one major European conflict at any one time.

Weller reminds us of the importance of keeping a wide lens on conflicts, arguing that Kosovo was pushed to the side by the international community during the London conference in 1992 to settle the broader conflict in the former Yugoslavia, and again by the international community's attitude that with the Dayton Accord's signing, the Yugoslav conflict was largely resolved. 'More radical elements in Kosovo saw this as confirmation of their view that Kosovo would only attract international interest if it launched its own armed campaign'. Kosovo, thus, has many lessons to offer to those interested in conflict management. The role of the international community, and especially the UN, was of central importance, as were the opportunities and constraints that local and international actors were presented with at a regional and global level. The UN was heavily involved in managing Kosovo's final status process between 2005 and 2008, when Kosovo finally declared independence, but throughout the period of the prolonged Yugoslav crisis from the early 1990s on, it cooperated with other governmental and NGOs who collectively have failed more than they have succeeded in protecting populations and states.

Like Kosovo, Northern Ireland was (and to some small extent remains) a secessionist conflict. Much longer and less violent, conflict management has consistently been focused on a consociational solution, despite many setbacks. Power-sharing institutions were first introduced in Northern Ireland in 1974, followed, after their collapse, by a prolonged period of direct rule by Westminster, albeit interspersed with multiple unsuccessful efforts to revive them. Thus, as with Cyprus, no real alternatives to power-sharing solutions have been offered in Northern Ireland. Indeed, as Adrian Guelke observes in Chapter 14, 'two principles have underpinned the design of Northern Ireland's political institutions, proportionality and parallel consent'. The predominance of the British, and to a lesser extent Irish, government in managing the conflict in Northern Ireland and their eventual success in doing so is an important dimension for broader considerations of conflict management in divided societies: states have a primary responsibility to manage conflicts within the boundaries of their own jurisdiction. This process, however, is complicated if states are in fact parties to the conflict, if they are challenged in their sovereignty and territorial integrity internally and externally, and if they have to manage the combined pressures of domestic and international public opinion. Yet, they can succeed in the face of these challenges if their interests become more enlightened and less narrowly focused and if they operate in a conducive regional and global environment – more constructive cooperation with the Republic of Ireland, the support of the peace process by the EU, and the sustained commitment by the United States at the highest level all form part of the explanation why conflict management in Northern Ireland eventually succeeded.

All the case studies expand on the primary challenges to designing plans to manage or resolve the conflicts, reflect on the current status and future prospects of the conflict and assess how the management process developed and what its weaknesses and strengths were. While this is not the place for a systematic case-by-case comparison, our understanding of the dynamics of conflict management in divided societies can be enhanced by pointing out common themes and draw some more general conclusions about the factors that have an impact on its long-term success or failure.

The five case studies in Part III offer a context-sensitive reflection on the issues raised in the earlier chapters on theories, processes and actors in conflict management. They reveal, unsurprisingly, a great deal of diversity in the way in which conflict in divided societies is managed and the conditions under which it might succeed or fail. Given that our empirical basis for generalization is too small to be authoritative, we can only draw some tentative conclusions at this stage, pending further more sustained comparative research. Yet, what we can do is point to and illustrate the conditions under which conflict management can achieve and sustain peace in divided societies. These conditions are best conceived of and structured according to three phases (negotiation, implementation and operation), three dynamics (leadership, diplomacy and institutional design) and three levels (local, regional and global) of conflict management.

Inclusive negotiations are important, yet they need not come at any price nor is their absence a recipe for disaster. In Northern Ireland, the talks were open to all parties provided they signed up to the Mitchell Principles on Non-violence. Once Sinn Féin did so, negotiations moved forward and eventually concluded with the 1998 Good Friday/ Belfast Agreement. Yet, with one of the main Unionist parties, the Democratic Unionists, having walked out of the negotiations as Sinn Féin entered, the Agreement was not fully inclusive, the subsequent referendum barely conclusive, and the implementation process soon stalled. Continued, high-level British, Irish and occasionally US engagement saved the process from collapse, and by 2010, following major revisions to the original Agreement and full engagement by the Democratic Unionists, it is fair to say that conflict management in Northern Ireland eventually turned out to be successful. Innovative institutional design, sustained and well-resourced diplomacy, and above all broad local commitment to peace can account for this.

The referendum mechanism for endorsing institutional designs that are the outcome of an internationally mediated conflict management process is not unique to Northern Ireland. Cyprus and Guatemala, too, have experienced the anxiety of a referendum process. Yet, in contrast to Northern Ireland, in both cases peace plans were defeated. This was partly due to a failure by mediators to appreciate fully the domestic political context in which a settlement was meant to take hold, but partly also illustrates the responsibility that local leaders have in bringing about peace. In Cyprus, Turkish Cypriots, for decades, had been viewed as the main problem to overcoming the island's partition, yet they overwhelmingly approved the 2004 Annan Plan whereas their Greek Cypriot compatriots refused to do so. The highly effective no-campaign among the Greek Cypriot community, however, was also made possible by a failure, especially of the EU, to use its leverage effectively. Greece, while eventually endorsing the Annan Plan, had threatened to veto the EU's ambitious 2004 enlargement unless the accession of Cyprus was decoupled from resolving the conflict on the island. As Brussels agreed to this, Greek Cypriot incentives to compromise vanished into thin air. In Guatemala, in contrast, the degree to which spoilers had an interest in continued conflict was underestimated. The reason for the referendum defeat here, however, was not, as in the Cypriot case, that one of the conflict parties did not realize its maximum demands, but rather that non-resolution of the conflict was far more profitable for too many.

The different outcomes of the settlement processes in Northern Ireland, Cyprus and Guatemala thus raise another question: could better institutional designs have led to more or earlier success. In the case of Northern Ireland, it took several revisions of the original 1998 Agreement and resolution of issues only alluded to in it (such as police reform) before an ostensibly stable settlement was achieved. In Cyprus and Guatemala, settlements clearly failed to inspire a consensus among majorities on both sides of the divide. Looking beyond these three cases, much like in Northern Ireland and Cyprus, settlements in Rwanda and Kosovo were very detailed and complex, whereas one of the major flaws identified in Guatemala was that the agreement was big on vision, but very light on content. Yet outcomes could not have been more drastically different: from genocide in Rwanda to a continuing status quo in Cyprus and to a reasonably well working political process in Northern Ireland. Consequently, negotiations and their outcome must be seen as but one phase in the conflict management process, its overall success depends as much on implementation and operation of agreements no matter how vague or detailed they are.

Having an actual agreement on a settlement clearly is important – Northern Ireland would not be where it is today without the 1998 Agreement. From this perspective, the current situation in Cyprus and Kosovo is not surprising – in neither case was there a 'proper' agreement between the parties, and more or less unilateral, international plans that give unequal weight to the concerns of both sides hardly lend themselves to successful implementation. Yet even in the absence of agreed settlements and in the aftermath of failure to reach a workable consensus, neither case has escalated into violence. This is to the credit of the parties, their external backers, and the continued engagement of international conflict managers. Not all of them have performed equally well or with complete good faith, yet even an imperfect status quo is preferable to renewed violence.

Yet, how can we explain that agreements in Guatemala and Rwanda have failed to live up to their initial promise? Rwanda highlights a weakness in the international system of conflict management: international focus on a conflict, and on the signing of a peace settlement, does not always also mean that focus will extend to the difficulties of implementing agreements. On the contrary, Rwanda signals that attention to a conflict is not always consistent, and the will to find a solution does not always translate into the provision of support in the critical next phases of implementation and operation when the international community loses interest and withdraws pressure, support and resources thus allowing conflict parties to revert all too easily into their old 'comfort zones' with devastating consequences.

In Guatemala, the lack of proper implementation structures was of critical importance: a broad vision for peace does not easily translate into reality in the absence of credible guarantees and enforcement mechanisms, especially when the military has high stakes in the conflict. One way around this dilemma is offered by the experience of Northern Ireland. Here, a 'choreography' of step-by-step agreements and trade-offs was painstakingly put together over time by the principal mediators that tied the different conflict parties into a process of at times very incremental progress and not without setbacks. Thinking beyond the incentives and pressures offered during negotiations and offering parties further rewards as they progress through implementation and operation can ensure their continued commitment to peace. The initial leap of faith required from local leaders to do so, often against the expressed preferences of their immediate constituents, still remains a stumbling block, but one that international mediators can help them to overcome, especially if they commit resources to 'prove' that a settlement is more advantageous than continuing, or reverting to, conflict. Such leverage, in both a positive and a negative sense, was absent in Cyprus once EU accession and conflict settlement were decoupled, and was insufficiently present in the Rambouillet negotiations over Kosovo.

Different local, regional and global conditions shape success in different phases of conflict management over time. Factors that lead to successfully completed negotiations are not necessarily the same as those that facilitate successful implementation and enable long-term stability of the operation of a settlement. In other words, skilled negotiators (i.e., local leaders) and mediators (i.e., external third parties) may reach a bargain over institutional design, but without adequate resources, often supplied externally, the full implementation of negotiated settlements is often impossible. Regional neighbours may be less important in terms of providing resources for the opening of negotiations, but their support is key in making sure that the impact of external spoilers during implementation and operation of agreed settlements is limited. Moreover, while negotiation and implementation phases of settlements often require a more forceful and determined external approach, longer-term 'over-involvement' of third parties is unlikely to generate the conditions of self-sustaining peace. This does not mean that external actors should completely disengage, but it begs the question whether the kind institutional designs that are sustainable without an international (military or security) presence really offer solutions. While we cannot answer this question conclusively, the analytical arguments and the empirical evidence in our volume suggest as important as the right institutional design and the correctly timed, designed and well-resourced international engagement may be, they cannot make up for shortcomings in local leadership. In other words, conflict management in divided societies cannot succeed unless there is a genuine commitment to peace among the parties to such conflicts.

## Notes

1 An overview of this debate on the (in)compatibility of building peace *and* democracy in post-war societies can be found in Wolff (2010a).
2 In the context of ethnic parties in Europe, political leadership and how it is shaped by institutional incentives is discussed in greater detail in Ishiyama and Breuning (1998). See also van Houten and Wolff (2007).
3 See O'Flynn (2007), Taylor (2009), and Wolff (2007, 2010a, 2010b) for recent surveys and critiques of the literature. Other approaches to conflict management that are more marginal in terms of their impact on academic debates and policy practice and are questionable in terms of their normative foundations include control techniques (Lustick 1979, 1980, 1993) and ethnic democracy (Smooha 1990; Smooha and Hanf 1992; Smooha and Järve 2005).
4 Apart from the principal works and authors covered below, see also the various engagements with ethnonational conflict management by Bastian and Luckham (2003), Benedikter (2007), Choudhry (2008), Darby and McGinty (2003), Ghai (2000), Hechter (2000), Henrard (2000), Jarstad and Sisk (2008), Lapidoth (1996), Noel (2005), Norris (2008), O'Flynn and Russell (2005), O'Leary *et al.* (2005), Reynolds (2002), Schneckener and Wolff (2004), Taylor (2009), Weller and Metzger (2008), Weller and Wolff (2005), Wilford (2001), Woelk *et al.* (2008) and Wolff (2003).
5 These dimensions of conflict management are well documented in the literature. On mediation, see, among others, Bercovitch (1991), Bercovitch *et al.* (1991), Gartner and Bercovitch (2006), Jackson (2000) and Kydd (2006). Implementation is discussed in detail in Stedman *et al.* (2003). External intervention more generally is examined in Walter (2002), Werner (1999), Werner and Yuen (2005), Zartman (1989) and Zartman and Touval (1985). The broader international environment of conflict management is treated in Brown (1996), Lake and Rothchild (1996), McGarry and O'Leary (2004), Rothchild and Roeder (2005), Walter (1999a, 1999b), Walter and Snyder (1999), Weller and Wolff (2005, 2008) and Wolff (2003).

# References

Bastian, S. and R. Luckham, eds. 2003 *Can Democracy Be Designed?*, London: Zed Books.

Benedikter, Thomas 2007 *The World's Working Regional Autonomies*, London: Anthem Press.

Bercovitch, Jacob 1991 'International Mediation', *Journal of Peace Research*, 28(1): 3–6.

Bercovitch, Jacob, J. Theodore Anagnoson and Donnette L. Wille 1991 'Some Conceptual Issues and Empirical Trends in the Study of Successful Mediation in International Relations', *Journal of Peace Research*, 28(1): 7–17.

Brown, Michael E., ed. 1996 *The International Dimensions of Internal Conflict*, Cambridge, MA: MIT Press.

Choudhry, Sujit, ed. 2008 *Constitutional Design for Divided Societies: Integration or Accommodation*, Oxford: Oxford University Press.

Darby, John and Roger McGinty, eds. 2003 *Contemporary Peacemaking*, Basingstoke: Palgrave.

Gartner, Scott Sigmund and Jacob Bercovitch 2006 'Overcoming Obstacles to Peace: The Contribution of Mediation to Short-Lived Conflict Settlements', *International Studies Quarterly*, 50(4): 819–40.

Ghai, Yash, ed. 2000 *Autonomy and Ethnicity*, Cambridge: Cambridge University Press.

Hechter, Michael 2000 *Containing Nationalism*, Oxford: Oxford University Press.

Henrard, Kristin 2000 *Devising an Adequate System of Minority Protection: Individual Human Rights, Minority Rights, and the Right to Self-determination*, The Hague, Boston, London: Martinus Nijhoff.

Ishiyama, John T. and Marijke Breuning 1998 *Ethnopolitics in the New Europe*, Boulder, CO: Lynne Rienner.

Jackson, Richard 2000 'Successful Negotiation in International Violent Conflict', *Journal of Peace Research*, 37(3): 323–43.

Jarstad, Anna K. and Timothy D. Sisk, eds. 2008 *From War to Democracy: Dilemmas of Peacebuilding*, Cambridge: Cambridge University Press.

Kydd, Andrew H. 2006 'When Can Mediators Build Trust?', *American Political Science Review*, 100(3): 449–62.

Lake, David A. and Donald Rothchild 1996 'Containing Fear: The Origins and Management of Ethnic Conflict', *International Security* 21(2): 41–75.

Lapidoth, Ruth 1996 *Autonomy: Flexible Solutions to Ethnic Conflicts*, Washington, DC: United States Institute of Peace Press.

Lustick, Ian 1979 'Stability in Divided Societies: Consociationalism v. Control', *World Politics*, 31(2): 325–44.

—— 1980 *Arabs in the Jewish State: Israel's Control of a National Minority*, Austin, TX: University of Texas Press.

Lustick, Ian 1993 *Unsettled States, Disputed Lands: Britain and Ireland, France and Algeria, Israel and the West Bank-Gaza*, Ithaca, NY: Cornell University Press.

McGarry, John and Brendan O'Leary, eds. 2004 *The Northern Ireland conflict: Consociational Engagements*, Oxford: Oxford University Press.

Noel, Sid, ed. 2005 *From Power Sharing to Democracy: Post-conflict Institutions in Ethnically Divided Societies*, Montreal: McGill-Queen's University Press.

Norris, Pippa 2008 *Driving Democracy: Do Power-sharing Institutions Work?* Cambridge: Cambridge University Press.

O'Flynn, Ian 2007 'Divided Societies and Deliberative Democracy', *British Journal of Political Science*, 37(4): 731–51.

O'Flynn, Ian and David Russell, eds. 2005 *Power Sharing: New Challenges for Divided Societies*, London: Pluto Press.

O'Leary, Brendan, John McGarry and Khaled Salih, eds. 2005 *The Future of Kurdistan in Iraq*, Philadelphia, PA: University of Pennsylvania Press.

Reynolds, Andrew, ed. 2002 *The Architecture of Democracy: Constitutional Design, Conflict Management and Democracy*, Oxford: Oxford University Press.

Rothchild, Donald and Philip G. Roeder 2005 'Dilemmas of State-building in Divided Societies', in *Sustainable Peace: Power and Democracy after Civil Wars*, eds. Philip G. Roeder and Donald Rothchild. Ithaca, NY: Cornell University Press, 1–25.

Schneckener, Ulrich and Stefan Wolff, eds. 2004 *Managing and Settling Ethnic Conflicts. Perspectives on Successes and Failures in Europe, Africa and Asia*, London: Hurst & Co.

Smooha, Sammy 1990 'Minority Status in an Ethnic Democracy: The Status of the Arab Minority in Israel', *Ethnic and Racial Studies*, 13: 389–413.

Smooha, Sammy and Theodor Hanf 1992 'The Diverse Modes of Conflict Regulation in Deeply Divided Societies', *International Journal of Comparative Sociology*, 33: 26–47.

Smooha, Sammy and Priit Järve, eds. 2005 *The Fate of Ethnic Democracy in Post-Communist Europe*, Series on Ethnopolitics and Minority Issues, Budapest: LGI Publications.

Stedman, Stephen John, Donald Rothchild and Elizabeth M. Cousens, eds. 2003 *Ending Civil Wars: The Implementation of Peace Agreements*, Boulder, CO: Lynne Rienner.

Taylor, Rupert, ed. 2009 *Consociational Theory: McGarry and O'Leary and the Northern Ireland Conflict*, London: Routledge.

Van Houten, Pieter and Stefan Wolff 2007 'The stability of autonomy arrangements: the role of external agents'. Presented at the 48th Annual Convention of the International Studies Association, Chicago, IL.

Walter, Barbara F. 1999a 'Designing Transitions from Civil War', in *Civil Wars, Insecurity, and Intervention*, eds. Barbara F. Walter and Jack Snyder. New York, NY: Columbia University Press, 38–69.

—— 1999b 'Designing Transitions from Civil War: Demobilization, Democratization, and Commitments to Peace', *International Security*, 24(1): 127–55.

—— 2002 *Committing to Peace: The Successful Settlement of Civil Wars*, Princeton, NJ: Princeton University Press.

Walter, Barbara F. and Jack Snyder 1999 *Civil Wars, Insecurity and Intervention*, New York, NY: Columbia University Press.

Weller, Marc and Barbara Metzger, eds. 2008 *Settling Self-determination Disputes: Complex Power Sharing in Theory and Practice*, Leiden and Boston: Martinus Nijhoff Publishers.

Weller, Marc and Stefan Wolff, eds. 2005 *Autonomy, Self-governance and Conflict Resolution: Innovative Approaches to Institutional Design in Divided Societies*, London: Routledge.

—— 2008 *Institutions for the Management of Ethnopolitical Conflicts in Central and Eastern Europe*, Strasbourg: Council of Europe.

Werner, Suzanne 1999 'The Precarious Nature of Peace: Resolving the Issues, Enforcing the Settlement, and Renegotiating the Terms', *American Journal of Political Science*, 43(3): 912–34.

Werner, Suzanne and Amy Yuen 2005 'Making and Keeping Peace', *International Organization*, 59(2): 261–92.

Wilford, Rick, ed. 2001 *Aspects of the Belfast Agreement*, Oxford: Oxford University Press.

Woelk, Jens, Francesco Palermo and Joseph Marko, eds. 2008 *Tolerance through Law: Self-governance and Group Rights in South Tyrol*, Leiden and Boston: Martinus Nijhoff.

Wolff, Stefan 2003 *Disputed Territories: The Transnational Dynamics of Ethnic Conflict Settlement*, New York, NY: Berghahn.

—— 2007 'Conflict Resolution between Power Sharing and Power Dividing, or Beyond?', *Political Studies Review*, 5(3): 363–79.

—— 2010a 'Building Democratic States after Conflict: Institutional Design Revisited', *International Studies Review*, 12(1): 128–41.

—— 2010b 'Consociationalism, Power Sharing, and Politics at the Centre', in *International Studies Encyclopedia*, ed. Robert A. Denemark. London: Blackwell Publishing, 535–56.

Zartman, I. William 1989 *Ripe for Resolution: Conflict and Intervention in Africa*, Oxford: Oxford University Press.

Zartman, I. William and Saadia Touval 1985 'International Mediation: Conflict Resolution and Power Politics', *Journal of Social Issues*, 41(2): 27–45.

# Part I

# Theories of conflict management

# 1 Consociationalism

## Power sharing and self-governance

*Stefan Wolff*

## Introduction

Consociationalism as a theory of managing conflict in divided societies has two predominant dimensions of institutional design that have emerged most clearly in its liberal consociational version: power sharing and self-governance.[1] Territorial approaches to conflict management in divided societies are occasionally treated as a separate approach in the literature, even though empirically power sharing and (territorial) forms of self-governance frequently coincide, by design or otherwise (Wolff 2009a). Proponents of (liberal) consociational power sharing have especially pointed out both the important connections between, and evolving complementarity of, consociational power sharing and territorial forms of self-governance,[2] thus seeking to fill a significant gap in conflict management theory.[3] While these empirical connections have been obvious for some time, conceptual links have only recently been established more systematically.[4]

This chapter aims to examine those links in more detail, including by empirical illustration. Engaging with critics of both power sharing and territorial self-governance, I offer a conditional theoretical and empirical defence of liberal consociationalism, thus also contributing further to the development of liberal consociational theory and practice and deepening the relationship between power sharing and territorial self-governance.

## Power sharing and self-governance in consociational theory

In the middle of the nineteenth century, the liberal philosopher John Stuart Mill in his *Considerations on Representative Government* expressed scepticism with regard to the possibility of democracy 'in a country made up of different nationalities' (Mill 1861, 230). While there clearly is empirical evidence that any system of government that permanently excludes specific segments of its citizens, on the grounds of race, ethnicity, religion, language or ideology, etc., eventually does so at its peril, democracy is the one system in which population diversity can be effectively accommodated without recourse to repression or assimilation. This is neither always easily accomplished, nor is there a blueprint for doing so. In fact, while Mill's dictum has been taken up as a challenge by scholars and practitioners of institutional design in divided societies to find ways in which democracy and diversity can be combined in a legitimate system of government, there is little consensus on how to do so. Alongside centripetalism and power dividing,[5] consociationalism is one of the approaches to make democracy possible in an ethnically diverse country. As a theory and a political practice, it is prominently associated with the work of Arend Lijphart, as well as more recently with that of John McGarry and Brendan O'Leary.

## The main characteristics of the power-sharing strategy

Arend Lijphart began to examine democratic consociational systems in the late 1960s, coining the very term when making reference to the political systems of Scandinavian countries and of the Netherlands and Belgium (Lijphart 1968, 1969). He followed up with further studies of political stability in cases of socially severely fragmented societies, eventually leading to his ground-breaking work *Democracy in Plural Societies* (Lijphart 1977).

The phenomenon Lijphart was describing, however, was not new. As a pattern of social structure, characterizing a society fragmented by religious, linguistic, ideological or other cultural segmentation, it had existed and been studied (albeit not as extensively) long before the 1960s. These structural aspects, studied by Lorwin (1971), among others, were not the primary concern of Lijphart, who was more interested in why, despite their fragmentation, such societies maintained a stable political process, and identified the behaviour of political elites as the main, but not the only, reason for stability. Furthermore, Lijphart (1977, 25–52) identified four features shared by consociational systems – a grand coalition government (between parties from different segments of society), segmental autonomy (in the cultural sector), proportionality (in the voting system and in public sector employment) and minority veto. These characteristics were, more or less prominently, present in all the classic examples of consociationalism: Lebanon, Cyprus, Switzerland, Austria, the Netherlands, Belgium, Fiji and Malaysia. Some of these consociations have succeeded, such as in Switzerland,[6] Austria, the Netherlands and Belgium, while others have failed, such as Lebanon, Cyprus, Fiji and Malaysia.

Lijphart's own thinking on consociational theory has developed considerably over the decades since he first introduced the concept into comparative politics, partly in response to the challenges that other scholars made against his assumptions and prescriptions. Lijphart engaged his critics most comprehensively in his book *Power Sharing in South Africa* (Lijphart 1985, 83–117) and in his contribution to Andrew Reynolds's *The Architecture of Democracy* (Lijphart 2002, 39–45). In the latter, he also offers a substantive revision of his original approach, now describing power sharing and autonomy (i.e., grand coalition government and segmental autonomy) as primary characteristics, while proportionality and minority veto are relegated to 'secondary characteristics' (Lijphart 2002, 39). Yet, in relation to his grand coalition requirement, Lijphart maintains his earlier position that this form of executive power sharing means 'participation of representatives of all significant groups in political decision making' (Lijphart 2002, 41).

Apart from Lijphart, the other main, and today predominant, thinkers on consociational theory and practice are John McGarry and Brendan O'Leary. In order to appreciate fully the current state of consociational theory, it is, therefore, useful to examine a collection of their joint and individual writings from 1987 to 2002, entitled *The Northern Ireland Conflict: Consociational Engagements* (McGarry and O'Leary 2004a), in particular its co-authored introduction on the lessons that Northern Ireland holds for consociational theory more broadly.[7]

Northern Ireland and its 1998 Agreement, McGarry and O'Leary maintain, 'highlights six important weaknesses in traditional consociational theory' (McGarry and O'Leary 2004b, 5). These are the failure to address the role of external actors; the trans-state nature of some self-determination disputes and the necessary institutional arrangements to address them; the increasing complexity of conflict settlements in which consociational arrangements form an important element but require complementary mechanisms to deal with 'the design of the police, demilitarization, the return of exiles to their homes, the management of prisoners, education reform, economic policy, and the promotion of language and other group rights' (McGarry and O'Leary 2004b, 13); terminological and conceptual inaccuracies, primarily associated with Lijphart's grand coalition requirement; the merits of preferential proportional electoral systems, i.e. STV; and the allocation of cabinet positions by means of sequential proportionality rules, i.e. the d'Hondt mechanism. In dealing with these weaknesses, McGarry and O'Leary offer both refinements of, and advancements to, traditional consociational theory. The refinements relate, first, to the technical side of consociational institutions, where the authors recommend STV instead of list-PR as an electoral system as it militates against the proliferation of micro-parties. Second, McGarry and O'Leary elaborate the usefulness of sequential proportionality rules, such as the d'Hondt mechanism or the Sainte-Laguë method, in the allocation of cabinet positions in order to avoid protracted bargaining between parties and increase parties' incentives to remain part of cross-communal coalitions.

McGarry and O'Leary's observations on external actors bring consociational theory into line with an established debate in international relations on the role of third parties in conflict resolution.[8] Equally importantly, their discussion of the provisions in the 1998 Agreement that go beyond domestic institutions and address the specific 'Irish dimension' of the Northern Ireland conflict reflects a growing awareness among scholars and practitioners of conflict resolution that many ethnic conflicts have causes and consequences beyond the boundaries of the states in which they occur and that for settlements to be durable and stable, these dimensions need addressing as well. In the case of the 1998 Agreement for Northern Ireland, McGarry and O'Leary highlight three dimensions: cross-border institutions which formalize cooperation between the Northern Ireland executive and the Irish government (the so-called North–South Ministerial Council) and renew British–Irish intergovernmental cooperation (the British–Irish Intergovernmental Conference); the explicit recognition by the two governments of the right to self-determination of the people in Northern Ireland and the Republic, i.e. the possibility for them to bring about, in separate referenda, a united Ireland if that is the wish of respective majorities; and new institutions of regional cooperation, incorporating the UK and Irish governments, and the executive organs of the other devolved regions in the UK and its dependent island territories in the Channel and the Irish Sea.

A final, and perhaps the most significant, advancement of the power-sharing dimension of consociational theory is McGarry and O'Leary's contention that Lijphart's grand coalition requirement is overstated, as 'what makes consociations feasible and work is joint consent across the significant communities, with the emphasis on jointness' (McGarry and O'Leary 2004b, 15). In other words, what matters for a democratic consociation 'is meaningful cross-community executive power sharing in which each significant segment is represented in the government with at least plurality levels of support within its segment' (O'Leary 2005a, 13). On that basis, McGarry and O'Leary distinguish 'unanimous consociations (grand coalitions), concurrent consociations (in which the executive has majority support in each significant segment) and weak consociations (where the executive may have only a plurality level of support amongst one or more segments)' (O'Leary 2005a, 13).

However, the subsequent assertion, also repeated in other writings, that '[c]onsociations become undemocratic when elites govern with factional or lower levels of support within their segments' (McGarry and O'Leary 2004b, 15) is not fully convincing. Assuming that 'support' means electoral support, a consociation is democratic or not if its executive emerges in free and fair elections, not if it fulfils certain numerical tests. Implicitly, what seems to be at stake is less the democratic credentials of the arrangement, than its consociational nature; especially the criterion of jointness which emphasizes equality and cooperation across blocs and some genuine consent among the relevant mass publics for a democratic consociation and thus excludes just any coalition, as well as cooptation of unrepresentative minority 'leaders'. By extension, an arrangement in which elites govern with low levels of support from within their segments might also prove less stable compared to one in which an executive can rely on broader levels of support. This was certainly true of Lebanon by the early 1970s, where the unreformed consociational mechanisms that had been in place since independence from France could no longer satisfy significant sections of Lebanese society.

The more recent writings by Lijphart, McGarry and O'Leary also indicate a clear move away from corporate and towards liberal consociational power sharing. The main difference between the two is that a 'corporate consociation accommodates groups according to ascriptive criteria, and rests on the assumption that group identities are fixed, and that groups are both internally homogeneous and externally bounded', while 'liberal ... consociation ... rewards whatever salient political identities emerge in democratic elections, whether these are based on ethnic groups, or on sub-group or trans-group identities' (McGarry 2007b, 172).[9] This is another important modification of consociational theory that addresses one of its more profound, and empirically more valid, criticisms, namely that (corporate) consociations further entrench and institutionalize pre-existing, and often conflict-hardened, ethnic identities, thus decreasing the incentives for elites to moderate (e.g., Horowitz 1985, 1991, 2003). However, this move away from corporate consociationalism in the literature is not entirely reflected in political practice: for example, Bosnia and Herzegovina, under the original Dayton Accords, Northern Ireland under the 1998 Agreement, Lebanon under the 1989 Ta'if Accord, Cyprus under the proposed (but rejected) Annan Plan all display features of predetermined arrangements based on ascriptive identities.

## The main characteristics of self-governance

In consociational theory the term 'autonomy' is frequently used to describe the second main dimension of institutional design alongside power sharing. In this abstract sense, it refers to the whole breadth of self-governance arrangements, be they territorial or non-territorial in nature.

Non-territorial or (national) cultural autonomy is usually advocated in cases where claimant groups are territorially not sufficiently concentrated. Such '[p]ersonal autonomy applies to all members of a certain group within the state, irrespective of their place of residence. It is the right to preserve and promote the religious, linguistic, and cultural character of the group through institutions established by itself' (Lapidoth 1996, 175).[10] It has its modern origins in Austro-Marxism, and is particularly associated with the work of Otto Bauer (1907) and Karl Renner (1918). It was widely applied in the period between the First and Second World Wars, and has seen a degree of resurgence in Central and

Eastern Europe after 1991, while also being incorporated into the Belgian federal model (see Smith 2010). Neither conceptually nor empirically is it much invoked in the contemporary literature on consociationalism as a strategy for managing conflict in divided societies, and I shall therefore not treat it at any further length here.

Territorial self-governance (TSG), on the other hand, is a strategy of conflict management in divided societies widely and predominantly employed in cases of territorially compact groups (Benedikter 2007; Hannum 1996; Lapidoth 1996; Suksi 1998; Wolff 2009a). Though it has generated a significant literature both within and without the consociational school of conflict management, as well as among its critics, there are considerable conceptual and empirical problems with the definition of TSG as a strategy of conflict management.[11] Moreover, much discussion has focused on just two forms of TSG – autonomy and federation.

Conceptually broader and more contested is the term autonomy. Beyond its general use in consociational theory describing both territorial and non-TSG arrangements, in the literature on TSG, autonomy often refers simultaneously to the specific territorial status of an entity within an otherwise unitary state (e.g., the Åland Islands in Finland) and the functional status of a particular level of government within a multilayered system (e.g., the autonomy of a federal state to make certain decisions independent of a federal government). Put differently, autonomy, which is one of the most frequently employed terms to describe territorial approaches to conflict management in divided societies, is used both in an abstract functional sense in the context of governance arrangements and as a concrete manifestation of TSG in a specific (often singular) sub-state entity in a given state.[12] It is therefore useful to trace the academic history of the concept of 'autonomy' and its practical application, as this illustrates how TSG as a tool of statecraft and as a tool of conflict management, especially in divided societies, have become more and more conceptually intertwined.

Tim Potier (2001, 54) noted some time ago that 'international lawyers have failed to come to any agreement on a "stable" workable definition for autonomy ... it escapes definition because it is impossible to concretize its scope. It is a loose and disparate concept that contains many threads, but no single strand.' In political science, too, the difficulty to pin down and conceptualize autonomy has been recognized:

> Overlapping cantonization and federalization there exists a grey area of territorial management of ethnic differences which is often found in conjunction with external arbitration. International agreements between states can entrench the territorial autonomy of certain ethnic communities, even though the 'host state' does not generally organize itself along either cantonist or federalist principles.
>
> (McGarry and O'Leary 1993, 32)[13]

Despite the difficulty of clearly defining what autonomy is, political scientists and international lawyers have not hesitated to propose a variety of definitions. In doing so, many focus on the functional aspect of autonomy, rather than its concrete territorial manifestation. Michael Hechter (2000, 114) describes political autonomy as 'a state of affairs falling short of sovereignty'. In Ted Robert Gurr's (1993, 292) understanding 'autonomy means that a minority has a collective power base, usually a regional one, in a plural society', and Harff and Gurr (2004, 221) define autonomy as 'a political arrangement in which an ethnic group has some control over its own territory, people, and resources but does not have independence as a sovereign state'. Hurst Hannum and Richard Lillich

(1980, 859) stated in their influential essay on the concept of autonomy in international law that 'autonomy is understood to refer to independence of action on the internal or domestic level, as foreign affairs and defense normally are in the hands of the central or national government, but occasionally power to conclude international agreements concerning cultural or economic matters also may reside with the autonomous entity'. In her extensive study on autonomy, Ruth Lapidoth defines territorial political autonomy as 'an arrangement aimed at granting a certain degree of self-identification to a group that differs from the majority of the population in the state, and yet constitutes the majority in a specific region. Autonomy involves a division of powers between the central authorities and the autonomous entity' (Lapidoth 1996, 175–6). Daftary (2000, 5) makes a similar point, emphasizing that such arrangements normally mean that 'powers are not merely delegated but transferred; they may thus not be revoked without consulting with the autonomous entity ... the central government may only interfere with the acts of the autonomous entity in extreme cases (for example when national security is threatened or its powers have been exceeded)'.

As a consequence of this wide range of definitions, there is little consensus over what forms of state construction actually qualify as 'autonomies'. Palley, for example, claims that '[p]olitical autonomy may range from devolution of power to small communities, through regionalism, to federal government' (Palley 1991, 5) and cites the examples of South Tyrol, Swedish speakers in mainland Finland and the Åland Islands, the German minority in Denmark and the Danish minority in Germany, Belgium, Switzerland and the Netherlands all as cases of autonomy. Elazar, in the introduction to his *Federal Systems of the World: A Handbook of Federal, Confederal and Autonomy Arrangements* identifies 91 'functioning examples of autonomy or self-rule, ranging from classic federation to various forms of cultural home-rule' in 52 different states (Elazar 1991), while Benedikter (2007) counts 58 regions across the world with territorial autonomy.

Regardless of the scope and detail of the above definitions, the one common feature they all share is the transfer of certain powers from a central government to that of the (thereby created) self-governing entity, and the relatively independent exercise of these powers. Such arrangements then can incorporate executive, legislative and judicial powers to varying degrees. Where they are used as an instrument for conflict prevention and settlement in divided societies, they ideally include such a mix of the three that enables the claimant groups to regulate independently the affairs central to the concerns of its members, which are normally easily identifiable as they manifest themselves in concrete demands. However, because such TSG arrangements fall short of full sovereignty, this often happens within the broader constitutional and legislative framework of the existing state and under the supervision of a central government or similar agencies.

It is important to bear in mind that TSG is seen here as both a tool of statecraft *and* a mechanism of conflict management in divided societies, specifically when compact ethnic groups make demands for self-determination. McGarry and O'Leary's definition of the broader concept of territorial pluralism is useful in this context:

> Territorial pluralism assists geographically concentrated national, ethnic, linguistic, or religious communities. It is not relevant for small, dispersed communities, including immigrant communities, for whom self-government is infeasible or undesirable. Territorial pluralism should be distinguished not just from group-based

(non-territorial) autonomy, but also from territorial self-government based on 'administrative', or 'geographic' criteria, including regional components of the state's majority community.

(McGarry and O'Leary 2010, 250)

Hence, not every form of TSG is relevant to this analysis. Federalism in Australia, Germany or the US, for example, is less relevant than in Switzerland; devolution in the UK and regionalization in France have greater significance than the application of the subsidiarity principle to local municipalities in Ireland. Thus, TSG as a tool of state construction employed for managing conflict in divided societies is best defined as the legally entrenched power of territorially delimited entities within the internationally recognized boundaries of existing states to exercise public policy functions independently of other sources of authority in this state, but subject to its overall legal order.[14] As such, TSG encompasses five distinct governance arrangements – confederation, federation, federacy, devolution and decentralization.[15]

- *Confederation: extensive self-rule without institutionalized shared rule.* This is an empirically rare form of voluntary association of sovereign member states which pool some competences (e.g., defence, foreign affairs and currency) by treaty without giving executive power to the confederal level of government. Relevant examples include Serbia and Montenegro under the terms of the 2003–6 constitution (which was never fully implemented), Switzerland between 1291 and 1848 (formally Switzerland retains the term confederation in its official name, functionally, however, it is a federation). The relationship between Republika Srpska and the Federation of Bosnia and Herzegovina also resembles a confederal arrangement.
- *Federation: extensive self-rule with institutionalized shared rule.* This implies a constitutionally entrenched structure in which the entire territory of a given state is divided into separate political units, all of which enjoy certain exclusive executive, legislative and judicial powers independent of the central government. Most commonly cited examples of federations as tool of conflict management in divided societies include India, Canada and Belgium, as well as Yugoslavia, the Soviet Union and Czechoslovakia.
- *Federacy arrangement: constitutionally entrenched extensive self-rule for specific entities.* A federacy enjoys similar powers and constitutional protection as federal entities, but does not necessitate territorial subdivisions across the entire state territory. In other words, federacy arrangements are a feature of otherwise unitary states, such as the Åland Islands (Finland), South Tyrol (Italy), Gagauzia (Moldova) and Crimea (Ukraine).
- *Devolution: extensive self-rule for specific entities entrenched in ordinary law.* Devolution can be applied to selected territories in a unitary state. The degree of legal protection is weaker and extends only to protection by 'regular' rather than constitutional laws. The primary example here is the United Kingdom with its four devolution settlements (London, Northern Ireland, Scotland and Wales).
- *Decentralization: executive and administrative powers at the local level.* Guided by the principle of subsidiarity, decentralization means the delegation of executive and administrative powers to local levels of government. It does not include legislative competences. Recent examples of the application of this form of TSG as a mechanism of conflict management in divided societies include Macedonia (under the 2001

Ohrid Agreement) and Kosovo (under the terms of its 2008 constitution and related 'Athisaari legislation').

## When are consociational institutional designs appropriate?

Discussing the 'appropriateness' of consociational institutional designs involves two distinct dimensions: their feasibility and their viability. Feasibility is about the primarily structural conditions under which different forms of power sharing and TSG, and combinations thereof, appropriately reflect the preferences of the immediate conflict parties. That is, the question is about the (structural) factors that determine the (institutional) outcome of negotiations and does not take account of the dynamics of negotiations that lead to agreement on a specific settlement.[16] Viability, in contrast, is about the degree to which a negotiated outcome (i.e., a set of institutions agreed between the conflict parties) in actual fact addresses the core demands and concerns of each conflict party to such an extent that they do not take recourse to violence but rather engage in a political process within the agreed institutional framework.

While there is significant overlap in terms of the factors that lead to the emergence of power-sharing and self-governance arrangements, it is useful to treat them initially separately for analytical purposes. The key structural factor to consider in relation to TSG is the territorial pattern of ethnic demography.[17] Among the proponents of TSG, there is relative consensus that such TSG institutions are generally needed in conflict situations involving territorially compact communities willing to accept self-governance in the area they inhabit as the way in which they express their right to self-determination.

In the following three types of situations power-sharing mechanisms are required, either in addition to, or instead of TSG arrangements: to accommodate local, politically relevant heterogeneity in the self-governing territory; to reflect the significance of the self-governing territory relative to the rest of the state; or to account for the significance of particular groups that lack compact settlement patterns. Power sharing as a result of efforts to accommodate local population diversity in the self-governing territory takes the form of a regional consociation, such as in South Tyrol and Northern Ireland. If the significance of the territory (or territories) in question relative to the rest of the state is high and necessitates power sharing at the centre, the institutional outcome is a sovereign consociation, such as in Belgium, Switzerland, or Iraq. Regional and sovereign consociations are not mutually exclusive but can occur together. Empirical evidence for this, exists, for example, in the Dayton Accords for Bosnia and Herzegovina, as well as in the arrangements in Brussels and Belgium. Where groups live dispersed such that territorial self-governance is not an option, yet their significance relative to the rest of the state and its population is high, sovereign consociations emerge, possibly in combination with non-territorial self-governance, such as in Lebanon under the National Pact and the Ta'if Accords, in Rwanda under Arusha Accords, or in Burundi under the Pretoria Protocol.

'Significance' is one of the less straightforward, but nonetheless important, key concepts of this analytical framework and relates to both territory and population. For states, territory possesses certain value in and of itself, including natural resources, the goods and services produced there and the tax revenue generated from them, and military or strategic advantages in terms of natural boundaries, access to the open sea, and control over transport routes and waterways. Additionally, for identity groups, territory very often is also important in a different way – as a crucial component of their identity. Territory is then conceptualized more appropriately as place, bearing significance in relation to the group's history, collective memories and 'character'. Yet, for identity groups, too, territory is, or can become, a valuable commodity as it provides resources and a potential power base, including natural resource presence, strategic location and cultural importance. Significance can also arise from the size of a particular population group, the wealth it has and/or generates (as expressed in GDP per capita), its control of particular sectors (security, public administration, business), and its electoral impact at the centre. If three or more of these indicators matter in relation to either territory or population, I define significance as 'high', for two indicators as 'medium' and for one or none as 'low'. The relevance of a medium level of significance for institutional design outcomes is initially difficult to assess, whereas it is more intuitively logical to hypothesize a particular (non-)outcome in relation to high and low significance.

As a starting point to explain the viability of consociational institutions, I take the observation that institutions designed to manage conflicts in divided societies in practice work as a package; that is, they 'interact in complex ways' (Belmont *et al.* 2002, 4). What matters, therefore, is that different dimensions of institutional design fit each other and the context in which they are to be implemented to enable overall outcomes that are conducive to the success of conflict settlements. (See Table 1.1.)

The existing literature on conflict management offers some insights on what contextual conditions need to be in place to enable sustainable settlements. As far as TSG is concerned, the consensus generally extends to the need for institutional arrangements to address the key conflict issues (including assignment of substantive powers to the self-governing entity, adequate financing for their discharge, clear delineation of competences held by the territorial entity and by the centre), to entrench the settlement achieved constitutionally, and to provide for effective dispute resolution mechanisms (e.g., Lapidoth 1996; McGarry and O'Leary 2010; Weller and Wolff 2005a).

Moreover, the establishment of appropriate power-sharing arrangements has a direct bearing on the success of TSG: governance arrangements within the self-governing territory must contribute to the settlement's workability at the local level, and relations with the centre must be structured in such a way that they adequately reflect the

*Table 1.1* Content and context as success conditions for consociational conflict management

| | | |
|---|---|---|
| **Content** | | Match of institutional bargain to structural conditions |
| | | Match of institutional arrangements to conflict issues |
| | | Appropriate dispute resolution mechanisms |
| | | Constitutional entrenchment |
| | | Proper financing |
| **Context** | Domestic | Parties' acknowledgement of each other's right to be part of the common state with their distinct identity |
| | | Parties' credible commitment to implementation |
| | | Absence of effective domestic spoilers |
| | External | Absence of effective external spoilers |
| | | International support for implementation |

significance of the self-governing entity relative to the rest of the state. Yet, the relationship is not linear; power-sharing institutions have their own 'success conditions', too.

Lijphart (1977, 53–103) identified several such 'favourable factors', based on his study of sovereign consociations in the 1960s and 1970s, but confusingly his favourable factors included both factors that enable the emergence of consociational arrangements as the outcome of a negotiation process and those that can ensure their subsequent success. Lijphart thus listed overarching loyalties, a small number of political parties in each segment, segments of about equal size, and the existence of some cross-cutting cleavages with otherwise segmental isolation. In addition, the small size of the territory to which a consociational structure is applied and the direct and indirect internal and external consequences of this, as well as a tradition of compromise among political elites were also emphasized by Lijphart as conditions enhancing the stability of the consociational settlement.

Since Lijphart's original analysis of success conditions, the literature on conflict management more broadly has developed various and increasingly sophisticated approaches to determining the factors that condition success. A broad distinction can be made between factors related to content (of the institutions put in place) and context (of their implementation and operation), though sometimes the distinction is difficult to pin down. As far as the impact of the content of any agreement goes, what matters primarily is the degree to which the institutional bargain achieved reflects the structural conditions of each conflict situation and the degree to which it addresses the concerns and demands of the conflict parties.[18] In addition, appropriate dispute resolution mechanisms should be part of an agreement and translated into institutional mechanisms. The proper financing of self-governance and the constitutional entrenchment of the agreement's provisions are two factors that are somewhat in a grey area between content and context. As they are quite frequently written into agreements, I consider them as part of content, while acknowledging that they are also part of its broader context.

Beyond the structural aspects that significantly shape the content of an agreed institutional design, two aspects are of particular significance: elite agendas and behaviour and the external environment. Concerning elite agendas and behaviour, three issues appear to matter most (Bogaards 1998; Lijphart 1977, 2002; McGarry and O'Leary 2004a, 2009a; Nordlinger 1972; Putnam 1988). First, 'the mutual understanding and acceptance of each side's concerns about survival, status, legitimacy, and cultural and political rights' needs to be reflected in settlements (Pearson 2001, 278) and parties need to acknowledge and protect institutionally each other's right to be part of the common state with their distinct identity. Second, elites must commit in word and deed to full implementation and subsequent operation of an agreement, they must be prepared to revisit it in whole or part in good faith if specific provisions in the original agreement do not or no longer work or if there is an expectation that a changing context might affect the effectiveness of specific provisions.[19] Third, elites need to retain as widely as possible the support of their constituents for the settlement to ensure that they can interact with each other with a relative degree of autonomy, not having to fear being outflanked within their own community. This is closely related to the extent to which all relevant political elites within each conflict party adopt a non-partisan approach when it comes to preserving the settlement and do not engage in mutual ethnic outbidding predicated on 'defending' communal interests rather than an inter-communal peace. Crucial for the success of any settlement (and process leading up to it) is thus the absence of effective spoilers at the domestic level.

Apart from these primarily domestic factors, it has been increasingly recognized that there is also an external dimension to the sustainability of any settlement (Brown 1996; Lake and Rothchild 1996; McGarry and O'Leary 2004a; Rothchild and Roeder 2005b; Walter 1999a, 1999b, 2002; Walter and Snyder 1999; Weller and Wolff 2005a, 2008; Wolff 2003). McGarry and O'Leary have also tied these aspects to their expansion of consociationalism. There are two factors widely accepted in the existing literature: the absence of effective external spoilers[20] and broad international support for the implementation (and operation) of agreements, including through donor funding and international/regional security guarantees.

Another external dimension affects content more than context: third parties, such as international governmental (e.g., UN, EU, AU, OSCE, OIC) and non-governmental organizations (Centre for Humanitarian Dialogue, Conciliation Resources, Concordis, Kreddha, Initiative on Quite Diplomacy), individual states (e.g., United States, Norway) and prominent individuals (e.g., Jimmy Carter, Martti Ahtisaari, George Mitchell) play a major role in mediating between the conflict parties during the negotiation phase of a conflict management process[21] and thus have a significant impact on the content of any settlement. Their involvement often commits them to long-term engagement beyond the negotiation phase, for example, by extending security guarantees or offering monitoring and verification of agreement implementation (Stedman *et al.* 2003; Walter 2002; Werner 1999; Werner and Yuen 2005; Zartman 1989; Zartman and Touval 1985).

## Consociationalism in practice: an empirical illustration

As outlined in the previous section, consociational theory is descriptive, predictive and explanatory: it can accurately describe institutions of conflict management in divided societies, predict their emergence and explain their stability. In terms of describing institutional arrangements, three dimensions are of particular importance: first, the nature of any TSG regime in place; second, the nature of local power-sharing institutions; and third, that of those at the centre. Regarding the predictive value of consociational theory, the contention here is that what matters is the compactness of groups in conflict (for self-governance arrangements), the heterogeneity of contested territories (for local power sharing) and the significance of groups and/or territories (for central power sharing). The explanatory function of consociational theory also involves three dimensions: the quality of leadership (among the conflict parties), the quality of diplomacy (i.e., the nature of third-party engagement in the conflict) and the quality of institutional design (i.e., the content of any agreement). Within the scope of this chapter, I limit myself to more extensive treatment of the descriptive and predictive functions.

I have selected seventeen cases of divided societies from Europe, Africa and Asia for the following analysis:[22] Brussels, Wallonia and Flanders in Belgium; the District of Brčko, the Federation of Bosnia and Herzegovina and Republika Srpska in Bosnia and Herzegovina; Aceh in Indonesia; the Kurdistan region in Iraq; South Tyrol in Italy; the districts of the Mitrovica region in Kosovo; Albanian-dominated districts in western Macedonia; Gagauzia in Moldova; Bougainville in Papua New Guinea; the Autonomous Region of Muslim Mindanao (ARMM) in the Philippines; Crimea in Ukraine; and Northern Ireland and Scotland in the United Kingdom.

As Table 1.2 indicates, only two of the seventeen regions (with the relevant qualifications) are not heterogeneous: Republika Srpska (BiH), and the Flemish Region (Belgium).

*Table 1.2* Groups and their corresponding territorial entities

| Case | Group/s | Territorial entity | Heterogeneity[i] | Significance |
|---|---|---|---|---|
| Belgium | Dutch speakers, French speakers | Brussels Capital Region | 85:15 | High |
| | Dutch speakers | Flemish Region | No | High |
| | French speakers, German speakers | Walloon Region | 98:2 | High |
| Bosnia and Herzegovina[ii] | Bosniaks, Croats | Federation of Bosnia and Herzegovina | (60:40) | High |
| | Serbs | Republika Srpska | No | High |
| | Serbs, Croats, Bosniaks | District of Brčko | 49:51 (35) | Low |
| Indonesia | Acehnese, Javanese, others | Nanggröe Aceh Darussalam | 70:30 (16) | Medium |
| Iraq | Kurds, Turkoman, Arabs, Assyrians, Chaldeans[iii] | Kurdistan Region | 95:5 | High |
| Italy | German speakers, Italian speakers, Ladin speakers | Province of South Tyrol/Region of Trentino-Südtirol | 64:36 (24) | Medium |
| Kosovo | Albanians, Serbs[iv] | Districts of the Mitrovica Region | 88:12 (7) | Medium |
| Macedonia | Macedonians, Albanians | Local districts in western Macedonia | 65:35 (25) | High |
| Moldova | Gagauz, Moldovans, Bulgarians, Ukrainians, Russians | Territorial Autonomous Unit of Gagauzia | 82:18 (5) | Medium |
| Papua New Guinea | Bougainvilleans | Province of Bougainville (North Solomons) | Yes | Medium |
| Philippines | Muslims, Catholics, Evangelicals, others | Autonomous Region of Muslim Mindanao | 90:10 | Medium |
| Ukraine | Ukrainians, Russians, Crimean Tatars | Crimea | 58:42 (24) | High |
| United Kingdom of Great Britain and Northern Ireland | Protestants, Catholics | Northern Ireland | 53:47 (43) | Low |
| | Scots, British | Scotland | 88:12 (7) | Medium |

[i]This is calculated as the ratio between the largest group and the total of all other groups. If local minorities make up more than 10% of the total, the share of the largest local minority group is indicated in parentheses. I do not examine here the extent to which heterogeneity is a result of recent, state-sponsored e/immigration. All calculation based on latest census data except where indicated otherwise.

[ii]There has been no census in Bosnia and Herzegovina since 1991, when the following data were established: total population – 4.38 million, Muslims – 1.9 million (43.5%), Serbs – 1.37 million (31.2%), Croats – 761,000 (17.4%). Current population estimates set the total resident population at 3.84 million. See www.bhas.ba/Arhiva/2007/TB/Demografija-hr.pdf.

[iii]Estimates according to UNDP data of 2004. See www.reliefweb.int/rw/RWFiles2005.nsf/FilesByRWDocUNIDFileName/KHII-6CC44A-undp-irq-31dec1.pdf/$File/undp-irq-31dec1.pdf.

[iv]Estimates according to Kosovo Government. See www.ks-gov.net/ESK/esk/pdf/english/population/Demographic%20changes%20of%20the%20Kosovo%20population%201948-2006.pdf.

With the exception of the Walloon Region (Belgium), all other regions display levels of diversity of at least 5 per cent local minorities.

All but two regions are distinct and clearly demarcated territories: only the situation in Macedonia and Kosovo is different inasmuch as the settlement areas of ethnic Albanians and ethnic Serbs, respectively, do not constitute a specific larger territorial entity but comprise relevant local government units only. However, the constitution of Kosovo specifically allows for the establishment of 'horizontal links' between local units of self-government, i.e., greater levels of cooperation on matters devolved into the competence of the local communes. This makes it conceivable that Serb-dominated communes can establish their own quasi-region. In contrast to similar provisions in the Iraqi constitution of 2005 (formation of regions from provinces/governorates), in the Kosovo case this does not mean a change in status or powers at the disposal of the quasi-region.

As far as the distinctiveness of the territories in question is concerned, two further observations are noteworthy. First, constitutional reforms in Macedonia following the 2001 Ohrid Framework Agreement, which established the principle of far-reaching decentralization, went hand in hand with redrawing the boundaries of local communes, thus rendering them more ethnically homogeneous. Second, two of the territorial entities – Gagauzia and ARMM – are, in fact not territorially contiguous, but rather a patchwork of territories whose populations decided by referendum that they wanted to be part of the respective territorial entity. In South Tyrol, similarly, the boundaries of the autonomous province were largely determined on the basis of the historical entity of South Tyrol, but some 'adjustments' were made to incorporate some predominantly German-speaking municipalities that would have otherwise been part of the province of Trentino. This flexible approach to boundary determination complements the broader liberal consociational approach that emphasizes self-determined over predetermined identities.

Table 1.3 summarizes the predictive 'success' of consociational theory as elaborated above along the three dimensions of TSG, and local and central power sharing, while the following three subsections provide an accompanying narrative that briefly describes the nature of the institutions in place.

### Forms of territorial self-government

With two exceptions, all relevant entities have distinct legal status and enjoy legislative and executive powers of their own and independently of the central government. The exceptions to this rule are Macedonia and Kosovo where territorial self-government exists only qua decentralization of power to local communes. While the degree of decentralization is quite substantial, the powers enjoyed by local communes do not include legislative powers.

In all other cases, the specific territories in which the groups reside have legal status as a whole and on their own, as predicted within the framework of consociational theory developed above. This takes different forms:

- Devolved government (one country, two cases): Scotland, Northern Ireland.
- Federacy (seven countries, seven cases): Brčko, Aceh, South Tyrol, Gagauzia, Bougainville, ARMM, Crimea.
- Federation (three countries, six cases): Brussels Capital Region, Flemish Region, Walloon Region, Federation of Bosnia and Herzegovina, Republika Srpska, Kurdistan Region.

Table 1.3 Institutional arrangements

| Self-governing territorial entity | Heterogeneity | Local power sharing | Significance | Central power sharing |
|---|---|---|---|---|
| Brussels Capital Region | 85:15 | Yes | High | Yes |
| Flemish Region | No | No | High | Yes |
| Walloon Region | 98:2 | No | High | Yes |
| Federation of Bosnia and Herzegovina | 60:40 | Yes | High | Yes |
| Republika Srpska | No | No | High | Yes |
| District of Brčko | 49:51 | Yes | Low | No |
| Nanggröe Aceh Darussalam | 70:30 | No | Medium | No |
| Kurdistan Region | 95:5 | Yes | High | Yes |
| Province of South Tyrol/Region of Trentino-Südtirol | 64:36 | Yes | Medium | No |
| Districts of the Mitrovica Region | 95:5 | No | Medium | Yes |
| Local districts in western Macedonia | 95:5 | No | High | Yes |
| Territorial Autonomous Unit of Gagauzia | 82:18 + political | No | Medium | Yes |
| Province of Bougainville (North Solomons) | Yes (political) | Yes | Medium | Yes |
| Autonomous Region of Muslim Mindanao | 90:10 | No | Medium | Yes |
| Crimea | 58:42 | No | High | No |
| Northern Ireland | 53:47 | Yes | Low | No |
| Scotland | 88:12 | No | Medium | No |

## Forms of local power sharing

One of my underlying assumptions about the combination of power sharing and TSG is that ethnic heterogeneity in the self-governing entity leads to the establishment of local institutions that guarantee power sharing between relevant identity groups. The results of the case analysis here are more ambiguous at first sight. Even assuming that heterogeneity is politically relevant only above the level of 10 per cent, there are still several cases that do not confirm this assumption: Aceh, Gagauzia, Crimea and Scotland. The case of Aceh is the one most difficult to explain, given the relative novelty of the arrangements and lack of data availability. From what little information is available, there are two issues. On the one hand, the majority of the non-Acehnese are migrant Javanese, who are widely seen as privileged representatives of Jakartan domination. Hence a local power-sharing arrangement would have given a say to precisely those against whom the Acehnese were rebelling. However, since the settlement, tensions have emerged between the Gayo, the largest 'native' non-Acehnese group, and the Acehnese. Here, future instability might have its sources in the lack of local power-sharing institutions.

In Scotland, during the first two terms of devolved government, the pro-union Labour Party governed first in a majority government of its own and then with the support of the Liberal Democrats in a coalition. The only decisively pro-independence Scottish National Party (SNP) achieved a plurality of votes in the 2007 elections (47 out of 129) and governed as a minority government until achieving an overall majority in the 2011 Assembly elections. From this perspective, the nature of the party system, at least in part, explains the lack of a power-sharing government: the SNP is the only decidedly pro-independence party, and none of the other major parties (Labour, Liberal Democrats, Conservatives) was keen to join it in government, but the political–ideological differences between them prevented them from forming an (anti-independence) coalition, even though numerically this would have been possible with the three parties commanding a total of 78 (out of 129) seats in the Scottish parliament. However, indirectly, and because of the balance of power in the parliament, the SNP needs to seek support from the other parties for its legislative programme which guarantees the major parties a certain degree of at least indirect influence on government policy.

In Gagauzia and Crimea, the situation is slightly different. In Crimea, coalition governments including ethnic Russians and ethnic Ukrainians have been the norm rather than the exception in regional politics, even though this has meant that the Crimean Tatar population (12.1 per cent of the Crimean population) has been excluded from executive power. Voluntary power-sharing coalitions, in this case at least, thus can have a potentially negative impact on inter-ethnic relations inasmuch as they can become a mechanism of exclusion rather than inclusion.

In Gagauzia, on the other hand, the chief executive of the autonomous government is directly elected and appoints his or her own cabinet. This kind of 'presidential system' is combined with a single-member plurality election system that has so far always resulted in a regional assembly that has been relatively representative of Gagauzia's ethnic make-up and has, qua committee scrutiny, checked the powers of the regional governor.

As predicted by the above outline of consociational theory, all other heterogeneous self-governing entities have guaranteed power-sharing mechanisms in place:

- Guaranteed representation in the regional executive: Brussels Capital Region, Federation of Bosnia and Herzegovina, Brčko, Kurdistan Region, South Tyrol, Bougainville, Northern Ireland;
- Parliamentary decision-making procedures (qualified or concurrent majority voting): Brussels Capital Region, Federation of Bosnia and Herzegovina, Brčko, Northern Ireland.

### Forms of central power sharing

In cases of highly significant territories power-sharing institutions exist at the level of the central government, except in the case of Crimea. Moreover, there are provisions in four cases of medium significance (Kosovo, Gagauzia, Bougainville, Mindanao), but these arrangements do not amount to power sharing in the sense of jointness in executive decision making between representatives of the self-governing entity and the centre.

In the case of Kosovo, arrangements extend to the guaranteed representation of the Serb and other non-Albanians communities in the government and to concurrent voting procedures on issues of vital interest in parliament. However, while the majority of Serbs lives in the districts of the Mitrovica region, there are other pockets of Serb settlement in central and southern Kosovo, and thus a guarantee of Serb representation and co-decision making does not equate to these guarantees applying to Serb representatives from Mitrovica per se.

In the cases of Gagauzia and Mindanao, representation of the self-governing entities in the central government is achieved qua cooptation. Central-level power sharing, therefore, is somewhat limited in that it only extends to the mandatory inclusion of members of the regional government into the national government. Thus, while regional representatives can participate in the national executive process, they do not have veto powers nor are there qualified or concurrent majority voting procedures in place that would increase the influence of regional representatives at the centre. Hence, the main benefit of these arrangements needs to be seen in both the symbolic recognition of the region (qua inclusion of its representatives into the central government) and in the establishment of formal channels of communication between regional and central executives (i.e., the institutionalization of a policy coordination mechanism).

In the case of Bougainville, local influence on central decisions is generally achieved through the establishment of consultation mechanisms aimed at creating consensus between the central and autonomous governments, and by reference to judicial arbitration where such consensus cannot be achieved. Moreover, any changes to the agreed and constitutionally entrenched structure of the institutions created by the 2001 Bougainville peace agreement require the consent of two-thirds of the representatives of Bougainville's parliament and the Bougainville government retains the right to be represented in any international negotiations potentially affecting the constitutional status and powers of Bougainville as stated in the 2001 peace agreement.

The situation in another case of medium significance is also of interest in this respect. In South Tyrol, no central-level power-sharing arrangements exist, but the settlement for South Tyrol technically creates a nested consociation with guaranteed power sharing at the level of the province (South Tyrol) and the region (Trentino-Südtirol), which is the next higher level of authority, and where South Tyrol is clearly of high, rather than medium significance.

In terms of the predictive value of consociational theory, this means that in both low-significance cases no central-level power sharing exists, while for a total of eight cases where the self-governing territory is of high significance, in seven central-level power sharing structures exist. In four out of seven medium significance cases, representation in executive and/or legislative branches of the central government is guaranteed. Where central-level power sharing institutions exist, they take the form of one or both of the following arrangements:

- Guaranteed representation in the central executive: Belgium, Bosnia and Herzegovina, Indonesia, Iraq, Kosovo, Macedonia, Moldova, Papua New Guinea;
- Parliamentary decision-making procedures (qualified or concurrent majority voting): Belgium, Bosnia and Herzegovina, Iraq, Kosovo, Macedonia, Papua New Guinea.

## Consociationalism: critique and defence

Consociationalism as an approach to managing conflict in divided societies has been, and continues to be, criticized from three perspectives: a theoretical one that it is built on an uncertain and changing conceptual basis; a normative one that it is undemocratic; and a pragmatic one that it does not lead to stable conflict settlements. All three critiques are interrelated, thematically and in terms of their authors, and they all reflect not only a (partial) rejection of the consociational strategy but also, directly and indirectly, advocacy for its two main rivals: centripetalism and power dividing.

Engaging with critics of consociationalism and offering a defence for it is complicated by the fact that most critiques focus on its power-sharing dimension, while critics of territorial approaches to conflict management equally see them in isolation despite significant empirical evidence to the contrary. This terminological, and to an extent conceptual, imprecision has also not been helped by Lijphart's own use for more than two decades of power-sharing democracy as by and large synonymous with consociational democracy (see Lijphart 1998, 100). Thus, I shall engage separately with both sets of critique and defend each approach individually, before offering a more 'joined-up' defence of consociationalism as a whole in the concluding section.

### Engaging critics of power sharing

The theoretical critique of power sharing is associated prominently with the work of Mathijs Bogaards (1998, 2000). Bogaards levels two challenges against Lijphart on the basis of conceptual, terminological, and typological problems within consociational theory. His first criticism is 'that Lijphart's recommendation of consociational democracy as against majoritarian democracy for plural societies does not derive from and cannot be supported with his empirical analysis of the performance of these types of democracy in plural societies' (Bogaards 2000, 417). Bogaards' second criticism, again based on a careful examination of Lijphart's writings, is that a 'lack of theoretical coherence [in terms of the underlying assumptions of consociational theory] shows in the considerable changes the favourable factors [for the success of consociational democracy] underwent in both number and content in the course of time' (Bogaards 1998, 476). Bogaards' twofold critique is well supported by the evidence he presents from Lijphart's writings up until the late 1990s,[23] but requires some qualification in light of Lijphart's own writings in the twenty-first century and in light of McGarry and O'Leary's development of consociational theory.

Lijphart himself responded directly to the first dimension of Bogaards' critique by accepting a degree of conceptual vagueness and reaffirming his definition of consociation as consisting of 'the four characteristics of grand coalition, autonomy, proportionality, and mutual veto' (Lijphart 2000, 425). Perhaps more importantly, Lijphart rejected the claim that because of the lack of overlap between consociation as a normative and an empirical type, no policy recommendations can be derived, emphasizing the 'beneficial character and practical value' of power sharing in divided societies that derives from the empirical analysis of actual conflicts and their management and the assessment of actual or potential alternatives (Lijphart 2000, 430).[24]

McGarry and O'Leary's early engagement with consociational theory particularly addressed Boogards' critique of Lijphart's discussion of the conditions conducive to the success of consociation as a strategy to manage conflict in divided societies. Bogaards (1998) pointed out that Lijphart's 'favourable factors' are essentially deterministic and thus in stark contrast to his otherwise 'voluntaristic stance'. In contrast to Lijphart, McGarry and O'Leary, as noted above, as early as 1993 identified three fundamental conditions for consociational systems to work that put much greater emphasis on elite behaviour, precisely what Bogaards (1998, 476) demanded. Part of the confusion here rests with Lijphart, part with Bogaards' exclusive focus on Lijphart and his specific reading of Lijphart's claims. Lijphart's favourable factors mixed conditions conducive to the emergence of power-sharing arrangements with those conducive to their stability and success in managing conflict in divided societies. McGarry and O'Leary (2004a) have since made this distinction more clearly, and subsequently (McGarry and O'Leary 2009c) elaborate further on elite motivations with specific reference to Northern Ireland. As I have argued above, systematic analysis of consociational theory (and practice) suggests that a distinction is both necessary and possible between its predictive and explanatory functions to determine precisely the factors that dictate when consociational structures are likely to emerge and when they provide for sustainable conflict management.

Normative and pragmatic full and partial rejections of the power-sharing strategy as an approach to conflict management in divided societies often go hand in hand. They focus on the diminished quality of a consociational democracy; the fact that power sharing entrenches ethnic cleavages; and that such arrangements are essentially unstable and easily end in deadlock. Complete rejectionists of the power-sharing strategy are considerably fewer in number than those who see partial value in it, especially as a means to facilitate a transition after civil war.

The out-of-hand rejections of power sharing made by Wilson (2009), Jarstad (2008) and Ghai and Cottrell (2008) are illustrative of this type of critique.

Wilson criticizes consociationalism in the Northern Irish context from the perspective of a counter-proposal: 'an "intercultural" alternative to consociationalism' that 'has at its heart the idea that one develops one's own complex identity through deliberation with others'; in other words, focusing on the need for 'reconciliation towards an integrated society conforming to the democratic norm that the individual citizen, rather than the "community", comprises the social unit, in line with the Universal Declaration of Human Rights' (Wilson 2009, 221). McGarry and O'Leary (2009c, 368–71) provide a robust rebuttal to Wilson's claims. Instead, I wish to focus on a more limited, but in some ways more critical point, which stands for a broader and more widely shared criticism of consociational power sharing: that is, that consociationalism favours and entrenches communal identities at the expense of individual identities and rights. This is a gross misreading of liberal, as opposed to corporate, consociationalism theory and practice. Lijphart (1995a), as well as McGarry and O'Leary (2008a, 2008b) have convincingly demonstrated both theoretically and with reference to practical examples that contemporary power-sharing practice favours self-determined over predetermined groups in its institutional prescriptions and arrangements.

The broadly corporate assumption of consociational power sharing also permeates Jarstad's criticism. Her criticism is conceptually focused narrowly – on corporate consociations – but extrapolates from their shortcomings a broader rejection of power sharing more generally. Thus, the claim that 'all power sharing systems have to settle the difficult issues of defining which groups should be represented and the share of seats for each group' (Jarstad 2008, 127ff.) is empirically not generalizable. It is true, to some extent, for the arrangements in Bosnia and Herzegovina (under the 1995 Dayton constitution), but not as far as other prominent examples go, such as Iraq (2005 constitution), Northern Ireland (1998 and 2006 Agreements) or South Tyrol (1972 Autonomy Statute). These latter cases, among others, are essentially liberal consociational institutional arrangements in the terminology of McGarry and O'Leary (2008a, 2008b). As already noted, the body of work by McGarry and O'Leary represents a significant further development of power-sharing theory beyond Lijphart, who is Jarstad's main reference point (see Jarstad 2008, 110), but even a closer reading of Lijphart's own work (e.g., Lijphart 1995a) reveals that he has for long argued that 'consociational institutions that follow the principle of ... "self-determination" are superior to those that are based on "pre-determination"' (Lijphart 2008, 6). Moreover, Jarstad's reading and interpretation of existing literature in this field appears to be limited, which leads to the erroneous claim that 'previous research on power sharing has underestimated the long-term negative consequences of power sharing on both democracy and peace' (Jarstad 2008, 106), ignoring the decades-long debate on the virtues, or lack thereof, of power-sharing arrangements.[25]

Even if one leaves these shortcomings in the conceptualization of power sharing aside, Jarstad's reservations about the long-term suitability of power sharing need some qualification. First, the claim that 'moderate actors are often excluded from a share of power' (Jarstad 2008, 107) may be empirically true in a number of cases, but it is far more difficult to demonstrate causality. Especially in cases where power-sharing governments emerge from an electoral process, the fact that power is to be shared in the executive is at best an indirect cause of the success of hardliners (see Mitchell *et al.* 2009). Lack of popular support, Jarstad's (2008) second reservation, is also rather more context dependent. In Bosnia and Herzegovina, for example, Serbs are strong supporters of the power-sharing arrangements created under the Dayton constitution, Bosniaks are more likely to advocate for recentralization and integration, while Croats to some extent would like to see a different set of reforms, namely those that would give them a greater share of power at the state level than they currently have.

Jarstad's (2008) claim that power sharing necessitates external intervention in order to become viable and thereby minimizes local ownership is of significant substance. Heavy-handed international intervention and long-term presence may, indeed, not be conducive to building a locally legitimate democratic state after conflict, but as Sisk has noted, 'extended commitments [by the international community] to war-torn societies need to be the norm, not the exception' if 'bringing about lasting peace through democratization in societies shattered by war' is to succeed (Sisk 2008, 256ff.). Jarstad's final reservation, that power sharing 'freezes ethnic division by group representation' (Jarstad 2008, 107) has been well rehearsed in the literature, but applies only to corporate consociations and thus cannot be generalized across the variety of power-sharing regimes established in post-conflict societies.

Ghai and Cottrell's (2008) critique of consociational power sharing, while drawing largely on the experience of Fiji, offers similar observations. It is less generalized in terms of the broader viability of power-sharing institutions, but it resonates well with some established critiques in their general concern, including the 'degrading of human rights', the downgrading of 'citizenship rights ... in favour of group rights, with an emphasis of community and custom prevailing over the rights of the individual' (Ghai and Cottrell 2008, 314). In the same way in which Jarstad also cannot but acknowledge that 'in many cases, the alternatives to power sharing are worse' (Jarstad 2008, 133), Ghai and Cottrell offer a significant caveat to their critique when accepting that it would be 'difficult to tell how Fiji would have fared under a different kind of dispensation, one emphasising a non-racial approach and providing incentives for cooperation across racial boundaries' (Ghai and Cottrell 2008, 314). But perhaps such a counter-factual already exists in the consequences of the introduction of the Alternative Vote system (AV) in 1999 which resulted in the two most radical parties in each community (indigenous Fijian and Indo-Fijian) taking the largest share in every election since then. AV, generally hailed by centripetalists such as Horowitz (1985, 2003, 2004) and Reilly (2001) as inducing moderation and cross-ethnic cooperation has clearly not functioned in Fiji as predicted by its proponents.[26] Having said that, this still leaves the question of whether non-power-sharing institutions would have led to more conciliatory political outcomes in Fiji. While Ghai and Cottrell cannot offer a conclusive answer to this question, their implicit endorsement of doing away with the corporate aspects of power sharing in Fiji, especially the communal electoral rolls, is consistent with the critique made by liberal consociationalists such as McGarry and O'Leary (2009a, 2009c), as well as by centripetalists such as Horowitz (1985, 1991, 2003), and therefore crosses conceptual boundaries.

The second category of 'rejectionists' comprises scholars who accept power sharing as a transitional mechanism, but have serious reservations about its long-term ability to induce stability and democracy in divided societies. Prominent authors here include Philip Roeder and the late Donald Rothchild, who, in the context of their theory of power dividing also assume the frequent necessity of transitional power-sharing arrangements as a step towards democratic institutions without power-sharing arrangements.[27] Similarly, Horowitz, who provides a centripetalist critique and alternative to power sharing has observed that '[c]ivil wars ... can sometimes be brought to an end with consociational arrangements, but the desirability and durability of such agreements are often in doubt' (Horowitz 2008, 1220). As power-dividing and centripetalist strategies are dealt with separately in this volume, I shall focus on three other recent partially rejectionist critiques of power sharing put forward by Sisk (2008), Murray and Simeon (2008) and Papagianni (2008).

The partial rejection of power sharing, i.e., its acceptance as only a transitional arrangement, is based on the empirically derived insight that such institutional arrangements, especially if internationally guaranteed, assure conflict parties that it is safe to commit to resolving remaining, and potentially new, disputes by political rather than military means. At the same time, however, critics' acceptance of power sharing as a transitional mechanism reflects concerns that power sharing in the long term may not be suitable for successful conflict management. At the same time, this approach is predicated on the assumption that it is in fact possible to make this transition from a period in which decisions are made in power-sharing institutions to one in which these institutions have been abrogated. One way of achieving this is a sunset or expiry clause according to which power-sharing institutions are limited to a specific period of time after the conflict. Here the primary success case is South Africa, which is analysed in great depth by Murray and Simeon (2008), who argue that the interim constitution of 1993 not only provided for power sharing in the period towards the eventual Constitution of South African agreed in 1996 but also included a set of constitutional principles to govern the negotiations of the Constitution, thus providing a double assurance to the parties that their essential concerns would not be neglected.

While South Africa provides empirical evidence that sunset clauses can work and maintain stability beyond the end of formal power-sharing arrangements, such agreements may not always be acceptable, especially to the politically weaker parties in such a deal. Sisk and Papagianni, in their respective contributions to this debate, offer alternatives. Sisk (2008, 254) recommends 'to encourage national dialogue processes on democracy that can allow for supplementary consensus building to occur outside formal institutions' and argues that 'such dialogues have the benefit of creating consensus first on possible institutional or procedural reforms following which implementation of reforms can be less controversial'. In a similar vein, Papagianni sees instrumental value in transitional power-sharing arrangements beyond merely assuring weaker parties in peace settlements: 'the goal of inclusion and elite bargaining in the transitional period is to secure the engagement of key political actors in the process and to channel differences among them through agreed-upon institutions and procedures' (Papagianni 2008, 63).

These critiques of power sharing as a long-term or permanent way of governance in divided societies are not as such rejections of power sharing, but rather attempts to move beyond what are often considered arrangements that are inferior in terms of the long-term stability and quality of democracy they provide. In this sense, they are not an alternative to liberal consociational power-sharing theory but in fact a strong endorsement of it, precisely because the focus on the principle of self-determination rather than predetermination in liberal consociational theory affords the possibility of the kind of institutional change required by proponents of only transitional power-sharing institutions. Liberal consociationalism is a theory conflict management in divided societies, not a theory of democracy in plural societies as such. This is an important distinction, one that often goes unappreciated by its critics (and sometimes by its advocates, too).

### Engaging critics of territorial self-governance

Similar to the debate over the utility of power-sharing institutions, the academic and policy communities are equally deeply divided over whether territorial approaches to conflict management in divided societies offer appropriate mechanisms to keep or restore peace while preventing the break-up of an existing state. The critique of TSG, however, is far more simplistic and mono-dimensional than that of power sharing, its main point being the assertion that territorial arrangements empower fundamentally separatist elites and their supporters and endow them with resources to pursue their agenda even more vigorously. For example, Cornell (2002, 252) in his analysis of ethnic conflicts in the Caucasus argues that the 'institution of autonomous regions is conducive to secessionism', a point that Roeder (1991) made more than a decade earlier in relation to Soviet ethnofederalism and later reiterated in a broader empirical study (Roeder 2007), in line with similar findings by Bunce (1999) Hale (2000, 2004) and Treisman (1997).

The failure, in particular of ethnic federations and federacies, is one of the most frequently voiced objections to the use of TSG arrangements for accommodating self-determination claims. While some of this literature (e.g., Cornell 2002) fails to appreciate that (renewed) conflict is a consequence of the abrogation of TSG arrangements rather than of their prior existence, there is also a more sophisticated recent trend in research on TSG, such as that by Chapman and Roeder (2007) and Brancati (2009). Similar to the charge of a democratic deficit levelled against power-sharing institutions, Chapman and Roeder (2007) demonstrate empirically that, from the perspective of long-term stable democratic outcomes, partitions are preferable to any other territorial settlement. Brancati (2009) similarly finds that 'political decentralization' (meaning in her definition, federation) has short-term positive effects; its long-term consequences, however, are more often than not negative for preserving peace, democracy and existing international boundaries.

While the authors referred to above are highly sceptical of TSG as a conflict-management approach, arguing that, rather than being a cure, territorial approaches induce conflict, others have presented empirical evidence to the contrary. TSG, in this view, thus offers an acceptable compromise to conflict parties. Gurr (1993, 301) argues that the 'recent historical track record shows that, on balance, autonomy arrangements can be an effective means for managing regional conflicts'. Wallensteen (2007, 175, 179) concurs with such a positive assessment, pointing out that 'since the Cold War, autonomy solutions have been of increasing interest' and that '[t]hus far, the territorial solutions negotiated since the end of the Cold War using autonomy or federation have not failed'. Saideman *et al.* (2002, 118) find that 'federalism reduces the level of ethnic violence', Bermeo (2002, 97) concludes that 'federal institutions promote successful accommodation' in cases of ethnic conflict. Rothchild and Hartzell (2000, 269) find that 'territorial autonomy ... combined with other safeguards ... can be used to reassure groups in deeply divided societies about their security and ability to exercise a limited authority' and that such 'arrangements may help to lay the foundation for a stable, accommodative politics'. Hartzell and Hoddie (2007, 169) offer statistical evidence that '[d]esigning a negotiated settlement or negotiated agreement to include [territorial power sharing] lowers the risk of a return to war'. Cohen (1997) and Schneckener (2002) similarly endorse the use of territorial approaches to resolving self-determination conflicts, while Harff and Gurr (2004, 186) argue that 'if no autonomy options are open to regionally concentrated groups, armed conflict may occur'.

There is no denying the fact that territorial approaches to conflict management in divided societies have a track record that is far from spotless. In several cases, TSG arrangements have failed to prevent the break-up of multinational states. In others, they have been unable to preserve or sustain peace between the conflict parties, and critics of territorial approaches have documented these cases well empirically and analytically (Bunce 1999; Bunce and Watts 2005; Cornell 2002; Hale 2000, 2004; Nordlinger 1972; Roeder 1991, 2007; Snyder 2000; Suberu 1993; Treisman 1997, 2007). However, many of these critiques are focused on federal arrangements alone and on the post-communist/post-Soviet region.[28]

In contrast, what is advocated here is a broader approach to understanding the utility of TSG as a conflict management mechanism in divided societies, emphasizing three aspects that are often neglected in critiques. First, territorial options for conflict management extend beyond federal and federacy (autonomy) arrangements. Devolution and decentralized local government offer viable alternatives that can satisfy self-determination demands without endangering the continued territorial integrity of an existing state. Second, TSG arrangements are adopted not only as negotiated settlements after civil wars fought over minority self-determination demands but also in the course of non-violent disputes. Hence, many arguments against the viability of TSG arrangements include a selection bias.[29] Third, and most importantly, no claim is made that TSG arrangements are a panacea in themselves, but rather that, when combined with other conflict management mechanisms in a more comprehensive institutional package, they can make an important contribution to maintaining peace and keeping international borders intact.

While the track record of TSG arrangements in managing conflicts in divided societies may be sketchy, it is far less disheartening than some of its critics suggest. TSG will retain its importance as an approach to conflict management also because self-determination movements will continue to demand it, including as a concession from the state in return for their refraining from demands for independence. Moreover, the track record, at least in Europe, of international involvement in the management of conflict in divided societies suggests that TSG is often considered a natural compromise by international mediators that allows states to preserve their territorial integrity and overall sovereignty and gives self-determination movements greater control over their own affairs. At the same time, TSG on its own is unlikely to provide sustainable conflict management, yet it can be a valuable mechanism within a broader package of measures aimed at accommodating the competing demands of different segments in divided societies. It is for that reason that, practically as well as theoretically, TSG is a natural complement to power sharing within a consociational strategy of conflict management.

## Conclusion

Consociationalism as an approach to managing conflict in divided society has a long history as a theory and a political practice, which has evolved significantly over time. Today it has two primary dimensions of institutional design (and prescription): power sharing and TSG. While these are obvious in consociational practice, their connection remains theoretically underexplored, both by supporters and critics of the consociational strategy of conflict management. Those critical of consociationalism as a whole often focus on its power-sharing dimension, while critics of territorial approaches to conflict management in divided societies normally ignore it altogether. Until recently, supporters of consociationalism, too, were largely oblivious to the significance of the (necessary) complementarity of power sharing and TSG. Yet, there is strong empirical evidence that the viability of consociational institutions increases when they combine both dimensions. Hartzell and Hoddie (2003, 2007), for example, argue that conflict settlements (after civil war) are the more stable the more they institutionalize power sharing across four dimensions – political, economic, military and territorial. Schneckener (2002) reaches similar conclusions in a study that is focused on European consociational democracies. These recent empirical findings confirm the conceptual and empirical links between con-sociation and federation that had already been established by Lijphart three decades ago, noting two crucial principles, namely that 'the component units [must] enjoy a secure autonomy in organizing their internal affairs ... [and] that they *all* participate in decision-making at the central level of government' (Lijphart 1979, 506). Following this path, McGarry and O'Leary (2010, 260) recently noted that 'some successful cases of territorial pluralism suggest that, at least with sizable nationalities, autonomy should be accom-panied by consociational power sharing within central or federal institutions. Such arrangements prevent majoritarianism by the dominant nationality, and make it more likely that minorities have a stake in the state.' This is in line with conclusions reached by Weller and Wolff, who argue that 'autonomy can only serve in the stabilization of states facing self-determination conflicts if it is part of a well-balanced approach that draws on elements of consociational techniques, moderated by integrative policies, and tempered by a wider regional outlook' (Weller and Wolff 2005a, 269).

This phenomenon of power sharing and TSG occurring in combination has been identified by several authors over the past years. Kettley *et al.* (2001, 4–5), Weller (2008b), and Wolff (2009a, 2009b) refer to it, albeit in somewhat different ways, as 'complex power sharing', O'Leary (2005a, 34–5) uses the term 'complex consociation', and Hartzell and Hoddie (2007) conceptualize it as 'highly institutionalized negotiated settlement'. Analytically, it is possible to explain both why such multidimensional institutional arrangements emerge and why they might have a greater chance of success. Empirically, Gurr (1993, 292) offered the initial evidence that 'some combination of ... autonomy and power sharing' offers reasonable prospects to accommodate minority demands. Based on the empirical discussion above, there is clearly some evidence of the sustainability of such arrangements, even though some of them are too recent to assess their longer-term success. A number of consociational arrangements from the cases examined above have proved relatively stable for at least a decade: Belgium (notwithstanding the recent deadlock over government formation), Bosnia and Herzegovina, Bougainville, Crimea, Gagauzia, Macedonia, Scotland and South Tyrol. Northern Ireland has, despite sig-nificant delays, achieved a remarkable institutional compromise that appears to endure. The settlements for Aceh and the Kurdistan Region, short-lived as they may be, nonetheless have so far provided a degree of institutional stability and peace that neither region had experienced prior to the settlement. Mindanao, on the other hand, has only achieved partial success in bringing peace to a troubled region of the Philippines, while Kosovo's post-independence experience is dominated by quasi-partition.

The empirical evidence that these cases offer also allows a number of conclusions with regard to the practice of consociational conflict management. Grand coalitions, proportionality and minority veto rights continue to play a role even in liberal consociational practice, but when it comes to power sharing, the emphasis has shifted more and more to cooperation and consensus among democratically legitimized elites, regardless of whether they emerge on the basis of group identities, ideology or other common interest. Institutional prescriptions have also become more flexible: parliamentary systems remain dominant, but the merit of collective or rotating presidencies has been acknowledged; PR list electoral systems are no longer the standard and only recommendation, but proportional preferential electoral systems (e.g., STV) have been tested successfully; power-sharing arrangements have also shifted from an earlier emphasis on representation rules and come to include participation rules (e.g., decision-making procedures that require qualified and/or concurrent majorities); and novel procedures to avoid protracted government formation have become part of the liberal consociational menu (e.g., the application of the d'Hondt rule) (Lijphart 2004; Norris 2008; O'Leary 2005a; O'Leary, Grofman, and Elklit 2005; Wolff 2005).

In order to protect individuals and groups against the abuse of power by majorities at the state level or the level of self-governing entities, liberal consociationalism offers three remedies – the establishment of TSG regimes, the replication of its core institutional prescriptions within the self-governing entity and the establishment and enforcement of strong human and minority rights regimes at both the state and sub-state levels.

The resulting more coherent integration of power sharing and TSG and the consequently greater emphasis on TSG as a complement to power sharing has enriched consociational theory in two ways. On the one hand, it has enhanced the selection of mutually reinforcing institutional options that can provide sustainable conflict management in divided societies. On the other hand, the systematic integration of the territorial and power-sharing strategies in theory and practice addresses a number of justified concerns among critics of either strategy individually. Power sharing within the self-governing entity can prevent abuses of minority groups that might become possible by empowering local majority populations, while power sharing at the centre ties the elites of self-governing entities to the centre, giving them a stake in the common state and minimizing the appetite for secession. In turn, self-governance for locally compact groups reduces the stakes of political competition at the centre and thus the likelihood of institutional deadlock. Moreover, the focus on self-determined identity groups in liberal consociationalism offers more flexibility and enables the longer-term change towards politics that are not entirely driven by narrow group interests. This is also reflected in the liberal consociational approach to TSG, which supports the principle of asymmetric devolution of powers, i.e. the possibility for some self-governing entities to enjoy more (or fewer) competences than others, depending on the preferences of their populations (McGarry 2007a).

According to O'Leary (2005b), liberal consociationalists prefer 'pluralist federations' in which co-sovereign sub-state and central governments have clearly defined exclusive competences (albeit with the possibility of some concurrent competences) whose assignment to either level of authority is constitutionally and, ideally, internationally protected, in which decision making at the centre is consensual (between self-governing entities and the centre, and among elites representing different interest groups), and which recognize, and protect the presence of different self-determined identities. This preference for pluralist federations, however, remains context dependent, and is not the default liberal consociational institutional design. In some circumstances, e.g., where ethnic communities are not ethnonationalist (i.e. demanding their own governance institutions), it is quite possible that a unitary state with power sharing at the centre will suffice as a mechanism to settle conflicts.

It is this flexibility in institutional design that makes liberal consociationalism an appealing strategy: the emphasis on the protection of self-determined (rather than predetermined) identity groups through ensuring their effective representation and participation in decision making especially in the executive and legislature and combining this with an approach to TSG that allows self-governing territories, too, to be defined from the bottom-up, rather than be prescribed top-down. In this sense liberal consociationalism is a truly, rather than deficient democratic strategy of conflict management in divided societies.

## Notes

1 This chapter draws, in part, on previously published work, including Cordell and Wolff (2009, 2010), Wolff and Weller (2005) and Wolff (2008a, 2008b, 2009a, 2009b, 2010a, 2010b).

2 See Lijphart (2002), McGarry (2007b), McGarry and O'Leary (2004b, 2010), (Norris 2008), O'Leary (2005a, 2005b), O'Leary and McGarry (2010), Weller and Metzger (2008) and Weller and Wolff (2005b). But see Lijphart (1979) for an early example of this observation.

3 Advocates of centripetalism and power dividing generally reject the idea of territorial self-governance for communities seeking self-determination as destabilizing, and variably propose 'non-ethnic' federalism or at least splitting communities across several territorial entities for a more nuanced account of the utility of federalism. See, for example, Horowitz (1985, 1990), Reilly (2001), Roeder and Rothchild (2005b), Sisk (1996) and Wimmer (2003). But see Horowitz (2007) for a more nuanced account of the utility of federalism. Analysts of TSG often neglect the power-sharing dimension of conflict management. See, for example, Benedikter (2007), Lapidoth (1996), and Safran (Safran and Máiz 2000). A notable exception focused on South Tyrol is Woelk *et al.* (2008).

4 See for example O'Leary (McGarry and O'Leary 2010; O'Leary and McGarry 2010; Weller and Metzger 2008; Weller and Wolff 2005b). But see Lijphart (1979) for an early example of this observation.

5 See Reilly and Roeder in this volume (Chapters 2 and 3).

6 Note that Roeder (this volume, Chapter 3) considers Switzerland an example of the power-dividing strategy for conflict management in divided societies.

7 The arguments put forward by McGarry and O'Leary in that volume have also been rehearsed elsewhere, e.g., McGarry and O'Leary (2006a, 2006b); as well as in Taylor's (2009) volume on consociational theory (McGarry and O'Leary 2009b, 2009c).

8 See, for example, contributions in Otunnu and Doyle (1998), Walter and Snyder (1999), Thakur and Schnabel (2001), Carment and Schnabel (2003), Diehl and Lepgold (2003), Pugh and Singh Sidhu (2003), Weller and Wolff (2008), van Houten and Wolff (2007) and Wolff and van Houten (2008).

9 Lijphart (1995b) made a similar point earlier, distinguishing between self-determined and predetermined identities.

10 This distinction between territorial and non-territorial autonomy is made by a number of other scholars as well, including Heintze (1997, 37–46; 1998, 18–24), Hechter (2000, 72ff.), and Potier (2001, 55–9). For a recent conceptual and empirical study of this phenomenon, see Smith (2010).

11 There have been a number of attempts in the past to conceptualize 'territorial solutions'. These include especially Benedikter (2007), Brancati (2009), Coakley (2003), Dinstein (1981), Ghai (2000, 2003), Hannum (1996), Lapidoth (1996), McGarry and O'Leary (2010), O'Leary and

McGarry (2010), O'Leary (2005b), Nordquist (1998), Wehengama (2000) and Wolff and Weller (2005).

12  See also the more detailed discussion on the use of the term in Benedikter (2007, 16–20), Elazar (1987, ch. 2) and Ghai (2000, 8–24).

13  More recently, McGarry and O'Leary (2010) use the term 'federacy' for such arrangements, noting that 'the grant of self-government is constitutionally guaranteed and cannot be revoked by the centre unilaterally' and that it 'normally applies to a part of the state's territory, and normally a small part (in population)', thus setting it apart from both devolution (lack of constitutional guarantee) and federation (application to the entire territory). Elazar (n.d.) defines federacy in similar terms as a relationship '[w]hereby a larger power and a smaller polity are linked asymmetrically in a federal relationship in which the latter has substantial autonomy and in return has a minimal role in the governance of the larger power. Resembling a federation, the relationship between them can be dissolved only by mutual agreement.'

14  The definition of self-governance has been adapted from Wolff and Weller (2005) and is identical to its usage in Csergo and Wolff (2009) and Wolff (2010a).

15  Note that as forms of state construction, each of these types of governance arrangement can be applied with their territorial boundaries cutting across or around the settlement areas of ethnic or national minorities. In our conceptualization of TSG as a simultaneous conflict prevention/management/settlement mechanism, our empirical analysis focuses on arrangements with the latter kind of territorial boundaries.

16  A more detailed discussion of this goes well beyond the scope of this chapter, and beyond consociational theory as such, and would require consideration of a whole raft of other factors in addition to the structural factors I am focusing on, including especially questions related to the nature and structure of the negotiations process leading to an agreement (see, e.g., Bercovitch 1991; Bercovitch *et al.* 1991; Gartner and Bercovitch 2006; Jackson 2000; Kydd 2006).

17  I am particularly interested here in intra-state rather than trans-state demography. The latter also shape institutional design, however, as discussed by McGarry and O'Leary in relation to Northern Ireland (McGarry and O'Leary 2004) and more generally (McGarry and O'Leary 2010). See also Wolff (2007) on 'para-diplomacy' as institutional expression of trans-state ethnic demography.

18  Pearson (2001) uses the notion of 'quality' in a similar context and meaning: 'whether they made sense from a social, geographic, or political perspective'.

19  This point is also made by Beardsley (2008), Werner (1999), Werner and Yuen (2005).

20  On the 'spoiler problem' more generally, see Stedman (1997).

21  Zartman (2007, 476) goes as far as stating that 'Peacemaking rests squarely in the hands of third parties'.

22  The selection of cases was based somewhat randomly on availability of relevant data and the degree of prior knowledge I had. Work on a more comprehensive dataset of cases is ongoing.

23  The latest of Lijphart's writings available to Bogaards when he formulated the second of his critiques (Bogaards 2000) was Lijphart's *Patterns of Democracy. Government Forms and Performance in Thirty-Six Countries* (Lijphart 1999).

24  This point is made in similar vein by Kerr (2005), McGarry (2007b), Norris (2008), O'Leary (2005a), Schneckener (2002), (Weller 2008a), Weller and Wolff (2006), and Wolff (2003), as well as various contributions in Noel (2005) and Weller and Metzger (2008).

25  Prominent contributors to the debate include Barry (1975a, 1975b, 2000), Bogaards (1998, 2000, 2003), Horowitz (1985, 1990, 1991, 1993, 2008), Lustick (1979), contributions in Noel (2005) and in O'Flynn and Russell (2005), Reilly (2001, 2006), and Wimmer (2003). For more recent manifestations of the debate, see contributions in Taylor (2009) and Wolff (2010b).

26  The broader debate on AV and the implications of the case of Fiji has been carried for the past five years by Fraenkel and Grofman (2004, 2006) and Horowitz (2004, 2006; 2008, 1235–6).

27  See Roeder (2005), Roeder and Rothchild (2005a), Rothchild and Roeder (2005a, 2005b).

28  Roeder (2007) is an important exception here in its more comprehensive global analysis.

29  Lake and Rothchild (2005, 110–11) sceptically argue that '[t]erritorial decentralization is likely to prove a stable and effective long-term solution only under an extraordinary conjunction of conditions ... [which] are unlikely to be present at the end of contemporary civil wars'. However, the more recent study by Hartzell and Hoddie (2007) suggests that even after civil wars TSG arrangements have a significant positive impact by lowering the risk of a return to war.

# References

Barry, Brian 1975a 'The Consociational Model and Its Dangers', *European Journal of Political Research* 3(4): 393–413.

—— 1975b 'Political Accommodation and Consociational Democracy', *British Journal of Political Science* 5(4): 477–505.

—— 2000 *Culture and Inequality*. Cambridge: Polity.

Bauer, Otto 1907 *Die Nationalitätenfrage und die Sozialdemokratie*. Vienna: Verlag der Wiener Volksbuchhandlung Ignaz Brand.

Beardsley, Kyle 2008 'Agreement without Peace? International Mediation and Time Inconsistency Problems', *American Journal of Political Science* 52(4): 723–40.

Belmont, Katharine, Scott Mainwaring and Andrew Reynolds 2002 'Introduction: Institutional Design, Conflict Management, and Democracy', in *Architecture of Democracy*, ed. Andrew Reynolds. Oxford: Oxford University Press, 1–13.

Benedikter, Thomas 2007 *The World's Working Regional Autonomies*. London: Anthem Press.

Bercovitch, Jacob 1991 'International Mediation', *Journal of Peace Research* 28(1): 3–6.

Bercovitch, Jacob, J. Theodore Anagnoson and Donnette L. Wille 1991 'Some Conceptual Issues and Empirical Trends in the Study of Successful Mediation in International Relations', *Journal of Peace Research* 28(1): 7–17.

Bermeo, Nancy 2002 'The Import of Institutions', *Journal of Democracy* 13(2): 96–110.

Bogaards, Matthijs 1998 'The Favourable Factors for Consociational Democracy: A Review', *European Journal of Political Research* 33(4): 475–96.

—— 2000 'The Uneasy Relationship between Empirical and Normative Types in Consociational Theory', *Journal of Theoretical Politics* 12(4): 395–423.

—— 2003 'Electoral Choices for Divided Societies: Multiethnic Parties and Constituency Pooling in Africa', *Journal of Commonwealth and Comparative Politics* 41(3): 59–80.

Brancati, Dawn 2009 *Peace by Design: Managing Intrastate Conflict through Decentralization*. Oxford: Oxford University Press.

Brown, Michael E., ed. 1996 *The International Dimensions of Internal Conflict*. Cambridge, MA: MIT Press.

Bunce, Valerie 1999 *Subversive Institutions: The Design and the Destruction of Socialism and the State*. Cambridge: Cambridge University Press.

Bunce, Valerie, and Steven Watts 2005 'Managing Diversity and Sustaining Democracy: Ethnofederal versus Unitary States in the Postcommunist World', in *Sustainable Peace: Power and Democracy after Civil Wars*, eds. Philip G. Roeder and Donald Rothchild. Ithaca, NY: Cornell University Press, 133–58.

Carment, David, and Albrecht Schnabel, eds. 2003 *Conflict Prevention: Path to Peace or Grand Illusion?* Tokyo: United Nations University Press.

Chapman, T., and Philip G. Roeder 2007 'Partition as a Solution to Wars of Nationalism: The Importance of Institutions', *American Political Science Review* 101(4): 677–91.

Coakley, John, ed. 2003 *The Territorial Management of Ethnic Conflict*, 2nd edn. London: Frank Cass.

Cohen, F. S. 1997 'Proportional versus Majoritarian Ethnic Conflict Management in Democracies', *Comparative Political Studies* 30(5): 607–30.

Cordell, Karl, and Stefan Wolff 2009 *Ethnic Conflict: Causes – Consequences – Responses*. Polity: Cambridge.

—— 2010. 'Power Sharing', in *The Routledge Handbook of Ethnic Conflict*, eds. Karl Cordell and Stefan Wolff. London: Routledge, 300–10.

Cornell, Svante E. 2002 'Autonomy as a Source of Conflict: Caucasian Conflicts in Theoretical Perspective', *World Politics* 54(2): 245–76.

Csergo, Zsuzsa, and Stefan Wolff 2009 'Regions of Nationalism in Europe', in *105th Annual Meeting of the American Political Science Association*. Toronto.

Daftary, Farimah 2000 *Insular Autonomy: A Framework for Conflict Settlement. A Comparative Study of Corsica and the Åland Islands*. Flensburg: European Centre for Minority Issues.

Diehl, Paul F. and Joseph Lepgold, eds. 2003 *Regional Conflict Management*. Lanham, MD: Rowman & Littlefield.

Dinstein, Yoran, ed. 1981 *Models of Autonomy*. New Brunswick, NJ: Transaction Books.

Elazar, Daniel J. 1987 *Exploring Federalism*. Tuscaloosa, AL: University of Alabama Press.

—— 1991 'Federal Systems of the World: A Handbook of Federal, Confederal and Autonomy Arrangements' (at: www.jcpa.org/dje/books/fedsysworld-intro.htm).

Fraenkel, Jon and Bernard Grofman 2004 'A Neo-Downsian Model of the Alternative Vote as a Mechanism for Mitigating Ethnic Conflict in Plural Societies', *Public Choice* 121: 487–506.

—— 2006 'Does the Alternative Vote Foster Moderation in Ethnically Divided Societies? The Case of Fiji', *Comparative Political Studies* 39(5): 623–51.

Gartner, Scott Sigmund and Jacob Bercovitch 2006 'Overcoming Obstacles to Peace: The Contribution of Mediation to Short-Lived Conflict Settlements', *International Studies Quarterly* 50(4): 819–40.

Ghai, Yash, ed. 2000 *Autonomy and Ethnicity*. Cambridge: Cambridge University Press.

—— 2003 'Territorial Options', in *Contemporary Peacemaking: Conflict, Violence, and Peace Processes*, eds. John Darby and Roger McGinty. Basingstoke: Palgrave, 184–93.

Ghai, Yash and Jill Cottrell 2008 'A Tale of Three Constitutions: Ethnicity and Politics in Fiji', in *Constitutional Design for Divided Societies: Integration or Accommodation?* ed. Sujit Choudhry. Oxford: Oxford University Press, 287–315.

Gurr, Ted Robert 1993 *Minorities at Risk: A Global View of Ethnopolitical Conflicts*. Washington, DC: United States Institutes of Peace Press.

Hale, Henry E. 2000 'The Parade of Sovereignties: Testing Theories of Secession in the Soviet Setting', *British Journal of Political Science* 30: 31–56.

—— 2004 'Divided We Stand: Institutional Sources of Ethnofederal State Survival and Collapse', *World Politics* 56: 165–93.

Hannum, Hurst 1996 *Sovereignty and Self-determination: The Accommodation of Conflicting Right*, 2nd edn. Philadelphia, PA: University of Pennsylvania Press.

Hannum, Hurst and Robert Lillich 1980 'The Concept of Autonomy in International Law', *American Journal of International Law* 74(4): 858–89.

Harff, Barbara and Ted Robert Gurr 2004 *Ethnic Conflict in World Politics*. Boulder, CO: Westview Press.

Hartzell, Caroline and Matthew Hoddie 2003 'Institutionalizing Peace: Power Sharing and Post-Civil War Conflict Management', 2(47): 318–32.

—— 2007 *Crafting Peace: Power-sharing Institutions and the Negotiated Settlement of Civil Wars*. University Park, PA: Pennsylvania State University Press.

Hechter, Michael 2000 *Containing Nationalism*. Oxford: Oxford University Press.

Heintze, Hans-Joachim 1997 'Wege zur Verwirklichung des Selbstbestimmungsrechts der Völker innerhalb bestehender Staaten', in *Selbstbestimmungsrecht der Völker – Herausforderung der Staatenwelt*, ed. Hans-Joachim Heintze. Bonn: Dietz, 16–59.

—— 1998 'On the Legal Understanding of Autonomy', in *Autonomy: Applications and Implications*, ed. Markku Suksi. The Hague: Kluwer Law International, 7–32.

Horowitz, Donald L. 1985 *Ethnic Groups in Conflict*. Berkeley, CA: University of California Press.

—— 1990 'Ethnic Conflict Management for Policymakers', in *Conflict and Peacemaking in Multiethnic Societies*, ed. J. V. Montville. Lexington, KY: Lexington Books.

—— 1991 *A Democratic South Africa? Constitutional Engineering in a Divided Society*. Berkeley, CA: University of California Press.

—— 1993 'Democracy in Divided Societies', *Journal of Democracy* 4(4): 18–38.

—— 2003 'Electoral Systems and Their Goals: A Primer for Decision-Makers', *Journal of Democracy* 14(4): 115–27.

—— 2004 'The Alternative Vote and Interethnic Moderation: A Reply to Fraenkel and Grofman', *Public Choice* 121(3–4): 507–17.

—— 2006 'Strategy Takes a Holiday: Fraenkel and Grofman on the Alternative Vote', *Comparative Political Studies* 39: 652–62.

—— 2007 'The Many Uses of Federalism', *Drake Law Review* 55(4): 953–66.

—— 2008 'Conciliatory Institutions and Constitutional Processes in Post-conflict States', *William and Mary Law Review* 49: 1213–48.

Jackson, Richard 2000 'Successful Negotiation in International Violent Conflict', *Journal of Peace Research* 37(3): 323–43.

Jarstad, Anna K. 2008 'Power Sharing: Former Enemies in Joint Government', in *From War to Democracy: Dilemmas of Peacebuilding*, eds. Anna K. Jarstad and Timothy D. Sisk. Cambridge: Cambridge University Press, 105–33.

Kerr, Michael 2005 *Imposing Power-Sharing: Conflict and Coexistence in Northern Ireland and Lebanon*, Dublin: Irish Academic Press.

Kettley, C., J. Sullivan and J. Fyfe 2001 'Self-determination disputes and complex power sharing arrangements: A background paper for debate' (at: www.intstudies.cam.ac.uk/centre/cps/download/background1.pdf; accessed 4 March 2009).

Kydd, Andrew H. 2006 'When Can Mediators Build Trust?', *American Political Science Review* 100(3): 449–62.

Lake, David A. and Donald Rothchild 1996 'Containing Fear: The Origins and Management of Ethnic Conflict', *International Security* 21(2): 41–75.

—— 2005 'Territorial Decentralization and Civil War Settlements', in *Sustainable Peace: Power and Democracy after Civil Wars*, eds. Philip G. Roeder and Donald Rothchild, Ithaca, NY: Cornell University Press, 109–32.

Lapidoth, Ruth 1996 *Autonomy: Flexible Solutions to Ethnic Conflicts*, Washington, DC: United States Institute of Peace Press.

Lijphart, Arend 1968 'Typologies of Democratic Systems', *Comparative Political Studies* 1(1): 3–44.

—— 1969 'Consociational Democracy', *World Politics* 21(2): 207–25.

—— 1977 *Democracy in Plural Societies*, New Haven, CT: Yale University Press.

—— 1979 'Consocation and Federation: Conceptual and Empirical Links', *Canadian Journal of Political Science* 12(3): 499–515.

—— 1985 *Power-Sharing in South Africa*. Vol. 24 of *Policy Papers in International Affairs*, Berkeley, CA: Institute of International Studies, University of California.

—— 1995a 'Self-determination versus Pre-determination of Ethnic Minorities in Power Sharing Systems', in *The Rights of Minority Cultures*, ed. Will Kymlicka. Oxford: Oxford University Press, 275–87.

—— 1995b 'Self-determination versus Pre-determination of Ethnic Minorities in Power Sharing Systems', in *The Rights of Minority Cultures*, ed. Will Kymlicka. Oxford: Oxford University Press, 275–87.

—— 1998 'Consensus and Consensus Democracy: Cultural, Structural, Functional, and Rational-Choice Explanations', *Scandinavian Political Studies* 21(2): 99–108.

—— 1999 *Patterns of Democracy: Government Forms and Performance in Thirty-Six Countries*. New Haven, CT: Yale University Press.

—— 2000 'Definitions, Evidence and Policy: A Response to Matthijs Bogaards' Critique', *Journal of Theoretical Politics* 12(4): 425–31.

—— 2002 'The Wave of Power Sharing Democracy', in *The Architecture of Democracy: Constitutional Design, Conflict Management and Democracy*, ed. Andrew Reynolds, Oxford: Oxford University Press, 37–54.

—— 2004 'Constitutional Design for Divided Societies', *Journal of Democracy* 15(2): 96–109.

—— 2008 *Thinking about Democracy: Power Sharing and Majority Rule in Theory and Practice*, London: Routledge.

Lorwin, Val R. 1971 'Segmented Pluralism: Ideological Cleavages and Political Cohesion in the Smaller European Democracies', *Comparative Politics* 3 (January): 153–6.

Lustick, Ian 1979 'Stability in Divided Societies: Consociationalism v. Control', *World Politics* 31(2): 325–44.

McGarry, John 2007a 'Asymmetry in Federations, Federacies and Unitary States', *Ethnopolitics* 6(1): 105–16.

—— 2007b 'Iraq: Liberal Consociation and Conflict Management', in *Iraq: Preventing Another Generation of Conflict*, eds. Ben Roswell, David Malone and Markus Bouillon. Boulder, CO: Lynne Rienner Press, 169–88.

McGarry, John and Brendan O'Leary 1993 'Introduction: The Macro-Political Regulation of Ethnic Conflict', in *The Politics of Ethnic Conflict Regulation*, eds. John McGarry and Brendan O'Leary. London: Routlegde, 1–40.

—— eds. 2004a *The Northern Ireland Conflict: Consociational Engagements*, Oxford: Oxford University Press.

—— 2004b 'Introduction: Consociational Theory and Northern Ireland', in *The Northern Ireland Conflict: Consociational Engagements*, eds. John McGarry and Brendan O'Leary. Oxford: Oxford University Press, 1–60.

—— 2006a 'Consociational Theory, Northern Ireland's Conflict and Its Agreement: Part 1. What Consociationalists Can Learn from Northern Ireland', *Government and Opposition* 41(1): 43–63.

—— 2006b 'Consociational Theory, Northern Ireland's Conflict and Its Agreement: Part 2. What Critics of Consociation Can Learn from Northern Ireland', *Government and Opposition* 41(2): 249–77.

—— 2008a 'Consociation and Its Critics: Northern Ireland after the Belfast Agreement', in *Constitutional Design for Divided Societies: Integration or Accommodation?* ed. Sujit Choudhry. Oxford: Oxford University Press, 369–408.

—— 2008b 'Iraq's Constitution of 2005: Liberal Consociation as Political Prescription', in *Constitutional Design for Divided Societies: Integration or Accommodation?* ed. Sujit Choudhry. Oxford: Oxford University Press, 342–68.

—— 2009a 'Must Pluri-National Federations Fail?', *Ethnopolitics* 8(1): 5–25.

—— 2009b 'Power Shared after the Deaths of Thousands', in *Consociational Theory: McGarry and O'Leary and the Northern Ireland Conflict*, ed. Rupert Taylor. London: Routledge, 15–84.

—— 2009c 'Under Friendly and Less-Friendly Fire', in *Consociational Theory: McGarry and O'Leary and the Northern Ireland Conflict*, ed. Rupert Taylor, London: Routledge, 333–88.

—— 2010 'Territorial Approaches to Ethnic Conflict Settlement', in *The Routledge Handbook of Ethnic Conflict*, eds. Karl Cordell and Stefan Wolff. London: Routledge, 249–65.

Mill, John Stuart 1861 *Considerations on Representative Government*. New York, NY: Liberal Arts Press.

Mitchell, Paul, Geoffrey Evans and Brendan O'Leary 2009 'Extremist Outbidding in Ethnic Party Systems is Not Inevitable: Tribune Parties in Northern Ireland', *Political Studies Review* 57(2): 397–421.

Murray, Christina and Richard Simeon 2008 'Recognition without Empowerment: Minorities in a Democratic South Africa', in *Constitutional Design for Divided Societies: Integration or Accommodation?* ed. Sujit Choudhry. Oxford: Oxford University Press, 409–37.

Noel, Sid, ed. 2005 *From Power Sharing to Democracy: Post-conflict Institutions in Ethnically Divided Societies*. Montreal: McGill-Queen's University Press.

Nordlinger, Eric A. 1972 *Conflict Regulation in Divided Societies*. Cambridge, MA: Harvard University Center for International Affairs.

Nordquist, Kjell-Åke 1998 'Autonomy as a Conflict-solving Mechanism: An Overview', in *Autonomy: Applications and Implications*, ed. Markku Suksi. The Hague: Kluwer Law International, 59–77.

Norris, Pippa 2008 *Driving Democracy: Do Power-sharing Institutions Work?* Cambridge: Cambridge University Press.

O'Flynn, Ian and David Russell, eds. 2005 *Power Sharing: New Challenges for Divided Societies.* London: Pluto Press.

O'Leary, Brendan 2005a 'Debating Consociational Politics: Normative and Explanatory Arguments', in *From Powersharing to Democracy*, ed. Sid Noel. Montreal: McGill/Queen's University Press, 3–43.

—— 2005b 'Powersharing, Pluralist Federation and Federacy', in *The Future of Kurdistan in Iraq*, eds. Brendan O'Leary, John McGarry and Khaled Salih. Philadelphia, PA: University of Pennsylvania Press, 47–91.

O'Leary, Brendan and John McGarry 2010 'The Politics of Accommodation: Surveying National and Ethnic Conflict Regulation in Democractic States', in *The Study of Politics and Ethnicity: Recent Analytical Developments*, eds. Adrian Guelke and Jean Tournon. Opladen: Barbara Budrich.

O'Leary, Brendan, Bernard Grofman and John Elklit 2005 'Divisor Methods for Sequential Portfolio Allocation in Multi-Party Executive Bodies: Evidence from Northern Ireland and Denmark', *American Journal of Political Science* 49(1): 198–211.

Otunnu, O. A. and Michael W. Doyle 1998 *Peacemaking and Peacekeeping for the New Century.* Lanham, MD: Rowman & Littlefield.

Palley, Claire (ed.) 1991 'Introduction', in *Minorities and Autonomy in Western Europe*, ed. Minority Rights Group International. London: Minority Rights Group International.

Papagianni, Katja 2008 'Participation and State Legitimation', in *Building States to Build Peace*, eds. Charles T. Call and Vanessa Wyeth. Boulder, CO: Lynne Rienner Publishers, 49–71.

Pearson, Frederic S. 2001 'Dimensions of Conflict Resolution in Ethnopolitical Disputes', *Journal of Peace Research* 38(3): 275–87.

Potier, Tim 2001 *Conflict in Nagorno-Karabakh, Abkhazia and South Ossetia. A Legal Appraisal.* The Hague: Kluwer International Law.

Pugh, Michael and W. P. Singh Sidhu 2003 *The United Nations and Regional Security: Europe and Beyond.* Boulder, CO: Lynne Rienner.

Putnam, Robert D. 1988 'Diplomacy and Domestic Affairs: The Logic of Two-Level Games', *International Organization* 42(3): 427–60.

Reilly, Benjamin 2001 *Democracy in Divided Societies.* Cambridge: Cambridge University Press.

—— 2006 *Democracy and Diversity: Political Engineering in the Asia-Pacific.* Oxford: Oxford University Press.

Renner, Karl 1918 *Das Selbstbestimmungsrecht der Nationen in besonderer Anwendung auf Österreich.* Leipzig and Vienna: Deuticke.

Roeder, Philip G. 1991 'Soviet Federalism and Ethnic Mobilization', *World Politics* 43(2): 196–232.

—— 2005 'Power Dividing as an Alternative to Power Sharing', in *Sustainable Peace: Power and Democracy after Civil Wars*, eds. Philip G. Roeder and Donald Rothchild. Ithaca, NY: Cornell University Press, 51–82.

—— 2007 *Where Nation-States Come From: Institutional Change in the Age of Nationalism.* Princeton, NJ : Princeton University Press.

Roeder, Philip G. and Donald Rothchild 2005a 'Conclusion: Nation-State Stewardship and the Alternatives to Power Sharing', in *Sustainable Peace: Power and Democracy after Civil Wars*, eds. Philip G. Roeder and Donald Rothchild. Ithaca, NY: Cornell University Press, 319–46.

Roeder, Philip G. and Donald Rothchild, eds. 2005b *Sustainable Peace: Power and Democracy after Civil Wars.* Ithaca, NY: Cornell University Press.

Rothchild, Donald and Caroline Hartzell 2000 'Security in Deeply Divided Societies: The Role of Territorial Autonomy', in *Identity and Territorial Autonomy in Plural Societies*, eds. William Safran and Ramón Máiz. London: Frank Cass, 254–71.

Rothchild, Donald and Philip G. Roeder 2005a 'Dilemmas of State-building in Divided Societies', in *Sustainable Peace: Power and Democracy after Civil Wars*, eds. Philip G. Roeder and Donald Rothchild. Ithaca, NY: Cornell University Press, 1–25.

—— 2005b 'Power Sharing as an Impediment to Peace and Democracy', in *Sustainable Peace: Power and Democracy after Civil Wars*, eds. Philip G. Roeder and Donald Rothchild. Ithaca, NY: Cornell University Press, 29–50.

Safran, William and Ramón Máiz, eds. 2000 *Identity and Territorial Autonomy in Plural Societies*. London: Frank Cass.

Saideman, S. M., D. J. Lanoue, M. Campenni and S. Stanton 2002 'Democratization, Political Institutions and Ethnic Conflict: A Pooled Time-Series Analysis', 1985–98', *Comparative Political Studies* 35(1): 103–29.

Schneckener, Ulrich 2002 'Making Power Sharing Work: Lessons from Successes and Failures in Ethnic Conflict Regulation', *Journal of Peace Research* 39(2): 203–28.

Sisk, Timothy D. 1996 *Power Sharing and International Mediation in Ethnic Conflict*. Washington, DC: United States Institute for Peace Press.

—— 2008 'Peacebuilding as Democratization: Findings and Recommendations', in *From War to Democracy: Dilemmas of Peacebuilding*, eds. Anna K. Jarstad and Timothy D. Sisk. Cambridge: Cambridge University Press, 239–59.

Smith, David J. 2010 'National Cultural Autonomy', in *The Routledge Handbook of Ethnic Conflict*, eds. Karl Cordell and Stefan Wolff. London: Routledge, 278–87.

Snyder, Jack 2000 *From Voting to Violence: Democratization and Nationalist Conflict*. New York, NY: Norton.

Stedman, Stephen John 1997 'Spoiler Problems in Peace Processes', *International Security* 22(2): 5–53.

Stedman, Stephen John, Donald Rothchild and Elizabeth M. Cousens, eds. 2003. *Ending Civil Wars: The Implementation of Peace Agreements*. Boulder, CO: Lynne Rienner.

Suberu, Rotimi T. 1993 'The Travails of Federalism in Nigeria', *Journal of Democracy* 4(4): 39–53.

Suksi, Markku, ed. 1998 *Autonomy: Applications and Implications*. The Hague: Kluwer Law International

Taylor, Rupert, ed. 2009 *Consociational Theory: McGarry and O'Leary and the Northern Ireland Conflict*. London: Routledge.

Thakur, Ramesh and Albrecht Schnabel 2001 *United Nations Peacekeeping Operations: Ad Hoc Missions, Permanent Engagement*. Tokyo: United Nations University Press.

Treisman, Daniel S. 1997 'Russia's "Ethnic Revival": The Separatist Activism of Regional Leaders in a Postcommunist Order', *World Politics* 49(2): 212–49.

—— 2007 *The Architecture of Government: Rethinking Political Decentralization*. Cambridge: Cambridge University Press.

Van Houten, Pieter and Stefan Wolff 2007 'The stability of autonomy arrangements: the role of external agents'. Presented at the 48th Annual Convention of the International Studies Association, Chicago, IL.

Wallensteen, Peter 2007 *Understanding Conflict Resolution*, 2nd edn. London: Sage

Walter, Barbara F. 1999a 'Designing Transitions from Civil War', in *Civil Wars, Insecurity, and Intervention*, eds. Barbara F. Walter and Jack Snyder. New York, NY: Columbia University Press, 38–69.

—— 1999b 'Designing Transitions from Civil War: Demobilization, Democratization, and Commitments to Peace', *International Security* 24(1): 127–55.

—— 2002 *Committing to Peace: The Successful Settlement of Civil Wars*. Princeton: Princeton University Press.

Walter, Barbara F. and Jack Snyder 1999 *Civil Wars, Insecurity and Intervention*. New York, NY: Columbia University Press.

Wehengama, G. 2000 *Minority Claims: From Autonomy to Secession*. Aldershot: Ashgate.

Weller, Marc 2008a *Escaping the Self-determination Trap*. Leiden: Martinus Nijhoff.

—— 2008b 'Settling Self-determination Conflicts: An Introduction', in *Settling Self-determination Disputes: Complex Power Sharing in Theory and Practice*, eds. Marc Weller and Barbara Metzger. Leiden: Martinus Nijhoff, xi–xvii.

Weller, Marc and Barbara Metzger, eds. 2008 *Settling Self-determination Disputes: Complex Power Sharing in Theory and Practice*. Leiden and Boston: Martinus Nijhoff Publishers.

Weller, Marc and Stefan Wolff 2005a 'Recent Trends in Autonomy and State Construction', in *Autonomy, Self-governance and Conflict Resolution: Innovative Approaches to Institutional Design in Divided Societies*, eds. Marc Weller and Stefan Wolff. London: Routledge, 262–70.

—— 2006 'Bosnia and Herzegovina Ten Years after Dayton: Lessons for Internationalized State Building', *Ethnopolitics* 5(1): 1–13.

—— 2008 *Institutions for the Management of Ethnopolitical Conflicts in Central and Eastern Europe*. Strasbourg: Council of Europe.

Weller, Marc and Stefan Wolff, eds. 2005b *Autonomy, Self-governance and Conflict Resolution: Innovative Approaches to Institutional Design in Divided Societies*. London: Routledge.

Werner, Suzanne 1999 'The Precarious Nature of Peace: Resolving the Issues, Enforcing the Settlement and Renegotiating the Terms', *American Journal of Political Science* 43(3): 912–34.

Werner, Suzanne and Amy Yuen 2005 'Making and Keeping Peace', *International Organization* 59(2): 261–92.

Wilson, Robin 2009 'From Consociationalism to Interculturalism', in *Consociational Theory: McGarry and O'Leary and the Northern Ireland Conflict*, ed. Rupert Taylor. London: Routledge, 221–36.

Wimmer, Andreas 2003 'Democracy and Ethno-Religious Conflict in Iraq', *Survival* 45(4): 111–34.

Woelk, Jens, Francesco Palermo and Joseph Marko, eds. 2008 *Tolerance through Law: Self-governance and Group Rights in South Tyrol*. Leiden and Boston: Martinus Nijhoff.

Wolff, Stefan 2003 *Disputed Territories: The Transnational Dynamics of Ethnic Conflict Settlement*. New York, NY: Berghahn.

—— 2005 'Electoral Systems Design and Power Sharing Regimes', in *Powersharing: New Challenges for Divided Societies*, eds. Ian O'Flynn and David Russell. London: Pluto, 59–74.

—— 2007 'Paradiplomacy: Scope, Opportunities and Challenges', *Bologna Center Journal of International Affairs* 10(1): 141–50.

—— 2008a 'Complex Power Sharing as Conflict Resolution: South Tyrol in Comparative Perspective', in *Tolerance through Law: Self-governance and Group Rights in South Tyrol*, eds. Jens Woelk, Francesco Palermo and Joseph Marko. Leiden: Martinus Nijhoff, 329–70.

—— 2008b 'Power Sharing and the Vertical Layering of Authority: A Review of Current Practices', in *Settling Self-determination Disputes: Complex Power Sharing in Theory and Practice*, eds. Marc Weller and Barbara Metzger. Leiden: Martinus Nijhoff, 407–50.

—— 2009a 'Complex Power-sharing and the Centrality of Territorial Self-governance in Contemporary Conflict Settlements', *Ethnopolitics* 8(1): 27–45.

—— 2009b 'Peace by Design? Towards "Complex Power Sharing"', in *Consociational Theory: McGarry and O'Leary and the Northern Ireland Conflict*, ed. Rupert Taylor. London: Routledge.

—— 2010a 'Approaches to Conflict Resolution in Divided Societies: The Many Uses of Territorial Self-governance', *Ethnopolitics Papers* (5) (at: http://centres.exeter.ac.uk/exceps/downloads/Ethnopolitics_Papers_No5_Wolff.pdf).

—— 2010b 'Consociationalism, Power Sharing, and Politics at the Centre', in *The International Studies Encyclopedia*, ed. Robert A. Denemark. London: Blackwell Publishing, 535–6.

Wolff, Stefan and Pieter van Houten 2008 'The external management of peace settlements: international organisations and conflict resolution in the Western Balkans and the Former Soviet Union'. Presented at the International Studies Association, 49th Annual Convention, San Francisco.

Wolff, Stefan and Marc Weller 2005 'Self-determination and Autonomy: A conceptual introduction', in *Autonomy, Self-governance and Conflict Resolution: Innovative Approaches to Institutional Design in Divided Societies*, eds. Marc Weller and Stefan Wolff. London: Routledge.

Zartman, I. William 1989 *Ripe for Resolution: Conflict and Intervention in Africa*. Oxford: Oxford University Press.

—— 2007 'Conclusion: The Use of Methods and Techniques in a Conflict's Lifespan', in *Peacemaking in International Conflict: Methods and Techniques*, ed. I. William Zartman. Washington, DC: United States Institute of Peace Press, 465–77.

Zartman, I. William and Saadia Touval 1985 'International Mediation: Conflict Resolution and Power Politics', *Journal of Social Issues* 41(2): 27–45.

# 2 Centripetalism

## Cooperation, accommodation and integration

*Benjamin Reilly*

Centripetal approaches to conflict management seek to foster peaceful politics by encouraging cooperation, accommodation and integration in divided societies. However, the specific institutional recommendations to achieve these goals differ enormously from those advanced by advocates of consociationalism, power dividing or territorial self-governance.[1]

## The main characteristics of centripetal approaches

Centripetalists believe that the best way to manage democracy in divided societies is not to replicate existing ethnic divisions in the legislature and other representative organs, but rather to put in place institutional incentives for cross-ethnic behaviour in order to encourage accommodation between rival groups. As such, they typically reject elite-driven approaches such as consociationalism, and the reification of ethnicity that goes with it, and instead seek to dilute the ethnic character of competitive politics and promote outcomes which favour the political centre. To do this, centripetalists place a premium on promoting cross-ethnic electoral and party systems that make politicians reliant on the votes of different ethnic communities to gain election. In so doing, they advocate political institutions that can help to break down the salience of ethnicity rather than fostering its representation.

Perhaps the clearest distinction between centripetalism and other approaches is found in their contrasting recommendations regarding the design of electoral systems. One of the most fundamental relationships in political science is that between electoral systems and the representation of minorities. Proportional representation (PR) is frequently advocated as a key reform in ethnically plural societies to ensure fair representation of minorities and majorities alike. However, because PR systems encourage smaller parties they tend to fragment the party system and can encourage parties to craft their appeals around narrow sectarian interests, such as ethnicity – precisely because they can be secure in gaining seats by appealing to a relatively narrow section of society. In addition, there is a difference between representation and power: a minority can be fairly represented in a legislature but remain completely shut out of political power in government.

For this reason, centripetalists often see PR as a cause of rather than a solution to problems of ethnic politics. Instead of focusing on minority representation, they recommend electoral rules which can make politicians reciprocally dependent on the votes of members of groups other than their own, and which more broadly favour multiethnic political parties rather than ethnically exclusive ones. Specific institutional reforms to achieve such outcomes include the use of cross-regional or vote-transfer electoral systems, political party laws which require cross-national party organization, and legislative selection procedures which encourage median, centrist outcomes. These and other kinds of institutions give parties and candidates electoral incentives to 'pool votes' across ethnic lines, centripetalists contend, and can thus encourage vote-seeking politicians to reach out across the ethnic divide and, in so doing, help to take the heat out of ethnic politics (Horowitz 1985, 1991).

In an earlier book on electoral engineering for divided societies (Reilly 2001), I examined the record of centripetalism as a conflict management strategy, and identified three facilitating components which seem to recur across different countries and contexts:

1   the presentation of *electoral incentives* for campaigning politicians to reach out to and attract votes from a range of ethnic groups other than their own, thus encouraging candidates to moderate their political rhetoric on potentially divisive issues and forcing them to broaden their policy positions;
2   the presence of multiethnic *arenas of bargaining* such as parliamentary and executive forums, in which political actors representing different identity groups have an incentive to come together and cut deals on reciprocal electoral support, and hence perhaps on other more substantial policy issues as well; and
3   the development of *centrist, aggregative and multiethnic political parties* or coalitions of parties which are capable of making cross-ethnic appeals and presenting a complex and diverse range of policy options to the electorate.

By what specific institutional designs can such desirable outcomes be encouraged in divided societies, where cooperation across social cleavages is, by definition, lacking? One approach is to structure electoral processes so as to require successful candidates to gain support across different regions of a country, thus helping to break down the appeal of narrow parochialism or regionalism. Another is to give campaigning politicians incentives to seek the second-preference votes of electors from rival ethnic groups under electoral systems which allow the expression of a gradation of political preferences. A third is to mandate some degree of multiethnicity within political parties and other representative bodies, via requirements that compel parties to put forward heterogeneous candidate lists or organize on a cross-regional basis, thus making parties themselves a potential site for multiethnic bargaining. While very different, these diverse strategies all represent examples of centripetal approaches to institutional design, in that they all seek to nudge the basis of representative democracy in divided societies away from the politics of ethnic solidarity and towards greater interethnicity.

## Centripetalism in practice

The 'distribution requirement' applied at presidential elections in Nigeria, Kenya and Indonesia is an example of the first kind of approach, which seeks to encourage cross-regional politics by requiring winning presidential candidates to gain not just a majority of the vote, but a spread of votes across different parts of the country, in order to be elected. Distribution requirements have been mostly used for presidential elections in large, ethnically diverse states in order to ensure that winning candidates receive a broad cross-national spread of electoral support, rather than drawing their votes from one region only. Nigeria, for instance, requires a president to win a majority overall and at least one-third of the vote in at least two-thirds of all states. The Kenyan constitution provides a similar threshold, requiring successful candidates to win a plurality of the vote overall as well one-quarter of valid votes cast in at least five of the eight provinces. In Indonesia, candidates for president must gain over 50 per cent of all votes nationally as well as at least 20 per cent in half of all provinces to avoid a second-round run-off.

There is disagreement among scholars as to the utility of devices, with some interpreting them as impotent or even harmful interferences with the democratic process, while others see them as important mechanisms for muting ethnic conflict and ensuring the election of broad, pan-ethnic presidents (Sisk 1996, 55). The empirical evidence to date reflects this divergence of opinion. In both Kenya and Nigeria, problems have arisen with the operation of such systems when no candidate has met the required cross-national vote spread or when an incumbent has died in office. But despite these problems, distribution requirements have remained a feature of national electoral politics, and in Nigeria have been extended to parliamentary elections as well via reforms that make national party registration dependent on the vote shares at local elections (Bogaards 2008, 54). In Indonesia, distribution laws seem more successful. For instance, incumbent president Susilo Bambang Yudhoyono won an overwhelming first-round electoral victory in 2009, easily amassing the necessary distribution of votes across the archipelago to take the presidency. Indeed, Yudhoyono provides a good example of the kind of president centripetalists endorse: centrist, moderate, with broad-based support from a range of different regions and groups. For similar reasons, distribution requirements have also been proposed (but not enacted) for presidential elections in Iraq (Wimmer 2003, 122).

For parliamentary elections, a more direct and potentially more powerful centripetal approach to electoral system design is to use vote-transfer electoral systems such as the alternative vote (AV) or the single transferable vote (STV), which ask voters to declare not only their first choice candidate, but also their second, third and subsequent choices among all candidates standing. Under AV rules, if no one gains an outright majority, these votes are transferred according to their rankings in order to elect a majority-supported winner. STV, as a proportional system, uses a quota rather than a majority threshold for election, but the same basic principle applies. While the best-known examples of such vote-transfer systems are the established democracies of Australia and Ireland, such systems have also been used in a number of ethnically divided developing democracies, including Papua New Guinea, Northern Ireland and Fiji, as well as for one-off elections in Estonia and Bosnia. AV and STV systems also have a history of use in several Canadian provinces and US cities. Related systems include the supplementary vote used for presidential elections in Sri Lanka and London mayoral elections, and variants of the Borda count which are used for parliamentary elections in Nauru and some seats in Slovenia (Reilly 2004). STV also has a well-established record of use in intra-parliamentary elections, such as the selection of upper houses in India and a number of other South Asian democracies.

Because they enable politicians to make deals for reciprocal vote transfers with their rivals, in ethnically diverse societies such systems can present vote-maximizing candidates with incentives to seek secondary preference votes from groups other than their own, so as to ensure the broadest possible range of support for their candidacy. To obtain such cross-ethnic support, candidates may need to behave accommodatively on core issues, tempering their rhetorical and policy positions so as to attract broader support. There is evidence of this practice occurring in very different types of multiethnic societies including Papua New Guinea, Fiji and Northern Ireland at different times.[2] However, the utility of using such systems in deeply divided societies remains a subject of debate: the accommodation-inducing potential of 'preference-swapping' is dependent on a range of facilitating conditions, including a competitive party system, an ethnically heterogeneous electorate and a degree of moderate sentiment existing in the community at large. For this reason, critics have pointed to the difficulties of inducing accommodation via electoral engineering, and questioned whether vote transfers have indeed promoted moderate outcomes in bipolar societies such as Northern Ireland and Fiji.[3]

Other centripetal electoral reforms seek to undercut the logic of ethnic politics by requiring political parties to present ethnically mixed slates of candidates for 'at-large' elections, thus making voter choice contingent, at some level, upon issues other than ethnicity. In multiethnic societies as diverse as Singapore, Lebanon and Djibouti, electoral laws require parties to include ethnic minorities on their candidate lists in multimember districts. As the electorate comprises voters from all groups in a given district, some degree of cross-ethnic voting is thus inevitable. However, these kinds of stipulations are often more tokenistic than substantive. In Singapore, for instance, parties and alliances contesting the fourteen multimember districts designated as 'Group Representation Constituencies' must include one or two candidates from designated ethnic minorities on their ticket – an arrangement which requires only a minimal degree of cross-ethnic voting, while guaranteeing that nine seats in the Singaporean parliament will be occupied by Malays, and five by Indians or other minorities. Today, the island states of the Comoros and Mauritius use similar measures to ensure ethnic minority representation via 'best loser' schemes for members of underrepresented groups or parties.

In Africa, a variety of cross-voting schemes to ameliorate ethnic divisions have been proposed over the years. An elaborate racial cross-voting scheme was included in the 1961 Rhodesian constitution to allow black voters to cast a vote in white electoral units and vice versa, as a means of moderating the potential election of extremists in either camp. However, the qualifications for each voter roll were based on a mix of income, property and education qualifications which seemed designed to maintain the economic superiority of whites, and few black electors ever registered or voted in the two elections (1962 and 1965) held under the 1961 constitution.[4] There is also the intriguing case of the 'constituency pooling' model proposed (but never implemented) in Uganda. According to Bogaards (2003), this was first introduced in the Ugandan electoral law of 1971 as a means of overcoming regional, ethnic and religious differences and encouraging the creation of national political parties. Under this proposal, candidates would stand for election in four different electoral districts at the same time: their 'basic' district and three 'national' districts. The candidate receiving the largest overall percentage of votes, combining both the 'basic' constituency and 'national' constituencies, would win the seat. Unfortunately for comparative purposes, not to mention the people of Uganda, Idi Amin seized power in a military coup and cancelled the elections.

Fiji provides another, even more complex, example of mandated cross-voting in the shape of the political system which existed there from independence in 1970 until the ethnically motivated coup of 1987. As in Lebanon, the ethnic balance of the 52-seat parliament was predetermined, with 22 seats reserved for Fijians, another 22 reserved for Indo-Fijians and the remaining 8 seats reserved for 'General Electors' (i.e. Europeans, Chinese and other minorities). In addition, 23 electorates were designated as 'national' seats which required voters from one ethnic community to vote for candidates from a different community, in order to ensure that elected members from these seats would have to draw a degree of cross-communal support from all groups. Like the abortive

Ugandan cross-voting model, the Fijian system required each elector to cast no fewer than *four* votes: one for their communal (co-ethnic) representative, and one each for a 'national' candidate from each of the other three designated communal groups. An indigenous Fijian voter, for example, would vote for a Fijian candidate in his or her communal electorate, and then cast three additional votes – one for a Fijian, one for an Indo-Fijian and one for a General Elector – in the appropriate national electorates.

Other cross-voting schemes mix centripetal and communal incentives. Lebanon's 'confessional' political system, in which both parliamentary seats and key executive offices are allocated on a sectarian basis, is perhaps the best-known example. To do this, the composition of Lebanon's 128-seat national assembly is preordained according to communal ratios, with an even split between Christians and Muslims, as well as specified seat balances for Sunni, Shia, Maronite, Druze and other confessional groups within each religious community. Key executive offices such as the presidency, prime ministership and the parliamentary speaker are also allocated on a confessional basis. Elections are contested by inter-confessional electoral alliances which must match the preordained confessional structure of each multimember electoral district. In practice, this requires electors to engage in a degree of cross-voting by choosing candidates who hail from outside as well as within their own confessional identity group. But the Lebanese model also has real drawbacks, fixing ethnic identities in place and making communal affiliation the basis of the entire political system.[5]

Similarly complex schemes for cross-voting have been a part of transitional constitutions in Cyprus, Bosnia, Northern Ireland, Burundi and elsewhere. In addition, informal practice of cross-ethnic vote pooling has been identified in the electoral politics of a number of ethnically plural states, such as Malaysia and Sri Lanka (Horowitz 1985). Despite a mixed record of success, the fact that so many different countries and conflicts have made recourse to the basic ideas of cross-voting, often without reference to or apparent knowledge of the experience of others, is a testament to the recurring appeal of this idea. Indeed, schemes for cross-voting featured in eighteenth-century constitutional debates in France and the United States as a means of tempering the interests and passions of different social groups and classes in representative bodies (Elster, 2003).

A related but distinct approach is via direct attempts to shape the nature of political parties and party systems. In particular, efforts to foster large, aggregative parties, and discourage sectional or minority ones, have been a distinctive feature of the 'third wave' of democratization (Reilly and Nordlund 2008). Again, one of the clearest examples is to be found in Indonesia – the world's most populous emerging democracy and largest Muslim country. There, parties must establish an organizational network across a set proportion of provinces (initially one-third, then two-thirds and now 60 per cent of all provinces), as well as offices in at least half of the districts or municipalities within these provinces, before they are allowed to contest the election, while a separate threshold has also been introduced to limit splinter parties. These rules are intended not just to make it difficult for regionally based or secessionist movements to organize (although an exception has been made for local parties in Aceh under the terms of the 2005 peace deal there), but also to promote the development of nationally focused political parties.[6] As such, the party law shares a common centripetal logic with Indonesia's presidential electoral system, which also includes (weaker) incentives for cross-regional support.

Political party engineering is also popular in other regions. In Africa, some twenty-two countries include requirements that parties have a national presence (Bogaards 2008, 48–66). But such exhortations are typically accompanied by overt bans on ethnic parties, and tend to have little impact on actual party development. In Latin America, ethnic parties are not a major issue, but there have been similar attempts to encourage aggregative and nationally oriented parties with a cross-regional organizational base in Colombia, Ecuador, Guatemala, Nicaragua, Honduras, Mexico and Peru. In Mexico, for example, parties must have at least 3,000 affiliates in ten out of the thirty-two states, or one-third of federal districts, while in Ecuador and Peru, parties must meet officially inscribed membership levels in at least half of all provinces. However Ecuador, which introduced spatial registration rules in the 1970s to combat party fragmentation, also provides a cautionary tale. There, the introduction of spatial rules helped to consolidate the party system, but at the cost of wiping out parties representing the country's indigenous minority, which relied on regionally concentrated Amerindian support (Birnir 2004).

## When are centripetal institutional designs appropriate?

As these divergent examples suggest, political engineering and institutional design to encourage centripetal outcomes is an uncertain process fraught with what some have characterized as an 'iron law' of unintended consequences (Bastian and Luckham 2003). But despite this, and the uncertain experience of some measures to promote cross-ethnic politics, centripetal political engineering remains popular, particularly in new democracies. The attractiveness of such reforms can be explained by several factors.

Theoretically, centripetalism draws upon core political science ideas about the nature of social cleavages, particularly Seymour Martin Lipset's (1960) classic arguments about the virtues of cross-cutting cleavages for democracy. The kinds of cross-voting schemes discussed above, for instance, all hinge on the idea that reinforcing social cleavages are a problem, and that general interests need to be given priority over group interests. Normatively, the virtues of political aggregation and centrism are advocated (sometimes instinctively) by policymakers schooled in the Anglo-American tradition of two-party politics. Empirically too, most centripetal reforms are more compatible with the development of aggregative, centrist party systems than alternatives such as consociationalism. Indeed, to many 'third wave' reformers, the integrative politics of fluid ethnic attachments and mass parties found in the immigrant societies of the United States, Australia, Canada represents the potential benefits of centripetalism in multiethnic societies. But the 'settler society' context of these new world democracies is very different from the deep-rooted antipathies found in parts of Africa, Asia or indeed Europe.

While many of the cross-voting schemes discussed above are of mostly historical interest, the most successful contemporary applications of centripetalism in deeply divided societies to date have been in societies where the facilitating demography favours vote-pooling – for instance, in countries where ethnic groups are either so numerous and small in size (e.g. Papua New Guinea) or so regionally dispersed and intermixed (e.g. Malaysia) as to make cross-ethnic voting a winning electoral strategy. These are relatively unusual configurations. Nonetheless, new democracies such as Indonesia, where political elites have embarked on an ambitious exercise in centripetal political engineering, offer promising but preliminary evidence of how aggregative party and electoral strategies can help to manage transitions to democracy in situations of great social diversity.

## Critiques

Centripetalism has attracted significant criticism on empirical and conceptual grounds. Empirically, critics point to the paucity of centripetal models in the real world; the limited application of cross-voting electoral systems, distribution requirements and other favoured devices; the difficulty in both forming and sustaining multiethnic political parties and coalitions in divided societies; and the ambiguous real-world experience of particular institutions such as the alternative vote.[7] However, many of these critiques focus on the experience of a few high-profile cases such as Northern Ireland or (recently) Fiji, but tend to ignore other larger but less well-known examples of centripetalism in action such as Indonesia or Papua New Guinea. For instance, the reintroduction of AV laws in Papua New Guinea and the subsequent reduction in electoral conflicts at the 2007 national elections has yet to be incorporated into comparative discussions of centripetalism. Neither has the success of the peacemaking process in Bougainville, which includes a number of centripetal reforms such as cross-voting reserved seats for women, youth and ex-combatants as well as AV presidential elections.[8]

Centripetalism is sometimes criticized for being essentially majoritarian in nature. As the logic of centripetalism is focused above all on the potential benefits of *aggregation* – of votes, of opinions, of parties – at one level, this is correct. G. Bingham Powell, for example, notes that political aggregation lies at the heart of what he calls the 'majoritarian vision' of democracy: 'the majoritarian view favours much greater aggregation, while the proportional view emphasizes the importance of equitable reflection of all points of view into the legislature' (Bingham Powell 2000, 26). But while centripetalism is indeed a majoritarian model, it is a majoritarianism of broad-based parties and inclusive coalitions – not a majoritarianism of 'ins' and 'outs', of ethnically defined majorities and minorities.

Interestingly, the majoritarian themes of the centripetal approach and their emphasis on aggregative, 'bridging' political parties are increasingly echoed by the scholarly literature on the political economy of development (Persson and Tabellini 2003). Both literatures, for example, advocate aggregative political institutions, majoritarian electoral processes and broad-based 'catch-all' parties or coalitions. These same recommendations are also prominent in the 'developmental state' literature on the optimum political arrangements for economic reform in new democracies (Haggard and Kaufman, 1995). Such recommendations suggest a growing convergence among different political science sub-disciplines on the benefits of aggregative and centripetal institutions for political development and stability.

## Conclusion

In practice, centripetalism, like other political-engineering models, is best seen an ideal type rather than a coherent, all-encompassing prescription. Indeed, in many cases of conflict management, a mixture of recommendations from different models can be and is applied. Thus a number of constitutional settlements and peace deals cited above including Bosnia, Fiji, Lebanon and Northern Ireland feature a mixture of centripetal, consociational and communal models of ethnic conflict management.

One explanation for this is the fact that, despite differences, there is some agreement on a number of broader issues. For instance, there is consensus on the capacity of political institutions to change political outcomes, and hence on the utility of political engineering. Common ground is also found in the central role ascribed to political parties and electoral systems as key institutional variables influencing the reduction – or escalation – of communal tensions in ethnically diverse societies. A third area of agreement is the broad acceptance of the need in divided societies to deal with the political effects of ethnicity directly, rather than wishing them away. At a minimum, this means some type of government arrangement that gives all significant groups access to power, either directly or indirectly. For this reason, consociationalists and centripetalists broadly agree on the desirability of some form of power sharing for divided societies, even as they disagree on the means to achieve it (Jarstad 2008).

The contemporary experience of these different approaches has varied depending on the severity of the conflicts at stake. In deeply divided post-war scenarios such as Bosnia, Northern Ireland and most recently Iraq, consociationalism remains the dominant approach. However, this trend is party driven by the United Nations' standard model of post-conflict democratization, which favours the use of PR elections and power-sharing governments in the immediate aftermath of a conflict (Reilly 2008). Elsewhere, in less catastrophic cases, the trend in many regions has been away from the ethnically based approach of consociationalism towards more fluid, centripetal models. Thus, there has been a marked shift away from consociationalism and towards centripetalism in many parts of the developing world, particularly in Asia and the Pacific, in recent years.[9]

## Notes

1 See the contributions in this volume by Roeder (Chapter 3) and Wolff (Chapter 1).
2 See Reilly (2001, chs. 4–6).
3 For a recent example, see Coakley and Fraenkel (2009).
4 See Bowman (1973, 34, 174).
5 For an excellent analysis, see Salloukh (2006).
6 For more on this, see Hillman (2010).
7 For a discussion, see Lijphart (1991); Fraenkel (2001); Lijphart (2004); Fraenkel and Grofman (2004).
8 For a partial exception, see, Reilly (2007).
9 For a book-length discussion of this trend, see Reilly (2006).

## References

Bastian, S. and Luckham, R. 2003 'Conclusion. The Politics of Institutional Choice', in Bastian, S. and Luckham, R. (eds.), *Can Democracy be Designed? The Politics of Institutional Choice in Conflict-Torn Societies*, London: Zed Press.

Bingham, Powell G. 2000 *Elections as Instruments of Democracy: Majoritarian and Proportional Visions*, New Haven, CT and London: Yale University Press.

Birnir, Jóhanna Kristín 2004 'Stabilizing Party Systems and Excluding Segments of Society? The Effects of Formation Costs on New Party Foundation in Latin America', *Studies in Comparative International Development* 39(3): 3–27.

Bogaards, Matthijs 2003 'Electoral Choices for Divided Societies: Multi-Ethnic Parties and Constituency Pooling in Africa', *Commonwealth and Comparative Politics* 41(3), 59–80.

—— 2008 'Comparative Strategies of Political Party Regulation', in Benjamin Reilly and Per Nordlund (eds.), *Political Parties in Conflict-Prone Societies: Regulation, Engineering and Democratic Development*, Tokyo: United Nations University Press.

Bowman, L. 1973 *Politics in Rhodesia*, Cambridge, MA: Harvard University Press.

Coakley, John and Fraenkel, Jon 2001 'Do preference transfers assist moderates in deeply divided societies? Evidence from Northern Ireland and Fiji', paper presented at the Annual Meeting of the American Political Science Association, Toronto, September.

Elster, Jon 2003 'Cross-voting', unpublished paper, Columbia University.

Fraenkel, Jon 2001 'The Alternative Vote System in Fiji: Electoral Engineering or Ballot-Rigging?', *Commonwealth and Comparative Politics* 39(1): 1–31.

Fraenkel, Jon and Grofman, Bernard 2004 'A Neo-Downsian Model of the Alternative Vote as a Mechanism for Mitigating Ethnic Conflict in Plural Societies', *Public Choice* 121: 487–506.

Haggard, Stephan and Kaufman, Robert 1995 *The Political Economy of Democratic Transitions*, Princeton, NJ: Princeton University Press.

Hillman, Ben 2010 *Political Parties and Post-Conflict Transition: The Results and Implications of the 2009 Parliamentary Elections in Aceh*, Centre for Democratic Institutions Policy Paper 1/10, Canberra: Centre for Democratic Institutions.

Horowitz, Donald L. 1985 *Ethnic Groups in Conflict*, Berkeley, CA: University of California Press.

—— 1991 *A Democratic South Africa? Constitutional Engineering in a Divided Society*, Berkeley, CA: University of California Press.

Huntington, Samuel P. 1991 *The Third Wave: Democratization in the Late Twentieth Century*, Norman, OK: University of Oklahoma Press.

Jarstad, Anna 2008 'Power-Sharing: Former Enemies in Joint Government', in Anna K. Jarstad and Timothy D. Sisk (eds.), *From War to Democracy: Dilemmas of Peacebuilding*, Cambridge: Cambridge University Press.

Lijphart, Arend 1991 'The Alternative Vote: A Realistic Alternative for South Africa?', *Politikon* 18(2): 91–101.

—— 2004 'Constitutional Design for Divided Societies', *Journal of Democracy* 15(2): 96–109.

Lipset, S. M. 1960 *Political Man: The Social Bases of Politics*, New York, NY: Doubleday.

Persson, T. and Tabellini, G. 2003 *The Economic Effects of Constitutions*. Cambridge, MA: MIT Press.

Reilly, Benjamin 2001 *Democracy in Divided Societies: Electoral Engineering for Conflict Management*, Cambridge: Cambridge University Press.

—— 2004 'The Global Spread of Preferential Voting: Australian Institutional Imperialism?', *Australian Journal of Political Science* 39(2): 253–66.

—— 2006 *Democracy and Diversity: Political Engineering in the Asia-Pacific*, Oxford: Oxford University Press.

—— 2007 'Political Engineering in the Asia-Pacific', *Journal of Democracy* 18(1): 58–72.

—— 2008 'Post-Conflict Elections: Uncertain Turning Points of Transition?', in Anna K. Jarstad and Timothy D. Sisk (eds.), *From War to Democracy: Dilemmas of Peacebuilding*, Cambridge: Cambridge University Press.

Reilly, Benjamin and Nordlund, Per (eds.) 2008 *Political Parties in Conflict-Prone Societies: Regulation, Engineering and Democratic Development*, Tokyo: United Nations University Press.

Salloukh, Basel F. 2006 'The Limits of Electoral Engineering in Divided Societies: Elections in Postwar Lebanon', *Canadian Journal of Political Science* 39(3): 635–55.

Sisk, Timothy D. 1996 *Power Sharing and International Mediation in Ethnic Conflicts*, Washington, DC: United States Institute of Peace Press.

Wimmer, Andreas 2003 'Democracy and Ethno-Religious Conflict in Iraq', *Survival* 45(4): 111–34.

# 3 Power dividing

## The multiple-majorities approach

*Philip G. Roeder*

Power dividing (also called the multiple-majorities approach) constitutes a strategy for building institutions in societies divided along cultural lines and, like power sharing and centripetalism, claims that institutional arrangements that diverge from the simple majoritarianism associated with Westminster parliamentarism can improve the chances for civil peace and democracy even in societies divided by deep ethnic or religious differences.[1] The power-dividing strategy differs from these other approaches to conflict management, however, in its emphasis on institutions that limit the privileged representation of these cultural communities in state policymaking to as narrow a domain as is realistically possible, that encourage political representation of as many other cultural groups and socioeconomic interests as possible, and that rely on civil society rather than the state as much as possible to provide the cultural needs of individuals who belong to different ethnic and religious groups (Roeder and Rothchild 2005; Roeder 2005).

## The main characteristics of the power-dividing strategy

The philosophical foundations of power dividing are principles of liberalism and pluralism; yet, power dividing describes not a philosophical ideal type, but a prudential strategy of institution building. First, the power-dividing strategy seeks to remove the most divisive issues from the jurisdiction of the government and to reserve these decision-making powers to individuals and civil society. The principles of liberalism were formed by the crucible of culture wars (particularly the English Reformation and Revolutions) that tore apart states and wasted lives, and so liberals from the start have been keenly aware of the dangers that arise when these issues are brought into the political realm and have long championed the cause of taking the most explosive cultural issues out of the hands of government, such as getting governments out of the business of writing books of common prayer. In the liberal strategy civil society and a robust associational life become primary means by which cultures preserve traditions. The state plays only a minimal role in this. Although this is rooted in deep liberal principles about the dignity and autonomy of each individual, in the power-dividing strategy it is a pragmatic principle: Power dividing seeks to lower the stakes in politics.

In terms of institutional arrangements to remove these issues from government the power-dividing strategy begins with extensive civil liberties, that is, restrictions on governments that protect individuals from the state; but this is a pragmatic rather than an ideological commitment. For example, where distributive and regulatory choices among cultures are likely to ignite lines of political division and to encourage escalation of political conflict, it is often preferable that civil liberties prohibit government from making decisions on these cultural issues. Liberals press for broad civil liberties with particularly strong guarantees of freedom of association; these are both barriers to government action and foundations for a civil society that can meet cultural needs. Thus, power dividing, first of all, divides decision-making rights between society and the government and constructs a high wall – in the United States it is the Bill of Rights enforceable in courts – to protect the decision rights that are set outside the reach of government such as decisions whether to support religion and which religions to support.

By empowering all citizens and all associations equally with civil liberties, the power-dividing strategy leaves to civil society rather than the state the decisions concerning which groups will form in order to meet the constantly evolving cultural needs of citizens. The power-dividing strategy grants similar political and civil rights to members of majorities and minorities – not only those currently recognized by the state, but also currently unrecognized groups and unforeseen cultural communities that may emerge in the future. These are not group rights, but rights of individuals with a freedom of association. The power-dividing strategy removes the government as much as possible from the dubious undertaking of deciding which cultural communities will be officially recognized and privileged with access to government decision making, funds collected through taxation, and the like. Alternatively, power-sharing solutions end up privileging some cultures (such as Catholic, Reformed and secular Netherlanders) at the expense of other macro-cultures (such as Buddhists and Hindus) that are not so privileged and at the expense of the microcultures (such as divorced and remarried Catholics or Calvinists in same-sex marriages) that diverge only partially from the prescriptions of the privileged cultures.[2]

Second, in its strategy for building institutions to make state policy, the power-dividing strategy is rooted in principles of pluralist democracy. In what remains of the state sector after many decision rights are reserved to individuals and civil society, the power-dividing strategy disperses governmental decision making both horizontally and vertically to multiple, functionally specific organs of government rather than concentrating this in a single supreme parliament-plus-government or dividing this between a central government and a single layer of general-purpose homeland or communal administrations. In this strategy many organs of the central government, where policy is made for all within the state, exercise definitive policymaking power within only a narrow realm, such as setting interest rates, collecting and distributing water, regulating securities markets, or establishing higher-education standards.

In designing jurisdictions at the sub-national level, power dividing devolves decision rights to multiple, cross-cutting jurisdictions, so that all devolved powers do not concentrate in the same political jurisdictions. School districts should not be coextensive with water basin districts, which in turn should not be coextensive with police districts, and so forth, and each of these should not be subordinated to or nested within an overarching regional jurisdiction. Thus, the power-dividing strategy warns against creating territorial (ethnofederal) or non-territorial (ethnocorporatist) autonomies that exercise powers across a wide range of policy domains.

In establishing decision-making rules within organs and local administrations, power dividing remains committed to the democratic principle that the majority must decide policy whenever possible. Power dividing sees privileging minorities through vetoes or supermajority requirements that permit the minority to frustrate the majority in policy-making as a denial of democracy. Thus, the division of powers does not mean a 'separation of powers with checks and balances' where policy must be approved by multiple organs, each of which exercises a veto. Instead, each organ is empowered to make policy by majority vote, but only in its narrow issue domain and sometimes only in that domain within a specific geographic jurisdiction. One exception to majority rule must be constitutional revision, particularly changes in the rights of individuals against governmental action: this must require either multiple referenda (separated in time) or approval by multiple governmental organs or both.

By establishing these organs to represent the public interest in varying configurations of majorities and minorities, power dividing institutionalizes a division of powers among the organs of the central government that lowers the likelihood that the same majority will dominate all organs and make all decisions; hence, the label 'multiple majorities'. That is, in its rules of representation, power dividing rejects the idea of adopting one electoral rule or principle of representation because it is superior to the others. Rather, power dividing prescribes varying the rules for representing society from organ to organ and among types of jurisdictions so as to represent different configurations of interests such as the division between business and labour over economic policy or between upstream and downstream dwellers in a common river basin.[3] In this way, power dividing accepts the pluralist amendment to the Westminster model that society is not simply divided into one majority and one minority, but is divided across issues among many majorities and many minorities that typically do not correlate well (Dahl 1961; Campbell *et al.* 1960; Lewis-Beck *et al.* 2008). The power-dividing strategy relies on institutions designed so that many different majorities can make policy (each in a specific domain) through their representatives in separate organs with distinct and limited jurisdictions. In this multiple-majorities strategy, while most decisions are made by majority rule, few decisions are made by the same majority because different organs represent society in alternative ways; taken together these represent cross-cutting cleavages in society.

In the power-dividing strategy ethnic and religious communities may be empowered to decide specific issues through decision-making organs in the central government that bring together representatives of the communities or in one or the other of many types of local administrations such as regional cultural agencies or city cemetery commissions. However, the agencies defined by any one cultural divide are empowered only in a narrow range of issues, such as burial of the dead. Overlapping, cross-cutting communities and interests are empowered in other organs to decide other issues, such as water resource management. This is particularly important in countries where cultural conflict has a potential to become severe: the power-dividing strategy attempts to avoid privileging the parties to the previous conflict in the post-settlement government as much as possible. If parties to previous conflict must be co-opted into post-settlement institutions or if there is no way to prevent these parties from reconstituting themselves within a post-settlement government, then first and foremost the power-dividing strategy divides decision making among multiple organs with different rules for representing society and with jurisdictions that are limited and drawn so as to make it more difficult to replicate the same cultural divide in every organ.

As detailed in the chapters on power sharing and centripetalism, these alternative strategies of conflict management tend to recommend very specific institutions to address conflict in divided societies. In contrast, power-dividing does not recommend specific institutions (such as list PR electoral rules, alternative vote or federalism), but a strategy that avoids the monopolism of any single mode of representation. Thus, in the central government the rules for representation of society should vary among organs so that the majority that makes decisions in one organ is unlikely to be the same majority that makes decisions in another organ. In this way the power-dividing solution seeks to complicate the task of constituting the same governing majority in every organ of power. Moreover, the power-dividing strategy warns that simple borrowing of institutions that result in multiple majorities in one country does not guarantee that they will produce multiple majorities in another. In culturally divided countries, the logic of power dividing requires identifying in each particular society alternative, cross-cutting divisions that do not replicate its cultural divide and are less likely to be trumped by cultural differences.

## Power-dividing institutional designs in practice

One illustration of power dividing – up to a point – is Switzerland, where ethnolinguistic identity has been only a latent basis for political action and seldom has represented an important political divide (Bogdanor 1988, 73; Steiner 1969, 290). In part the low salience of ethnicity is attributable to the good fortune of demographic patterns, because differences in language, religion and urban–rural residence cut across one another (Steiner 1974, 255; Government of Switzerland 1993, vol. 16, tables 2.002–2.004). Even so, good power-dividing institutions are an equally important factor. The low salience of ethnicity owes much to the fact that Switzerland embeds the rights of ethnic groups in a set of rights shared by many other, often more salient, groups. Today linguistic groups share similar rights with religious and class groups. All of these groups must express many of their claims through a common set of cantonal decision rights that divide and sometimes trump all three types of social cleavage. Moreover, for the development of individual cultural communities, the Swiss rely heavily on civil society and private action. Indeed, Switzerland, like the United States, comes closer to the ideal of limited government than most established democracies. (For example, government spending, as a share of GDP, is 47 per cent higher in Switzerland's four neighbours than in Switzerland (United Nations 2001).) The Swiss government is about one-third smaller than its neighbours (even after taking into account the different size of the countries) and leaves many more decisions to the private sector or civil society.

In Swiss governmental decision-making processes no one configuration of interests is privileged (Schoch 2000, iv). Switzerland's bicameral legislature represents the Swiss people by two different formulae – neither of which privileges ethnicity. The collective presidency balances ideological (left–right), cantonal, religious and ethnolinguistic representation. Decisions may be made by direct democracy in referenda and initiatives, by consensus in the federal institutions, or in cantonal or communal institutions. At every level of government many decisions are made by agencies of self-administration (*Milizverwaltung*), such as the water-supply system in the high valleys of Valais (Linder 1994, 52–4). As Jürg Steiner and Robert H. Dorff (1985, 53) conclude, 'it becomes less clear as to how much Swiss decision processes are federal or unitary … The main impression is the great amount of variation from one decision process to another' (also see Steiner 1987). In sum, the Swiss have not created a simple ethnic or religious power-sharing constitutional order; they have empowered civil society and multiple majorities in government, so that winners and losers do not accumulate along cultural lines (cf. Steiner 1998, 19).

Many more examples of power-dividing constitutions are found in the ten West Coast and Rocky Mountain states (minus Utah) of the United States. All have plural executives, with an average of six elected statewide executive officers such as governor, secretary of state, attorney general and superintendent of public instruction, and many maintain elected statewide boards, such as board of education, public service commission or corporations commission, sometimes elected by districts. At the local level all ten states maintain at least four times as many special-purpose governments (such as school districts, natural resources districts or fire districts) as general-purpose governments (including counties and municipalities); often the former are led by their own elected leaders, and exercise autonomous revenue-raising, spending and regulatory authority.[4] The constitution of California, for example, provides for direct statewide election of eight constitutional officers plus election by district of members of the State Board of [Tax] Equalization. Each officer exercises autonomous decision powers, so that no one executive organ exercises authority across all domains, much to the consternation of any governor who aspires to remake California politics in her or his own image. One important consequence for divided societies: The plural executive has made it difficult for any one party to dominate all executive organs – even in a state with only two important parties. Thus, at no time since at least 1955 has one party simultaneously controlled all elected executive offices in California.[5] Both parties have had some wins in each election. At the local level California maintains seven times as many special-purpose governments as general-purpose governments, the highest ratio for all fifty states (United States 2009). In the 1990s the state controller listed over 57 different types of special districts that performed over 30 different functions such as providing education, fire protection, flood control, water and sewage, mass transit, air pollution control, hospitals, ports and airports (Hyink and Provost 1998, 163). Most of these special-purpose governments are led by elected leaders, the remainder by appointees or ex officio representatives of other governments (Bell and Price 1991, 298). The cross-cutting jurisdictions and diversity of representation formulae have produced multiple majorities, not the domination of policy by one majority: Majorities in one organ, such as Christian fundamentalists who control a school district, find it difficult to sweep into power across all organs. The dispersion of power and multiplication of cross-cutting lines of division throughout the state have meant that most citizens are parts of a majority in some organs and that no one divide, such as race, urban versus rural, or north versus south has come to dominate political conflict.

The most obvious divergence from the power dividing strategy in Switzerland and California is the initiative – the right of citizens to propose constitutional amendments and to adopt these in one election. The power-dividing strategy recommends much stronger guarantees of the rights of individuals and private associations, including rights to build minarets. These might include a provision that constitutional amendments require two or more popular votes separated by at least one year or that the popular vote be confirmed by the national legislature or constitutional court as well.

## When are power-dividing institutional designs appropriate?

Power dividing, as illustrated by the examples of Switzerland and the western American states, has tended to emerge through slow accretions of institutions in response to limited demands from specific constituencies. Alternatively, power dividing is unlikely to emerge spontaneously in a bargain among a limited number of parties that have already escalated conflict to extreme levels such as a civil war, believe they share few common interests that could be represented by cross-cutting groups, and object to participation in the negotiations over the design of post-conflict institutions by groups that did not fight in the war. Where the parties demand power sharing as a condition for setting down arms, there are likely to be few if any alternatives to power sharing.

The prospects for introducing power dividing increase under three conditions – where political conflict is multidimensional rather than only cultural, where negotiations over institutional design involve more parties representing diverse interests rather than just the leaders of the cultural communities, and where occupying powers exercise extensive authority in the design of institutions. First, power dividing is more likely to emerge and easier to impose before a single cultural divide has come to monopolize politics, that is, before more and more issues on the policy agenda have been transformed into battle-grounds among cultural communities. Thus, power dividing is easiest to adopt when ethnic or religious conflict is still of low intensity and low salience to most issues. For example, it would probably have been easier to implement power dividing in Belgium in the 1950s or even in the 1970s than today, after decades of ever deepening and widening ethnic conflict, particularly since the introduction of power sharing between Flemish and Walloon communities. Second, power dividing is more likely to emerge when many, diverse interests are empowered to participate in the negotiations over institutional design. This may be subject to some manipulation when the convenors of constitutional conventions control the agenda and the invitation list: by dividing the design of specific organs among multiple working groups with broad representation of interests and experts relevant to each organ, the convenors can improve the prospects for adopting a power-dividing constitution. Third, power dividing is easier to impose when occupying powers have greater say in the design of institutions. In instances where occupying powers have considerable discretion, such as in the design of Bosnia's 1995 constitution, these powers can impose power-dividing rather than power-sharing institutions.

## Critiques

Criticisms of power dividing hit the mark on two points, but miss it on a third. The first criticism concerns the practicality of the strategy when conditions are hostile to its introduction (as outlined in the previous section): it is more difficult to implement power dividing after civil wars when the parties resist it and demand only power sharing. Yet, as will be explained in the next section, this demand for power sharing by the parties themselves should attune us to the very danger contained in power sharing and why those concerned for the longer-term survival of peace within a country should be most resistant to power sharing at exactly the moment it appears to be the only option: power sharing is a quick fix to end one round of conflict, but raises the risk of later recurrence of con-flict at still greater intensity. Power dividing provides a better chance to mitigate that deep divide.

A second criticism adds that power dividing can exact a price in the coordination and coherence of policy: power dividing increases the likelihood that policy will become incoherent across issue areas where policies adopted by one organ are not well integrated with policies adopted by another organ. A particular manifestation of this lack of coor-dination may be higher spending and taxes, where each organ responds to the demands of its particular majority seeking greater government benefits but no single organ is responsible for the entire governmental budget (Berry 2009). This incoherence is accepted by power dividing as part of a trade-off among three undesired consequences that all alternative strategies must confront in deeply divided societies – the risk that policy will be imposed across the board by a single majority on an unwilling minority, deadlock across a broad range of policies, and incoherence among policies. One remedy for the incoherence is more coordination among organs, such as a strong party organization can provide (Berry 2009, 148–78). Yet, in a divided society this coordination across organs increases the risk of a single ethnic or religious majority dominating the minority in all policy arenas. Both power sharing and power dividing are attempts to avoid this majoritarian danger, but they differ in how they lower this: Power sharing gives minorities vetoes, power dividing limits the cultural majority to only a narrow policy domain. The consequence of minority vetoes under power sharing is increased likelihood of deadlock across many policy domains. Power dividing limits the likelihood of deadlock, by allowing policy to be decided in other organs by majorities other than the cultural majority. The risk that arises when majorities vary from organ to organ is incoherent policy, but this is less threatening to the survival of peace, democracy and the state than domination by a single majority or deadlock.

A third criticism, that power dividing places excessive faith in the ability of political institutions to structure conflict, is misdirected. Certainly power dividing shares with power sharing and centripetalism the claim that institutions can have an effect on conflict, by shaping the incentives associated with different patterns of conflict and cooperation, but none claims that this effect must be determinative. All that power dividing claims is that political institutions are seldom neutral in their effects on the prospects for conflict management and, to the extent that these institutions have an effect, it is preferable, when possible, to rely on power dividing rather than the alternatives. That is the point explored more fully in the next section.

## Advantages of power-dividing institutions

The case for power dividing is not primarily normative; it is prudential. The case is based on the consequences of institutional structures, but power dividing does not guarantee specific outcomes, for political institutions do not have a deterministic effect. Instead, the case for power dividing speaks of increasing the likelihood of outcomes by shaping the institutional constraints that empower some actors in politics and affect the relative efficiency of different patterns of cooperation and conflict. In this regard, each alternative strategy should be judged not against some unspecified ideal (a comparison in which all strategies come up short), but against one another so as to identify their strengths and weaknesses relative to the known alternatives. Power sharing's advantage, as noted in the previous sections, comes in providing a quick solution to end intense conflicts (Walter 2002, 27–31, 80–1). Power dividing provides a strategy more likely to avoid coming to such an intense conflict in the first place or re-escalating conflict after the end of the most recent round of fighting. Unfortunately, the two strategies cannot be adopted sequentially: as noted by Roeder and Rothchild (2005, 12–15) in what we labelled the 'dilemma of power sharing', once a state has begun to govern itself under power sharing it is unlikely to make the shift to power dividing and may have locked in to a course more likely to bring a recurrence of escalating conflict (also see Brancati 2009).

In evaluating the three alternative strategies, the case for power dividing is based first of all on a prudential claim about the consequences of each strategy for developments at three levels of society: at the individual or micro-level, power dividing is more likely to lead to free development of individual identities that are multiple, situation specific and cross-cutting. At the group or meso-level, power dividing is more likely to lead to a vibrant civil society and less likely to lead to organizational monopolies that cartelize or pillarize society. At the statewide or macro-level, power dividing is more likely to lead to robust state political institutions that can weather many diverse conflicts rather than falling to the one overarching cultural conflict. All three of these consequences are essential to the maintenance of peace within the state and to democratic survival. This causal claim is rooted in an institutionalist assertion that, insofar as political institutions can shape the incentives that encourage different patterns of identities, social organization and political dynamics, it is prudent to design political institutions to foster or permit pluralism to emerge at the individual, group and state levels.

### Micro-level: plural versus omnisalient individual identities

By not privileging one set of cultural identities in politics, power dividing, unlike power sharing and centripetalism, seeks to give greatest opportunity for individuals to develop multiple, situation specific, cross-cutting identities. In the context of ethnically or religiously divided societies the power-dividing or multiple-majorities strategy begins from the constructivist view that often the politicization of ethnic identities (and sometimes even the invention of such identities) is endogenous to the political process (Brass 1991) and in the absence of political–institutional constraints identities tend to be more fluid (Nagel 1994; Waters 1990; Roeder 2007). Situations in which politicized ethnic or religious identities become monopolistic (or *omnisalient*) and either crowd out or subsume all other identities in the public space are often pathological situations as existed in Yugoslav or Rwandan communities in the run-up, and during, the severe (genocidal) violence these societies experienced in the 1990s.[6] In evaluating the alternative strategies we should ask the following question about political–institutional constraints on the public expression of individual identities under each arrangement: to what extent do political institutions create incentives for individuals to conform to monopolistic ethnic or religious identities in public?

By its commitment to extensive and defensible civil liberties, the power-dividing strategy is more likely to empower each individual to develop her or his own identities through individual networks of associations, public expression and public debate. Compared to the alternatives, power-dividing institutions lower the incentives for individuals to enter social relations only through identities associated with deep cultural divides privileged by the political institutions, and create fewer strong political–institutional obstacles to initiation of new identities. When individuals enter social relationships, it is more likely under power dividing, compared to power sharing or centripetalism, to be through groups that are associated with one of the alternative, often cross-cutting identities that are salient only for limited purposes. For example, power-dividing institutions structure politics so that for individuals to construct a temporary policy majority on a specific issue, it is often more efficient to focus on interests and identities that cut across cultural divides. Unlike the centripetalist strategy, these are less likely to be coalitions among the dominant cultural groups, but coalitions of individuals with shared interests on a specific issue, for whom their identity as members of an ethnic or religious group is not the most salient identity they possess on that issue. In many situations it is their other identities – as teachers, downstream water consumers, investors or labourers. Thus, power dividing stresses the capacity of governmental institutions to shape the configuration of identities that are expressed by individuals in their relationships beyond the family. All political–institutional strategies have an effect on identities, but the dispersal of power among separate, independent governmental organs with alternative forms of representation increases the likelihood that individuals will see in many instances that their identities that are most salient in relationships beyond the family are not their identity as a member of a cultural community. The multiple-majorities strategy seeks to create institutional arrangements in which citizens are more likely to see themselves as members of various, cross-cutting, situation-specific configurations of majorities and minorities in society.

Alternatively, the power-sharing and centripetal strategies typically privilege one configuration of majority and minorities – and often through predetermined governmental formulae. Where institutions empower one configuration of ethnic or religious groups, leaders of those groups may use their powers inside their autonomous homelands or corporate communities to cultivate monopolistic or *omnisalient* identities through separate schooling, public celebrations and a constant din of media propaganda. Because cross-cutting identities compete with and potentially erode the unity and boundaries of the cultural communities led by the privileged leaders, these leaders have strong incentives to use their powers to make it difficult for other identities to be expressed publically. They may even convert such decision rights as control over assembly halls, public squares, printing presses, or broadcasting towers into coercive tools to block the public expression and possibly even the emergence of competing identities. Yet, even in a democratic society where less coercive means are used this power of institutions and institutionally empowered politicians to increase the salience of specific cultural divides may be felt. For example, in India, according to Ramesh Dutta Dikshit (1975, 125) the reorganization of state boundaries to correspond with those of linguistic communities has elevated language so that it is 'the main factor of cleavage between the states of India' and 'language has begun to play mischief ... to the detriment of national unity'.

### Meso-level: civil vs. pillarized society

Power dividing does more than power-sharing and centripetalist strategies to reduce the likelihood that leaders of specific cultural communities will hold an extensive advantage in organizational resources that they can wield to shape associational life and to construct or maintain a 'cartelized' or 'pillarized' society. (Pillarization – from the Dutch *verzuiling* – refers to the segmentation of society among comprehensive, integrated subcultures, each of which encapsulates individuals' associational life from cradle to grave; see Lijphart 1968.) In evaluating the alternative strategies, it is important to ask two questions about the distribution of organizational resources and the organization of society: first, do political institutions empower leaders of ethnic or religious groups (more than the leaders of other groups) with organizational resources to facilitate collective action by their followers? Second, do political institutions empower leaders of ethnic or religious groups (more than the leaders of other groups) with the coercive capabilities to block collective action by their rivals?

Power dividing disperses organizational resources and is less likely to lead to concentration of these in only a few hands. As a consequence, leaders of ethnic and religious groups, as only a few out of many empowered leaders, have less of an advantage over the leaders of other groups in the resources to co-opt loyalists and coerce rivals into pursuing their interests only through organizations of the cultural community that support the leaders' agendas. In this the power-dividing strategy recognizes the resource mobilization school's insight that it is often the relative availability of resources for collective action that determines which interests – whether ethnic, religious, or other – get organized and mobilized in society (McCarthy and Zald 1987; Leites and Wolf 1970). Political institutions can shape the distribution of these resources, which in turn shape the configuration of groups that are organized in society. By empowering not only ethnic or religious majorities and minorities, but also multiple cross-cutting majorities and minorities, the power-dividing strategy seeks to foster development of multiple associations along multiple dimensions of social cleavage (cf. Lipset 1981). In short, as an analyst of political opportunity structures (Tarrow 1989) notes, political institutions constitute an important constraint on whether mobilizing ethnic or religious groups (rather than another type of group) is the most efficient strategy for ambitious social entrepreneurs seeking to achieve a particular goal. The power-dividing strategy limits the realms in which it is prudent to achieve collective ends through ethnic or religious networks and expands the number of realms in which other types of associations are more efficient or effective. Thus, compared to the alternatives, power dividing is less likely to lead to an organizational cartel or pillarized society and more likely to create conditions for the development of a civil society of many NGOs.

Alternatively, power sharing tends to privilege the leaders of specified cultural communities with resources such as ready-made organizations and hierarchical chains of command, including the governments of autonomous governments, which are not available to the leaders of other interests; that is, power sharing tends to concentrate organizational resources in these hands. Because power-sharing arrangements tend to skew the distribution of organizational resources in this way, social entrepreneurs with other interests to press, such a forming a chamber of commerce or a labour union, are more likely to find it expedient to frame their ambitions in terms of rights of one of the cultural communities and to work within cultural networks. They may find that attempts to express independent interests that divide or cross-cut the cultural communities are blocked or made more costly by the empowered leaders of cultural communities. Even in the absence of extensive coercion from the empowered leaders, power sharing favours pillarization, because it makes working through cultural networks a less costly (more efficient) strategy. For example, in Belgium prior to the introduction of power sharing 'civil-society networks were essentially national, with at most dependent regional "wings"'. But now 'former national structures are dis-aggregating' as 'regional and community civil-society networks have emerged to "shadow" and influence the new regional and community authorities'. The authorities have encouraged this restructuring because 'the pilarised [*sic*] structure enables the elite leadership of each to deliver "its" pillar in negotiations' (Fitzmaurice 1998).

### Macro-level: robust versus fragile democratic institutions

Democratic institutions designed according to this power-dividing strategy are less likely to facilitate the escalation of political conflict and more likely to weather conflicts. In evaluating the contribution of the three alternative institutional strategies to the survival of civil peace and democracy in the face of conflict, it is important to ask four questions that bear on issues of opportunities, incentives and capabilities for escalation of cultural conflict and the balance of coercive capabilities: first, concerning opportunities and incentives, to what extent do political institutions provide leaders of cultural groups opportunities to monopolize the governmental agenda and transform more policy debates into cultural conflicts, and incentives to escalate demands to challenges to the constitutional order? Second, concerning capabilities, to what extent do political institutions make escalation (or re-escalation) of political conflict and challenges to the constitutional order more or less costly? Third, concerning the coercive balance, to what extent do political institutions distribute coercive and defensive capabilities to deter escalation of both demands and means by ethnic or religious leaders seeking to change the existing constitutional arrangement by expanding the powers of one part of government at the expense of others? Fourth, also concerning this balance, to what extent do political institutions deter the predation of government on the rights of individuals and groups in society?

First, power dividing makes it more difficult for cultural groups to monopolize the policy agenda. That is, the combination of power divided among governmental organs and power divided between government and individuals is more likely to reduce the stakes in government bargaining in three ways that make it more difficult to link all policy issues on the government's agenda to the cultural conflict and to escalate cultural demands on government. (a) Power dividing takes many decisions out of the hands of government and trusts to civil society and private initiative to fulfil many of the aspirations of individuals for such things as religious expression. That is, it raises the transaction costs of getting the governmental organs to act on issues reserved to the private sector, because the government lacks the power to act on such issues and must confront other government organs, including the courts, which can be used to block such action. (b) Power-dividing institutions in divided societies give cultural politicians less agenda control in government and so fewer opportunities to frame all issues as cultural conflicts. Thus, it is less likely that all issues that do reach the government will become battle-grounds in which larger constitutional issues involving the allocation of decision rights to cultural communities are fought over by the leaders of ethnic or religious groups. Where many more decisions are made in diverse centres of state policymaking, with different majorities and minorities, it is more likely that many agenda items will remain isolated issues with relatively lower stakes and not linked to a single overarching high-stakes cultural divide. (c) Power dividing lowers the cultural stakes on issues that do fall within the jurisdiction of the government by making it less likely that winners and losers will correlate with cultural divides and less likely that wins and losses across issues will be cumulative for members of cultural majorities and minorities. So, a loss as a member of *the* minority specific to one issue – such as the allocation of water in a river basin – does not jeopardize one's gains as a member of *the* majorities specific to other issues – such as interest rates or education policy. Power dividing gives cultural leaders and their followers less reason to fear tyranny by a single cultural majority across issue areas.

Alternatively, power sharing gives the major empowered cultural politicians expanded agenda control and the means to frame agenda items as cultural conflicts. More threatening still to civil peace and democracy is the fact that power sharing creates incentives for cultural leaders to reframe their demands as challenges to the allocation of decision rights in the existing constitutional order: particularly, but not exclusively, for the leaders of autonomous homelands, nothing privileges a policy claim more than framing it as an expression of the sovereign right of the cultural community to exercise certain powers – a strategy in ethnofederations that has come to be known as 'playing the sovereignty card'. Power sharing also provides incentives to mimic such claims: Any claim by one cultural-group leader to expanded decision rights, such as sovereign control over natural resources in the homeland of the cultural community, must be matched by the leaders of other cultural groups, because cultural-group leaders who make no such demands will end up with a diminished share of state powers and decision making. Power sharing may even unravel through a domino effect of escalating challenges. To illustrate: in the Soviet Union after *perestroika* political institutions gave leaders of homelands privileged access to central decision-making organs, where they came to control the policy agenda. These homeland leaders used their agenda control in order to reframe all issues that did get to the central bargaining table, such as economic reform or environmental protection, into claims for expanded powers for the homeland administrations vis-à-vis the central government. But these soon turned into competitive constitutional claims and escalation of constitutional challenges was one way to protect a cultural community from the demands of others. In late 1991, as Russia's reformist leaders under Boris Yeltsin demanded a larger voice in the governing of the Soviet Union, and actually began making decisions for the whole union unilaterally, leaders of other republics like Belarus and Ukraine at first followed suit to demand an expanded voice, but then decided to leave the union altogether, because they did not want to be members of a union where the lion's share of governmental powers was held by the new Russian government.

Second, by dispersing institutional weapons, power dividing raises the costs of organizing an assault on the constitutional order. Under power-dividing institutions, before a significant assault can be mounted, coalitions must be formed among many groups with independent control over coercive capabilities. Where society is composed of a multitude of fluid interests arrayed along multiple dimensions rather than pillarized among stable camps, it becomes harder to assemble and hold together a winning coalition of challengers from outside government. If the assault on the existing constitutional order begins within an organ of government, it must build a coalition of organs to mount a potent challenge; where the organs of government are divided by a multitude of interests the transaction costs of organizing such a challenge from within the government rise.

That is, power dividing avoids the concentration of institutional weapons in the hands of a few office holders. Philip Selznick (1960, 2) notes that control over governmental decision rights can become institutional weapons 'used by a power-seeking elite in a manner unrestrained by the constitutional order' and that these decision rights can be used to challenge that constitutional order. In divided societies the incentive for leaders of ethnic or religious groups to escalate challenges to the government increases when these leaders have the means to back their demands by inflicting losses (or threatening to inflict such losses) on the government. Power dividing, like the other strategies, does create institutional weapons, but power dividing disperses institutional weapons, so that leaders of ethnic groups and religious communities, as only one of many empowered leaders, have fewer institutional weapons at their ready disposal. By dispersing rather than concentrating institutional weapons among many countrywide and local majorities, the power-dividing strategy raises the transaction costs associated with escalating stakes and means in bargaining over cultural or other issues.

In particular, power dividing decreases the likelihood that cultural leaders can coerce the government or other cultural leaders in the government by threatening or creating governmental deadlock. By creating independent organs with specialized decision authority, power dividing is more likely to protect efficient decision making in most areas even if deadlock paralyses one or a few organs. In addition to the main general-purpose decision-making bodies of the central government such as national assemblies, power-dividing arrangements include independent special-purpose administrations with countrywide jurisdiction. At the local level, city and county governments exist alongside independent administrations for school boards, water districts, and so forth. Without minority vetoes in these other organs and with the unlikelihood that one majority will dominate all organs, cultural-community leaders are less able to threaten deadlock on these other issues, such as water delivery, until other leaders deliver on core cultural-group demands.

Alternatively, power sharing lowers the relative transaction costs of escalation, because it concentrates many of the institutional weapons for assaulting the constitutional order in the same few hands. By giving the leaders of cultural groups pieces of the state, power sharing multiplies the number of escalatory options available to these leaders, so that they can undertake escalation piecemeal through incremental or 'salami' tactics in order to induce others to give them what they demand. Particularly threatening to the constitutional order is power sharing with consensual decision making that places vetoes in the hands of cultural-group leaders: A veto in decisions of a grand coalition of the central government gives ethnic or religious leaders the power to paralyze the national decision-making process until the leaders of other ethnic or religious groups give in on major constitutional issues. This potent institutional weapon poses a threat to the legitimacy and stability of a democracy. To illustrate: in the Soviet Union following perestroika, the homeland leaders had many escalatory options at their disposal, such as withholding revenues from the central government or refusing to implement all-union policies in their homelands. These were relatively low-cost options in the period of *Perestroika* and so these ploys became a common way for ethnopoliticians to back up their demands. Yet, after decision making transferred to the Council of the Federation in the summer of 1990, where the leaders of each union republic wielded veto power, negotiations over policy, particularly economic reform and a new union treaty, bogged down as these leaders played a game of brinkmanship, threatening mutual disaster by withholding agreement until the others made concessions.

Third, power dividing is more likely than the alternative strategies to create a robust balance of coercive governmental capabilities that protects the constitutional order from predation by one part of government against the others: in the face of shifting challenges from different organs of government, the existing distribution of powers among governmental organs has more powerful defenders than challengers in each small crisis. This dynamic rather than static balance is more likely to deter future challenges to the distribution of powers. In this way, power dividing responds to a central dilemma in power sharing when attempting to distribute coercive governmental capabilities among empowered groups that are often predetermined (relatively static) and divided along a single dimension, such as ethnicity or religion. On one side of this dilemma is the problem of escalating claims that challenge the existing distribution of power: If the initial distribution of governmental powers favours one party to power sharing, there is little to prevent centralization or devolution of still more powers into its hands at the expense of other groups. This change may even be peaceful if the preponderance of power is known to all sides, because the weaker side will know that resistance is futile. Ethnofederalism and ethnocorporatism under power sharing can be particularly destabilizing in this regard (Lake and Rothchild 2005; Roeder 2009), where governmental powers tend to accumulate in two foci – the central government and the ethnic governments. Not only does this tend to define all policy disputes as majority–centre versus minority–periphery, but it tends to concentrate coercive governmental capabilities to back up demands in the hands of the leaders of these two decision-making foci. Blocking predation by one side or the other becomes a central concern in the constitutional design of power sharing. Thus, designers of stable one-dimensional power sharing typically try to design an initial equal distribution of power. Yet, this is where the other side of the dilemma arises – the risk of escalating means (including violence): at the point of relative equality of coercive governmental capabilities among groups, the likelihood of escalation of means is highest (Wittman 2001; Benson and Kugler 1998).[7] That is, insofar as estimates of the likelihood of victory in a showdown of coercion and counter-coercion are derived from the balance of capabilities, it is at the point of equal power that the parties are most likely to hold incompatible expectations of victory and both or all conclude that escalation of means (even to violence) will pay off.

The power-dividing strategy is more likely to avoid this dilemma, because under power-dividing institutions it is easier to assemble a temporary coalition of governmental defenders of the constitutional order than a coalition of governmental challengers; and knowledge of this is likely to deter challenges. By dispersing powers among central-government organs and among sub-national jurisdictions, and by dividing these along multiple dimensions rather than a single (cultural) dimension, power dividing limits the institutional weapons in the hands of any group in control of one of these organs or jurisdictions. Because power dividing disperses institutional weapons, a challenge by one organ or jurisdiction is likely to remain more limited due to the higher transaction costs associated with the necessity of organizing a broad coalition of organs or jurisdictions to pose a more substantial challenge. On the other hand, any claim that the power of one organ or type of jurisdiction should be increased is likely to inspire a defensive coalition of other organs and jurisdictions that may not share policy preferences, but see this reallocation of decision-making authority as a diminution of their organs' place in the government. Because the challengers have limited means at their disposal, the coalition in defence of the status quo need mobilize only a small coalition to turn back this challenge, even if most other members of organs sit on their hands and do nothing on behalf of the constitutional order.

In this way, power dividing is more likely than power sharing to deter predation on the decision rights of other organs of government and to deter the escalation of conflict: the leaders of majorities in different governmental organs that control institutional weapons estimate the outcome of escalation of demands and escalation of means by measuring the relative leverage they have to induce others to act in desired ways. This leverage is measured by their ability to back their demands with action that is costly to other government leaders, such as embargoing national taxes collected in their jurisdictions, delaying decision making at the centre through vetoes, initiating campaigns of terrorist violence, or conducting warfare. They must also consider their ability to withstand such coercion by others. Mutual deterrence depends on the balance of leverage that each side has over the other. The dispersion of institutional weapons among multiple organs divided by multiple dimensions of interest more successfully deters constitutional challenges by one governmental organ against others because there is less reason to expect success.

Fourth, power dividing is more likely to create a robust defence of the rights of cultural minorities in society against the predation of governmental organs. Power dividing is based on the logic that if a government organ infringes on the rights of cultural minorities, members of the cultural majority, particularly those who are minorities on other issues, are more likely to desert their cultural leaders and jump to the defence of the minority, *to the extent* they share a vested interest in preserving the rights of minorities in many other situations. Moreover, minorities are more likely to have allies within the majority cultural community *to the extent* the civil liberties guaranteed minorities are not only rights of *the* cultural minority against the majority, but also rights of minorities (such as divorced and remarried Catholics) *within* the majority and minority communities. In power dividing the rights of majorities and minorities – and not just cultural majorities and minorities – are identical: the liberal regime grants the same civil liberties of association and expression to all groups – not simply ethnic or cultural groups, but industrial, commercial, labour and public service groups as well. And so, many more members of the cultural majority and minorities are likely to recognize shared interests in defending the rights of minorities against governmental infringement. For example, in the United States when some members of the religious majority have attacked the rights of religious minorities, such as the right of Native Americans to use peyote in religious rituals, other members of the religious majority, notably members of mainstream Protestant denominations that share civil liberties with the religious minority, have been among the minority's strongest allies (Pevar 1983). These members of the majority fear that their own First Amendment rights would be threatened if the courts decided against Native Americans.

In stark contrast, the allocation of decision rights in power sharing (particularly where these are institutionalized in communal organs or autonomous governments) privileges ethnic or religious groups over other groups and some of these cultural groups over others. Because the empowered groups become isolated from the 'disfranchised' groups, both 'non-cultural' groups, such as labour and business, and cultural groups excluded from the power-sharing arrangement have no interest in defending the rules of a game that discriminate against them and, in fact, have an incentive to change those rules that privilege specific cultural groups at their expense. If the government begins to prey upon the special rights of cultural groups, these other elites are unlikely to jump to the defence of the privileged groups and may even press the government to encroach on these privileges. For example, in the Russian Federation in the 1990s leaders of Russian provinces (oblasts) expressed deep resentment at the special prerogatives accorded many non-Russian republics within the federation and were among the leading advocates pressing Moscow to strip away these prerogatives and equalize the rights of regional governments.

## Conclusion

In addressing the problem of conflict management, the power-dividing strategy stresses a prudential, long-term view: institutional design should not only address the issue of ending a current conflict that may have already become intense, but should seek to shape politics in future years in ways that avoid escalation or re-escalation of conflict to such intensity. As an institutionalist strategy power dividing stresses that political institutions can structure the identities that people express in public (and even how they see themselves), the collective efforts in which they join to achieve goals they cannot reach individually and their engagement in politics. On the last, power dividing builds on a well-researched causal chain that political institutions empower some political actors more than others to use some tactics more than others and to turn to either nongovernmental or governmental institutions to serve their collective aspirations. Early institutionalists, such as James Madison, recognized that conflict is inherent in politics and so the goal of institutionalists has not been to end conflict, but to encourage participants to press claims and to select means for pressing those claims that are unlikely to challenge the constitutional order.

In ethnically or religiously divided societies, the power-dividing strategy stresses institutions that create more incentives for individuals to reach across the boundaries of cultural communities in more aspects of their lives and particularly in politics. It stresses institutions that lower the stakes in politics by creating incentives for individuals to fulfil more of their aspirations through a multitude of private associations rather than governmental action. In politics, power-dividing institutions reduce the agenda control of cultural leaders, limit their coercive capabilities, and constrain their ability to use their place within government to diminish the powers and liberties of others, so that ethnic or religious leaders are no more privileged than the leaders of other interest groups. Power dividing protects cultural minorities from predation by either government or others through extensive, defensible civil liberties. The case for power dividing is not an ideology or ideal type, but a strategy of pragmatic steps in the politics of divided societies taken to increase the likelihood that on any issue citizens are more likely to use moderate means to pursue limited objectives that do not threaten the constitutional order with ethnic or religious predation, deadlock and violence.

## Notes

1 For the other strategies, see Wolff (Chapter 1) and Reilly (Chapter 2) in this volume.
2 Indeed, so potent is this power to discriminate among cultures that many argue for the use of power-sharing institutions in order to empower more moderate leaders, such as moderate Muslims, at the expense of radicals within their communities.
3 As an illustration of multiple majorities see Faust's (1996) discussion of the special formula in the Federal Reserve that Congress used to represent shared and diverging interests concerning inflation.
4 These data are from the websites of the individual state governments and from United States (2009). The median for all 50 states is under 1.4 special-purpose governments per general-purpose government.
5 Hyink and Provost (1998), updated from lists of constitutional officers posted on Wikipedia.
6 On Rwanda, see Clark in this volume (Chapter 10).
7 A significant body of theory and evidence in international relations also supports the contention that power parity increases the likelihood of violence while preponderance decreases this; see Organski (1958), Bueno de Mesquita and Lalman (1992) and Kugler and Lemke (1996).

## References

Bell, C. and Price, C. 1991 *California Government Today*, Pacific Grove, CA: Brooks/Cole Publishing.
Benson, M. and Kugler, J. 1998 'Power Parity, Democracy, and the Severity of Internal Violence', *Journal of Conflict Resolution*, 42: 196–209.
Berry, C. 2009 *Imperfect Union: Representation and Taxation in Multilevel Governments*, New York, NY: Cambridge University Press.
Bogdanor, V. 1988 'Federalism in Switzerland', *Government and Opposition*, 23: 69–90.
Brancati, D. 2009 *Peace by Design: Managing Intrastate Conflict through Decentralization*, New York, NY: Oxford University Press.
Brass, P. 1991 *Ethnicity and Nationalism: Theory and Comparison*, New Delhi: Sage.
Bueno de Mesquita, B. and Lalman, D. 1992 *War and Reasons: Domestic and International Imperatives*, New Haven, CT: Yale University Press.
Campbell, A., Converse, P., Miller, W. and Stokes, D. 1960 *The American Voter*, New York, NY: Wiley.
Dahl, R. 1961 *Who Governs? Democracy and Power in an American City*, New Haven, CT: Yale University Press.
Dikshit, R. D. 1975 *The Political Geography of Federalism: An Inquiry into Origins and Stability*, New York, NY: Wiley.

Faust, J. 1996 'Whom Can We Trust to Run the Fed? Theoretical Support for the Founders' Views', *Journal of Monetary Economics*, 37: 267–83.

Fitzmaurice, J. 1998 'Diversity and Civil Society, New Order? International Models of Peace and Reconciliation' (Report No. 9) Belfast: Democratic Dialogue (available online at: http://cain.ulst. ac.uk/dd/report9/report9d.htm).

Government of Switzerland 1993, *Eidgenössische Volkszählung 1990: Sprachen und Konfessionen*, vol. 16, Bern: Bundesamt für Statistik.

Horowitz, D. 1985 *Ethnic Groups in Conflict*, Berkeley, CA: University of California Press.

Hyink, B. and Provost, D. 1998 *Politics and Government in California*, New York, NY: Longman.

Kugler, J. and Lemke, D. (eds) 1996 *Parity and War: Evaluations and Extensions of the War Ledger*, Ann Arbor, MI: University of Michigan Press.

Lake, D. and Rothchild, D. 2005 'Territorial Decentralization and Civil War Settlements', in P. Roeder and D. Rothchild (eds.) 2005 *Sustainable Peace: Power and Democracy after Civil Wars*, Ithaca, NY: Cornell University Press.

Lewis-Beck, M., Jacoby, W., Norpoth, H. and Weisberg, H. 2008 *The American Voter Revisited*, Ann Arbor, MI: University of Michigan Press.

Leites, N. and Wolf, C. 1970 *Rebellion and Authority: An Analytic Essay on Insurgent Conflicts*, Chicago, IL: Markham.

Lijphart, A. 1968 *The Politics of Accommodation: Pluralism and Democracy in the Netherlands*, Berkeley, CA: University of California Press.

—— 1972 *Democracy in Plural Societies*, New Haven, CT: Yale University Press.

Linder, W. 1994 *Swiss Democracy: Possible Solutions to Conflict in Multicultural Societies*, New York, NY: St Martin's Press.

Lipset, S. 1981 *Political Man: The Social Bases of Politics*, expanded and updated edition, Baltimore, MD: Johns Hopkins University Press.

McCarthy, J. and Zald, M. 1987 'Resource Mobilization and Social Movements: A Partial Theory', in M. Zald and J. McCarthy (eds.), *Social Movements in an Organizational Society*, New Brunswick, NJ: Transaction Books.

Nagel, J., 1994 'Constructing Ethnicity: Creating and Recreating Ethnic Identity and Culture', *Social Problems*, 41: 152–76.

Organski, A. 1958 *World Politics*, New York, NY: Alfred Knopf.

Pevar, S. 1983 *The Rights of Indians and Tribes*, New York, NY: Bantam Books.

Roeder, P. and Rothchild, D. (eds) 2005 *Sustainable Peace: Power and Democracy after Civil Wars*, Ithaca, NY: Cornell University Press.

Roeder, P. 2005 'Power Dividing as an Alternative to Ethnic Power Sharing', in P. Roeder and D. Rothchild (eds.) 2005 *Sustainable Peace: Power and Democracy after Civil Wars*, Ithaca, NY: Cornell University Press.

—— 2007 *Where Nation-States Come From: Institutional Change in the Age of Nationalism*, Princeton, NJ: Princeton University Press.

—— 2009 'Ethnofederalism and the Mismanagement of Conflicting Nationalism', *Regional and Federal Studies*, 19: 203–19.

Schoch, B. 2000 'Switzerland – A Model for Solving Nationality Conflicts?', Frankfurt: Peace Research Institute.

Selznick, P. 1960 *The Organizational Weapon: A Study of Bolshevik Strategy and Tactics*, Glencoe, IL: Free Press of Glencoe.

Steiner, J. 1969 'Nonviolent Conflict Resolution in Democratic Systems: Switzerland', *Journal of Conflict Resolution*, 13: 295–304.

—— 1974 *Amicable Agreement Versus Majority Rule: Conflict Resolution in Switzerland*, revised edition, Chapel Hill, NC: University of North Carolina Press.

—— 1987 'Consociational Democracy as a Policy Recommendation: The Case of South Africa', *Comparative Politics*, 19: 361–72.

—— 1998 'Consociational Theory and Switzerland – Revisited Thirty Years Later'. Paper presented at the Center for European Studies conference on the Fate of Consociationalism, Cambridge, MA: Harvard University.

Steiner, J. and Dorff, R. 1985 'Structure and Process in Consociationalism and Federalism', *Publius: The Journal of Federalism*, 15: 49–55.

Tarrow, S. 1989 *Struggle, Politics, and Reform: Collective Action, Social Movements, and Cycles of Protest*, Ithaca, NY: Cornell University Center for International Studies.

United Nations 2001 Department of Economic and Social Information and Policy Analysis, Statistical Division, *Statistical Yearbook*, New York, NY: United Nations.

United States Census Bureau 2009 *Statistical Abstract of the United States: 2010*, Washington, DC (available online at: www.census.gov/statab/www).

Walter, B. 2002 *Committing to Peace: The Successful Settlement of Civil Wars*, Princeton, NJ: Princeton University Press.

Waters, M. 1990 *Ethnic Options: Choosing Identities in America*, Berkeley, CA: University of California Press.

Wittman, D. 2001 'War or Peace?'. Unpublished manuscript, Santa Cruz: University of California, CA.

# Part II

# Processes and actors

# 4    The diplomacy of conflict management

*I. William Zartman*

States have always sought both to pursue and to reduce conflict, as they work to maximize their security, the primary goal of foreign policy. Conflicts that are winnable are to be pursued, to the degree that the stakes are important and the means are available to the state; conflicts that are not or are damaging to the states are to be reduced. This goes for both one's own conflicts and the conflicts of others; the latter, again, to the extent that they matter to the third party state (Charillon 2002, Aggestam and Jerkeck 2009). Over time, however, the weights of these considerations have evolved somewhat, and the means by which they have been conceived and conducted have also developed. Hence a consideration of the diplomacy of conflict resolution could well focus either on the constancy of its prime parameters, despite the contextual changes in which it operates, or on the new emphases that have evolved, despite the constancy of the basic process. This discussion will do the latter, with the understanding that claims about what is new are usually only highlighting shifts in emphasis rather than total novelties.

Four such shifts in emphasis are significant to the topic. *Security* has moved from exclusive application to the state to inclusive application to its population as well. *Prevention* has come to orient states' policies beyond simply reaction to conflict and crises. The *scope* of states' concerns has expanded from purely bilateral or at most regional to global interests. The *arena* of conflict has shifted from a primarily interstate to a largely intrastate level. Each will be examined in turn for its role in the evolution of the diplomacy of conflict resolution, although together all four form an interrelated ball of wax. At the end of each of the four analyses, the positive effects of the change will be noted.

## Security

International relations were long treated as interstate relations, and when domestic conflicts were involved, it was as incidents concerning state security. This is still strongly true, but at the same time, there is a rising concern on many fronts about human security, the security of people, populations and human lives (HSRP 2008). This concern is reflected in the significant rise in importance of humanitarian conditions, emergencies and intervention, bypassing the state and often holding the state responsible for the plight of its citizens. Humanitarian efforts are the turf of non-governmental organizations (NGOs), both as direct interveners and as advocates who seek to mould public opinion and state policy. But they are also the stuff of state actions, as they lead diplomacy into areas that were earlier considered out of bounds.

The no-fly zone in northern (Kurdish) Iraq in 1991 and the relief operation in Somalia in 1992 were the first two UN operations justified as humanitarian interventions, in areas where the US and other Security Council members had no direct interest. Arguably, the UN intervention in the crumbling state of Kampuchea (Cambodia) after 1990 was a humanitarian operation, even though not justified as such, where most of the UNSC member had no direct interest but all were impelled by the murderous insecurity of the Cambodian people. On the other side of the policy divide, the same UNSC members (except, later in Operation Turquoise, France) avoided intervention in the Rwandan genocide where no national interests were at stake, but were roundly criticized by public opinion and by other states for their inaction (or for one-sided action in the case of France).

In addition, a growing number of conflict resolution or management demarches driven by concern for human security have marked a number of countries' foreign policy. Norway has developed a calling to mediation, notably in offering good offices to Guatemalans in 1985 and Palestinians and Israelis in the Oslo negotiation in 1993 and then in seeking to mediate the internal conflict in Sri Lanka in 2007. A unique institutionalized multilateral effort is the Office of the High Commissioner on National Minorities of the Organization for Security and Cooperation in Europe (OSCE), specifically devoted to the prevention and settlement of minority conflicts (Meerts and Coulaloglu 2011).[1]

Most notably, the shift to human security has brought about two major reorientations in international law that pose important problems still awaiting a lengthy political and legal examination. One is the Responsibility to Protect (R2P); the other is universal jurisdiction. R2P replaces the standard but dangerous doctrine of sovereignty as protection, accepted since the Peace Treaties of Westphalia of 1648, with the equally dangerous notion of sovereignty as responsibility (Deng et al. 1996; Evans and Sahnoun 2002; Ban 2009; Zartman 2010). The first protects the state from external interference, particularly from stronger states, giving it the right to do what it wants with its population, whereas the latter protects the population against its own state, empowering others – particularly stronger states – to intervene to accomplish that protection if the state does not live up to its responsibilities to its own people. The dangers are evident, to the people in the first case and to the smaller states in the second. The international community has not yet worked out the limits and thresholds of the new doctrine, and the risks involved have caused it to take a less prominent place interstate politics and discussion after the mid-2000s – despite being adopted by the UN Summit in 2005 – than in the previous decade. Nevertheless, the new doctrine is on the table, giving a criterion for action in conflicts contradictory to that of the previous doctrine.

Universal jurisdiction and international criminal courts have had the same effect and as a result are undergoing the same type of defining debate. Where formerly legal accusations and more broadly class action suits could be brought against individuals within the plaintiff's country, universal jurisdiction opens such suits for crimes against humanity to be brought against defendants outside the country by plaintiffs only broadly concerned. Furthermore, political leaders and followers can be indicted and tried for crimes against humanity by international tribunals, either with global jurisdiction similar to that of the International Court of Justice, as in the International Criminal Court (ICC), or else with jurisdiction limited to a specific country, as in the International Tribunals on Yugoslavia, Rwanda and Sierra Leone. All of these legal innovations carry the issue of human security directly into the offending state, with incontrovertible effect.

These various mechanisms that reflect new directions in security, away from state to human concerns, pose major problems of orientation and contradiction. While human security policy in regard to the Kurds was consistent with the rest of US policy towards Saddam Hussein's Iraq, the implications of action in Somalia and Rwanda were complicating for the US as for other countries, and in the end brought heavy opprobrium for getting out and for not getting in, respectively. R2P was, in part, the consequence, but the doctrine immediately poses the implementary question: when and how? The invasion of Iraq in 2003 could be claimed to be the first major application of R2P but it met widespread world condemnation because the required UNSC majority for a specific mandate was not available, even though intervention in Iraqi Kurdistan in 1999, Kosovo in 1999 and Macedonia in 2001, occurred without UNSC authorization. Thereafter, for the rest of the decade, the responsibility to protect human security became elusive, despite opportunities to do so in Zimbabwe, Congo, Darfur and Sri Lanka, among others. When the doctrine was revived in 2011 in Libya, it ran into embarrassing consequences and posed embarrassing questions in regard to a similar situation in Syria. Because of the authority of the action, universal and international criminal courts jurisdiction over human security issues poses major problems for conflict management efforts towards the states in question. Mediation in Sudan and Uganda has been seriously impeded by ICC indictments brought against Omar al-Bashir, the president of Sudan, and Joseph Kony, the rebel guru in Uganda. Mediatory relations between Great Britain and the Middle East have been seriously complicated by the threats of suits to be brought against Israeli public figures over the Gaza incursion of January 2009. Diplomacy to resolve conflicts over state security is often at cross purposes with efforts to protect human security.

As an extreme example, a salient case of conflict in the current era concerns the basis of self-determination. Since the end of the First World War, the overriding policy guideline has been that of national self-determination. The effect of the doctrine was originally extremely limited, applying only to selected empires, the Austro-Hungarian and Ottoman. An attempt was made to create new states that approximated the territorial limits of major nationalities. When the doctrine was carried to its logical application, as by the Egyptian Wafd movement, to justify post-colonial independence, it was summarily rejected, to be applied to European colonies only a war later. After the Second World War, the term 'national' was given an equally restricted definition, referring only to constituted colonial territories and thereby slipping into a new guideline defined as state self-determination (Emerson 1960). The notion was further limited, locked in by the application of *uti possedetis* to sanctify often badly drawn colonial boundaries and to launch states on the process of constructing a state nation, in the absence of a nation-state (Thompson and Zartman 1975; Gordon 1971; Shedahi 1993; Staravoitova 1997). In both periods, many ethnic groups were crammed into states dominated by one majority, pieces of which were often assigned to other states. State self-determination has strengthened its hold over post-Cold War conflict management, dominating the settlements over the break-up of Yugoslavia and the Soviet Union and disregarding human (ethnic) criteria. Post-Cold War self-determination in Africa followed the same state criterion in regard to Eritrea, Somaliland, and (stretching it) Southern Sudan although with a nod to national criteria at the same time. Yet, self-determination claims by Albanians in Macedonia, Serbs in Kosovo, Armenians in Azerbaijan, Indians in Chiapas, Tamils in Sri Lanka and Diolas and others in Casamance have been rejected, despite some internal measures in some of the cases. National self-determination would have caused major squabbles and conflicts over the shape of the new units, a fact that doubtless played a large role in the diplomatic adoption of state self-determination as the criterion.

Nonetheless, significant diplomatic efforts have been made to advance human security in the midst of conflict. The initial intervention in Somalia in 1992 was the result of a shock imparted to the Bush administration by the famine. The same administration issued the 1990 Christmas warning on Kosovo in the face of impending mass killing, which then took place towards the end of the decade and finally brought on diplomatic efforts at Rambouillet and then the NATO bombings in 1999 to eventually bring about Kosovo's independence in 2008. Diplomatic and then physical interventions in Haiti in the early and again late 1990s and then in 2010 were the result of compelling attention to human security. UN mediation in the intrastate conflicts in El Salvador in the 1980s and Guatemala in the 1990s was impelled by the same concern.

## Prevention

Certainly in past times, diplomacy sought to prevent crises among states, and one can well analyse and even judge interstate relations as an exercise of 'normal diplomacy', an ideal type akin in international relations to 'normal politics' in comparative politics. Normal diplomacy is based on the notion, contained in official instructions, that the prime task of ambassadors is to promote good relations between the home and the host state (Satow 1917; de Callieres 1716/2001), and, by extension, to prevent conflicts between them. It works, as testified by the literally innumerable conflicts that have not taken place or have not escalated into worse violence, and by some specific cases where a diplomat was the agent of prevention. The history of diplomacy emphasizes this focus, but the delicate balance that characterized the Cold War carried with it a particular emphasis on crisis prevention (Brecher and Wilkenfeld 1997). The focus, of course, was on bipolar relations.

But the focus on prevention of conflicts was earlier, deeper and now more pronounced in the post-Cold War period. It should be understood, to begin with, that the word 'conflict' is subject to confusing usage, referring both the a simple incompatibility between positions and at other times to the violent expression of that incompatibility. Conflict per se is an inevitable, even useful, aspect of human relations; even when passive conflict – the state of incompatibilities of positions – becomes active through escalation, it is part of normal relations. However, it also carries the seed of violence, if parties become too strongly attached to their positions and feel that further escalation into violence will enable them to prevail. It is necessary to examine and deal with conflicts before they become violent, in order to prevent crises but also to understand the source of the violence when it does occur. Therefore the aim is to tend conflicts before they escalate into violence, fend off conflicts that are in the violent stage, and mend conflicts that have been deescalated from violence (Hamburg 2008; Cohen and Albright 2008; Zartman 2010).

In strategic terms, conflicts tend to take the form of a Prisoners' Dilemma Game (PDG) where an outcome favourable to the opponent is the worst possible, worse than continued conflict. Normally, the conflict is continued by each party in order to attain its preferred outcome, by means that can either be violent, political or simply suspended; most conflicts follow one of the latter two paths – political or suspended. Conflict management refers to efforts to keep the conflict on those two levels; only if the incompatibilities that give rise to the conflict are removed can one talk of conflict resolution. If one party's goal becomes simply to prevent the other party from attaining *its* preferred outcome, possibilities for conflict management begin to appear, and when the parties decide that continued conflict or stalemate is the outcome most to be avoided, those possibilities become salient, as in a Chicken Dilemma Game (CDG) (Snyder and Diesing 1977; Goldstein 2010). Conflict prevention then means elimination or blockage of the means of pursuing the conflict that are violent and tending conflicts before they become so.

It was secretary-general Dag Hammarskjöld who pressed the notion of preventive diplomacy and then his distant successor, Boutros Boutros-Ghali, who brought it back into prominence, after a Cold War interlude. During the 1990s, preventive diplomacy was also addressed by academic analysis within nongovernmental research organizations. The Council on Foreign Relations undertook a group study on *enforcing restraint: collective intervention in internal conflicts* where legitimacy was linked to a collective decision but also to the effectiveness of international organizations facing new challenges (Damrosch 1993). The US Institute of Peace published a strategic toolkit and analysis for conflict prevention by Michael Lund (1996). Under the inspiration of David Hamburg, the Carnegie Corporation set up its Commission on Preventing Deadly Conflict that sponsored a broad collection of investigations into prevention (Holl 1997; Jentleson 2000; Zartman 2001).

On the official side, the 2000 meeting of the G-8 foreign ministers in Japan produced the G-8 Miyakazi Initiative for Conflict Prevention that laid out a strategy of 'chronological comprehensiveness' covered structural prevention, early and late prevention and post-conflict peace building. A notable attempt to address the questions of measures and mandates was the Swedish initiative in connection with the Swedish presidency of the European Union (EU) in the first half of 2001, based on a 1999 report, *Preventing Violent Conflict*, that was designed to focus and energize Swedish and eventually EU policy to develop a culture of prevention. (Foreign Ministry 1997, 1999; ISIS 1999; Björkdal 1999)

These various paths of attention came together in the Canadian-sponsored International Commission on Intervention and State Sovereignty (ICISS), whose 2001 report *The Responsibility to Protect*, took up the same theme to state that although 'the primary responsibility for the protection of its people lies with the state itself, where a population is suffering serious harm, as a result of internal war, insurgency, repression or state failure, and the state in question is unwilling or unable to halt or avert it, the principle of non-intervention yields to the international responsibility to protect' (Deng *et al.* 1996; Deng and Zartman 2002). It also declared, in bold type, that 'prevention is the single most important dimension of the responsibility to protect', and sought to shift the debate from the 'right to intervene' to the 'responsibility to protect'. Prevention is divided into structural or root-cause prevention and direct (operational) or conflict prevention, and military intervention is circumscribed by a just cause threshold, precautionary and operational principles and right authority (Evans and Sahnoun 2001, I: xii–xiii, 22–7, 47–69). These concerns then found their place, along with the R2P doctrine, in the secretary-general's High Level Panel that was unanimously adopted by the General Assembly at the 2005 World Summit.

The subsequent decade, however, saw the doctrine of prevention running aground on the same sorts of difficulties as had the doctrines of R2P and human security. As in the previous case, the shoals were practical and conceptual. Practical difficulties concern the implementation of prevention. The UN doctrine on peacekeeping, as constituted in 'Chapter VI.5' not written in the Charter, is that peacekeeping forces (PKF) are rigorously held to keeping a peace already agreed to rather than intervening in situations of violence; the Mission of the UN in Congo (MONUC) stretched this doctrine towards intervention when it learned that no peace had been agreed to in Eastern Congo, but possible UN prevention was dodged in 1997 in Congo-Brazzaville on the grounds that peace had not taken hold (Zartman 2000; Zartman 1998). Preventing conflicts not yet violent from becoming so, a rising emphasis of the prevention doctrine, is even more difficult, for it amounts to telling sovereign states not to pursue their conflict with external or, more seriously, internal enemies (Zartman 2010; Anstey and Zartman 2011). Since intrastate conflict often arises from deprivations imposed by a narrowly based government or discriminations imposed on internal rivals, such advice and efforts to implement it are sharply resented by target states and their leaders. Governments carrying out a policy of violent conflict against an identified – and, almost necessarily, demonized – internal or external enemy are not likely to take kindly to external attempts to prevent their efforts for the defence of the country or regime.

The conceptual difficulties are similar to those of human security, and they underlie the practical difficulties. 'What to prevent when' is a major operative as well as conceptual question. Early prevention is the most difficult to justify, for the chances of the foreseen event's taking place are highly uncertain and, if prevented, never to be proven. Commentators call for early action to validate early warning, but the guarantees of a tropical storm warning turning into a tropical storm are inconclusive (Zartman and Faure 2005). Warnings and intervention to prevent Israel from carrying out expansionist policies that arguably will take it to Masada, or Egypt from carrying out repressive policies that predictably will introduce a Muslim Brotherhood takeover, or Iran from carrying out nuclear policies that will assuredly feed its persecution complex inevitably complicate attempts to cultivate better relations with the target countries. On the other hand, 'early late' prevention efforts, before the conflict has reached the crisis or 'too late' stage, have major obstacles of over-commitment to overcome that earlier action would have avoided.

Nonetheless, preventive diplomacy has achieved notable successes in conflict management, and even resolution. The two preventive interventions in Macedonia by both physical and diplomatic means in 1992 and 2001 are frequently cited as the model cases. Russian diplomatic intervention in the Nagorno–Karabakh conflict in 1994 brought a management of the conflict that still holds, providing a potential basis for resolution (Mooradian and Druckman 1999; Hopmann and Zartman 2010). The dissolution of the Soviet Union gave rise to some notable cases of preventive diplomacy in the Baltic States, in Ukraine and elsewhere in the so-called Near Abroad (Hopmann 2001; Jentleson 2000). Congo-Brazzaville in 1993 was an excellent case of African preventive diplomacy, unfortunately unmatched in the revival of the conflict in 1997 (Zartman and Vogeli 2000).

## Scope

The twentieth century displayed a striking spread of state concerns beyond the bilateral and the regional, at an astonishing pace. The two World Wars linked a European and an Asian theatre of operations; the Cold War made them one. Great power concerns have always extended beyond their immediate neighbourhood; superpower concerns became global. Businesses became multilateral corporations that drew on world markets and outsourced and offshored their production around the globe (Friedman 2009). The most notable sign of globalism is the rise of a multinational corporation with a secret, mobile headquarters, a corporate culture, multinational branches and international cadres, funding from diaspora and organized criminal sources, IT and electronic communications, and state security penetration to attack a worldwide range of targets, named The Base (Al-Qaeda). Diplomacy has truly been globalized.

There are three reasons for this extension of diplomacy and national interests around the world: strategic interests, new national interest and human security (again). *Strategic interests* have a strongest effect on great and superpowers, as far away events have an increasingly direct effect on their concerns and welfare. Although the colonial era has passed, the former metropoles maintain their historic interest and economic ties, as well as political relations, with their former colonies. Superpower strategic concerns more often tended to be pre-emptive, demanding an interest in order to prevent the other superpower from gaining a foothold, rather than deriving from direct interest in Third World areas. Cold War interest rushed in to fill the vacuum left by colonial withdrawal; when the Cold War ended, the decline of pre-emptive interests produced a similar withdrawal, and the Third World burst out into its own conflicts, liberated from the constraints that their Cold War protectors had imposed. At that point, strategic interests returned in their own right, as the US is drawn into Sudan, Darfur, Somalia, Philippines and the Sahara and Sahel by concern about Al-Qaeda, and into Congo, Korea and Burma by concern for stability in a strategic and unstable neighbourhood. But other great powers and members of the UNSC find themselves responsible for the course of events in troubled areas, including Congo, Libya, Syria, Sudan, Cambodia, Afghanistan and Palestine, because of their position in the UN and because of their concept of interests that goes beyond their immediate neighbourhood.

*National interests* have gone some way (not all the way) in the minds in many capitals in moving from national interests that are qualified as 'narrow' to those termed 'enlightened'. The first have long been dominant in diplomatic and Realist thinking, much as was the doctrine of sovereignty as protection. They relate to a geostrategic concern for national independence, territorial integrity and protection of the country's way of life and standard of living (Morgenthau 1948). The latter, enlightened interests, are concerned with the maintenance of collective agreements and reciprocal security, under the Liberal or Institutionalist perspective that reciprocity is an important interest for the assurance of mutual security (Ikenberry 2001). Thus, it is important for states to cooperate in managing far-flung conflicts and to conceive of their interests in terms of mutual assurances of security and stability. In a memorable statement, Ambassador Christopher Hill (2005) indicated that the purpose of the six-party talks was to convince North Korea (DPRK) that its security would be better assured by taking its place in the international community than by unilateral measures that only threaten the other members of that community. Managing distant conflicts builds on that notion and fact of an international community with reciprocal obligations that reduce conflict and justify intervention.

*Human security* provides a powerful motivation for the global extension of diplomacy beyond the direct effect noted above. Whereas states were formerly concerned with their own state security, as under the rubric of narrow national interests, or with reciprocal state security obligations, as under the notion of enlightened national interests, they now find themselves drawn into conflicts where they have no state interest at all but where the horror of the human condition compels a response. The effect of this new criterion for action has already been discussed, above, but its impact on the scope of diplomatic activity is relevant to the consideration of globalism in conflict management. Striking examples are the unexpected intervention of the US in the Somali situation in 1992 and of NATO in Libya in 2011, justified only by humanitarian concerns (unlike some other humanitarian interventions as in Kurdistan which were justified by strategic concerns as well). But the effect is equally notably evidenced in the diplomacy of other states. The most marked example is Norway, which has no national interests, enlightened or otherwise, in East or West Asia or Latin America, but extended important efforts into the mediation of the Guatemalan, Israeli and Sri Lankan conflicts, for purely humanitarian reasons.

In such cases, the combined reasons of strategic, enlightened national and humanitarian interest stretch the notion of interest far beyond its earlier definitions. Even smaller states have become involved in conflict management around the world, and have put their reputations on the line in the search for solutions. As in case of other sources of shift in emphasis, this stretch is not unilinear; it has its ebbs and flows. Overstretch causes domestic reaction and the country pulls back to a reduced circumference of interests. Then new events pull on the reasoning of strategy, enlightenment and/or humanity and the country or countries are impelled back into conflict management. The dynamic is interesting: a country may return to an expanded role invigorated, or timid, or pushed by a public reaction or electoral change, or it may pull back further, although the record of the US shows that isolationism can produce a more timid response but scarcely a full pullback from world events and interests.

Nonetheless, global interest has led to notable successes in conflict management, and even resolution. The multiple roles of Norway in Guatemala, Israel and Sri Lanka, outside its sphere of interest, have been noted. More broadly, the Scandinavian countries have been active in East Africa in development diplomacy. The US played the decisive role in bringing independence to Namibia and an end to the South African conflict with Angola, and was helpful in the change of regime in South African itself (Lyman 2009). The US was pulled in to the conflicts in Afghanistan and Pakistan by its cold war interests in the 1980s and by its anti-terrorist interests in the 2000s, but the area, along with Central Asia in general, was long beyond US interests. More broadly, the attention of the Security Council members was drawn to Kosovo and Cambodia in intense diplomatic efforts at conflict management, in new extensions of their previous interests.

## Arena

While internal conflicts, from riots to revolutions, have pockmarked normal politics and normal diplomacy over millennia, the post-war and then post-Cold War eras have seen a notable decrease of interstate wars and a corresponding increase of intrastate conflict. Despite or because of the touchiness of numerous pairs of interstate relations, escalation to war has become rare; in some deep-seated cases, such as India–Pakistan, Israel–Palestine, Morocco–Algeria, Iran–Israel, among others, mutual assured destruction (MAD) stalemates reminiscent of the Cold War have frozen the conflict and prevented a cataclysm from erupting. At the same time, the end of the Cold War brought into question the power, authority and centrality of the state in economy, society and polity in much of the Third and Second World. Democracy legitimized opposition and removed the monopoly of power from government; free enterprise encouraged competition and shattered a centralized economy; the end of bipolarity undercut foreign support for single-party regimes and shredded the philosophical support for democratic centralism and the general will. In addition, attempts to create a state nation in the absence of a nation state sidelined traditional nations, tribes and ethnic groups and, contrarily, raised their salience when central state efforts were weakened. The result has been an absolute rise in internal, often ethnic, conflicts to challenge the weakened state and foster the collapse of post-independence social contracts, increasing in numbers in the 1990s followed by a decline and then rise again in the first 2000 decade (data contained in the Minorities at Risk Project (MAR) (2009) and the Uppsala Conflict Data Program (UCDP) (2010).

Internal conflicts are a different kind of animal from interstate conflicts. Intrastate conflicts are often referred to as asymmetric, an insightful but not complete characterization. They involve unequal parties in terms of both power and legitimacy: the state is the stronger of the two parties, at least through much of the conflict, and the state is the sovereign, legitimate actor. This means that the rebels have to lead a triple struggle against odds – for attention, for power and for legitimacy. But they do have an equalizing weapon, and that is commitment. Unlike a state, their cause is their only cause, and they are dedicated fanatics in its pursuit, taking up arms to call attention to their grievance. They have to, or they would soon be overwhelmed by the normal calculations of power. They seize the opportunity to claim legitimacy as spokespersons for their deprived and discriminated population and then seek to destroy the legitimacy of the state as ruler of the whole political system (Zartman 1995). The result has been a challenging need to revise the nature of conflict management diplomacy, to overcome obstacles to entry into negotiations, to reconceptualize attainable outcomes and retool for effective intervention.

*Diplomacy* is generally beyond the experience of the rebels and beyond the intentions of the state. At least initially, the rebels are a badly organized, inchoate body, with any political sense subsumed under the military demands of the struggle. Later in the struggle, if it is long enough, they can develop the elements of a proto-state, further complicating the nature of the conflict. If an agreement to manage or resolve the conflict finally comes, it poses the problem of rebuilding the state, to some extent if the conflict is only managed and to a greater extent as diplomacy moves towards conflict resolution where the challenges of 'business as usual during remodelling' are enormous. When states make peace among themselves, the signing units generally remain intact and continue operations; when the parties end an internal conflict, they are under deep internal strains and have to construct new relations within the political system.

Rebels frequently are simply not organized to act and think as negotiators and are in need of training to be able to participate in conflict management. During a decade of armed struggle, RENAMO had only a vague idea of what it was fighting for, as opposed to against, and needed training and coaching in meeting the Mozambican government in negotiations. The same problem faced the several Darfuri rebel groups in Sudan, the RUF in Sierra Leone and the UNITA in Angola. Even when the goal (independence) was clear in the rebels' minds, the requirements of give and take in a situation where their victory was not acquired were foreign to the rebels' abilities, as in the case of the Polisario in Morocco, Hamas in Palestine, the FARC and ELN in Colombia and the LTTE in Sri Lanka. Thus, mediation is needed, not only to bring the parties together on an agreeable outcome but to train the parties how to act in looking for such an outcome. The same problem plagues many of the movements involved in the uprisings in the Arab Spring, who know clearly what they are against but less precisely what they are for, and how to negotiate a viable new order.

A particular problem is the multiplication of rebel movements as the conflict moves towards negotiation and, presumably, resolution. Mediators and negotiators dealing with rebel movements often seek to split the movement and play on its factionalism in order to find leadership – often the political as opposed to the military wing – willing to talk conflict reduction. But what is often a necessary tactical move can work in the opposite direction. Rebel factions see that their movement as a whole won concessions – including willingness to negotiate – from the government by continued resistance; so they break ranks with the main movement to hold out for their own benefits or sometime to race to an agreement before the main body. The proliferation of rebel movements as the conflict goes on tests the process of conflict management. Proliferation was destructive to negotiations in Liberia and Darfur (Zartman 2005; Mutwol 2009; Brooks 2008; Zartman and Faure 2011).

Another aspect of the need to reorient conflict management diplomacy concerns the role of the intervening military (Hoffman 2009). The world's armed forces are undergoing serious reconceptualization as the conflicts they deal with shift from interstate to intrastate. Conventional military tasks and tactics are totally out of place in handling rebellions. The intervening military is a third force, unable to rely on the official armed forces or on the rebels, and cast in a role that is not simply one of supporting the state's self-defence. The military is often a peacemaker and institution rebuilder in its own right, while at the same time a police force to restore local security. This challenge is predominant in many current intrastate conflicts, from the Trans-Sahel Initiative to the military missions in Darfur and eastern Chad to the large theatres of operation in Iraq, Afghanistan and Pakistan.

*Entry* is a particular challenge for internal conflict management (Maundi *et al.* 2006). The state generally resists mediation, since it is interference in internal affairs and implies that the state cannot handle its own problems. Mediation is generally a boost to the weaker, internal party, and it raises the question of recognition and position as equals in the negotiations, the prime goal of the rebels, who seek state recognition as valid spokesman for the cause or the people it claims to represent.

A particular challenge to diplomatic entry is the practice of 'diplomacy as usual' that is dominant in most situations of internal conflict. As noted, the conduct of normal diplomacy is based on the premise that the ambassador's job is to cultivate good relations between his/her country and the host country. This lends the ambassador to adopt the state's position on the rebellion and to turn a blind eye to the fact that, whatever their merits, rebellions are generally an indicator of a problem. In large and underdeveloped countries, embassies are concentrated in the capital, away from the scene of the conflict and away from intelligence and understanding of the conditions of the area. This problem troubled US policy in the second half of the 1990s as the government of president Sese Seko Mobutu collapsed, and it continued to limit a positive US role in the subsequent phases of the War of the Zairian Succession.

*Outcomes* in internal conflict are also of a different nature than in interstate wars. The restoration of peace between two sovereign states, with resolving attention to issues (such as boundary disputes) that started the conflict, and the return to the states' daily business is a far cry from internal settlements that tend to involve the creation of a new political system and the readjustment of social groups' roles and practices. DDRR(R) require new facilities through which to retrain the demobilized forces, a new combined military force within which to reintegrate the former enemies, and a functioning economy within which to reinsert the unemployed soldiers. The economy needs rebuilding, which often involves social restructuring, ethnic integration, infrastructural reconstruction and new investments. The polity has to be restructured to involve former excluded forces and new institutions must be installed and begun to run. Some of this may be part of an interstate peace settlement too, to be sure, but in no way in the depth and complexity that internal peace settlements require.

As current research on the durability of peace agreements (Fortna 2004; Walter 2002; Gartner and Melin 2009; Collier *et al.* 2003) shows, there is a high tendency for conflict areas to return to conflict (the Conflict Trap) and that durability is associated with international monitoring and attention, as well as attention through peace dividends to initial and conflict-driven grievances. The challenge for conflict diplomacy is to maintain attention and engagement in the conflict area long after the peace agreement is signed, a demanding requirement in the face of donor fatigue and distraction by other new or renewed conflicts. The international community is simply not tuned to the need for long-term support for peacebuilding efforts. The story of Haiti is instructive, where it took a full collapse of the peace process of the mid-1990s to finally get a long-term international commitment for sustained attention in the 2000s, then again challenged by the 2009 earthquake. Similar problems of the lack of sustained commitment have weakened peace diplomacy in Palestine, Congo, Lebanon and Northern Ireland, among others.

Nonetheless, conflict management diplomacy has produced a few notable successes that have overcome these challenges to negotiation, entry and outcomes. Mozambique and South Africa, both in the early 1990s, are important instances of internal conflict management and even resolution diplomacy. Negotiations for Namibian independence in the late 1970s and throughout the 1980s ended in a solid resolution in 1988 but were essentially interstate. Other cases can be cited for progress, although their lingering recurrence calls into doubt their ultimate success; such are the negotiation of Sudan's Comprehensive Peace Agreement, concluded in 2005, whose application in the 2010 elections was pro forma and the 2011 referendum led to renewed violence; the 1987 Taif agreement on Lebanon that certainly ended the violence with conflict management but left the conflict far from resolution; the Angolan negotiations of the 1990s that never managed the conflict until Jonas Savimbi was killed in 2002. Other such attenuated cases abound.

## Conclusion

This chapter has been designed to highlight developments in conflict management diplomacy, involving security, prevention, scope and arena. In all of these areas, the evolution concerns a shift in emphasis rather than a sharp innovation or reorientation. However, the final point in analysing these changes is that they can frequently complicate the practice of normal interstate diplomacy, making the achievement of good relations between states more difficult to attain. Human security arouses conflicting interpretations among allies, prevention requires measures that make it difficult to mind one's own business, global outreach takes countries into area where they do not traditionally belong and intrastate conflicts bring out the maxim that mediating is meddling.

## Notes

1 The original mandate for the HCNM provided as follows (Conference for Security and Co-operation in Europe 1992: 9): 'The High Commissioner will provide "early warning" and, as appropriate, "early action" at the earliest possible stage in regard to tensions involving national minority issues which have not yet developed beyond an early warning stage, but, in the judgment of the High Commissioner, have the potential to develop into a conflict within the CSCE area, affecting peace, stability or relations between participating States, requiring the attention of and action by the Council or the CSO.'

## References

Aggestam, Karin and Jerneck, Magnus, eds. 2009 *Diplomacy in Theory and Practice*. Malmo: Liber.
Anstey, Mark, Meerts, Paul, and Zartman, I. William, eds. 2011 *The Slippery Slope to Genocide: Reducing Identity Conflicts and Preventing Genocide*. Oxford: Oxford University Press.
Ban, Ki-moon 2009 'Implementing the Responsibility to Protect'. Report of the Secretary-General, 12 January, A/63/677. United Nations.

Björkdahl, Anita 2000 'Developing a Toolbox for Conflict Prevention', *Preventing Violent Conflict – The Search for Political Will Strategies, and Effective Tools*. Stockholm: Swedish International Peace Research Institute, appendix I.

Brecher, Michael and Jonathan Wilkenfield (1997). *A Study of Crisis*. Ann Arbor, MI: University of Michigan Press.

Brooks, Sean 2008 'Enforcing a Turning Point and Imposing a Deal', *International Negotiation*, 13(3): 415–42.

Charillon, Frederic, ed. 2002 *Politique étrangère: Nouveaux regards*. Presses de Sciences Pô.

Collier, Paul *et al.* 2003 *Breaking the Conflict Trap*. World Bank. Washington, DC: World Bank.

Cohen, William and Albright, Madeleine, eds. 2008 *Preventing Genocide*. Washington, DC: United States Institute of Peace.

Conference for Security and Cooperation in Europe (1992) *The Challenges of Change* (CSCE Helsinki Document; available online at: www.osce.org/documents/mcs/1992/07/4048_en.pdf; accessed 10 May 2010).

Damrosch, Lori, ed. 1993 *Enforcing Restraint*. Council on Foreign Relations.

de Callieres, François 1716/2001. *On the Manner of Negotiating with Princes*. Boston, MA and New York, NY: Houghton Mifflin.

Deng, Francis *et al.* 1996 *Sovereignty as Responsibility*. Washington, DC: Brookings Institute.

Deng, Francis M. and Zartman, I. William 2002 *A Strategic Vision for Africa: The Kampala Movement*. Washington, DC: Brookings Institution.

Emerson, Rupert 1960 *From Empire to Nation*. Boston, MA: Beacon Press.

Evans, Gareth and Sahnoun, Mohamed, eds. 2001 *The Responsibility to Protect*. International Commission on Intervention and State Sovereignty.

Foreign Ministry, 1997 *Strategi för konfliktförebyggande og konflikthantering*, Stockholm: Foreign Ministry Ds 1997: 18.

—— 1999 *Preventing Violent Conflict – A Swedish Action Plan*, Stockholm: Foreign Ministry, Ds 1999: 24.

Fortna, Page 2004 *Peace Time*. Princeton, NJ: Princeton University Press.

Friedman, Thomas 2009 *The World is Flat*. London: Penguin.

Gartner, Scott and Melin, Molly 2009 'Assessing Outcomes: Conflict Management and the Durability of Peace', in Jacob Bercowvitch, Victor Kremenyuk and I. William Zartman, eds., *The SAGE Handbook on Conflict Resolution*. London: Sage.

Goldstein, Joshua 2010 'Chicken Dilemmas: Crossing the Road to Cooperation', in I. William Zartman and Saadia Touval, eds., *International Cooperation*. Cambridge: Cambridge University Press.

Gordon, David 1971 *Self-Determination and History in the Third World*. Princeton, NJ: Princeton University Press.

Hamburg, David 2008 *Preventing Genocide*. Boulder, CO: Paradigm.

Hill, Christopher, 2005 'The Beijing Accord and the Future of the Six Party Talks', briefing at USIP, 28 Sept.

Hoffman, Frank 2009 'Hybrid Threats: Reconceptualizing the Evolving Character of Modern Conflict', Strategic Forum, Institute for National Strategic Studies, National Defense University.

Holl (Lute), Jane, ed. 1997 *Preventing Conflict*. Carnegie Commission for Preventing Deadly Conflict, New York.

Hopmann, P. Terrence 2001 'Disintegrating States: Separating without Violence', in I. William Zartman, ed. *Preventive Negotiations*. Lanham, MD: Rowman & Littlefield.

Hopmann, P. Terrence and Zartman, I. William, eds. 2010 *Negotiating the Nagorno–Karabakh Conflict*. Special issue of *International Negotiation* 15(1).

HSRP 2008 *miniAtlas of Human Security*. Human Security Report Project, Human Security Research Group (World Bank, Simon Fraser University, School for International Studies) (available online at: www.miniatlasofhumansecurity.infor/en/access.html; accessed 14 October 2008).

Ikenberry, John 2001 *After Victory*. Princeton, NJ: Princeton University Press.

ISIS 1999 *Restructuring for Conflict Prevention and Management: EU Restructuring Conference Report and Comments*, Brussels: International Security and Information Service, Europe.

Jentleson, Bruce, ed. 2000 *Opportunities Missed, Opportunities Seized*. Lanham, MD: Rowman & Littlefield.

Lund, Michael 1996 *Preventing Violent Conflicts*. Washington, DC: US Institute of Peace Press.

Lyman, Princeton 2009 *Supporting South African Independence*. Washington, DC: Institute of Peace Press.

Minorities at Risk Project 2009 'Minorities at Risk Dataset'. College Park, MD: Center for International Development and Conflict Management (available online at: www.cidcm.umd.edu/mar; accessed 30 May 2011).

Maundi, Mohammed *et al.* 2006 *Getting In.* USIP

Meerts, Fedor and Coulaloglu, Tassos 2011 'Between Mediation and Negotiation: The High Commissioner on National Minorities', in Mark Anstey, Paul Meerts and I. William Zartman, eds. *The Slippery Slope to Genocide: Reducing Identity Conflicts and Preventing Genocide.* Oxford: Oxford University Press.

Mooradian, Moorad and Druckman, Daniel 1999 'Hurting Stalemate or Mediation?', *Journal of Peace Research*, 36(6): 709–27.

Morgenthau, Hans J. 1948 *Politics among Nations*. New York, NY: Knopf.

Mutwol, Julius 2009 *Peace Agreements and Civil, Wars in Africa*. Amherst, NY: Cambria.

Saferworld, 2000 *Preventing Violent Conflict: Opportunities for the Swedish and Belgian Presidencies*, London: Saferworld and International Alert.

Satow, Ernest 1917 *A Guide to Diplomatic Practice*. London and New York, NY: Longmans.

Shedahi, Kamal 1993 *Ethnic Self-Determination and the Break-up of States*. London: IISS.

Staravoitova, Galina 1997 *National Self-Determination*. Occasional Paper 27, Watson Institute for International Affairs, Brown University.

Snyder, Glenn and Diesing, Paul 1977 *Conflict among Nations*. Princeton, NJ: Princeton University Press.

Thompson, Scott and Zartman, I. William, 1975 'At the First OAU Session', in Yassin Elayouty, eds. *The OAU after Ten years*. Boulder, CO: Westview.

Uppsala Conflict Data Program (UCDP) 2010 'UCDP Database' Uppsala: Uppsala University (available online at: www.ucdp.uu.se/database; accessed 30 May 2011).

Wallensteen, Peter, ed. 1997 *International Intervention: New Norms in the post-Cold War Era?* Uppsala: Uppsala University Department of Peace and Conflict Research, report 45.

Walter, Barbara 2002 *Committing to Peace*. Princeton, NJ: Princeton University Press.

Zartman, I. William, ed. 1995 *Elusive Peace: Negotiating an End to Civil Wars*. Washington DC: Brookings Institution.

—— 1998 'An Apology Needs a Pledge', *New York Times*, 1 April.

—— ed. 2001 *Preventive Negotiations*. Lanham, MD: Rowman & Littlefield.

—— 2005 *Cowardly Lions: Missed Opportunities to Prevent Deadly Conflict and State Collapse.* Boulder, CO: Lynne Rienner.

—— 2010 *Preventing Identity Conflicts leading to Genocide and Mass Killings*. International Peace Institute.

Zartman, I. William and Faure, Guy Olivier, eds. 2005 *Escalation and Negotiation in International Conflicts*. Cambridge: Cambridge University Press.

Zartman, I. William and Faure, Guy Olivier, eds. 2011 *Engaging Extremists: Timing, Trade-Offs and Diplomacy*. Washington, DC: Institute of Peace Press.

Zartman, I. William and Katharina Vogeli 2000 'Prevention Gained and Prevention Lost: Collapse, Competition and Coup in Congo', in Bruce Jentleson, ed. *Opportunities Missed, Opportunities Seized*. Lanham, MD: Rowman & Littlefield.

# 5 Quiet diplomacy

## Preventing conflict through discreet engagement

*Craig Collins and John Packer*

## Introduction

'Diplomacy' describes the conduct of international relations through the interaction of official representatives of governments or groups. It encompasses a broad range of activities and approaches that vary according to actors and situations, but which aim generally to exchange information, negotiate agreements and maintain or improve (usually bilateral) relations. Something akin to diplomacy has been practised for as long as organized societies have been in contact with one another, and it is a fundamental and inescapable foreign policy tool of the modern state.

A recent development is the emergence of 'quiet diplomacy' as a form of diplomacy which may be employed as a tool for conflict resolution between or within states particularly concerning divided societies. It gained particular relevance as conflict in the post-Cold War period shifted in nature from predominantly inter- to intrastate, providing an approach for third-party actors to assist in addressing ostensibly intrastate tensions on the grounds of broader, i.e. *inter*state, security implications. The specific content and practice of quiet diplomacy, however, is neither clearly defined nor widely known. This is due in part to a lack of any comprehensive assessment of what types of engagement qualify, and how they are undertaken. A survey of the literature reveals no precise understanding or terminology on the subject, with multiple definitions often invoked simultaneously. At the same time, concepts are not clear in practice, and activities often overlap.

This chapter seeks to provide an overview and assessment of quiet diplomacy as a distinct approach which uses specific tools to address, resolve and prevent violent conflict and its recurrence. It also outlines briefly the development of one successful approach, its current contribution to conflict resolution, and future prospects.

## Overview and definitions

At the nexus of international affairs and violent conflict, quiet diplomacy generally describes confidential, non-coercive assistance of an impartial third party who seeks to create conditions in which disputing parties can address – and ultimately resolve – their differences before they lead to violence or recur (where there may already have been violence). Experience has shown that such assistance, when provided discreetly and at an early stage, can help avert crises by tempering confrontational approaches and building receptiveness to peaceful solutions that target both the root and proximate causes of tensions.

This chapter assesses quiet diplomacy in particular as the practice of preventive diplomacy through quiet means, notably through the use of 'persuasion', 'suasion',[1] 'influence', and other non-coercive techniques. Preventive diplomacy is taken to encompass approaches to the pacific settlement of disputes as identified in UN Charter Article 33[2] when applied *before* the outbreak or escalation of violence (Peck 1998, 132). Such activities are distinguished from coercion or the use of force, though non-coercive diplomacy may well take place in contexts where these factors are present and even welcomed by parties – notably in the form of preventive deployment to achieve the stabilization necessary for diplomacy and other political processes to proceed.[3]

Quiet diplomacy is a particular option for diplomacy which can be undertaken via various practices, but it has specific characteristics and generally employs specific techniques. It is defined herein as 'third-party' intergovernmental engagement distinct from the traditional diplomacy of an interested party or government. It is high-level, or Track I, interaction with official decision makers, though it may include Track II (with non-officials) or Track I ½ (blended) processes. In contrast to traditional diplomacy, third-party engagement is characterized by disinterest, independence, neutrality and impartiality. Disinterest describes a party acting with no interest other than a mandated and typically public one. Within its mandate, the third party may exercise a degree of independent decision-making power apart from a state or organization, though there can also be interested, and often dependent, third parties – including to the organizations they represent or even to the parties to the conflict (Collins and Packer 2005, 10–11). With regard to neutrality and impartiality, the former refers generally to the position of the third party regarding the *issues* in dispute (and the outcome) – i.e., to be neutral towards these – while the latter applies to her/his position relative to the parties.

In terms of techniques, quiet diplomacy is not public, and much less megaphone diplomacy; nor is it secret, but rather is defined by confidentiality and discretion (Collins and Packer 2005, 11). Whereas public diplomacy may play to domestic constituencies, and megaphone diplomacy seeks to call international attention (and, presumably, pressure) to address a given situation, the aim of quiet diplomacy is to create a safe space in which parties can evaluate positions and interests, weigh options and consider independent and impartial advice without the public scrutiny that risks their losing face or may encourage a hardening of their positions. Discretion therefore makes quiet diplomacy a distinctive approach – though, like others, one which may be more or less robust.

In this light, quiet diplomacy differs from normal diplomacy, which is based (as noted by Zartman in this volume, Chapter 4) on the interaction of ambassadors to promote good relations between home and host states and to prevent conflicts between them. Quiet diplomacy, on the other hand, is most often employed to prevent or resolve violent conflicts which may arise *within* states as a result of tensions between state authorities and one or more of the communities of which the state is comprised, or between communities (though the state is rarely neutral). These are the predominant conflicts of the post-Cold War period.

## Development and history

Less than a decade after the founding of the United Nations, its second Secretary-General, Dag Hammarskjöld, became a prominent early practitioner and proponent of quiet diplomacy, citing often the merit of what he also referred to as private diplomacy. In the shadow of then-recent history, he repudiated the inter-war belief that public diplomacy could 'provide insurance of peace', noting instead that 'a ruthless group of rulers' had misused the mass media 'to build strong public support for [their] wildest aspirations ... and thus to place an additional weapon in the hands of those who wanted to lead the world in the direction of war' (Hammarskjöld 1958). Public fora presented 'the temptation to play to the gallery' and created the risk that 'positions once taken publicly become frozen, making a compromise more difficult' (Falkman 2005, 131). Hammarskjöld felt strongly that 'the rules of the game, and the specific position of the Secretariat inside the system, force the Secretariat in its activities as representative of the Organization as a whole to apply what is now often called quiet diplomacy' (Falkman 2005, 132). Discretion enabled the Secretary-General to work with member countries to resolve highly sensitive, even *internal*, issues.

Hammarskjöld 'perfected a style of active but quiet diplomacy ... successful in a series of seemingly hopeless situations. He improvised a variety of original instruments', including 'various experiments in "good offices"' (Urquhart 1972, 596). His engagements in the Suez Crisis and Congo were early examples of a quiet diplomatic approach to engage parties discreetly to address threats to the peace, as was the work of his UN colleague Ralph Bunche with Israel and its neighbours, and in Congo, Cyprus and Kashmir. In subsequent years, UN envoys, special representatives, and the secretary-general himself sought to use the Good Offices function of the secretary-general to de-escalate tensions in, among other situations, the Cuban Missile Crisis, the withdrawal of Soviet forces from Afghanistan, and conflicts in Bougainville, Cambodia, El Salvador and Sierra Leone.[4]

Practice in the UN and elsewhere was, and indeed remains, largely ad hoc, reactive, and personality driven. Institutionalized mechanisms, with dedicated staff, clear mandates and commensurate resources, are largely absent in the international system. As such, it is more accurate to say that quiet diplomacy did not so much 'develop' as an approach as was 'used' in various situations from the 1950s to the 1990s. Lessons were identified (and in some cases even learned), but no one particular approach was elaborated or employed in a systematic way.

Regional, sub-regional and other intergovernmental organizations, as well as a small group of non-governmental actors, began to play a quiet role as new institutions, capacities and opportunities emerged. The EU, for example, has since 1996 appointed Special Representatives to twenty-three different countries, while the OSCE Chairman-in-Office has similarly appointed Personal Representatives with mandates relating to specific thematic issues or situations. These actors have been called upon to assist conflict resolution efforts through space provision and dialogue, as in the case of the EU Special Envoy for the Middle East Peace Process,[5] and the OSCE Personal Representative to the Nagorno–Karabakh conflict.[6] The Secretary-General of the League of Arab States, special envoys of the Commonwealth Secretary-General, and former Presidents Jimmy Carter of the United States and Martti Ahtisaari of Finland have engaged respectively at official level in intrastate conflict situations in Lebanon, Fiji, North Korea and Indonesia, among others.

A related development is the emergence of so-called 'eminent persons' groups to perform or assist with preventive diplomacy. The African Union has a Panel of the Wise, the ASEAN Regional Forum (ARF) has a Register of Expert and Eminent Persons, ECOWAS has a Council of the Wise, and the Pacific Islands Forum has appointed Eminent Persons Groups for occasional fact-finding missions. Unfortunately, aside from the fact-finding missions and the ad hoc involvement of eminent persons in some situations,[7] these

potentially useful instruments for preventive diplomacy remain to be fully oper-
ationalized. Eminent persons, panels and other representatives have in some cases not
been named, their mandates remain undefined or they simply have not been called upon
to act. The small number of individuals who could play a role often lack specific
knowledge, skills and support – in the form of human and financial resources – to do so,
while the organizations they represent tend to lack the experience and credibility that
might encourage parties to seek their assistance or accept a well-intentioned offer. The
lack of institutionalization – namely the development of pre-standing, properly resourced
mechanisms, and their operationalization – remains a principal obstacle to proactive and
effective engagement.

### The OSCE High Commissioner on National Minorities

In this context, the establishment in 1992 of the High Commissioner on National Minorities (HCNM) of the Organization for Security and Cooperation in Europe (OSCE)
represents a milestone in the development of the practice of quiet diplomacy. The
HCNM was the first, and remains the only, intergovernmental mechanism dedicated
specifically and *solely* to the prevention of violent conflict. With the first High Commissioner taking up his responsibilities in January 1993, the HCNM has since accumulated
nearly two decades of experience engaged actively in some eighteen states and providing
assistance in various forms to many others and to the OSCE in general. Beyond discretion, the HCNM has developed and implemented a specific approach to quiet diplomacy
which seeks to address both root and proximate causes of conflict before they escalate
into violence – or to avoid the recurrence of conflict in a post-conflict situation.

The heads of state or government of the participating states of the (then) Conference
for Security and Cooperation in Europe (CSCE) signed the Helsinki Final Act in 1975
with a number of key commitments on politico-military, economic and environmental,
and human rights issues. Following the 1990 Charter of Paris for a New Europe, the
OSCE was eventually established in 1994. Principal among the organization's preventive instruments is the HCNM, which was created as an instrument of independent and
impartial action to work 'at the earliest possible stage' to prevent inter-ethnic conflict
through quiet diplomacy. All OSCE participating states committed to cooperate with the
High Commissioner on the basis of common concern and interest.

The High Commissioner's role is future-oriented, consensus-based and cooperative,
such that specific actions are taken in consultation with the states concerned. Using quiet
diplomacy and offering advice and assistance, which may range from reforming legislation or negotiating bilateral treaties, to discussing questions of public policy concerning
language use and education, the HCNM is well placed to act before tensions escalate.
Importantly, the mandate of the HCNM (which is in fact granted to an individual of 'the
highest integrity') has been held over almost eighteen years by just three experienced
diplomats/politicians. In chronological order, they have been: former Netherlands Foreign
Minister Max van der Stoel (January 1993 through June 2001); former Swedish top diplomat Rolf Ekéus (July 2001 through June 2007); and former Norwegian Foreign Minister
Knut Vollebaek (July 2007 to the present). With such full-time and long service, the
HCNM benefits from the undivided attention of highly qualified individuals who are
viewed as credible and impartial international public servants. In their work, they
have been supported by a staff of now thirty political, legal and area specialists, project
officers and administration who provide the HCNM with research, analysis and advice,

planning, logistics and other essential counsel, technical and administrative assistance. Internationally recognized independent experts have also been invited to elaborate general recommendations endorsed or issued by the HCNM.

Of particular interest is the methodology developed by the HCNM, which is based on a problem-solving approach rather than a traditional hard-bargaining, power-based approach (Peck 2001, 564). Typically, the HCNM begins his work with on-site visits, meeting with representatives from all sides, including senior government officials (not least including presidents, prime ministers, and other relevant ministers); opposition parties; representatives of minority groups; civil society groups; and parties in neighbouring states (Peck 2001, 570). Through information-gathering and analysis, he attempts to gain an understanding of the core interests and positions of all parties, seeking at the same time to develop relationships with the major parties (not least, the leading personalities), in order to engage them in a cooperative problem-solving process. They use international and other norms already recognized by the parties as the basis of their recommendations, which seek to address directly the causes of tensions, or create effective institutions and mechanisms to this end. Reflections on whether and how the HCNM 'mediates' have been advanced, including the idea coined by Steven Ratner that the HCNM is a 'normative intermediary' who shapes solutions and clarifies positions held by parties on the basis of international law and other norms (Ratner 2000), and that the HCNM even contributes a form of 'soft jurisprudence' in analysing situations according to the applicable norms (Packer 2000).

## Other developments

In recent years, the UN and some regional, sub-regional and other intergovernmental organizations have sought to develop their institutional capacity and credibility, share experience, and assist parties to reduce tensions in specific situations.

Believing that a direct exchange with some analysis of experience would contribute to enhancing practice, a highly regarded practitioner (and the first HCNM), Max van der Stoel, brought together Secretaries-General and senior officials from fifteen intergovernmental organizations for a July 2005 'Consultation on Options and Techniques for Quiet Diplomacy' to share and discuss the what and how of their work in this area. It was the first – and to date the only – meeting to allow a full-day discussion at the level of Secretary-General about quiet diplomacy as a method of preventing violent conflict.[8]

Had such a meeting been convened only a few years before, the question of *whether* to offer third-party assistance to member states regarding domestic situations would have been an overriding concern. There was still in 2005 a general disinclination towards such involvement, and many considered it precluded from their mandates. It was therefore significant that many officials were willing to explore directly the question of *how* to engage. There was broad agreement that growing interdependence means instability in one state has regional implications, and that regional, sub-regional and other intergovernmental organizations are well placed to play a third-party role to address threats. Furthermore, UN Charter provisions encourage the engagement of regional organizations to address emerging conflicts according to the principles of subsidiarity and complementarity (see Chapters VI and VIII of the UN Charter).

Three promising developments emerged from the July 2005 Consultation. First, it was noted that although such activities may not be expressed in the mandate of the secretary-general or the organization, the need for responses to developing situations had usually put it on their agendas. Second, on paper, some organizations already possess bodies which could become pre-standing preventive mechanisms that might act as third-party facilitators or mediators.[9] Lastly, regional or other intergovernmental actors appear to agree on the value of stimulating processes that could result in formal invitations from member governments for third-party facilitation. It was suggested that an offer (from a willing secretary-general) of assistance might be well received if the assistance inspires confidence and provides practical recommendations without publicity – thus making it easier for parties to consider and accept them.

More recent developments have included: creation in the UN Department of Political Affairs of a Mediation Support Unit; establishment in the Organization of American States of a new Department for Crisis Prevention and Special Missions (now Sustainable Democracy and Special Missions); a meeting of former Commonwealth special envoys with Max van der Stoel to share, assess and consolidate their experience; and engagements by the League of Arab States in Somalia and the Organization of the Islamic Conference in Iraq (to name just some instances). A number of IGOs are increasingly receptive to engagement by donors and non-governmental actors to share experience and develop knowledge and skills, with intergovernmental officials participating in workshops, seminars and capacity-building initiatives, and Secretariats collaborating directly with other organizations (as in the case of the AU and a group of NGOs), the deployment by the UN Mediation Support Unit of experts to support the work of other intergovernmental organizations, and the Mediation Support Unit's participation in an international Mediation Support Network comprising mainly non-governmental mediation actors.

The general picture is one of increasing appreciation of the logic of prevention, the value of quiet, preventive diplomacy, and the need to develop capacity for effective practice. In his term as UN Under-Secretary-General for Political Affairs, Ibrahim Gambari spoke much of the need to make good offices *better* (Gambari 2006). New thinking and some resources have been dedicated to this effort, and with some impact in concrete situations. In a number of regions and situations, however, the demand for effective facilitation and mediation far outstrips supply, and even good *enough* offices would be notable progress.

## The current role of quiet diplomacy

The primary function of quiet diplomacy is to create conditions in which disputing parties can address and ultimately resolve their differences before they lead to violence, thus helping to avert crises by moderating confrontational approaches and building receptiveness to pacific solutions that target the root and proximate causes of tensions. Diplomatic tools available include structuring and facilitating dialogue, and creating political space for interested parties to address options (and, it is hoped, find solutions) regarding recurrent issues, from contested matters of identity and diversity management, to resource distribution and participation in political processes. The third-party actor can also rally 'friends', or what might be called 'fourth parties', who may not be centrally involved in the conflict but may hold interests and may help to create positive conditions and incentives.[10]

Within this basic function, the key contribution of quiet diplomacy is problem-solving, generating recommendations and persuading governments and other actors to consider the consequences of certain kinds of action or inaction. The task goes far beyond encouraging dialogue or articulating consequences. The problem-solver can facilitate contacts and processes between actors, and bring a cross-contextual expertise gained from other situations. S/he essentially helps to find or construct solutions, which can take the form of advice on policy and law in relation to, *inter alia*, political organization and participation, access to public goods, elections, decentralization, constitutional reform, citizenship policies, maintenance of identities, language use, education, cultural policy and financing, and bilateral relations including the conclusion and implementation of treaties (Collins *et al.* 2006, 11). In effect, this proactive approach describes a catalytic and mobilizing agent pursuing the public interest of dispute resolution and violence prevention. Discretion and confidentiality are essential to the success of such efforts, which run the risk of being perceived and/or portrayed as intrusive – i.e. unwanted – intervention in domestic affairs, rather than the collaborative assistance of a trusted partner.

Creating conditions consists largely of creating political space for dialogue and establishing and maintaining confidence. Both objectives are enhanced by developing relations at an early stage and building confidence, trust and local knowledge – including personal contacts – all of which may be drawn upon, especially if events should take a negative turn. This 'capital' complements and enhances problem-solving efforts by maximizing the impact of the abovementioned notions of persuasion, suasion and influence. Through early, long-term relation-building, the third-party actor is better able to identify and then draw attention to the enlightened self-interest of parties to a conflict, devising genuine and workable solutions to real problems, advancing argument, and using experience and prestige to influence (Collins and Packer 2005, 12). This requires credibility on the part of the third party, born of recognized status, experience and skill, for which commensurate resources are needed. It also requires the capacity to deliver expert assistance and otherwise be useful.

A broad range of techniques may be employed, from confidential bilateral exchanges, multiparty discussions or round-tables, technical consulting, and facilitating access to other sources of advice and/or the financial and material resources necessary for policy implementation. Finally, the function also involves an advisory role which reflects back to the international community the lessons learned from particular situations. Thus, the problem-solver is an advocate within their organizational framework who also can inform and suggest structural, procedural and normative developments (and provision of resources) which may further facilitate conflict prevention in the future (Collins *et al.* 2006, 9).

The principal options through which to apply these techniques are facilitation, mediation, good offices and special envoys, of which the latter two may differ from the others in form and function, but might involve, or evolve to include them or elements thereof. The options are neither exhaustive nor exact, and they overlap conceptually and in actual use.

## Facilitation

Facilitation describes third-party engagement which provides a forum, space and environment conducive to dispute settlement. Other facilities and services may be provided as appropriate, notably communications. Such provision may be minimal or substantial depending on the situation and (most importantly) the will of the parties.

Facilitated mediation describes a more substantive third-party engagement which actively seeks to solve the matters in dispute by bridging positions and advancing alternatives.

These engagements work best at the earliest possible stage, when the sources of conflict are identified and addressed before tensions or violence emerge. The facilitator may maintain her/his independence and impartiality by basing actions and recommendations on international norms recognized by the parties concerned.

Historically, facilitation appears most effectively accomplished quietly, as elaborated and exemplified by the OSCE HCNM. It is generally practised before conflict dynamics emerge, and until or after the early operational conflict phase. It requires the consent (usually pre-established by the mandate of the mechanism) and cooperation of the parties and/or state concerned.

Effective facilitation can address root and proximate causes of conflict by creating conditions for parties to initiate and maintain their own dialogue process, communicating and interpreting international norms, recommending politically feasible solutions in line with those norms, explaining the advantages of adherence, and mobilizing support for conformity and implementation. It is characterized by independence, cooperation, impartiality, confidentiality, trust and credibility. Quiet facilitation may include gathering and analysing information, use and development of inside contacts, persistence, tactical use of media, and megaphone diplomacy when quiet options are exhausted (Kemp 2001, xv).

## Mediation

Mediation, a voluntary and ad hoc tool, is 'related to but distinct from the parties' own negotiations, (and) can be a non-coercive, non-violent [and often non-binding] form of intervention of a third party to affect, change, resolve, modify or influence a conflict' (Bercovitch 1997, 130). In mediation, parties seek the assistance of, or accept an offer of help from, an outside actor to change their perceptions or behaviour without resorting to the use of force or the authority of law. It may involve the commitment of parties to respect the determinations and decisions of the mediator.

A mediator may act as a 'catalyst, educator, translator, resource-expander, bearer of bad news, agent of reality, and scapegoat' (Stulberg 1987, in Bercovitch 1997, 136). Her/his objectives are 'to change the physical environment of conflict management, to influence the perception of what is at stake, and to stimulate the parties' motivation to reach a peaceful outcome by using subtle pressure' (Bercovitch 1997, 139). Mediators may seek to problem-solve and improve relationships between the parties concerned.

Mediation can contribute to issue definition, determine process, methods and procedures, and identify and explain (but not exactly wield) carrots and sticks. It involves, *inter alia*, direct contact with parties, trust and confidence-building, arranging for interactions, identification of underlying issues and interests, transmission of messages between parties, and ensuring that the interests of all parties are discussed. The mediator may choose the meeting site, control the pace and physical environment of meetings, highlight common interests and help devise acceptable outcomes, suggesting (and taking responsibility for) compromises and helping parties save face (Touval and Zartman 1985, 137–8).

## Good offices

Perhaps the most prominent example of third-party engagement has been the 'good offices' function of the heads of intergovernmental organizations. Though enshrined in the charters or dispute resolution mechanisms of a number of organizations, the precise meaning and practice of the term are rarely elaborated. The ambiguity of the good offices function – in one definition described as 'action taken to bring about or initiate negotiations, but without active participation in the discussion of the substance of the dispute' (Darwin 1998) – has permitted considerable freedom of action for those who have chosen to provide it.

The provision of good offices figures most prominently at the outset of a conflict management effort, gaining entry at the good office provider's own initiative, with consent or by invitation of parties. It may include enquiries, fact-finding, determination of legal rights and specific duties, facilitation and mediation. Acting as an intermediary involves the transmission of messages between parties, encouragement of an exchange of information, explanation and interpretation of messages to a receiving party, and formulation of objectives for the process. Through good offices, the third party may propose procedures for continued exchanges and negotiations, and communicate with other actors (Skjelsbaek 1991, 111).

### Special envoys

Special envoys are (ideally) respected, experienced and impartial individuals, typically senior or retired diplomats or politicians, dispatched by the authority of a third party to help reduce tensions and resolve disputes preferably before they have escalated. Their engagement, often by invitation of governments involved in conflicts, is usually short-term, to collect information, promote dialogue, make recommendations on issues of concern, and suggest courses of action. As envoys generally have limited power to move parties to comply, their involvement is most effective before stakes in a conflict have risen. Actions of the envoy at an early stage are more likely conciliatory and non-threatening and may accordingly help maintain the permission – implicit or explicit – of sponsoring organizations and their member states to engage parties in other ways.

Functions of a special envoy range from fact-finder/observer to active engagement with parties in communications and negotiations. The envoy seeks to earn trust, provide advice, counsel and recommendations, and may act as an intermediary, negotiator, mediator, and/or conduit to other instruments or processes. S/he may also contribute process and goal definition, catalyse institution-building or other means of addressing sources of conflicts, provide early warning for the outside community, and express (where appropriate) grievances of parties before the international community.

## Strengths and weaknesses

In an increasingly interdependent world, effective conflict prevention requires cooperative and coordinated – indeed, orchestrated – action at an early stage. This is especially true in addressing complex inter-group tensions such as identity-based conflicts, which have predominated in recent years. Once violence breaks out, the chances for successful diplomacy are substantially reduced, leaving costly options and the uncertain outcomes of more coercive forms of intervention. Quiet diplomacy presents an attractive approach to engage parties to help address sensitive issues *before* tensions escalate. It is of particular relevance in the intrastate context, where concerns over violations of sovereignty (and/or the impression of meddling) are a significant obstacle to outside involvement, and where the state may be a party to the conflict. A quiet, assistance-oriented approach can make possible the early and long-term engagement necessary to develop solutions to seemingly intractable problems by reducing the risks for state authorities to accept assistance, and by developing the confidence in the proposed solutions of the parties that must live with the results.

Acting quietly can facilitate access to actors and information, establish and maintain confidences, and create space for ad hoc or sustained dialogue. Confidentiality contributes to building trust, which in turn enables contact over the long term to identify and address underlying issues through problem-solving, the provision of advice and expertise, and the mobilization of resources. The institutionally based problem-solver is more likely to remain engaged from initial contact to implementation of agreements, even providing technical assistance with specific measures. Quiet diplomacy is therefore a potentially more durable approach than the more common disengagement – often precipitous – of the international community after a peace agreement is signed. Through persistence and sustained involvement, it can reduce the risk of parties falling into the 'conflict trap'.

Although principally involving official decision-makers, quiet diplomacy allows the third party to go beyond peace agreements and, to an important extent, beyond the political theatre of high-profile talks. It encourages conciliation and accord by facilitating confidential communication between parties, bridging differences and allowing parties to re-evaluate positions and reach agreements without losing face. High-level interaction presents the possibility of affecting potentially significant systemic change, including institutional development, constitutional reform, and policy measures around highly sensitive issues underlying inter-group tensions. It was observed with regard to the work of the first OSCE HCNM that it 'isn't always easy for domestic political leaders, backed by ethnic majorities, to be seen to be listening to foreign advice on issues as sensitive as treatment of ethnic minorities' (Michael Ignatieff in Kemp 2001, xv). Quiet diplomacy is about reducing the costs for parties to listen to and accept such advice. It is also about devising durable solutions which impact the day-to-day lives of individuals and groups in divided societies.

Quiet diplomacy is generally not a power-based approach. Intergovernmental and non-governmental third parties have a limited range of carrots and sticks at their disposal, promising instead forum provision, facilitation and, hopefully, the expert knowledge to offer something of value including frameworks and prospects. Their success depends on persuasion, suasion and influence to more gently nudge or pull parties toward solutions based on self-interest. This can be seen as a limitation, but an agreement reached without sanctions or incentives may hold when outside pressure, support and interest fade, as they so often do. In the case of failure or backsliding, the quiet approach can give way to more public tactics, to call attention to a situation and/or seek the support of actors with other tools at their disposal. In either case, the absence of public scrutiny, albeit temporary, can keep stakes lower and permit the active ripening of the conflict for further positive steps.

Conflict prevention, preventive diplomacy, and by association quiet diplomacy, nevertheless face a number of obstacles to their effectiveness and impact. In spite of the relatively minor cost, low risk and evident benefits of proactively addressing the grievances which cause conflict, several important lacunae delay or prevent action, in particular the lack of political will, and the limited credibility and capacity of potential third-party actors. At the political level, leaders take a relatively short-term view of priorities, and benefit little from truly preventive activities which require long-term commitments and whose outcomes (and the attribution of credit for them) are not always clear.

Quiet diplomacy is more effective if mechanisms are already in place, in other words, already agreed and at hand. Early action otherwise requires negotiation of the situation/ issue to be addressed, *and* a parallel negotiation of the mechanism to address it. This is too complicated and time-consuming to allow a rapid response, and virtually precludes *proactive* initiatives. It also entails transaction costs which are hardly affordable and have distorting effects at a time of crisis. With regard to credibility and capacity, credibility derives largely from demonstrated experience, which in turn depends on knowledge, skills and resources. The current reality is that institutional capacity for conflict prevention remains weak throughout the international system, opportunities are often missed (Zartman 2005), offers of engagement are sometimes rejected, and experience and the credibility that comes with it are not developed.

Sovereignty and the principle of non-interference also remain important barriers to potentially useful outside engagement. In addition to the remarkably resilient West-phalian conception of sovereignty, even in the face of clear and irreversible erosion in various areas, experience and the predominant discourse has been about 'intervention' and 'interference'. Unfortunately, the intervention paradigm and terminology (used to unfortunate effect by practitioners) connote intrusion, which is, not surprisingly, unwanted and rejected. Any desirable assistance therefore technically requires an 'invitation'. Remarkably, however, many potential third parties (i.e. at intergovernmental level) only recently began to appreciate that they might *offer* their support, and take measures to secure an invitation, or at least the consent or acquiescence of the parties concerned. Of course, credibility and the ability to offer something of value are essential to an offer being accepted. Timely and targeted political support can bolster such offers and improve substantially the chances of success.

In many regions reconciliation of the practice of prevention with the principle of non-interference remains the primary challenge to developing institutionalized preventive capacities, with several charters of regional and other intergovernmental organizations (following the United Nations) prohibiting 'interference', and certainly precluding 'intervention', in the internal affairs of their member states. However, the established principle of non-interference should not be equated with a policy of non-cooperation or non-involvement.

When actors apply a cooperative approach, effectively assisting governments in responding to various challenges and emerging threats, this methodology is more likely to secure intergovernmental engagement and cooperation. Indeed, on the basis of state consent, sovereignty would be 'fully respected and in the end enhanced, especially in the case of weak and so-called fragile states whose capacities and effective control would be strengthened' (Collins *et al.* 2006, 12). Such engagement is arguably encouraged if not exactly prescribed and supported by the fundamental principles of the basic instruments of a number of intergovernmental organizations, most notably deriving from duties of cooperation and the good faith connected with them.

Institutional capacity also remains a significant part of the problem. Most existing international institutions were designed to manage interstate conflicts. Intrastate, inter-group conflicts continue to be difficult for such institutions to manage. While some secretaries-general have seen their roles enhanced in this regard, such as the OSCE which strengthened the mandate of the secretary-general in 2004, other secretaries-general enjoy significantly less leeway to pursue diplomatic actions independently of member states, which often oppose involvement in internal situations. Indeed, for some secretaries-general it was even controversial to attend the biennial UN High-Level

Meetings without consulting and receiving approval from the foreign ministers of their member states. In some instances it is the alternating chairmanship or presidency of the organization which has been given an enhanced role, such as in ASEAN and the ASEAN Regional Forum. However, the temporary periods of rotating presidencies do not promote the development of sustained conflict prevention strategies and processes over time.

There are few actors with an expressed mandate and appropriate human and financial resources to support their work. Few departments or offices exist for which quiet diplomacy or conflict prevention is a principal (much less their only) responsibility, and the few relevant officials who might play a role have, historically, limited knowledge and skills in dialogue and mediation processes or of the recurring issues in dispute (such as discrimination, political participation, resource management, etc.) and the proven or useful approaches to address them. Financial resources, even basic travel budgets to allow visits to sites and for meetings with governments and other parties, are also lacking. Mandates may be ambiguous or even constraining, placing the burden on the individual actor to think creatively and take risks to create space for meaningful action. Absent pre-standing institutional support (and institutional memory), the effectiveness and impact of quiet diplomacy can accordingly be highly dependent upon the individual practitioner, and especially her/his willingness and ability to proactively take and sustain initiative, identify or create and then capitalize on opportunities, secure commitments and mobilize support for the process and outcomes. This is a lot to ask, and often too much for uncertain or inexperienced actors facing daunting challenges with modest or divided political support.

In terms of the approach itself, the generally non-coercive, interest-based character of quiet diplomacy is less apt to work in 'hot' conflicts where the soft power of persuasion meets the hard power of military might (Sri Lanka serves as an example of this). The high-level nature of contacts, whether senior government officials or the representatives of communities, may leave out legitimate voices and have limited impact in the day-to-day lives of people living with violence. It also carries the risk that processes only address proximate causes, securing political agreements rather than implementation of specific measures which can contribute to transform destructive inter-group dynamics. Underlying causes which remain unaddressed are likely to re-emerge.

## The future of quiet diplomacy

A few significant trends in international politics, economics and security point to the increasing relevance of quiet diplomacy as a tool to resolve conflict in divided societies. Deepening interdependence, widespread and long-term economic uncertainty, and growing environmental strains each present compelling rationales – and opportunities – for promoting and pursuing discreet, proactive and non-coercive approaches to address tensions and prevent the eruption of socio-political violence.

Continuing, and indeed increasing interconnectedness, integration (not least of global capital markets) and interdependence make it easier for conflict to threaten security beyond national borders. This is less a question of degree or depth as it is one of the immediacy of effects, since technology in particular has enabled events in far-flung places to impact others in significant ways in real time, rendering geographic separation less meaningful and all of us less secure. Proximity nevertheless remains highly significant in the security realm, as internal conflicts spill across borders in the form of displaced populations and migration, market instability, organized crime and direct violence, provoking the concern and potential involvement of neighbouring states and kin-groups. Violent conflict has, in these and other areas, an inescapable regional, and often global, dimension.

Appreciation of these broad security threats, and recent experience of the limits of power (exemplar is the USA in Iraq), have been accompanied by a renewed interest in multilateralism, given that cross-border issues by definition require an international response, and by a more evident appreciation for diplomacy over hard power, to address causes rather than symptoms. The recent US National Security Strategy is indicative of and likely to feed the trend, influencing international discourse and policy and producing important knock-on effects in its implementation. Institutional development at inter-governmental level is another reflection of the trend, as member countries seek to use multilateral institutions, in particular regional, sub-regional and 'extra-regional' organizations,[11] to address security challenges. States and the institutions themselves also better understand the broad impact of violent conflict, and the need for and positive potential of proactive and cooperative approaches to addressing and preventing destructive and destabilizing situations.

As Nye observed almost fifteen years ago, the globalized economy 'has undermined states' sovereignty and independence, and so undermined the power and legitimacy of many governments' (Nye 1996, 72). This trend has continued, and in some areas accel-erated. Economic changes have also threatened, or created the perception of threat to many group identities and communities. Such groups are accordingly more 'susceptible to the parochial political appeals of political, national, and ethnic demagogues' (Nye 1996, 73). As the gradual erosion of sovereignty continues, states which lack a strong central government are at greater risk for communal conflict, as 'established mechanisms for mediating conflicts lose force in delegitimized states' (Nye 1996, 73). Ethnic identities are seen to offer alternative grounds of legitimacy.

The ongoing financial and economic crisis, in addition to provoking social displace-ment and tensions on a global scale, is drastically tightening budgetary resources at the national level and stimulating the search for more cost-effective approaches. With global military expenditures approaching USD 1.5 trillion, annual costs of military operations in Iraq and Afghanistan around USD 140 billion, UNDPKO's latest peacekeeping budget nearly USD 8.4 billion, and the annual costs of the ICTY and ICTR around USD 300 million (in their nineteenth and sixteenth years, respectively, of operation), donor countries should have ample motivation to explore other options. Indeed, the impact of these considerable sums, spent largely *in response to* already tremendously costly conflicts, is uncertain enough, or at least so costly, that some adjustment of prio-rities would be merited in any fiscal climate. By way of comparison, the relative cost of effective prevention can be seen in the latest budget of the OSCE HCNM. At less than USD 4.1 million, the difference between prevention and the cost of post-conflict recon-struction, rehabilitation, and the broader peace-building enterprise is stark, and takes on greater significance in these times of belt-tightening and budget-cutting. Money is scarce, but questions of national and international security remain as pressing as ever.

New pressures from environmental degradation and population growth, including population movement and competition for increasingly scarce resources (such as arable land, fresh water and energy), will also create conditions for potential new conflicts, requiring creative diplomatic solutions. Natural resources figure prominently in many contemporary conflicts, often in low-income countries in which resource depen-dence and the licit and illicit export of commodities creates or exacerbates a cycle of under-development and violence. Many resource-rich countries suffer the so-called 'resource curse', experiencing poor economic development, endemic corruption and civil strife. The combination of resource dependence and grievances of economically marginalized groups around, *inter alia*, unequal distribution of the benefits of resource extraction, are often at the root of inter-group tensions and violence. In the worst case, resource exploitation can fund violence directly, and violence and instability facilitate illegitimate access to these resources. Tensions over access to, and the use of, natural resources such as forests and water that are indispensable to sustainable livelihoods and development can also lead to conflict – especially in the face of increasing pressures from environmental damage or degradation.

Diplomacy and mediation have a crucial role to play. In one study of nearly 600 mediation attempts in some 240 different conflicts from 1945 to 1990, Bercovitch found that preventive mediation appears to be more effective at addressing certain issues than others, with resource-related disputes seeing the highest rate of success (Bercovitch 1996, 241–58). If past experience is a guide, quiet diplomacy may be a particularly effective tool.

At the same time, many existing conflicts remain unresolved and continue to have serious implications for international peace, security, stability and development. Experience presents a strong case for redoubled efforts to pursue the pacific resolution of these disputes, including through quiet diplomacy. The same applies to the challenges of state fragility where assistance with governance can have a determinative effect in moving societies away from chaos or collapse and towards stability and development. The 2007 IPI study *Global Political Violence* argues that the most important factor in the post-Cold War decline in the number and intensity of armed conflicts is 'the unprecedented upsurge of international activism designed to stop ongoing wars and prevent old ones restarting' (Mack 2007, 3, 5). This and other studies – and the experience of a number of actors in diverse situations – provide evidence that quiet diplomacy can contribute to further reduce the number of conflicts by preventing future situations from turning violent, and by enhancing prospects not only for sustainable negotiated agreements but for the long-term resolution or management of the underlying causes. The number of violent conflicts remains high. Their devastating impact and the cost of typically reactive international responses underscore the urgent need for more effective, less costly and truly preventive alternatives. Quiet diplomacy offers one proven option.

## Notes

1 The authors consider 'persuasion' to involve the use of argumentation or discourse, while 'suasion' is accomplished through reference to non-specific or general perspectives (e.g., moral or cultural norms).
2 Article 33 of the Charter of the United Nations stipulates:

   (1) The parties to any dispute, the continuance of which is likely to endanger the maintenance of international peace and security, shall, first of all, seek a solution by negotiation, enquiry, mediation, conciliation, arbitration, judicial settlement, resort to regional agencies or arrangements, or other peaceful means of their own choice.
   (2) The Security Council shall, when it deems necessary, call upon the parties to settle their dispute by such means.

3 This was the case for the UN Preventive Deployment in Macedonia from 1995 to 1999.

4 On the UN more specifically, see Kittikhoun and Weiss in this volume (Chapter 6).
5 Miguel Ángel Moratinos was appointed EU Special Envoy for the Middle East peace process in 1996. His mandate was to establish close contact with all parties, first and foremost Israelis and Palestinians, but also with states in the region – Syria, Lebanon, Jordan and Egypt – and to contribute towards peace. Moratinos' appointment sought to add a political dimension to the Union's economic weight in the Middle East. The current EU Special Representative in the Middle East is Marc Otte. Other EUSRs are working with various mandates in Afghanistan, Bosnia and Herzegovina, FYR Macedonia, the Great Lakes Region, Kosovo, Moldova, Southern Caucasus and Sudan.
6 The OSCE Chairman-in-Office appointed in August 1995 a Personal Representative on the Conflict Dealt with by the OSCE Minsk Conference. Ambassador Andrzej Kasprzyk of Poland was appointed in July 1996. The Personal Representative's mandate was, *inter alia*, to: 'assist the CiO in achieving an agreement on the cessation of the armed conflict in Nagorno–Karabakh' and 'facilitate a lasting comprehensive political settlement of the conflict in all its aspects'.
7 ECOWAS called upon members of its then-Council of Elders to assist in moderating election-related tensions in Ghana in 2008.
8 The consultation was co-chaired by John Packer. To frame the discussion, the authors prepared and circulated to invitees a draft discussion paper cataloguing options for and techniques of quiet diplomatic third-party engagement.
9 As noted previously, the ASEAN Register of Expert and Eminent Persons, the AU Panel of the Wise, and the ECOWAS Council of the Wise.
10 See John Packer, 'Reflections on Implementation Mechanisms of Selected Autonomy, Self-Rule and Similar Arrangements', in Boltjes (2007, 69–85); specifically for a short summary of the idea of 'fourth parties', see the non-attributed summary of discussions from a conference held at Sitges, Spain, in 2005, in Boltjes (2007, 1–47, at 7–8).
11 Organizations whose membership is not limited to a geographic region, such as the Commonwealth, the International Organization of the Francophonie and the Organization of the Islamic Conference.

## References

Bercovitch, Jacob 1996 'Understanding Mediation's Role in Preventive Diplomacy', *Negotiation Journal*, 12(3), July.
—— 1997 'Mediation in International Conflict: An Overview of Theory, a Review of Practice', in Zartman, I. W. and Rasmussen, J. L. (eds.), *Peacemaking in International Conflict*. Washington, DC: US Institute of Peace.
Boltjes, Miek (ed.) 2007 *Implementing Negotiated Agreements; The Real Challenge of Intrastate Peace*. The Hague: TMC Asser Press.
Collins, Craig 2010 'Consultation of SGs Seeks to Enhance Diplomatic Means of Preventing Violent Conflict', *Human Rights Tribune des droits humains*, 11(3) (available at: www.hri.ca/pdfs/HRT%20Volume%2011,%20No.3%20Autumn%202005.pdf; accessed 15 November).
Collins, Craig, Erik Friberg and John Packer 2006 *Overview of Regional Organizations*. The Hague: European Centre for Conflict Prevention.
Collins, Craig and John Packer 2005 *Options and Techniques for Quiet Diplomacy*. Stockholm: Folke Bernadotte Academy.
Darwin, H. G. 1998 'International Disputes', in Victor Umbricht, *Multilateral Mediation: Practical Experiences and Lessons*. Boston, MA: Martinus Nijhoff.
Hammarskjöld, Dag 1958 'The Element of Privacy in Peacemaking'. Speech delivered at Ohio University, 10 February 1958 (available at: www.un.org/depts/dhl/dag/docs/privacy.pdf; accessed 10 January 2010).
Falkman, Kaj 2005 'To Speak for the World: Speeches and Statements by Dag Hammarskjöld'. Stockholm: Atlantis. From speech by Dag Hammarskjöld at the University of California, Berkeley, 25 June 1955, 2005.

Gambari, Ibrahim A. 2006 'Making Good Offices Better: Enhancing UN Peacemaking Capabilities', speech delivered to the Center for Strategic and International Studies, Washington, DC, Statesmen's Forum, 27 February.

Glanz, James 2009 'The Economic Cost of War', *New York Times*, 28 February 2009 (available at: at www.nytimes.com/2009/03/01/weekinreview/01glanz.html; accessed 2 March 2010).

Kemp, Walter A., ed. 2001 *Quiet Diplomacy in Action: The OSCE High Commissioner on National Minorities*. The Hague: Kluwer Law International.

Mack, Andrew 2007 *Global Political Violence: Explaining the Post-Cold War Decline*. New York, NY: International Peace Academy.

Nye, Joseph Jr. 1996 'International Conflicts after the Cold War', in Managing Conflict in the Post-Cold War World: The Role of Intervention. Report of the Aspen Institute Conference, 2–6 August 1995. Aspen, CO: Aspen Institute.

Packer, John 2000 'Making International Law Matter in Preventing Ethnic Conflict: A Practitioner's Perspective', *New York University Journal of International Law and Politics*, 32(3) (spring): 715–24.

Peck, Connie 1998 *Sustainable Peace: the Role of the UN and Regional Organizations in Preventing Conflict*. Lanham, MD: Rowman & Littlefield.

—— 2001 'The Role of Regional Organizations', in Crocker, Chester A., Fen Osler Hampson and Pamela Aall (eds.), *Turbulent Peace: The Challenges of Managing International Conflict*. Washington, DC: US Institute of Peace Press.

Ratner, Steven 2000 'Does International Law Matter in Preventing Ethnic Conflict?', *New York University Journal of International Law and Politics*, 32(3) (spring): 591–698.

Skjelsbaek, Kjell 1991 'The UN Secretary-General and the Mediation of International Disputes', *Journal of Peace Research*, 28(1): 99–115.

Stulberg, Joseph 1987 'Taking Charge/Mediating Conflict', Lexington, KY: DC Heath, as quoted in Bercovitch, 'Mediation in International Conflict: An Overview of Theory, a Review of Practice', in Zartman, I. W. and Rasmussen, J. L. (eds.), *Peacemaking in International Conflict*, Washington, DC: US Institute of Peace, 1997.

Touval, Saadia and I. William Zartman 1985 *International Mediation in Theory and Practice*. Boulder, CO: Westview Press/Foreign Policy Institute, SAIS, Johns Hopkins University.

Urquhart, Brian 1972 *Hammarskjöld*. New York: W.W. Norton & Company.

Zartman, I. William 2005 *Cowardly Lions: Missed Opportunities to Prevent Deadly Conflict and State Collapse*. Boulder, CO: Lynne Reinner.

# 6 Imperfect but indispensable

## The United Nations and global conflict management

*Anoulak Kittikhoun and Thomas G. Weiss*[1]

The United Nations plays a distinctive role in conflict management in divided societies, which we critically examine in three ways. The first offers an overview in theory of relevant UN bodies and mechanisms; particular attention is devoted to the roles and powers of the Security Council, the General Assembly, and the Secretary-General and Secretariat. The second surveys these UN entities in the historical practice of conflict resolution from the Cold War to the post-Cold War and contemporary periods; it highlights the nature of the international system and problems in each period, and accordingly the evolution in UN thinking and practice. We end by arguing that the UN has been blessed with a number of strengths as a conflict management instrument but simultaneously plagued by some key structural flaws.

## UN conflict management in theory

As part of its overall responsibility for maintaining international peace and security – the fundamental reason behind the world organization's establishment – the UN's work in conflict management draws on two broad mechanisms conferred upon it in Article 1.1 of the UN Charter: peaceful settlement of disputes and collective security enforcement. In this section, we use the term 'conflict management' broadly to encompass prevention, management and resolution. For the UN in practice, they are linked and often pursued simultaneously.

### Peaceful settlement of disputes

The UN is not required to manage or resolve any conflicts – the Security Council may address them if they constitute threats to international peace and security. Indeed, Chapter VI of the Charter urges the conflicting parties to 'first of all, seek a solution by negotiation, enquiry, mediation, conciliation, arbitration, judicial settlement, resort to regional agencies or arrangements, or other peaceful means of their own choice' (Article 33.1) (see Mani 2007, 301–8). These methods and mechanisms have long been used in international diplomacy and law and are not UN inventions. The UN's particular task is to encourage disputing parties to resort to them. When they are unable or fail to do so, the UN then employs these mechanisms to assist belligerents to resolve their differences.

### Collective security enforcement

While a large chunk of its conflict management involves the use of peaceful mechanisms, the UN, unlike its predecessor the League of Nations or any other international organization, has the legal power to use coercion. The general reason is simple as spelled out in the opening sentences of the Charter's Preamble, namely 'to save succeeding generations from the scourge of war, which twice in our lifetime has brought untold sorrow to mankind'.

The central idea behind the theory of collective security is that peace can best be preserved or established when states join together automatically to prevent any of their members from using force against one another (Gordenker and Weiss 1993, 3–7; Claude 1956). Accordingly, states must be normatively committed in favour of the peaceful settlement of disputes and against the use of force except to punish aggression or use it after a Security Council decision – in short, to see the interest of the international community of states as one's national interest. This theory flies in the face of history as well as the theory of realism (Mearsheimer 1994/1995, 26–30); it has also proved equally inapplicable in civil as well as international wars.

Nevertheless, given the ugly realities of confrontation that returned almost before the ink dried from state signatures on the Charter, only a limited version of this vision for collective security was put into place with the creation of the main body for dealing with conflicts – the UN Security Council. We now survey the role and power of this institution, as well as the other two important UN organs – the General Assembly and the Secretariat.

### The Security Council

Designated as the principal organ to maintain international peace and security (Article 24.1), the Security Council is, on paper at least, the most powerful international organ ever devised to regulate high politics. Its recommendations and resolutions are binding and must be carried out by member states (Article 25). In most cases, the council would usually urge (Article 33.1) and 'call upon the parties to settle their dispute' (Article 33.2) by peaceful means, 'investigate' the facts (Article 34), 'recommend appropriate procedures or methods of adjustment' (Article 36.1), or have the dispute be referred to it for more direct consideration (Article 37.1).

The teeth of the council lie in Chapter VII, which enables it to define 'the existence of any threat to the peace, breach of the peace, or act of aggression' (Article 39) and to undertake any measures, including such non-forcible measures as economic sanctions and arms embargoes (Article 41) and the ultimate forcible sanctions of outside military force (Article 42). Although it is often assumed that military means should always be the last resort or applied fairly and proportionally, nothing in the Charter explicitly prescribes such criteria (Luck 2006, 22–7). While the notion of ratcheting up pressure is implied by the order of the articles, an argument could be made that deploying military force sooner rather than later could be more effective and humane.

Effectively, Chapter VII gives the Security Council the legal power to set precedents and create international law, punish norm and law breakers, and intervene in the domestic jurisdiction of any state – without consent. In this regard, Chapter VII enforcement is the only instance that member states can decide that paramount UN principles such as sovereignty (Article 2.1) and non-intervention (Article 2.7) are not sacrosanct. As the guardian of these principles, the council is the only authority that can authorize such violations.

To guard the *ideals* of peace and security, the Security Council subscribed to the *reality* of power politics by allocating five permanent seats (P-5) to the most powerful victorious states after the Second World War (United States, Soviet Union, China, United Kingdom and France) – giving each a 'veto' over decisions. These special rights and responsibilities meant the absence of pretensions of equality among members large and small (Luck 2006, 9–15). At the same time, mandatory council decisions have an additional credibility so that warring parties should think twice before opposing resolutions that are backed up by the great powers' combined might. At the same time, the procedures also preclude collective action against one of the P-5 as it would make matters worse and perhaps lead to a third world war.

Balance of sorts is created through electing ten members, with five new states assuming a two-year term each January 1st. While until 1965 there were only six elected members, the influx of newly independent states led to calls for Charter reform, which resulted in adding four additional elected members. Ever since, and especially in the 1990s, numerous calls have been made to change the composition and procedures of the Security Council (e.g. High-level Panel 2004, Ch. XIV). Yet every proposal causes as many problems as it solves, and UN constitutional change appears unlikely (Weiss 2005).

A conflict can be brought to the attention of the Security Council in three ways: by any member state, usually a permanent or elected member of the council or a party to a conflict; by the General Assembly; or by the Secretary-General. Before officially placing it on the agenda, council members convene informally and consider the practicality and legality of involvement (a procedural discussion not subjected to veto). Sometimes, the dispute is referred to a regional body (Chapter VIII) if it is more suited, or to the International Court of Justice (ICJ) if legal issues are involved. When there are broad agreements, the issue is tabled for full deliberation – including having relevant parties make their cases and members propose resolutions. Much of the work takes place out of the limelight – that is, in private sessions during which the council's president (rotating each month), the P-5, or the Secretary-General and his senior staff or representatives attempt to work out possibilities for compromise with the disputing parties.

### The General Assembly

Compared to the Security Council, the 192-member General Assembly is a relatively weak arena for conflict management and resolution. Although the Charter stipulates that the assembly may discuss 'questions relating to the maintenance of international peace and security', it must defer any action to the council 'either before or after discussion' (Article 11). General Assembly resolutions, which require two-thirds majority present and voting (Article 18), are non-binding. Hence, while the Security Council's resolutions are 'decisions', the General Assembly's resolutions are 'recommendations'. Furthermore, the assembly is only able to recommend 'measures for the peaceful adjustment' of disputes (Article 14), which do not include coercion. Finally, Article 12 forbids the assembly, unless the council 'so requests', from making any recommendation on an armed conflict while the smaller and more powerful body is considering it.

### The Secretary-General and Secretariat

The UN Secretary-General participates in formal meetings of the Security Council and General Assembly on international conflicts. In supporting the work of these bodies, the Secretary-General, through the Secretariat, is the principal UN organ that monitors political developments, collects and distributes information, provides analysis, serves as point of contact for member states and non-governmental actors, and implements decisions of the council and assembly. The Secretary-General's role is especially important when it comes to providing 'good offices' (to facilitate confidential communication between conflicting parties whose negotiations have broken down or do not exist), setting up an inquiry such as a fact-finding mission, appointing special representatives and peace envoys for conflict mediation and resolution, and overseeing political and peacekeeping missions for conflict management (see Ramcharan 2008, ch. 4). The political power of the Secretary-General lies in Article 99, which grants him the ability to 'bring to the attention of the Security Council any matter which in his opinion may threaten the maintenance of international peace and security'.

The invocation of Article 99 is rare – only three times in sixty-five years – because much of the Secretary-General's work revolves around what Dag Hammarskjöld called 'quiet diplomacy' (Ramcharan 2008). Unlike the public theatre of intergovernmental forums, including the Security Council and the General Assembly, where conflicting parties often come to vent their grievances, the Secretary-General usually works behind the scenes with these parties to reach political compromises that they can claim as their own. Not resorting to Article 99 is understandable because the Secretary-General requires the support of council members to move ahead. If they are unwilling to raise an issue, there is little sense in the UN's head doing so.

The crucial Secretariat units assisting the Secretary-General in conflict management and resolution are the Department of Political Affairs (DPA), Department of Peacekeeping Operations (DPKO), Department of Field Support (DFS), Office for the Coordination of Humanitarian Affairs (OCHA) and Peacebuilding Support Office (PBSO).

DPA is responsible for political analysis, peacemaking and preventive diplomacy, including supporting UN peace envoys (e.g. Cyprus, Myanmar, Lebanon) and political missions (e.g. Somalia, Nepal, Iraq), as well as more comprehensive peacebuilding support missions (e.g. Central Asia, Central African Republic) and serving as a focal point for UN electoral assistance to member states. In a joint conflict prevention initiative with the UN Development Programme (UNDP), DPA has recently developed the capacity to deploy 'Peace and Development Advisers' (PDAs) to countries of potential conflict where the UN does not have political or peacekeeping missions (e.g. Guyana, Ecuador, Fiji). Reporting jointly to DPA and UNDP, their jobs are 'to provide political advice to [UN] Country Teams working in politically sensitive contexts and develop and guide specific initiatives aimed at defusing tensions and promoting dialogue' (UNDPA 2009, 17).

Another recent and relevant initiative is the creation of a DPA Mediation Support Unit to provide technical advices and best practices for UN and other regional organizations' mediators, which is supported by a small Standby Team of conflict resolution experts in ceasefires, power-sharing or constitutional arrangements who can be deployed on short notice. This Norwegian-funded squad, likened to a UN 'SWAT team for conflict mediation' (UNDPA 2008, 6) has already been deployed to offer expert advice in Kenya, Somalia, Darfur, Nepal, Iraq and the Solomon Islands.

When ceasefires or temporary agreements are in place but the conflict has not been resolved, the UN's time-tested tool is peacekeeping. Lightly armed UN soldiers (e.g., in Sudan, Darfur, Cyprus, Lebanon or Congo) are supervised by DPKO and supported by DFS (which also provides administrative support to DPA-managed political missions). In some cases, such as Cyprus or Lebanon, DPA supports the political envoys and missions working towards conflict resolution while DPKO overseas the peacekeeping operations that manage conflicts. In others, such as Sudan or Timor-Leste, DPA-run political missions give way to DPKO-managed peacekeeping ones. In yet other instances, such as Sierra Leone, peacekeeping operations end and special political missions begin for peacebuilding. For Afghanistan, an extraordinary arrangement has been set up so that this 'political mission' is run by DPKO.

When humanitarian needs are a predominant factor behind UN decisions (virtually all since the end of the Cold War), OCHA is also a partner in extended in UN system efforts to manage and resolve the conflict (Hoffman and Weiss 2006). Finally, a new office established in 2005, PBSO supports the Peacebuilding Commission – an advisory body of both the Security Council and General Assembly – in the longer-term recovery and reconstruction of post conflict societies.

## UN conflict management in practice

While in many ways the division of the UN's history into the periods before and after the fall of the Berlin Wall is simplistic, it captures a fundamental reality for the discussion of international conflict management (Weiss *et al.* 2010, chs. 1–4). The end of the East–West divide made more ambitious UN efforts a reality, which becomes clear in the following discussion.

UN work reflects the interplay among structural realist, liberal institutionalist and constructivist expectations about the role, power and ability of an international organization. The United Nations should be viewed not as unitary but as three linked components that interact: the 'First UN' as the arena for member state decision-making, especially the Security Council and General Assembly; the 'Second UN' of secretariat heads and staff members (Claude 1956, 1996); and the 'Third UN' of those non-governmental organizations (NGOs), experts, commissions and academics who are independent of the UN proper but deeply involved in its activities (Weiss *et al.* 2009). This broader embrace is not only an accurate reflection of reality but also crucial to understanding distinctive UN contributions to conflict management theory and practice such as peacekeeping, preventive diplomacy and the responsibility to protect.

### *The Cold War period*

In this section, we highlight UN attempts to resolve key conflicts in the post-1945 period – focusing on notable achievements and ideational innovations as well as operational failures and missed opportunities.

### *The Security Council and the reality of collective security*

First, the liberal institutionalist instinct for cooperation that created the United Nations extended into a concrete attempt to help resolve the conflict between Arab countries and Israel following the latter's 1948 declaration of independence. Invoking Chapter VII, the Security Council ordered a ceasefire and eventually created an observer mission under Chapter VI – the United Nations Truce Supervision Organization (UNTSO). The mission was unarmed but its utility to the belligerents in deterring truce violations is suggested by the fact that six and a half decades later, UNTSO is still operating. Successfully freezing aspects of the war is one thing, but a genuine peace between Israel and its Arab neighbours, and a resolution of the underlying reasons for the original outbreak of the armed conflict, is quite another.

During the 'hottest' phase of the Cold War, regarding conflicts in key divided nations – from Germany to China and Vietnam – the Security Council was unable to act because a P-5 member actually vetoed or would have vetoed proposed actions. The only time that collective security arguably was employed took place in divided Korea in 1950. But even here, it was only because the Union of Soviet Socialist Republics (USSR) was temporarily boycotting the Security Council to protest Taiwan's occupation of the 'China' seat. This international pouting allowed the United States and its allies to pass a resolution under Chapter VII authorizing military actions – the first and only time during the period – to 'defend' the pro-Western South Korea from Soviet and Chinese allied North Korea.

### *The General Assembly and the Uniting for Peace Resolution*

While the Charter accorded primary conflict management responsibility to the Security Council, its paralysis because of superpower political confrontation allowed the General Assembly to assume a role. In fact, the first occurrence followed the return of the USSR to the council when its veto forced the United States to take the Korean crisis to the assembly. At the time, the numbers in the General Assembly favoured Washington's position – most of Latin America stood behind the United States, and most of Africa and Asia remained under colonial domination. Hence, the assembly passed resolution 377, the 'Uniting for Peace Resolution', to endorse the continuation of US-led military actions in support of South Korea. While a truce went into effect in 1953, Korea today is still divided, and the conflict between its northern and southern parts remains unresolved with the additional complication of nuclear weapons.

Deadlocks in the Security Council, this time by British and French vetoes, also made way for the assembly to take action when Britain, France and Israel invaded Soviet-backed Egypt for nationalizing the Suez Canal in 1956. Fearing a possible East–West confrontation if the Soviets were to intervene (Lowe *et al.* 2008, 291), Washington invoked the Uniting for Peace Resolution to call for a ceasefire and a withdrawal of forces. The General Assembly then created the United Nations Emergency Force (UNEF I) to supervise troop disengagement and serve as a buffer between Israel and Egypt.

While Uniting for Peace remains on the books, pressure from the General Assembly increasingly has taken the form of uniformly supportive views from what came to be known as the 'Third World' (and more recently, the 'Global South') composed of the newly independent states of Africa, Asia, the Middle East and Latin America whose interest was institutionalized in the Non-Aligned Movement. These voices were important in compelling the Security Council to take actions in what were hitherto considered 'domestic affairs' in two divided societies dominated by racist policies – white-majority rule in Rhodesia and South Africa.

The Security Council passed a resolution under Chapter VII declaring the domestic situation in Rhodesia 'a threat to the peace' after it declared unilateral independence and, for the first time, ordered limited mandatory economic sanctions in 1965 that were to become 'comprehensive' by 1968 (see Stedman 1991). And after voluntary sanctions were imposed on South Africa from 1963, the council made them mandatory in 1977. While the precise effects of UN sanctions in ending apartheid are debatable, they revealed the costs of isolation (Klotz and Crawford 1999). These precedents foreshadowed subsequent council decisions that were far more intrusive; and overall, UN actions helped to move towards a resolution of the underlying conflicts, which took place with changes in domestic politics and the elections of 1981 and 1994 creating black-majority rule.

*The Secretary-General and the invention of peacekeeping*

While the first Secretary-General, Trygve Lie, failed to play a meaningful role in the Korean conflict once he enraged the USSR by siding with the West, it was a 'successful failure' that taught subsequent Secretariat heads to manoeuvre better on the margins of power politics. And it illustrated the importance of constructivist ideas and agency, most notably those behind the concept of peacekeeping, in subsequent efforts at conflict management even if collective security was impossible during much of the Cold War. In this regard, peacekeeping was not simply a 'fallback position', as realists maintain (Mearsheimer 1994/1995, 34) but also 'one of the great innovations of the international conflict resolution system' (Bercovitch and Jackson 2009, 69). As the independent UN Intellectual History Project has documented, peacekeeping ranks among the most significant accomplishments of the world body (see Jolly *et al.* 2009, ch. 10; Ramcharan 2008, ch. 7). The answer to Page Fortna's extensively researched book, *Does Peacekeeping Work?* (2008), is 'yes' – that is, the presence of peacekeepers do make a difference in terms of prolonging the peace after the conclusions of the nastiest civil wars. While success is not automatic and there have been spectacular failures as described below, Fortna shows that peacekeeping often works because it demonstrates and increases the benefits of peace; decreases uncertainty by monitoring compliance and disarmament; reduces the chances and increases the costs of a return to war; and prevents political abuse.

The intellectual forces behind UN peacekeeping and its principles were then Canadian foreign (and later Prime) Minister Lester Pearson and Secretary-General Dag Hammarskjöld – both of whom would win separate Nobel Peace Prizes. The idea was actually foreshadowed by Trygve Lie; while the distinguished diplomat and political scientist Ralph Bunche, another Nobel Peace laureate, was instrumental in setting up UNTSO – a model for subsequent UN peacekeeping. But it was Pearson during the 1956 Suez crisis who proposed in the General Assembly that the world organization, by and under the Secretary-General, deploy an 'international police force that would step in until a political settlement could be reached' (Harrelson 1989, 89). Because peacekeeping was to go further than Chapter VI but did not involve Chapter VII enforcement, Hammarskjöld poetically referred to its authorization as being somewhere in 'Chapter VI and a half' (Urquhart 1972, 1987).

As defined by former Under-Secretary-General Marrack Goulding, peacekeeping is 'United Nations field operations in which international personnel, civilian and/or military, are deployed with the consent of the parties and under United Nations command to help control and resolve actual or potential international conflicts or internal conflicts which have a clear international dimension' (Goulding 1991, 9; Goulding 2003). Traditionally, such UN activities involved observing the peace (monitoring ceasefires) and keeping the peace (acting as an interpositional buffer between belligerents in agreed disengagement zones).

UNEF I is widely recognized as the first peacekeeping mission and an early success. Another is the UN Disengagement Observer Force (UNDOF) in the Golan Heights. Since 1977, no major incident has occurred between Israel and Syria. The key ingredients and principles for successful traditional peacekeeping reflect this effort: consent and cooperation of the parties before and during operations, full support of the Security Council, willingness of states to contribute troops and resources, clear and precise mandate, and non-use of force except in self-defence and as a last resort to enforce the mandates (see Urquhart 1990, 198; Liu 1992; Diehl 2005).

However, an operational black eye for UN peacekeeping came when it tried to resolve a hodgepodge of conflicts in a divided Congo in the early 1960s. The divides were manifold: an anti-colonial struggle (versus Belgium), a secessionist conflict (by Katanga), a proxy war and a divided government (between the US-backed national president and the Soviet-supported prime minister). Invoking Article 99 for the first time, Hammarskjöld drew the Security Council's attention to the crisis. It subsequently authorized the Secretariat to create the UN Operation in the Congo (UNOC), which ultimately went beyond traditional peacekeeping and served an enforcement function against Katanga. Some troop contributors resisted UN command and withdrew their soldiers. Others, including France and the USSR, withheld payments; and the Uniting for Peace Resolution was used once again to continue the massive operation. Hammarskjöld's role was so significant during this period – and so negative for the Soviet-backed party to the conflict – that Moscow called for the Secretary-General's replacement with a troika of representatives from Western, socialist and newly independent countries. The Security Council rejected the proposal, and Hammarskjöld continued to mediate until his untimely death in a 1961 crash in the eastern Congo. Three years later, ONUC left a still unified country. But this 'accomplishment' came with perceptions of UN partiality and near political and financial bankruptcy. Some would dispute whether the underlying conflict was ever adequately addressed, for which the return of another huge UN Mission in the Congo (MONUC) in 1999 serves as proof and continues in 2011.

Another operational quandary was the UN Interim Force in Lebanon (UNIFIL) – authorized by the Security Council as a face-saving mechanism to allow Israel to withdraw troops in 1978 following its invasion in southern Lebanon. UNIFIL's early difficulties stemmed from problems like those in the Congo, namely an unclear mandate, uncooperative warring parties, absence of central authority and great-power disagreement (see Skogmo 1989; Erskine 1989). Despite these setbacks, UNIFIL's presence contributed to preventing more widespread fighting. Again, a lid was kept on the conflict's cauldron, and the mission has become part of the local infrastructure and politics. Like other operations – including UNTSO, UNDOF and the UN Peacekeeping Force in Cyprus (UNFICYP), created in 1964 to separate warring Greek and Turkish Cypriots – UNIFIL continues to operate today because genuine conflict resolution has not occurred.

This is hardly surprising. Traditional peacekeeping was not supposed to resolve conflicts but to buy time for negotiations and motivate the parties. However, the award of the 1988 Nobel Peace Prize recognizes that UN peacekeeping has 'under extremely difficult conditions, contributed to reducing tensions where an armistice has been negotiated but a peace treaty has yet to be established' (Nobel Committee 1988).

### The post-Cold War and contemporary periods: change and continuity

Constructivist ideas would prove not only useful in understanding the end of the Cold War (Wendt 1992, 421–2). After initiating 'new thinking' in the Soviet Union's governance, its General-Secretary Mikhail Gorbachev extended the idea to the management and resolution of international conflicts by reinvigorating multilateralism and peacekeeping in the late 1980s (Berridge 1991; Weiss and Kessler 1991). The idea was persuasive even to

Ronald Reagan, during whose tenure UN-bashing became a favourite American pastime and no new peacekeeping missions were launched. As a liberal institutionalist would expect, insignificant problems with 'relative gains' meant that cooperation became possible when tensions between great powers were not fierce (Keohane 1998, 88). And so, what was the impact on UN conflict management?

The UN Good Offices Mission in Afghanistan and Pakistan (UNGOMAP) was created in 1988 as a face-saving measure for the Soviet Union to withdraw from the 'bleeding wound' of Afghanistan. UNGOMAP reported the Soviet withdrawal after the fact; but its small size and lack of resources and weak mandate meant that the agreements on peace, disarmament and elections were a dead letter. The ensuing power vacuum was filled later by the Taliban. Nonetheless, this was one of the flashpoints in US–USSR relations in which the UN played a useful role as in three other flashpoints of Central America, Kampuchea (later Cambodia) and Namibia. After UN-sanctioned US-led forces overthrew the Taliban in 2001, the UN returned with an integrated political mission to help in the reconstruction as well as humanitarian relief and electoral assistance.

UN efforts in the late 1980s paved the way for a vast expansion of its operations with the definitive end of the Cold War (Weiss *et al.* 2010, chs. 3–4). A crucial factor was the importance of humanitarian justifications to motivate outside intervention in what had previously been largely off-limits, beginning in northern Iraq in 1991 and continuing in Somalia, Haiti and elsewhere (Hoffman and Weiss 2005). In general, much of the UN's post-Cold War work in conflict resolution lies beyond traditional 'Chapter VI.5' peacekeeping but falls short of Chapter VII enforcement. If anything, the legal basis for many of the new kinds of operations might be either very close to war-fighting or beyond both Chapters VI and VII and very close to state-building. Either way, they involve crafting solutions to 'identity' conflicts inside sovereign states rather than the traditional Cold War interstate disputes.

The first new group of UN security operations in the post-Cold War era – so-called 'second-generation' peacekeeping – involved extraordinary intrusions into a state's domestic jurisdiction with its grudging consent. Starting in Namibia, El Salvador, Mozambique, and expanding much more in scope in Cambodia and eventually in East Timor and Kosovo, these operations aimed to help previously divided societies move towards consolidation and legitimate governance after civil wars. The tasks included what Secretary-General Boutros Boutros-Ghali at the time described as 'disarming the previously warring parties and restoration of order, the custody and possible destruction of weapons, repatriating refugees, advisory and training support for security personnel, monitoring elections, advancing efforts to protect human rights, reforming or strengthening governmental institutions and promoting formal and informal processes of political participation' (Boutros-Ghali 1992, para. 21).

In Kosovo, for example, after the 'illegal but legitimate' (Independent Commission on Kosovo 2000, 6) North Atlantic Treaty Organization's (NATO) bombardment that began when UN mediation had failed to end Serbian atrocities, the Security Council authorized a massive international civil and security presence (UNMIK). For the first time, several international organizations were integrated under unified UN leadership: the UN (for administration), NATO (for security), UN High Commissioner for Refugees (for humanitarian efforts), the Organization for Security and Cooperation in Europe (for democratic institution-building) and the European Union (for reconstruction and some administrative functions since Kosovo's 2008 independence declaration). And while the jury is still out on this and other UN 'trusteeships' including Cambodia and East Timor (see Yannis 2004; Caplan 2005; Chesterman 2005), the likely alternative of no UN involvement would have resulted in considerably more violence and possibly genocides. Judging by the relative absence of recurrent large-scale conflicts, the UN's record in these kinds of operations is thus 'commendable' and 'ranging from mixed to transformative' (Doyle and Sambanis 2007, 327; Paris 2004; 2007, 412–16). Indeed, the *Human Security Report* (2005) credits UN involvement with having reduced total deaths from wars and total number of wars in the post-Cold War period. The 2006 establishment of the Peacebuilding Commission led to efforts in Sierra Leone, Burundi, Central African Republic and Guinea-Bissau; and lessons for future conflict management should result.

While the end of the Cold War has allowed the UN to play a more prominent and relatively successful role in post-civil war situations (Fortna 2008), it has also brought new challenges to conflict management in divided societies still embroiled in intrastate violence. Superpower behaviour and misbehaviour during the Cold War dictated UN action and inaction, but their rivalry also led to financial and military resources that propped up fragile states and regimes. The drying up of such resources (Reno 1997, 496), in addition to the impact of globalization and technology, led weak states and non-state actors, including criminal gangs, militias and terrorist networks, to invent new and more violent ways to survive in what has been labelled 'new wars' (Kaldor 1999).

The economies sustaining many ongoing civil wars reflect plunder, smuggling, drug trafficking and the sale of other illicit commodities. Those who benefit have an interest in continued violence rather than peace and can become 'spoilers' (Stedman *et al.* Cousens 2003). Belligerents fight for control over territory and access to resources in the midst of civilian populations who are often the targets of violence. Ethnic cleansing, mass rape, scorched earth campaigns, purposeful starvation and attacks on humanitarian aid workers are a standard bill-of-fare. These tactics are not 'new', but their coming together and intensity are more apparent than in the past (Hoffman and Weiss 2006).

Most UN involvement in these situations – as illustrated by the mid-late 1990s 'third generation' peacekeeping quandaries in Somalia, Rwanda or the Balkans – have been viewed as disastrous or at least disappointing. These 'war-fighting' operations, or 'peace enforcement' in UN parlance, are without the consent of the state to which they are deployed and have three aims: to impose order in a conflict without a comprehensive peace accord; to enforce no-fly zones or humanitarian corridors in an ongoing war; and to forcefully impose the terms of a peace agreement in which one or more of the parties defect (Doyle and Sambanis 2007, 332). After an initial bullishness (Boutros-Ghali 1992) following a string of initial successes in the late 1980s and early 1990s that 'created a kind of inebriation in New York and a feeling that the UN could not put a foot wrong' (Goudling 1999, 162), Boutros-Ghali's *Supplement to An Agenda for Peace* (1995) and the subsequent comprehensive review panel on peace operations chaired by Lakhdar Brahimi (2000) suggested that the UN avoid such operations.

In ethnically divided Rwanda on the eve of the 1994 genocide, for example, the UN actually pulled back its miniscule traditional peacekeeping mission (UNAMIR) – replicating earlier mistakes in Somalia and Bosnia. The UN had been successful in helping the parties achieve a peace agreement in 1993 to 1994 but could do little when it was not fully implemented. When genocide occurred, the Security Council – still smarting from the perceived failure in Somalia in 1993 – debated intervention instead of acting. Ironically, Rwanda was a non-permanent member in 1994, but no one asked for any explanation or responsibility for the genocide. After 800,000 deaths, 2 million internally displaced and 2 million refugees, the council authorized two military operations.

While these helped stabilize parts of the country and provide humanitarian relief, they had the effect of protecting many of the mass murderers. Kofi Annan, who then headed the DPKO that 'buried' the warnings from UNAMIR about mass killing plans, would later acknowledge the world organization's systemic failure to prevent the genocide (Annan 1999b; see also Dallaire 2004; Barnett 2002). The UN presently has no mission in Rwanda, but has been active in the surrounding divided countries with MONUC and a DPKO-administered political mission in Burundi (BINUB).

In short, the post-Cold War period has witnessed a dramatic increase, for good or ill, in the UN's profile in managing and resolving conflicts around the world. While the General Assembly has been sidelined, the Security Council reassumed its primary responsibility in peace and security; and the Secretariat under two active Secretaries-General – Boutros Boutros-Ghali (1992–6) and Kofi Annan (1997–2006) – innovated. Boutros-Ghali's 1992 *An Agenda for Peace* put forward four categories of UN conflict resolution activities – peacemaking, peacekeeping, peace enforcement, and post-conflict reconstruction or peacebuilding – which 'still defines the conceptual framework through which … the UN thinks about its work in the political field' (Myint-U and Scott 2007, 94). Boutros-Ghali was also responsible for two UN firsts: an enforcement mission under its command (Somalia) and a preventive deployment mission (Macedonia).

Kofi Annan played a leading role in calling for military intervention for human protection purposes and in overseeing the UN's vast expansion in operations and its quasi-state role in post-conflict societies. He and the world organization won the 2002 Nobel Peace Prize for these efforts. Current Secretary-General Ban Ki-moon draws considerable criticism for being low-key and bereft of big ideas. However, in his administration UN operations have broken new records for expenditures and troops as well as fielded the largest-ever operation in Darfur, pushed Myanmar to allow post-cyclone humanitarian relief, continued to emphasize zero-tolerance for sexual abuse by UN peacekeepers (a policy initiated by his predecessor), mediated between Russia and the West on Kosovo (Wedgewood 2009; Crossette 2009), and strengthened the Secretariat for conflict prevention and preventive diplomacy (UNDPA 2007/2008).

## Structural strengths and weaknesses

The United Nations is neither the oldest international organization – many began in the nineteenth century (Murphy 1994) – nor the one with the most financial resources. But in the field of international conflict management and resolution, some of its operational strengths and weaknesses have already been singled out. Here we stress structural ones.

### *Unique legitimacy and moral authority*

One of the main strengths of UN conflict management is its unparalleled 'dispute resolution machinery and processes, a venue for communication and coordination, opportunities for quiet diplomacy, and a normative framework' (Bercovitch and Jackson 2009, 69). Most importantly, its universal membership provides unrivalled legitimacy. As former Under-Secretary-General Shashi Tharoor points out, 'the UN embodies world opinion, or at least the opinion of the world's legally constituted states. When the UN Security Council passes a resolution, it is seen as speaking for … humanity as a whole, and in so doing it confers a legitimacy that is respected by the world's governments, and usually by their publics' (2003, 68–9). To address the most intractable of conflicts, the

UN's seal of approval through a Security Council decision is extremely useful for the mobilization of financial resources, political will and moral support – both for a UN operation itself as well as for regional organizations and coalitions of the willing deployed under subcontracts.

Even though the structural composition of the council is a perennial concern, it is 'no more relevant' to the legitimacy of UN actions than any structurally flawed 'national parliament that passes a law' (Tharoor 2003, 69). And lest we forget, while the P-5 can block action, no resolution can pass without the concurrence of at least four non-permanent members (to make up nine affirmative votes if all P-5 agree). This reality constitutes a 'sixth veto' that lends more legitimacy and representativeness to the Security Council than is commonly realized. Other major powers might well deserve P-5 privileges, but the real problem has not been the size, composition or veto. It is disagreement among those with privileges. Reforming the Council would not automatically translate into more agreements to resolve conflicts – indeed, it might result in fewer.

Universal legitimacy is vital when it comes to international mediation and peace-making, especially under the auspices of the secretary-general. He (not yet she) is generally seen as embodying impartiality, neutrality and moral authority – much more than other mediators, especially from major powers whose carrots and sticks are far more substantial but whose disinterestedness and legitimacy are doubtful. Working with the secretary-general, his representatives, or through other UN channels could make recalcitrant parties stop fighting and negotiate – allowing them to be seen as cooperating with world opinion rather than appearing weak or losing face.

Legitimacy, moral authority and experience in state-building constitute UN comparative advantages that the United States and the United Kingdom, for instance, are discovering (Dobbins *et al.* 2005). After going to war in Iraq in 2003 without Security Council approval, it was necessary to return to the UN and ask for help in the post-war rebuilding and conflict resolution. In 2004, the UN dispatched Lakhdar Brahimi, who as the Secretary-General's Special Representative, conducted negotiations that led to 'a deep revision' in the American plan for post-war governance (Gordenker 2005, 39, 52). Under extremely difficult conditions, the UN's political mission in Iraq (UNAMI) has since contributed to: organizing 'elections and the drafting of a new constitution in 2005; monitoring and reporting on human rights; aiding refugees and the internally displaced ... assisting with economic development and reconstruction', and recently, brokering 'political dialogue and reconciliation among Iraqi political groups and communities' (UNDPA 2009, 7).

Thus, even an unreformed Security Council is recognized as the body to impart collective legitimization – whether for mediation, enforcement or post-conflict reconstruction. While such regional organizations as NATO, ad hoc coalitions of the willing, or fantasies about 'a league of democracies' may attract more resources and firepower for a particular conflict, they simply do not possess the same legitimacy as the UN. The UN's legitimacy suggests a division of labour – whether it is a UN leadership role (e.g., Kosovo), a joint peacekeeping role with a regional organization (e.g., Darfur), a supporting political role (e.g., Iraq and Afghanistan) or even a mere approval before (e.g., Somalia) or after the fact (e.g., Liberia) role.

While the independence of the Secretary-General or his representatives is obvious, it can make efforts at mediation problematic when a belligerent has more to lose than gain from mediation. Moreover, when a conflict fails to be resolved or even escalates in the midst of outside assistance, the UN is a readily available 'scapegoat' – which Kofi Annan commented was the meaning of 'SG' for too many states. But those with either unreasonable expectations or seeking a convenient source to blame when efforts go poorly should recall that 'those who need a whipping boy must be careful not to flog him to death' (Tharoor 2003, 76).

### International norms setter and promoter

Another unrivalled structural strength of the UN has been its ability to generate and promote international norms and ideas that shape how the world manages and resolves conflicts. As the UN Intellectual History Project argues in its capstone volume, *UN Ideas That Changed the World* (Jolly *et al.* 2009, ch. 10), many agreed international initiatives and frameworks would not have been as prominent or developed as rapidly without UN sustenance. These include replacing conflict with the rule of law, preventive diplomacy, peacekeeping and, more recently, the responsibility to protect (R2P), human security and international criminal pursuit. In line with the shifts in the *scope* of interests (from bilateral/regional to global) and the *arena* of conflicts (from interstate to intrastate) that William Zartman identifies in this volume (Chapter 4), the UN has been leading the efforts in making two other crucial shifts – a redefinition of *security* from state to people and a focus on *prevention* rather than reaction. It is worth exploring briefly the impact of the UN's conflict management efforts from this constructivist perspective.

First, replacing might by the rule of law has been thoroughly institutionalized since the birth of the UN – efforts that Hugo Grotius started but could only dream about in the seventeenth century. While brute economic and military power still dominate the underlying problems and solutions to most armed conflicts, the legal context in which countries go to war has changed to such an extent that they can no longer attack other states or their own peoples without challenge or attention from the international community of states. We do, however, acknowledge that for conflicts involving external succession and even internal self-determination, international law as a conflict management tool remains largely untested.

Second, as Bertrand Ramcharan (2008) chronicles, preventive diplomacy is one of the clearest and most innovative UN ideas – originating in the Secretariat through the work of Ralph Bunche in the 1950s and developing further by Hammarskjöld. While it is easier to point to what fails, instances of UN mediators' successes in preventive diplomacy are impressive: from U Thant (who helped prevent the Cuban Missile Crisis from escalating) and Javier Pérez de Cuéllar and Álvaro de Soto (who negotiated the end to El Salvador's long civil war) to Martti Ahtisaari (who received the 2008 Nobel Peace Prize for 'constructive contributions to the resolution of conflicts' with his UN mandates in Kosovo as well as other efforts in Central Asia, the Horn of Africa, Northern Ireland and Indonesia).

Third, while we have already mentioned the intellectual forces behind peacekeeping, the responsibility to protect and broader human security ideas dramatically illustrate another contribution, namely the shift in the dominant metric away from states toward individuals caught in the cross hairs of violence. Since its emergence as the subject and title of the 2001 report by the International Commission on Intervention and State Sovereignty (ICISS), R2P was endorsed by the 2005 World Summit and has since shaped international responses to egregious violations of human rights and mass atrocities (genocide, war crimes, ethnic cleansing and crimes against humanity). The central normative tenet of R2P is the redefinition of state sovereignty as contingent and not absolute (Thakur 2006, 244–63; Weiss 2007). Each state has a responsibility to protect its citizens from mass killings. If that state is unable or unwilling to exercise that responsibility, or is itself a perpetrator of atrocities, its sovereignty is abrogated while the responsibility to protect devolves to the international community of states, ideally acting through the Security Council. Hence, R2P's relevance to conflict management is that it sees sovereignty as including a state's responsibility and as protecting its populations as the foundation for enduring peace and reconciliation. Normative advance does not necessarily translate into robust action, as situations in Darfur and the Democratic Republic of Congo illustrate. The norm can also be abused – as was the case in Iraq, Georgia and Myanmar – although misrepresenting and then clarifying it can lead to its strengthening (Badescu and Weiss 2010). And despite the risks as indicated by Zartman in this volume (Chapter 4), that a policy option exists at all for the use of force with UN sanction for human, and not state, protection breaks significant new ground for international relations. Moreover, the fact that R2P contains the 'responsibility' to *prevent* and *rebuild* in addition to *react* adds significantly to UN conflict management (Weiss, 2007; Evans 2008; Bellamy 2009).

As for the idea of human security, which grew from UNDP's concept of 'human development', the UN initially had followed a narrower approach in concentrating on armed attacks against civilians, forced displacement, denial of humanitarian assistance, targeting of humanitarian and peacekeeping personnel, and the humanitarian impact of sanctions (Annan 1999a). Later, it became clear that conflict management not only requires reacting to immediate threats to individuals but the structural prevention of armed conflicts by addressing their socio-economic root causes. To Kofi Annan (2001), the UN thus must move from 'a culture of reaction' to 'prevention' (see also Hampson and Malone 2001). The debate between those who advocate a narrower concept of human security as 'organized threats' to individuals (MacFarlane *et al.* 2006) and those who see the linkages to broader development issues (High-level Panel 2004) should not conceal the significant advance in conceptualization within UN circles.

Related to the ideas of protecting peoples and conflict prevention is the creation of international criminal tribunals (e.g., for the former Yugoslavia and Rwanda) and mixed local and international ones (e.g., for Cambodia and Sierra Leone) designed to pursue and bring to justice perpetrators of severe conflict-related crimes (Goldstone and Smith 2008). These courts along with the establishment of the International Criminal Court are steps toward universal jurisdiction, a quest that began in the late 1940s as a result of the Nuremberg and Tokyo tribunals. Some suggest, however, that these tribunals may actually inhibit peacebuilding and national reconciliation, and that they may well prolong armed conflicts because they create disincentives for parties to reach agreements if they fear being brought to trial – the refusal of Sudan to cooperate with the ICC to prosecute those responsible for genocide in Darfur (in violation of a 2005 Security Council resolution) is an illustration. While it is premature to evaluate definitively the results of these international efforts at judicial pursuit, the hope is that they ultimately may deter violence by making belligerents and governments think twice before fighting in the first place or at least make them respect more often the laws of war (Wallensteen 2002, 11; Mani 2007, 312).

### Competing international norms and laws

Ironically, universality also leads to inclusiveness and the presence of competing values and norms – e.g. sovereignty versus human rights, peaceful versus coercive mechanisms.

There is no view that is not on the agenda. Worse, without a structure to facilitate the pursuit of common goals, there are always different interests, inconsistent values, and double standards. Although elevating the value of protecting peoples has entered international policy debate, the most formidable collective bastion of state sovereignty and national interests remains the United Nations. Unbridled sovereignty constitutes the single most important structural flaw in moving toward a future in which global challenges, including conflict management, require global solutions (Weiss 2009, ch. 1).

The UN is thus at a severe disadvantage in most contemporary conflicts that involve intrastate tensions – ethnic, religious, tribal, communal, socioeconomic, etc. – where sovereignty issues are pronounced. These conflicts are extremely challenging to manage let alone resolve in the face of weak and failing states as well as non-state parties that are 'amply supplied with arms, obsessively secretive, inexperienced in negotiation, lacking transparent lines of authority, undisciplined, unfamiliar with the norms of international behaviour' (Goulding 1999, 161). Almost all resist outside intervention.

As in the cases of the Balkans in the 1990s or the Sudan today, the inability of the Security Council to act effectively not only reflects the inability of the major powers to formulate consistent policies but also the ability of the conflicting parties to play them off against each other (e.g. Russia vs. the West in the former, China vs. the West in the latter). This is hardly surprising as the council is neither impartial nor above the vagaries of changing world politics. While the independence of the Second and Third UNs is important as argued above – whether coming up with new mechanisms or new ideas – Realists are correct that it pales in comparison with the politics of major states in the First UN. This reality too is double-edged: the willingness of dominant powers to use the UN does not translate into conflict resolution if disputants refuse; at the same time, the UN's role in conflict-management is compromised if there are perceptions of partiality or undue influence. As Peter Wallensteen notes, the UN in this case risks 'becoming just another actor in the conflict, applauded by some, abused by others' (2002, 250).

## The nature and structure of the UN

The major structural weakness in corralling the world organization's strengths is the lack of overarching central authority. The sum of 192 member states means that decisions too often reflect the lowest common denominator of national parts rather than any larger global interest. In spite of Article 99, the UN has no military of its own, not even a modest 'rapid reaction force'; it has no independent funds (the organization often begs, borrows and steals whatever personnel it requires, including soldiers); and it cannot refuse to act even when there is a vast discrepancy between the nature of an assigned task and the resources made available. The fact that the UN increasingly focuses on 'human security' also means that priorities are sometimes difficult to establish if there is nothing that is not on the agenda (MacFarlane *et al.* 2006).

Last but not least, a continuing problem with the current UN's conflict management structure is ineffective coordination and competition among its various moving parts – something the neat UN organigram does not convey. Writing from experience, Goulding remarked that in the UN system 'there are well-known jealousies and competition between its programmes, funds and agencies, each of which has its own intergovernmental policy-making body, its own mandate, its own sources of funding and its own chain of command' (1999, 166). UN staffer and part-time academic Jean-Marc

Coicaud goes further and points to 'the tensions between the diplomatic culture shaping UN headquarters and the demands of the field, the gap between the administrative capacities of the United Nations in New York and the needs on the ground, and the endemic communication difficulties with the United Nations itself' (2007, 35). The turf battles among DPA, DPKO, OCHA and their respective field missions – as well as tensions with other members of the dysfunctional and decentralized UN family along with international NGOs – are well documented (Weiss 2009, ch. 3). The silver lining is that at least some UN organizations will be present in most war zones.

## Conclusion

Like Mark Twain, who read his own obituary, periodic reports of the UN's demise are exaggerated. There certainly is room for improvement in both the First UN and the Second UN, but narrowly bounded state sovereignty undoubtedly will remain for the foreseeable future the largest constraint on international efforts to manage and resolve armed conflicts. The UN's distinctive contributions since 1945 – ideational as well as operational – bring to mind the timeless wisdom attributed to Dag Hammarskjöld, its great second Secretary-General: 'the United Nations was not created to take humanity to heaven, but to save it from hell'. In short, the UN remains, as Barack Obama (2008) reminded us, 'an indispensable – and imperfect – forum', a precious and useful if highly flawed instrument for international conflict management in divided societies.

## Notes

1 Anoulak Kittikhoun is a political affairs officer in the Asia and Pacific Division of the United Nations Department of Political Affairs and was Research Associate at the Ralph Bunche Institute for International Studies and Adjunct Lecturer in Political Science at Brooklyn College. Thomas G. Weiss is Presidential Professor of Political Science and Director of the Ralph Bunche Institute for International Studies at the Graduate Center, the City University of New York.

The views expressed in this chapter are personal and in no way represent the views of the authors' institutions. The authors thank the editors and participants in the International Studies Association workshop in February 2010 for valuable comments on an earlier draft.

## References

Annan, Kofi 1999a *Protection of Civilians in Armed Conflict*, Report of the Secretary-General, UN Security Council Document S/1999/957 (8 September 1999), New York: United Nations.
—— 1999b 'Statement on receiving the report of the Independent Inquiry into the Actions of the United Nations During the 1994 Genocide in Rwanda' (16 December 1999), New York: United Nations.
—— 2001 *Prevention of Armed Conflict*, Report of the Secretary-General, UN General Assembly Document A/55/985 and UN Security Council Document S/2001/574 (7 June 2001), New York: United Nations.
Badescu, Cristina G. and Thomas G. Weiss 2010 'Misrepresenting R2P and Advancing Norms: An Alternative Spiral?' *International Studies Perspectives* 11(4): forthcoming.
Barnett, Michael. 2002 *Eyewitness to a Genocide: The United Nations and Rwanda*, Ithaca, NY: Cornell University Press.
Bellamy, Alex J. 2009 *Responsibility to Protect: The Global Efforts to End Mass Atrocities*, Cambridge: Polity Press.

Bercovitch, Jacob and Jackson, Richard 2009 *Conflict Resolution in the Twenty-first Century: Principles, Methods, and Approaches*, Ann Arbor, MA: University of Michigan Press.

Berridge, G. R. 1991 *Return to the UN*, London: Macmillan.

Boutros-Ghali, Boutros 1992 *An Agenda for Peace: Preventive Diplomacy, Peacemaking and Peacekeeping*. Report of the Secretary-General, UN Document A/47/277-S/24111 (17 June 1992), New York: United Nations.

—— 1995 *A Supplement for An Agenda for Peace*. Report of the Secretary-General, UN Document A/50/60-S/1995/1 (3 January 1995), New York: United Nations.

Brahimi, Lakhdar 2000 *Report of the Panel on United Nations Peace Operations*. UN Document A/55/305 – S/2000/809, New York: United Nations.

Caplan, Richard 2005 *International Governance of War-Torn Territories: Rule and Reconstruction*, New York, NY: Oxford University Press.

Chesterman, Simon 2005 *You, the People: The United Nations, Transitional Administration, and State-Building*, New York, NY: Oxford University Press.

Claude, Inis 1956 *Swords Into Plowshares*, New York, NY: Random House.

—— 1996 'Peace and Security: Prospective Roles for the Two United Nations', *Global Governance* 2(3): 289–98.

Coicaud, Jean-Marc 2007 *Beyond the National Interest: The Future of UN Peacekeeping and Multilateralism in an Era of US Primacy*, Washington, DC: US Institute of Peace Press.

Crossette, Barbara 2009 'For Europeans, Ban Remains an Enigma', *UNA–USA World Bulletin*, 7 October 2009.

Dallaire, Roméo 2004 *Shake Hands with the Devil: The Failure of Humanity in Rwanda*, Toronto: Brent Beardsley.

Diehl, Paul 2005 'Forks in the Road: Theoretical and Policy Concerns for 21st Century Peace-keeping', in Paul Diehl (ed.), *The Politics of Global Governance: International Organizations in an Interdependent World*, Boulder, CO: Lynne Rienner.

Dobbins, James, Jones, Seth G., Crane, Keith, Rathmell, Andrew, Steele, Brett, Teltschik, Richard and Timilsina, Anga 2005 *The UN's Role in Nation-Building: From the Congo to Iraq*, Santa Monica, CA: RAND Corporation.

Doyle, Michael W. and Sambanis, Nicholas 2007 'Peacekeeping Operations', in Thomas G. Weiss and Saw Daws (eds.) *The Oxford Handbook on the United Nations*, Oxford: Oxford University Press.

Erskine, E. A. 1989 *Mission with UNIFIL*, London: Hurst.

Evans, Gareth 2008 *The Responsibility to Protect: Ending Mass Atrocity Crimes Once and for All*, Washington, DC: Brookings Institution Press.

Fortna, Virginia Page 2008 *Does Peacekeeping Work? Shaping Belligerents' Choices after Civil War*. Princeton, NJ: Princeton University Press.

Goldstone, Richard J. and Smith, Adam M. 2008 *International Judicial Institutions: The Architecture of International Justice at Home and Abroad*, London: Routledge.

Goulding, Marrack 1991 'The Changing Role of the United Nations in Conflict Resolution and Peace-keeping', Speech given at the Singapore Institute of Policy Studies, Singapore (13 March 1991).

—— 1999 'The United Nations and Conflict in Africa since the Cold War', *African Affairs*, 98 (391): 155–66.

—— 2003 *Peacemonger*. Baltimore, MD: Johns Hopkins University Press.

Gordenker, Leon 2005 *The UN Secretary-General and Secretariat*, New York, NY: Routledge.

Gordenker, Leon and Weiss, Thomas G. 1993 'The Collective Security Idea and Changing World Politics', in Thomas G. Weiss (ed.), *Collective Security in a Changing World*, Boulder, CO: Lynne Rienner.

Hampson, Fen Osler and Malone, David 2001 *From Reaction to Conflict Prevention: Opportunities for the UN System*, Boulder, CO: Lynne Rienner.

Harrelson, Max 1989 *Fires All Around the Horizon: The UN's Uphill Battle to Preserve the Peace*, New York, NY: Praeger.

High-level Panel on Threats, Challenges and Changes 2004 *A More Secure World: Our Shared Responsibility*, New York: United Nations.

Hoffman, Peter J. and Weiss, Thomas G. 2006 *Sword & Salve: Confronting New Wars and Humanitarian Crises*, Lanham, Maryland: Rowman & Littlefield.

*Human Security Report: War and Peace in the 21st Century* 2005 Human Security Centre, University of British Columbia, New York, NY: Oxford University Press.

Independent Commission on Kosovo 2000 *Kosovo Report: Conflict, International Response, Lessons Learned*. Oxford: Oxford University Press.

International Commission on Intervention and State Sovereignty 2001 *The Responsibility to Protect*, Ottawa: International Development Research Centre.

Jolly, Richard, Emmerij, Louis and Thomas G. Weiss 2009 *UN Ideas that Changed the World*, Bloomington, IN: Indiana University Press.

Kaldor, Mary 1999 *New and Old Wars: Organised Violence in a Global Era*, Cambridge UK: Polity Press.

Klotz, Audie and Crawford, Neta C. 1999 *How Sanctions Work: Lessons from South Africa*, New York, NY: Palgrave MacMillan.

Liu, F. T. 1992 *United Nations Peacekeeping and the Non-Use of Force*, Boulder, CO: Lynne Rienner.

Lowe, Vaughan, Roberts, Adam, Welsh, Jennifer and Zaum, Dominik 2008 *The United Nations Security Council and War: The Evolution of Thought and Practice Since 1945*, New York, NY: Oxford University Press.

Luck, Edward C. 2006 *The UN Security Council: Practice and Promise*, London: Routledge.

Keohane, Robert O. 1998 'International Institutions: Can Interdependence Work?' *Foreign Policy* 110: 82–96.

MacFarlane, S. Neil and Khong, Yuen Foong 2006 *Human Security and the UN: A Critical History*. Bloomington, IN: Indiana University Press.

Mani, Rama 2007 'Peaceful Settlement of Disputes and Conflict Prevention', in Thomas G. Weiss and Saw Daws (eds.) *The Oxford Handbook on the United Nations*, New York, NY: Oxford University Press.

Mearsheimer, John J. 1994/1995 'The False Promise of International Institutions', *International Security* 19(3): 5–49.

Murphy, Craig 1994 *International Organization and Industrial Change: Global Governance since 1850*. New York, NY: Oxford University Press.

Myint-U, Thant and Scott, Amy 2007 *The UN Secretariat: A Brief History*, Boulder, CO: Lynne Rienner.

Nobel Committee 1988 *Press Release on The Nobel Peace Prize 1988* (September 29, 1988) (available at: http://nobelprize.org/nobel_prizes/peace/laureates/1988/press.html).

Obama, Barack 2008 'Announcement of National Security Team'. 1 December (available online at: http://change.gov/newsroom/entry/the_national_security_team).

Paris, Roland 2004 *At War's End: Building Peace After Civil Conflict*, Cambridge: Cambridge University Press.

—— 2007 'Post-Conflict Peacebuilding', in Thomas G. Weiss and Saw Daws (eds.), *The Oxford Handbook on the United Nations*, Oxford: Oxford University Press.

Plesch, Dan 2008 'How the United Nations Beat Hitler and Prepared the Peace', *Global Society* 22(1): 137–58.

Ramcharan, Bertrand G. 2008 *Preventive Diplomacy at the UN*. Bloomington, IN: Indiana University Press.

Reno, William 1997 'War, Markets and the Reconfiguration of West Africa's Weak States', *Comparative Politics* 29(4): 493–510.

Skogmo, Bjorn 1989 *UNIFIL: International Peacekeeping Lebanon*, Boulder, CO: Lynne Rienner.

Stedman, Stephen John 1991 *Peacemaking in Civil War: International Mediation in Zimbabwe, 1974–1980*. Boulder, CO: Lynne Rienner.

Stedman, Stephen John, Rothchild, Donald and Cousens, Elizabeth M. (eds.) 2003 *Ending Civil Wars: The Implementation of Peace Agreements*, Boulder, CO: Lynne Rienner.

Tharoor, Shashi 2003 'Why America Still Needs the United Nations', *Foreign Affairs* 82(5): 67–80.

Thakur, Ramesh 2006 *The United Nations, Peace and Security: From Collective Security to the Responsibility to Protect*, New York, NY: Cambridge University Press.

UN Department of Political Affairs (UNDPA) 2007/2008 'Politically Speaking', *Bulletin of the United Nations Department of Political* Affairs, winter: 1–24.

—— 2008 'Politically Speaking', *Bulletin of the United Nations Department of Political Affairs*, summer–fall: 1–24.

—— 2009 'Politically Speaking', *Bulletin of the United Nations Department of Political Affairs*, spring: 1–24.

Urquhart, Brian 1972 *A Life in Peace and War*. New York, NY: Harper & Row.

—— 1987 *Hammarskjold*. New York, NY: Knopf.

—— 1990 'Beyond the Sheriff's Posse', *Survival* 32(3): 196–205.

Wallensteen, Peter 2002 *Understanding Conflict Resolution: War, Peace and the Global System*, London: Sage.

Wedgewood, Ruth 2009 'Competence and Charm', *Forbes Magazine*, 24 September 2009.

Weiss, Thomas G. 2005 *Overcoming the Security Council Reform Impasse: The Implausible versus the Plausible*, Berlin: Friedrich Ebert Stiftung, Occasional Paper 14.

—— 2007 *Humanitarian Intervention: Ideas in Action*. Cambridge: Polity Press.

—— 2009 *What's Wrong with the United Nations and How to Fix It*. Cambridge: Polity Press.

Weiss, Thomas G., Carayannis, Tatiana and Jolly, Richard 2009 'The 'Third' United Nations', *Global Governance* 15(1): 123–42.

Weiss, Thomas G. and Daws, Sam (eds.) 2007 *The Oxford Handbook on the United Nations*, Oxford: Oxford University Press.

Weiss, Thomas G., Forsythe, David P., Coate, Roger A. and Pease, Kelly-Kate 2010 *The United Nations and Changing World Politics. 6th Edition*. Boulder, CO: Westview Press.

Weiss, Thomas G. and Kessler, Meryl A. 1991 *Third World Security in the Post-Cold War Era*, Boulder, CO: Lynne Rienner.

Wendt, Alexander 1992 'Anarchy is What States Make of It: The Social Construction of Power Politics', *International Organization* 46(2): 391–425.

Yannis, Alexandros 2004 'The UN as Government in Kosovo', *Global Governance* 10(1): 67–81.

# 7 Regional origins, global aspirations

## The European Union as a global conflict manager

*Nathalie Tocci*

## Introduction

The European Union (EU) has emerged as an actor in conflict resolution beyond its borders at the turn of the twentieth century, concomitantly with the development of its fledging foreign policy. Despite being a newcomer to the field, the EU's history and tradition in conflict resolution is far older, being inextricably tied to its very emergence and *raison d'être*. The EU in fact represents the (unfinished) product of one of the greatest and most successful conflict resolution endeavours worldwide. It is the outcome of an idea: securing peace in post-Second World War Western Europe through integration and the ensuing creation of dependable expectations that interstate disputes would be settled in peaceful ways (Deutsch *et al.* 1957; Haas 1968; Mitrany 1966). This same idea also created the legitimizing narrative for the eastern enlargement and the perceived imperative of reuniting Europe in the aftermath of the Cold War. More recently, the founding idea of the European Community as a peace project has led the EU to engage in conflict resolution beyond its borders as and when it entered the foreign policy realm in the 1990s.

The aim of this chapter is to explain the EU's role in conflict resolution beyond its borders by addressing the EU's objectives, the evolution of its policies, its strengths, weaknesses and its future prospects in this field. In doing so, it argues that all of the above-mentioned aspects of the EU in conflict resolution are fundamentally shaped by the Union's self-perception and nature as a 'peace-through-integration project' within its frontiers. As regards conflict resolution, what the EU aspires to achieve, how it has articulated its policies, and what its strengths, weaknesses and future prospects are, are all inextricably tied to what the Union is and what it represents.

## The emergence of the EU as an actor in conflict resolution: aims and evolution

In view of its nature and self-perception as a peace project, from the outset the EU's foreign policy objectives have prioritized conflict resolution. In the 1993 Maastricht Treaty, when the EU specified for the first time its foreign policy aims, conflict resolution stood out amongst them, alongside promoting international security, regional cooperation, democracy, the rule of law and human rights (Article J.1). Since then, the EU has remained firm on its objectives. The EU Security Strategy, first outlined in 2003, explicitly called upon the Union to engage in a full range of conflict resolution activities, spanning from conflict prevention, to crisis management and post-violence rehabilitation (Council of the EU 2003, 12). Likewise, the 2009 Lisbon Treaty states that the Union's external action would aim at 'preserving peace, preventing conflicts and strengthening international security' (Art III-193(2c)).

The EU's approach to conflict resolution is broad, mirroring on the one hand the expansion of the notion of security within the international arena and on the other the EU's internal predisposition towards the subject. The EU emerged as an actor in conflict resolution beyond its borders at the turn of the millennium, as and when the international community's approach was evolving through the notions of peacebuilding and, later, of human security (see Zartman's contribution in this volume, Chapter 4). Reflecting broader international trends, the EU's understanding of peace thus not only entailed brokering of agreements between warring parties, but also included a wide array of measures aimed at protecting the rights and security of individuals. These measures included both short-to-medium-term efforts aimed at securing ceasefires, demobilisation, disarmament, peacekeeping and reconstruction and longer-term activities aimed at good governance, security sector reform, judicial reform and transitional justice, democracy, civil society development, human rights protection and socio-economic development (Commission of the EC 2001a). This broad and organic approach to peacebuilding, dovetailed with the EU's internal instincts, whereby the Treaty on European Union identifies a clear link between the EU's internal nature and its external projection. In fulfilling its foreign policy aims in fact, the Treaty argues that the EU would be 'guided by, and designed to advance in the wider world, the principles which have inspired its own creation, development and enlargement' (Article III-193(1)). In other words, having secured peace internally, the Union's foreign policy vocation would be to promote peace externally, drawing on and promoting the principles upon which it is founded. These principles include democracy, human rights, fundamental freedoms and the rule of law (Articles I-2 and I-3), alongside interstate cooperation and integration. Inherent in the EU's approach to conflict resolution is thus the link drawn between principles such as human rights, democracy, the rule of law and regional cooperation on the one hand, and the prevention and resolution of conflicts on the other. The former, while being viewed as ends in themselves, are also considered as instrumental to achieving the latter, as demonstrated by Europe's own history (Commission of the EC 2001a, 2001b; Kronenberger and Wouters 2005).

Turning to what kind of solutions the EU advocates in conflict situations, in view of its own nature as a sovereignty-sharing entity committed to the respect of international law, the Union has typically prioritized the territorial integrity of states alongside the respect for group and individual rights within them. In most cases, the Union has called for federal and/or power-sharing solutions to intrastate conflicts. Where secession is avoided, autonomy, federal and consociational models are viewed as the best recipes to reconcile the metropolitan state's territorial integrity and its accompanying claims to property restitution and refugee return, with the minority community's calls for collective rights and self-determination. Hence, the Union's support for the Annan Plan in Cyprus (Council of the EU 2004), its mediation of the State Union of Serbia-Montenegro (Council of the EU 2001; Commission of the EC 2002), its role in brokering the Ohrid Framework Agreement in Macedonia (Ilievski and Taleski 2009), its active engagement in the functioning of the complex two-entity state of Bosnia and Herzegovina (Recchia 2007) and its support for the proposals by the United Nations (UN), the Organization for Security and Cooperation in Europe (OSCE) and the Minsk Group in the Abkhaz, South Ossetian and Nagorno Karabakh conflicts (Coppieters 2004), respectively. In other cases, the Union has promoted instead the extension and respect of individual, cultural and minority rights within multicultural unitary states. In the case of Turkey's Kurds for example, the EU has supported and pressed for the entrenchment of individual human rights, effective political participation and the extension of cultural and minority rights to Kurdish citizens, possibly also including elements of decentralized governance (Commission of the EC 1998, 20; Commission of the EC 2004b, 167).

Despite its innate resistance to the philosophy of separation, the EU has supported secession in a few rare cases. Two such examples are the Western Balkans and the Middle East. In the case of the former, the Union was unable to prevent the break-up of Yugoslavia in the early 1990s, which, in the EU's view, culminated with Kosovo's independence in 2008. In some instances, the EU did strive to prevent secession in the region, as evidenced by its support for the ill-fated State Union of Serbia and Montenegro between 2003 and 2006. But also in this case the EU ultimately accepted the ineluctability of secession. The second case is that of the Middle East, where the Union, since the late 1990s, has persistently called for a two-state solution along the 1967 borders in Israel–Palestine. In this case, the EU's unshakable commitment to Israeli self-determination and security (not least in view of Europe's history), and its ensuing appreciation of the individual and collective rights of the Palestinians has led to firm support for a two-state solution. Yet even in these two cases in which the EU has atypically supported independent statehood as a mechanism to resolve conflict, the Union's philosophy of conflict resolution has transpired through the attempted promotion of schemes for interstate regional cooperation and bilateral integration with the EU. Hence, the EU's commitment to regional integration in the Western Balkans through the Stability Pact for South Eastern Europe and the South East European Cooperation Process, and in the southern Mediterranean through the 1995 Euro-Mediterranean Partnership and the 2008 Union for the Mediterranean. Regardless of the questionable success of these regional and bilateral cooperation initiatives, their very existence testifies to the EU's instinctive support for cooperation models which draw from, and attempt to replicate, the Union's own history.

While the EU's aims and ethos in conflict resolution are fairly consistent and clearly traceable to its very nature, its practice in the field has been far more erratic. The Union's baptism in conflict resolution was marked by dismal failure followed by its greatest foreign policy success. In both cases, the prime explanatory factor is the EU's own nature, which, as we shall see below, accounts for both the EU's structural flaws as well as its principal strengths in conflict resolution. The EU's entry into the foreign policy realm with the 1993 Maastricht Treaty[1] took place amidst the eruption and aggravation of war in Yugoslavia. In this context, the Union displayed all the weaknesses inherent in its nature as an association of states reluctant and unable to share sovereignty and act in unison in international affairs. Intra-European divisions and the ensuing immobilism of the Union underpinned Europe's utter failure to prevent and put an end to war on its borders. The EU's acknowledged failure to deal with the unfolding tragedy in the Balkans both pushed it to equip itself in the foreign policy realm, particularly in the security and defence fields, and generated the imperative to contribute to the stabilization of the Western Balkans. In the words of former Enlargement Commissioner Olli Rehn (2006): 'Too often in the 1990s, Brussels fiddled while the Balkans burned. We must not risk this happening again'. To many observers, success in the Western Balkans is viewed as the quintessential litmus test for the effectiveness of EU foreign policy (International Commission on the Balkans 2005). Were the Union to fail again, the credibility of its foreign policy and conflict resolution ambitions could be irredeemably shattered.

Whereas the Balkans in the 1990s flagged the Union at its worst, generating the imperative to act in conflict resolution, Eastern Europe provided the opportunity for the EU to develop its conflict resolution techniques, redeeming its credibility. Concomitantly with and in the aftermath of the Yugoslav wars, the EU embarked on what is commonly considered as its greatest foreign policy success: the eastern enlargement (Smith 1999). While being a unique case of EU foreign policy, the enlargement policy was significant in so far as it determined many of the conflict resolution templates and mechanisms which the Union subsequently elaborated and applied within and beyond the context of enlargement. Above all the eastern enlargement taught the Union how to draw on its assets as a *sui generis* entity in order to provide frameworks of governance and generate incentives for conflict resolution.

At the 1993 Copenhagen European Council, the Union set out the political (as well as economic, legal and technical) conditions for a candidate country to be admitted to the EU. These included the stability of institutions guaranteeing democracy, the rule of law, human rights and the protection of minorities, as well as ensuring good neighbourly relations. The accession policy also developed instruments to induce compliance with the above mentioned conditions. In the annual Progress Reports, the European Commission reviewed the performance of the applicant countries, taking as a reference point the rights and obligations enshrined in the EU *acquis communautaire* as well as in other bodies of law such as the European Convention on Human Rights. On the basis of these reports, the EU published Accession Partnership documents spelling out the short (1–2 years) and medium-term (3–4 years) priorities that candidates had to fulfil in order to move the accession process forward. The successive steps in this process – such as being recognized as a candidate, opening accession negotiations, opening and closing the over thirty chapters of the *acquis*, signing and ratifying the accession treaty, and entering the EU – were all conditioned to the aspirant members' fulfilment of EU conditions. In order to aid compliance, the EU also provided financial and technical assistance, which, while primarily tailored to supporting a candidate's capability to adopt and implement the *acquis*, also reserved funds for human rights, democracy and reconciliation projects.

Within the context of enlargement, the EU also carried out specific conflict resolution initiatives in Eastern Europe. The 1995 Stability Pact promoted by French Prime Minister Balladur was intended to diffuse minority and border tensions in Central and Eastern Europe. Unless the candidates settled their most salient disputes, they would be prevented from opening accession negotiations. Although the Pact was a political and non-legally binding document, its inbuilt incentives promoted agreements between Slovakia and Hungary (1995) and later between Romania and Hungary (1996), and entrusted the OSCE with a role in monitoring border and minority arrangements.

## Current role, strengths and weaknesses

Since the late 1990s, EU conflict resolution activities have spanned beyond Eastern Europe, including neighbouring regions such as the Balkans, the Caucasus and the Middle East, as well as areas further afield in Africa and Central Asia. These activities have encompassed both short- and medium-term actions aimed at civilian and military crisis management, conflict settlement and rehabilitation, as well as longer-term endeavours tailored to state-building, democratization and societal reconciliation.

Within the realm of the Common Foreign and Security Policy (CFSP) and the Common Security and Defence Policy (CSDP), the EU generally engages in short to medium-term actions in conflict zones. These include diplomatic mediation efforts carried out by the High Representative of the EU and the EU's Special Representatives in conflict regions around the globe – specifically in Afghanistan, the African Great Lakes Region, Bosnia, Central Asia, Kosovo, Macedonia, the Middle East, Moldova, the South Caucasus and Sudan. Furthermore, within the context of the CSDP, the EU, at the time of writing in 2011, was engaged in military and civilian operations aimed at peacekeeping, security sector reform, judicial reform and border monitoring in regions such as the Balkans (EUFOR-Althea, EUPMøBiH, EULEX Kosovo), the former Soviet Union (EUBAMøMoldova and Ukraine, EUMM Georgia), the Middle East (EUPOL COPPS, EUBAM Rafah, EUFOR Libya, EUJUST-LexøIraq), South Asia (EUPOL Afghanistan) and Africa (EU NAVFOR Somalia, EU Somalia Training Mission, EUPOL RD CONGO, EUSEC RD Congo). These CSDP missions have an average duration of one to two years.

Turning to longer-term conflict resolution actions, we find EU aid and technical assistance programmes alongside EU contractual arrangements with third parties. Assistance and contractual arrangements are intended to foster sustainable structural change both within and between third countries, which in turn induces conflict prevention, resolution and transformation. Development is the first policy area in which EU assistance and contractual arrangements have aimed at inducing the structural transformation of third countries (Marantis 1994). The European Development Fund (EDF) has increasingly focused on democracy, good governance, human rights and reconciliation beyond the more traditional socio-economic development projects in the African, Caribbean and Pacific Group of States (ACP). In the Fourth Lomé Convention, as amended in 1995, the Union set out the procedures to hold a human rights dialogue in the context of political dialogue with the ACP countries. The ensuing 2000 Cotonou Agreement spelled out that human rights would be 'essential elements' of the Agreement (Article 8) and that negative measures would be considered by the EU in the event of persisting third-country non-compliance in the sphere of human rights (Article 96). On this basis, the Union ventured in using different forms of negative incentives to ACP states, taking action against Haiti (2001), Ivory Coast (2001), Fiji (2001) and Zimbabwe (2002) (Portela 2005).

Closer to home, EU conflict resolution policies have been deployed in the Balkans, the former Soviet space and the southern Mediterranean, applying *mutatis mutandis* the lessons from the Eastern enlargement. In view of its impotence during the Balkan wars and particularly after the 1999 Kosovo war, the EU intensified its relationships with the Western Balkan countries in the twenty-first century. At a multilateral level, applying the lessons from the Stability Pact for Eastern Europe, the EU launched the South East European Cooperation Process and actively supported the Stability Pact for South Eastern Europe, both aimed at inducing reconciliation and regional cooperation. Also drawing from the lessons of enlargement, the EU intensified its bilateral contractual relations with the Western Balkan countries, particularly when (at the 2000 Feira European Council, reconfirmed at the 2003 Thessaloniki European Council) the EU declared its intent to eventually integrate the Balkans into its fold. The EU launched the Stabilization and Association Process (SAP) with these countries, intending to give rise to Stabilization and Association Agreements (SAAs), which would pave the way into the accession process. The SAAs include an 'essential elements' article (Article 2) mentioning democracy, international law and human rights, alongside a 'non-execution' article allowing the EU to adopt proportional negative measures in the event of a material breach of these agreements. Furthermore, the EU also inserted Balkan-specific conditions related to refugee return, cooperation with the International Criminal Tribunal for the Former Yugoslavia and regional cooperation.[2] Until 2007, the financial instrument targeted to the Western Balkans was the Community Assistance for Reconstruction, Development and Stabilization (CARDS), which was partly devoted to democratic reform (Article 105). In 2007 and in view of the Western Balkans' gradual inclusion in the accession process, CARDS was replaced by the Instrument for Pre-Accession.

In the former Soviet space, the EU articulated its bilateral relations through the Partnership and Cooperation Agreements (PCAs). In the context of these agreements, the EU provided cooperation in the spheres of trade, culture and technology, while institutionalizing political dialogue and inserting a human rights 'essential elements' (Article 2) and 'non-execution' article (Article 93). Furthermore, under the Technical Assistance for the Commonwealth of Independent States (TACIS) programme, the EU supported both socio-economic development and projects aimed at strengthening the rule of law, good governance, human rights and democracy.

Turning south, the EU also formalized its relations with the southern Mediterranean countries. At a multilateral level, the 1995 Barcelona Declaration affirmed the EU and southern Mediterranean countries' commitment to the promotion of peace, security and shared prosperity through multilateral dialogue at foreign ministers, senior officials, parliamentary and civil society levels. Moreover, like the SAAs and the PCAs, the bilateral Association Agreements (AAs) signed and ratified by the EU and the southern Mediterranean countries all include 'essential elements' (Article 2) and 'non-execution' (Article 79) clauses (Bartels 2004). Lastly, in the context of the Euro-Mediterranean Partnership (since 2008 the Union for the Mediterranean), the EU has supported economic development, redressing socio-economic imbalances, good governance and human rights reforms through its financial assistance instrument (MEDA).

Finally, since 2003, the EU has developed a European Neighbourhood Policy (ENP), which rhetorically placed a visibly higher emphasis on political questions compared with its predecessor policies (Tocci 2007). Indeed, the ENP declaredly aims to promote the EU's values as a means to spread peace, stability, security and prosperity in the southern and eastern neighbourhoods. It also aspires to strengthen the EU's contribution to the solution of regional conflicts (Commission of the EC 2004a, 6). The ENP's 'eastern dimension' was bolstered in 2009 through the 'Eastern Partnership', which rather than replacing the ENP represents an attempt to reinvigorate the EU's engagement with the eastern neighbours in the aftermath of the 2008 Russia–Georgia war. The ENP's founding documents, alongside the operational Country Strategy Papers and the ensuing Action Plans (APs), agreed bilaterally with five eastern and seven southern neighbours by 2007, emulate the logic of the accession policy, specifying country-specific political, governance as well as conflict-related actions that should be undertaken in order to progress with deeper ties with the EU. In practice, this has been truer for some neighbours than for others. In countries such as Georgia, Moldova and the Palestinian Authority, the APs have specified detailed reform priorities in the areas of institutions and governance, elections and electoral laws, human rights, fundamental freedoms and minority rights, and the development of civil society. In cases such as Azerbaijan or Israel, reform priorities have been set out in brief, vague and open-ended ways (Emerson *et al.* 2007). In 2007, the financial instrument of the ENP – the European Neighbourhood and Partnership Instrument (ENPI) – became operational, replacing MEDA for the southern Mediterranean countries and TACIS for the eastern neighbours.

In addition to these geographic policy instruments, the EU has also elaborated thematic instruments directly or indirectly related to conflict resolution. Since 1994 the EU has established the European Initiative for Democracy and Human Rights (EIDHR), applied worldwide but thematically focused on democracy and human rights. The EIDHR has spent approximately €100–140m per year and its programmes have aimed at supporting human rights of individuals suffering from poverty and social exclusion; supporting the rights of minorities, ethnic groups and indigenous peoples; supporting the development of civil society and specifically groups working on human rights education, training and awareness raising; justice and the rule of law; and promoting democratic processes. The advantage of the EIDHR is that it does not require the assent of third states and the funds can be used by international and local NGOs and international agencies. More recent and aimed at the more short-term dimensions of peacebuilding is instead the Instrument for Stability (IfS), with a budget of approximately 1.8bn in the 2007–13 financial period. The IfS includes both a (non-humanitarian) crisis response component and a Peacebuilding Partnership designed to improve communication with conflict parties by financing Track II diplomacy, early warning and the provision of conflict expertise and training by civil society actors (Duke and Courtier 2010).

### EU strengths as a sui generis actor in conflict resolution

As pointed out by Hill (2001), the EU's role and corresponding strengths in conflict resolution can be twofold. First, the EU framework of governance, law and policy can offer a conducive context for conflict resolution. Second, the Union can generate incentives for peace, which are often not available to other states, international organizations and NGOs engaged in conflict resolution. The strengths of the EU as a framework and as an actor are inextricably tied to each other and to the Union's nature. Indeed most of the incentives which the EU can offer in the context of its conflict resolution policies are embedded in its internal institutional, legal and policy frameworks (Tocci 2004).

### EU assets as a framework of governance

When conflict countries are in the process of accession or have a realistic prospect of entering it, the Union's multilevel framework of governance could raise the prospects for reconciliation by transforming the meaning of sovereignty, identity, borders and security, all highly contested issues in conflict situations.

Although the EU is predominantly shaped and constituted by its member states, through its policies and institutions it mitigates the black-and-white legalistic differences between monolithic and divided sovereignty. Sovereignty in practice is shared and no longer absolute and undivided. Decision-making and implementation in a given policy domain is determined by a particular allocation of competences between levels of government. While different levels of government remain legally distinct, they become practically interrelated through different channels of communication and policy procedures (Marks *et al.* 1998; Hooghe and Marks 2001). The supranational level penetrates the national and sub-national levels as several competences are dealt with either exclusively or in part by it. As a result, the role of the state within the EU is fundamentally transformed, as levels of government become increasingly interdependent and the search for indivisible sovereignty becomes obsolete. The EU framework also increases the scope for sub-national roles in EU policymaking. There where member states accord pronounced roles to federated entities, these roles could be enhanced further within the EU, thus possibly reducing the appetite for secession within minority communities.

In particular, when a member state allows for a limited exercise of external sovereignty by federated entities, the importance of this could be magnified by allowing federated entities to participate in EU decision making within the Council of Ministers. Since the apposite Treaty revisions in 1991, several federal member states such as Germany and above all Belgium have made use of this possibility, allowing ministers from sub-national governments to represent their member state when a particular Council legislates in areas of sub-state competence (Kerremans and Beyers 2001).

Similarly, the EU framework induces a transformed understanding of identity and citizenship. The EU adds weight to a concept of citizenship which prioritizes civil, political, economic and social rights, over national or community affiliations. By fostering the view of a more 'civic' rather than 'ethnic' understanding of citizenship and identity, the Union could contribute to conflict resolution. Through its very existence, the EU framework can also foster the development of multiple rather than exclusive identities (Diez 2002). EU citizenship becomes an additional layer of identification, which does not compete with national (and sub-national) identities. The additional layer of EU citizenship allows the understanding of identity to have two or more, rather than a single dimension.

The transformed meaning of borders within the EU could also raise the potential for conflict resolution. The liberalization of the movement of goods, services, capital and persons within the Union dilutes the meaning of territorial boundaries between member states. In addition, Commission funds have been created to make interstate borders more permeable, by supporting institutionalized interregional associations and networks, which have turned several border regions straddling member states into 'spaces of governance in their own right' (Christiansen and Jorgensen 2000, 66). The creation of European borderlands in areas of potential conflict is evident in cases such as Alto Adige/South Tyrol. As such, in intra or interstate conflicts where the drawing or redrawing of territorial boundaries is contested, the EU framework could raise the potential for agreement. Within states instead, EU regional policy and structural funds could induce decentralization. In some conflicts, decentralization may be part of the solution, yet the existence of conflict may render the mere discussion of decentralization taboo subject. In these cases, EU regional policy may raise the acceptance of internal administrative boundaries with member states, thus facilitating reconciliation. An interesting case in point is that of regional decentralization in Turkey. In Turkey there is a knee-jerk reaction against decentralization, due to fears of Kurdish secession. Within the context of the accession process however, in 2004 the government presented a bill to parliament providing for administrative reform, including *inter alia*, steps towards decentralization. The proposal was made in light of the Commission's recommendations and articulated in terms of the EU's regional and cohesion policies. The reform is yet to pass, being stalled as much by domestic opposition as by the ailing state of Turkey's accession process. However the very fact that the bill was proposed is indicative of the depoliticizing potential of the EU when it comes to decentralization.

Finally, the EU framework can increase individual, communal and state security, facilitating conflict resolution, particularly when reconciliation is hindered by mistrust between conflict parties. EU membership can be viewed as a powerful guarantee of state security. It is far less likely that a state would be attacked (both from the outside and less still from the inside) as an EU member state. EU membership can also act as an important guarantee of individual security through its legal system enshrining human rights, non-discrimination, equal opportunities and fundamental freedoms through Treaties, the *acquis communautaire* and the Charter of Fundamental Rights. Furthermore, individuals in member and candidate states, required to be members of the Council of Europe, have the right to individually bring cases to the European Court of Human Rights and be awarded compensation under it. In addition, under the 1997 Treaty of Amsterdam, Articles 6 and 7 allow for the suspension of the voting rights of a member state in the event of serious breaches of democracy, human rights and the rule of law. The full respect of individual rights does not make the Union insensitive to group rights however. Article 151 of the Treaty of Amsterdam recognizes regional diversity as a European value worth preserving. Within the accession process, one of the 1993 Copenhagen political criteria is the respect for minority rights. The Treaty of Lisbon amended the Treaty on European Union now including minority rights amongst the principles of the EU itself (Article 2). The EU also draws from the norms of pan-European organizations such as the Council of Europe and the OSCE and their emphasis on group rights. Going further, in order to safeguard communal security the Union has accepted exemptions to the full implementation of the *acquis* in its Treaties of Accession in special cases. One such case is the exemptions accorded to the Swedish-speaking Åland Islands in Finland. The Union had also signalled its willingness to accept derogations to the full implementation of the *acquis* had the Greek Cypriots and Turkish Cypriots accepted the 2004 Annan Plan.

*EU strengths as an actor in conflict resolution*

The EU framework could thus add new and innovative options for conflict resolution for those countries in, or in the process and with the prospect of entering the European Union. But not only adding alternative options requires the EU, as an actor, to be able to convey them. Moreover, for the EU to play a role in conflict resolution beyond its borders, it must be able to generate incentives for conflict resolution beyond the confines of enlargement as well. What are the strengths of the EU as an actor in conflict resolution, compared to other states, international organizations and NGOs engaged in peace efforts?

First, the EU can use policies of conditionality in conflict resolution: i.e., the promise/ threat or granting/infliction of a benefit/punishment in return for the fulfilment/violation of a predetermined condition. Positive and negative conditionality is a strategy in conflict resolution which is not unique to the EU and is typically employed by principal mediators (Cortright 1997; Dorussen 2001; Touval and Zartman 1989). However the EU, in view of its nature, can offer a far more varied set of benefits and punishments compared to other principal mediators. In the case of states, international organizations and NGOs, conditional benefits and punishments normally include aid, trade preferences, investments or sanctions (Baldwin 1985), as well as security guarantees, recognition and membership of international organizations (Walters 1999). In the case of the EU, benefits and punishments include a greater range of options, which are embedded in the integration nature of the EU and in the ensuing contractual relationships it develops with third countries. EU benefits (and punishments) include the granting (and withdrawing) of trade preferences, membership in the customs union and in aspects of the single market, financial and technical assistance, cooperation in the fields of economics, science, technology, environment, energy, infrastructure, education and culture, institutionalized forms of political dialogue, and inclusion in EU programmes, institutions and agencies.

Given this broader range of options, the value/cost of EU incentives is often higher than what other actors engaged in conflict resolution can offer, potentially raising the prospects for conflict resolution. Value/cost is determined by the objective nature of the benefit/punishment on offer. Naturally, when full membership is an option, the EU's potential leverage on a conflict is higher than in cases where relations are based on association, partnership or financial assistance. This begs the question of whether the EU can significantly influence third states in conflict that it cannot or does not wish to fully integrate. Indeed this is the core dilemma underlying the European Neighbourhood Policy, which was born precisely to find an alternative to full membership for aspirant EU members. Amongst these EU aspirants are several conflict countries such as Georgia and Moldova. Yet equally important is also the subjective value of EU benefits: the perceived value by the recipients within a conflict. Hence, for example, the more a conflict party identifies with 'Europe' or the more dependent it is upon it, the greater the perceived value of EU offers. Following this logic, even in countries such as Moldova, Georgia or Armenia which the EU does not wish to integrate, EU actors could in principle add important incentives for conflict resolution.

In view of the wide set of possible benefits and punishments, the EU has also developed rather sophisticated channels to offer, promise, threaten and inflict them in the context of its contractual relations. Hence, for example, EU conditionality can be not only positive or negative, but also *ex ante* or *ex post*: i.e., either conditions are fulfilled before the contract is signed, or conditions specified in an agreement must be respected otherwise the contract may be suspended. In between these two extremes, conditionality can be exerted over time, and not exclusively at the time or after the delivery of specified benefits. The case of the 1993 Copenhagen criteria for EU membership is an example of *ex ante* conditionality, while the 'human rights clause' in EU Association Agreements, Stabilization and Association Agreements and Partnership and Cooperation Agreements is an example of *ex post* conditionality. Financial and technical assistance instead lends itself to a constant exercise of conditionality over time, given the divisible nature of the benefit on offer. While these types of conditionality are all available to the EU in principle, in practice the Union has declared and demonstrated its preference for *ex ante* and positive conditionality and its reluctance to engage in negative and *ex post* conditionality (Commission of the EC 2003, 11; 2001b, 8–9).

The Union has also developed sophisticated methods to deliver its benefits through the use of gatekeeping, benchmarking and monitoring. These techniques were first developed in the context of the eastern enlargement, in which the Union benchmarked and monitored the progress of the candidate states and allowed them to proceed along the successive steps of the accession process (Grabbe 2001). However these very same techniques have been replicated in the context of other forms of contractual relationships, and above all in the context of the ENP (Kelley 2006). Furthermore, the delivery of EU benefits has been made either directly conditional on peace efforts, such as the case of the 1995 Stability Pact in Eastern Europe, or indirectly related to conflict resolution by affecting policy fields linked to the conflict resolution agenda, such as the EU's conditions regarding the abolition of the death penalty in Turkey, which had an indirect impact on the Kurdish question.

Second, the EU's nature and its extensive contractual relationships with third states generate an EU propensity to induce conflict resolution through socialization. Socialization takes place through the institutional, political, economic and wider societal contact and dialogue between the EU and third states (Checkel 1999). Socialization does not simply aim at altering a conflict party's cost–benefit calculus, but rather at inducing a voluntary transformation of its perceived interests and values. Through participation in or close contact with the EU's institutional framework, EU actors engage in dialogue, awareness raising, persuasion, argumentation, as well as shaming and denunciation vis-à-vis conflict parties. Conflict parties, in turn, may alter their beliefs, priorities and strategies in a manner conducive to conflict resolution.

The principal forums through which the EU induces socialization is through its institutionalized dialogues with third state executives in the context of its contractual relations, including the Association Councils, the Partnership and Cooperation Councils and the Stabilization and Association Councils. Specific human rights dialogues are also held with China and several ACP countries in the context of the Cotonou Agreement (known as 'Article 8 dialogues'). In the context of these dialogues, the EU has discussed issues such as the signing and ratification of international covenants, the death penalty, torture and ill-treatment, discrimination, children's and women's rights, the freedoms of expression and association, democratization and good governance. Socialization can also take place at parliamentary level, through inter-parliamentary delegations including Members of the European Parliament and parliamentarians from third states. Socialization can take place through other means as well. Through technical committees, training programmes, twinning and selective participation in EU programmes a third state may be socialized into accepting the EU's professed norms in the sphere of conflict resolution. In addition, under the ENP socialization can also take place at non-official levels, through educational and youth exchanges, enhanced mobility for researchers, facilitated contact between NGOs, regional and local authorities, and business in the EU and the ENP countries (Commission of the EC 2006).

Finally, the EU can induce conflict resolution through the passive enforcement of rules and norms. Rather than highlighting the logic of reward and punishment through conditionality, this mode of EU action hinges on a system of rule-bound cooperation. EU benefits are not delivered as a recompense for a third country's compliance with specified conditions, and punishments are not threatened and imposed in order to disincentivize a violation. Third-state obligations rather constitute the necessary rules making mutually beneficial cooperation with the EU possible. For passive enforcement to work, there must be a clear set of legally defined and definable rules embedded in EU contracts, rather than conditions which the EU simply considers politically desirable. Hence, it is far easier for the EU to use passive enforcement in the context of accession, whereby the candidate country is called upon to implement the legally-binding *acquis* and to respect the European Convention of Human Rights as well as the EU Charter on Fundamental Rights. Beyond enlargement, passive enforcement relies on the rules of customary public international law. Community law requires that all Community-based agreements with third states are interpreted and implemented in accordance with international law. As such, the EU has the legal obligation to respect the peremptory rules of international law including international human rights law and international humanitarian law, applicable and relevant in conflict contexts. This means that the EU can neither break the rules itself nor assist others in doing so. The EU cannot therefore, through the measures of cooperation embedded in its contractual agreements, acquiesce to a third state's breaking of the peremptory norms of international law by recognizing, aiding or assisting such violations within the confines of EU agreements. Cases in point regard the violation of international humanitarian law in the Occupied Palestinian Territory (OPT) or in the occupied Western Sahara by Israel and Morocco respectively, and the EU's obligation to avoid acquiescing to such violations by facilitating these violations within the context of EU–Israel and EU–Morocco association agreements (EMHRN 2006).

## EU weaknesses as an actor in conflict resolution

When discussing the EU's structural weaknesses in foreign policy in general and conflict resolution (or rather crisis management) in particular, topping the list of concerns are the EU's inability to act rapidly and cohesively and its limited capabilities in the security and defence realm. Underpinning these critiques are the structural limits of the EU, notably the frequent inability to forge consensus between member states and member states' unwillingness to devolve sovereignty in the foreign policy realm; an unwillingness which has not been fundamentally overturned with the Lisbon Treaty. All these critiques are certainly valid to greater or lesser extents in different conflict contexts. As discussed above, the wars in the Balkans and the EU's inability to react to them rapidly and decisively highlighted the EU's limits in preventing and putting an end to violence in its backyard. Yet rather than concentrating on these well-known limits, in what follows I shall focus on another frequent limit of the EU in conflict resolution: its lack of credibility. It is the absence of credibility which often explains why the EU does not deliver on its potential in conflict resolution; potential which, as discussed above, has more to do with the EU's nature as a *sui generis* actor able to contribute to long-term conflict transformation, rather than with its unmet aspirations to engage in crisis management as a state-like actor.

The EU's potential as a framework and as an actor in conflict resolution hinges on the EU's credibility. Credibility depends on a third state's perception of the EU's capacity and will to carry out its declared commitments in the sphere of conflict resolution. In the case of conditionality, credibility is related to the Union's track record in delivering/withdrawing promised benefits when and only when the specified conditions are fulfilled/violated. Credibility in passive enforcement entails cooperating when and only when the rules governing engagement are respected. Credibility also impinges on socialization, given that a particular norm is more likely to be assimilated when all parties, including the EU, are steadfast in their respect of it.

The EU often falls short in terms of credibility, thus losing its effectiveness, when the conduct of its external relations is driven by political imperatives, operating beyond the blueprint of declarations, laws and contractual relations. An effective EU conflict resolution policy would necessitate automatic entitlement to rights and benefits when obligations are fulfilled and automatic withdrawal of or non-entitlement to benefits when they are not. Yet there is never such automaticity in practice. Beyond the contract lie the political imperatives of EU actors, which go beyond the promotion of peace, human rights and international law. Both the granting and the withdrawal of a benefit require consensus within the Union. For an association agreement or an accession treaty to come into force, there must be unanimity of the member governments and ratification by national parliaments and the European Parliament. Such consensus depends on the fulfilment of conflict countries' promises and obligations vis-à-vis the EU. But it also depends on other factors that are motivated by underlying political or economic imperatives. Hence, for example, EU policy towards Georgia's conflicts is heavily conditioned by the EU's and particular member states' sensitivities towards Russia, based on geopolitical as well as energy security reasons. In the Middle East, several member states view the protection of Israel and close relations with it as being of the utmost priority, over and above the promotion of conflict resolution. Europe's history of anti-Semitism has generated a deep-felt EU preference – particularly within some member states – to maintain close relations with Israel irrespective of its conduct, a preference which is magnified further by economic interests underpinning EU–Israel relations. Another EU priority in the Middle East is to seek close, cooperative and complementary relations with the United States, which has generated strong EU incentives, felt particularly by Atlanticist member states such as the United Kingdom and Italy, to accommodate American interests, strategies and policies in the conflict.

## Future prospects for the EU in conflict resolution

By representing probably the most innovative and successful experiment in conflict resolution worldwide, the EU's entry into the foreign policy realm and its declared commitment to promote conflict resolution beyond its borders is a welcome development. As this chapter has argued, the EU's strengths both as a framework for and as an actor in conflict resolution are rooted in its nature as an entity promoting rights, law, and interstate cooperation and integration. By way of conclusion, I shall briefly turn to the Union's future prospects in this field, highlighting the challenges lying ahead.

Given the inextricable bind between the EU's internal nature and its strengths in external conflict resolution, the progress in the integration project through constitutional and institutional reform is of the essence. In this respect the ratification of the Lisbon Treaty in 2009, after five years of soul-searching and failed attempts comes as an important step forward, allowing the EU to lift its gaze and focus again on the world around it. More specifically, the reforms in EU foreign policymaking, including the appointment of a 'double hatted' EU High Representative/Vice President of the Commission and the creation of an External Action Service open the possibility for a rationalization of the EU's external policies formerly conducted separately by the Commission and the Council. These reforms can certainly help in improving the rapidity and cohesiveness of EU policies, as well as develop further the EU's ethos, identity and aims as an actor in conflict resolution.

Beyond constitutional and institutional reform, three policy areas require particular attention if the EU is to fulfil its potential in conflict resolution and work on its structural weaknesses in the field. First, is the imperative to maintain its current commitments in the context of enlargement towards the Western Balkans and Turkey. The critical role played by the EU in stabilizing the war-torn Balkans and inducing intra and interstate integration in the region has hinged on the deepening of its bilateral relations with the Western Balkan countries through the SAP (Tocci 2007, 89). In addition, the EU-inspired reforms in the fields of rights and governance have promoted reconciliation both in the Balkans and between the Turkish state and its Kurdish citizens (Tocci 2007, 53–77). Moreover, particularly when it comes to Turkey, the credibility of the Union is at stake more broadly. The EU's accession process with Turkey, rightly or wrongly, is viewed by many as signalling the Union's stance towards Islam and the values upon which the EU stands. If the EU's rejection of Turkey were to be viewed as an affirmation of an exclusivist and essentialist European identity, the Union's credibility both as a framework for and as an actor in conflict resolution would be seriously undermined both in the Muslim world and beyond.

Second, it is essential for the Union to develop a credible alternative to its enlargement policy. As discussed throughout this chapter, the enlargement process played a critical role in shaping the EU's ethos, methods and strengths in conflict resolution beyond its borders. Yet at the same time, the EU finds itself entrapped in the logic of enlargement (Kelley 2006), attempting to replicate its templates and techniques but reluctant to proceed further with the enlargement process towards new aspirant members. This has generated frustration beyond the Union's borders while at the same time it has emptied the perceived content of alternative policy frameworks such as the ENP. In order for the EU to capitalize on its conflict resolution assets it is thus essential that it succeeds in developing a credible, valuable and thus effective policy in its wider neighbourhood.

Finally, the EU has elevated 'effective multilateralism' as a dominant value and goal in its foreign policy (Council of the EU 2003; Peterson *et al.* 2007). In the sphere of conflict resolution, the EU has indeed prioritized working alongside other states (e.g., the United States) and international organizations (e.g., the UN). In the period ahead and in response to the changing global order, EU actors will need to adapt their multilateral conflict resolution policies to the rise of new states and international forums, particularly if the Union is intent in contributing to conflict resolution beyond its immediate neighbourhood. However, as and when the EU engages with conflicts further afield and with a rising number of state and non-state actors, it is essential that it remains firm in practice and not only in principle to its ethos and methods in conflict resolution. Only in this case will the EU be able to truly represent a constructive and novel force in conflict resolution, willing and able to export externally some of the lessons painfully learnt and applied on the continent.

## Notes

1 Prior to the 1993 Maastricht Treaty, the member states of the European Community cooperated in the foreign policy realm through the European Political Cooperation. However it is only with the Maastricht Treaty and its ensuing revisions (i.e. the 1997 Amsterdam, the 2000 Nice and the 2009 Lisbon Treaties) that the EU explicitly acquired a foreign policy dimension through the Common Foreign and Security Policy.
2 For example, the EU has insisted that Serbia's cooperation with the ICTY, including the arrest and transfer of Radovan Karadžić and Ratko Mladić, is a precondition for the entry into force of the SAA between the EU and Serbia.

## References

Baldwin, D. 1985 *Economic Statecraft*, Princeton, NJ: Princeton University Press.

Bartels, L. 2004 'A Legal Analysis of Human Rights Clauses in the EU's Euro-Mediterranean Association Agreements', *Mediterranean Politics*, 9, 368–95.

Checkel, J. 1999 'Norms, Institutions and National Identity in Contemporary Europe', *International Studies Quarterly*, 43, 83–114.

Christiansen, T. and Jorgensen, J. E. 2000 'Transnational Governance "above"' and "below" the State: The Changing Nature of Borders in the new Europe', *Regional and Federal Studies*, 10(2): 62–77.

Commission of the EC 1998 *Regular Report on Turkey's Progress Towards Accession*.

—— 2001a *Communication from the Commission on Conflict Prevention*, COM(2001) 211.

—— 2001b *The EU's Role in Promoting Human Rights and Democratization in Third Countries*, COM(2001) 252.

—— 2002 *Staff Working Paper on the Federal Republic of Yugoslavia*, COM(2002) 163 (available online at: www.ec.europa.eu; accessed December 2002).

—— 2003 *Wider Europe-Neighbourhood: A New Framework for Relations with our Eastern and Southern Neighbours*, COM(2003) 104.

—— 2004a *European Neighbourhood Policy Strategy Paper*, Brussels, COM (2004) 373 (available online at: http://ec.europa.eu/world/enp/pdf/strategy/strategy_paper_en.pdf).

—— 2004b *Regular Report on Turkey's Progress Towards Accession*.

—— 2006 *Communication from the Commission to the Council and the European Parliament on Strengthening the European Neighbourhood Policy*, COM (2006) 726 final, Brussels, 4 December (available online at: http://ec.europa.eu/world/enp/pdf/com06_726_en.pdf).

Coppieters, B. 2004 'EU policy towards the Southern Caucasus', paper presented at the European Parliament, Committee of Foreign Affairs, Brussels, January.

Cortright, D. 1997 'Incentives and Cooperation in International Affairs', in D. Cortright (ed.) *The Price of Peace: Incentives and International Conflict Prevention*, New York, NY: Carnegie Corporation of New York, Rowman and Littlefield, 3–20.

Council of the EU 2001 *General Affairs Council Meeting*, 26 February 2001 (available online at: www.consilium.europa.eu; accessed May 2006).

—— 2003 *A Secure Europe in a Better World. European Security Strategy*, 12 December 2003 (available online at: http://ue.eu.int/pressdata/EN/reports/78367.pdf).

—— 2004 *Council Conclusions on Cyprus*, 26 April 2004 (available online at: www.consilium. europa.eu; accessed May 2004).

Deutsch, K. *et al.* 1957 *Political Community and the North Atlantic Area: International Organization in the Light of Historical Experience*, Princeton, NJ: Princeton University Press.

Diez, T. 2002 'Why the EU Can Nonetheless be Good for Cyprus', *Journal of Ethnopolitics and Minority Issues in Europe*, 2 (available online at: www.ecmi.de).

Dorussen, H. 2001 'Mixing Carrots with Sticks: Evaluating the Effectiveness of Positive Incentives', *Journal of Peace Research*, 38(2): 251–62.

Duke, S. and Courtier, A. 2010 'EU Peacebuilding: Concepts, Players and Instruments', in S. Blockmans, J. Wouters and T. Ruys (eds.) *The EU and Peacebuilding*, Leiden: Asser Press.

Emerson, M., Noutcheva, G. and Popescu, N. 2007 'ENP after Two Years: Time Indeed for an ENP Plus', *Working Paper*, Brussels: CEPS (available online at: www. ceps.eu).

Euro-Mediterranean Human Rights Network 2005 *A Human Rights Review of the EU and Israel – 2003–2004*, Copenhagen: Euro-Mediterranean Human Rights Network.

Grabbe, H. 2001 'How Does Europeanisation Affect CEEG? Conditionality, Diffusion and Diversity' *Journal of European Public Policy*, 8(6): 1013–31.

Haas, E. 1968 *The Uniting of Europe: Political, Social and Economic Forces*, Stanford, CA: Stanford University Press.

Hill, C. 2001 'The EU's Capacity for Conflict Prevention', *European Foreign Affairs Review*, 6(3): 315–33.

Hooghe, L. and Marks, G. 2001 *Multi-level Governance and European Integration*, Lanham: Rowman & Littlefield.

Ilievski, Z and Taleski, D. 2009 'Was the EU's Role in Conflict Management in Macedonia a Success?', *Ethnopolitics*, 8(3–4): 355–67.

Kelley, J. 2006 'New Wine in Old Wineskins: Promoting Political Reforms through the New European Neighbourhood Policy', *Journal of Common Market Studies*, 44(1): 29–55.

Kerremans, B. and Beyers, J. 2001 'The Belgian Sub-national Entities in the EU: Second or Third Level Players?', in C. Jeffrey (ed.), *The Regional Dimension of the European Union*, London: Frank Cass, 41–55.

Kronenberger, V. and Wouters, J. (eds.) 2005 *The EU and Conflict Prevention: Policy and Legal Aspects*, The Hague: Asser Press.

International Commission on the Balkans 2005 *The Balkans in Europe's Future*, Sofia.

Marantis, D. 1994 'Human Rights Democracy and Development: The European Community Model', *Harvard Human Rights Journal*, 7: 1–32.

Marks, G. *et al.* (eds) 1998 *Governance in the European Union*, London: Sage.

Mitrany, D. 1966 *A Working Peace System: An Argument for the Functional Development of International Organization*, Chicago, IL: University of Chicago Press.

Peterson, J., Aspinwall, M., Boswell, C. and Damro, C. 2007 'The Consequences of Europe: Multilateralism and the New Security Agenda', *Mitchell Working Paper 7*, Edinburgh: Europa Institute.

Portela, C. 2005 'Where and Why Does the EU Impose Sanctions?', *Politique européenne*, 17: 83–111.

Recchia, S. 2007 'Beyond International Trusteeship: EU Peacebuilding in Bosnia and Herzegovina', *Occasional Paper*, 66, EU Institute for Security Studies, Paris.

Rehn, O. 2006 'Brussels Must Offer the Balkans a Credible Future', *Financial Times*, 3 April.

Smith, K. E. 1999 *The Making of EU Foreign Policy, The Case of Eastern Europe*, London: Macmillan.

Tocci, N. 2004 'Conflict Resolution in the European Neighbourhood: The Role of the EU as a Framework and as an Actor', *EUI Working Paper* 29, Florence.

—— 2007 'Can the EU Promote Democracy and Human Rights through the ENP? The Case for Refocusing on the Rule of Law', *EUI Working Papers*, Florence 9 (available at: www.iue.it/LAW/Events/ENP/Papers/PaperTocci.pdf).

—— 2007 *The EU and Conflict Resolution. Promoting Peace in the Backyard*, London: Routledge.

Touval, S. and Zartman, W. I. 1989 'Mediation in International Conflict', in K. Kressel D. G. Pruitt and Associates (eds.), *Mediation Research, the Process and Effectiveness of Third Party Intervention*, San Francisco, CA: Jossey-Bass Publishers, 115–37.

Walters, B. 1999) 'Designing Transitions from Civil War', *International Security*, 24(1): 127–55.

# 8 Limited capabilities, great expectations

## The African Union and regional conflict management

*John Akokpari*

## Introduction

The transformation of the 39-year-old Organization of African Unity (OAU) to the African Union (AU) in July 2002 was met with optimism. The OAU had become anachronistic in a post-Cold War era characterized by a new set of challenges and opportunities. The birth of the AU raised hopes of a new dawn for Africa against a backdrop of the OAU's demonstrated inability to resolve speedily conflicts that had plagued the continent. There were expectations on the AU to restore the continent's largely tattered image under the broader African renaissance agenda (Mathews 2008, 25). Due in part to limited resources and partly to the inability to prevent conflicts from occurring, military intervention and peacekeeping have become the dominant approaches to conflict resolution by the AU and its subregional organizations. Africa's notoriety as a theatre of incessant, often seemingly intractable, conflicts is well known. Since the 1960s, it has witnessed no fewer than 30 conflicts, which claimed close to 10 million lives and which cost more than US$ 250 billion (Murithi 2005, 82). By the beginning of 2010, the UN had deployed 20,000 peacekeepers, the largest contingent in Africa, in the Democratic Republic of the Congo (DRC). While the record of the AU in conflict resolution remains mixed at best in its eight years of existence, it would be grossly unfair to dismiss the efforts, even achievements, of the organization in this direction. Since 2002, the AU has been able to resolve a few of Africa's conflicts, although the post-conflict peace in some of these countries remains tenuous.

This chapter analyses the role of the AU in resolving conflicts using its intervention in the conflicts in Burundi, Somalia, Ivory Coast and Darfur as case studies. It argues that while the AU has set out good intentions and is theoretically committed to conflict resolution, its record in this area has been remarkably unimpressive. While it ended the conflicts in Burundi and Ivory Coast, it failed to bring peace to Somalia and Darfur. The inability of the AU to position itself firmly as a credible actor of conflict resolution stems from a litany of factors, including its failure to address the root causes of conflicts, inadequate financing of its peace operations, the reluctance of member states to contribute resources, including troops to its peacekeeping operations (PKOs) and the tendency of the AU to rely on external actors. The next section reviews the different positions of the OAU and the AU on conflict resolution; the following analyses the efforts of the AU in conflict resolution, focusing mainly on peacekeeping, while the subsequent highlights some of the challenges facing the AU in its efforts at conflict resolution. The conclusion briefly reflects on the AU's future as an actor in conflict resolution.

## Continental approach to conflict resolution: the old and the new

The OAU and the AU adopted different, in fact contrasting, postures on conflict resolution. While the former adopted a reluctantly reactive position, the latter adopted a more proactive stance. Although the Charter of the OAU established a Commission of Mediation, Conciliation and Arbitration (CMCA) under Article XIX to resolve conflicts (OAU 1963), this organ had limited powers, authority and scope. Essentially, the CMCA served as an agency to persuade warring factions to end hostilities or prevent their escalation through mediation. The mediatory intervention of the CMCA was therefore to be a last resort as 'member states pledge[d] to settle all disputes among themselves by peaceful means' (art. XIX). By this provision, moreover, the OAU implicitly relied on the commitment of member states to abide by their pledges. The bulk of Africa's conflicts in the 1960s and 1970s were border related and were an almost inevitable consequence of the arbitrary boundary demarcations imposed by colonialism. The objective of the CMCA was therefore to ensure the timely diffusion of such border demarcation-related tensions through mediation and arbitration. The OAU did not foresee the huge possibility of complex intrastate conflicts in the future and thus to position itself for such eventualities. Emerging out of, or at least informed by the ideas of Kwame Nkrumah, one of Africa's first radical anti-colonial leaders, the OAU's *raison d'être* was the rapid decolonization and the eventual unification of the continent against neo-colonialism (Foltz 1991). The imperative to decolonize Africa eclipsed the urgency for establishing proactive conflict resolution mechanisms (Okoth 2008, 23).

Historically, besides the ill-fated, Nigerian-led OAU military intervention in Chad in 1982, the organization showed a truncated capacity to resolve many of Africa's high-profile conflicts. The Angolan war of the 1970s, the Ethiopian–Somali border conflict which began in the 1960s, the conflict over the Ogaden region, the long-running conflict in south Sudan and the 1994 Rwandan genocide, to name just a few, raged in the full view of the OAU. The OAU's weakness in conflict prevention was further revealed in its lack of action when it stood by as full-scale hostilities re-erupted and escalated between Ethiopia and Eritrea in June 1998. Even more glaring, fighting intensified between rebels and the government of Guinea-Bissau at the same time that the OAU summit of the heads of states and governments was taking place in nearby Burkina Faso in 1998. In its usual practice the OAU only issued a declaration condemning the violence and calling for the restoration of calm (Akokpari 1999, 12). By 1999, the OAU eventually intervened in the Guinea-Bissau conflict with the deployment of the Economic Community of West African States (ECOWAS) Monitoring Group (ECOMOG), a force drawn largely from French-speaking West African countries (Adebajo 2004a, 7). Generally, the OAU's record at violent conflicts of any kind was dismal (Sesay 1982; Okoth 1987).

If the need for decolonization limited the OAU ability to be proactive in resolving conflicts, its institutional setup was even more inhibiting. The respect for the sovereign equality of states and in particular the principle of 'non-interference in the internal affairs of states' enshrined in Article III of the OAU Charter prevented the organization from undertaking any robust conflict resolution initiatives (Foltz 1991). Meant to preserve the hard-won independence, the principles on sovereignty and non-interference were strictly adhered to, keeping the OAU at bay as conflicts raged and refugee problems overwhelmed countries (Jonah 1994). Equally worrisome, the policy of non-interference provided salutary conditions for some African leaders to commit acts of bad governance, including corruption, dictatorship, partisanship and sometimes persecution of their own populations without fearing the risk of intervention by an external force (Feldman 2008, 267). Such acts of impunity as in the cases of Siyad Barre's Somalia, Mobutu Sésé Seko's Zaire (now Democratic Republic of the Congo, or DRC), Mengistu Haile Mariam's Ethiopia, Samuel Doe's Liberia, to name just a few, generated resentment, rebellion and prolonged violent conflicts. Mainly as a result of its inaction, the OAU was described, in the words of one observer, as 'a toothless talking shop, a silent observer to the atrocities being committed by its member states' (Murithi 2008, 72).

In contrast to the OAU, the AU in principle demonstrated a commitment to a proactive approach to conflict resolution attested to by at least three developments. First, Article 4(h) of the Constitutive Act of the AU grants it 'the right to intervene in a member state pursuant to a decision of the Assembly in respect of grave circumstances, namely war crimes, genocide and crimes against humanity' (African Union 2000). This was a radical positional shift, from 'non-interference to non-indifference' (Mwanasali 2008). While respecting the sovereign existence of member states, the AU by this provision prioritized conflict prevention and resolution, i.e., the rights of individuals over those of states. The AU, moreover, underscored the emergence of such important developments as the respect for human rights, concerns for human security, the need for humanitarian interventions and the responsibility to protect, which have characterized the post-Cold War global dispensation. Together, these developments rendered obsolete the sanctity of sovereignty, which guided the relations among states since the Peace Treaties of Westphalia in 1648. The AU accepted that sovereignty was no longer sacrosanct, absolute or fixed; it was now relative and its respect was to be weighed against the larger security and safety of people (Weiss *et al.* 2001; Sarkin 2008)· Accordingly, the AU sent a clear message to potential dictators that the days of impunity under the lame and inept OAU were over. Importantly, by declaring an intention to intervene in member states, albeit under specified circumstances, the AU set itself apart, at least in theory, as an actor of conflict resolution from the OAU.

Second, the Constitutive Act established a Peace and Security Council (PSC) as one of the key organs of the AU. Although provided for in the AU Constitutive Act, the PSC was only officially launched in May 2004 following the election of its fifteen members. Membership in the PSC was based on a number of criteria, including peacekeeping experience; financial contribution to the AU's Peace Fund; capacity to pay; and commitment to constitutional governance (Adebajo 2008, 133). Expected to function like the UN Security Council, Article 7 of the Protocol on PSC vests it with the mandate to exercise overall responsibility over issues of peace and security by preventing, managing and resolving conflicts (Cilliers and Sturman 2004). Advised by a panel of five eminent persons (Panel of the Wise),[1] the PSC is responsible for the deployment of the African Standby Force (ASF) to be established under the AU's broader security architecture (Sarkin 2008, 59). Mandated by Article 13 of the Constitutive Act, the ASF is to be established by 2010, composed of the combined standby brigades of the AU's five regional blocks – ECOWAS, the Southern Africa Development Community (SADC), the East African Community (EAC), the Economic Community of Central African States (ECCAS) and the Arab–Maghreb Union (AMU). The key rationale for the establishment of the ASF is to have a contingent ready for expeditious deployment to conflict spots. Composed of military, police and civilian segments, the ASF is expected to have 40,000 peacekeepers in place by 2010 (Dersso 2009; Potgieter 2009). In addition to using military means, Article 20 of the PSC protocol also mandates it to encourage civil society 'to participate actively in the efforts aimed at promoting peace, security and stability in Africa'. A Continental Early Warning System (CEWS) is to be established under the PSC. Using appropriate 'early warning indicators', including economic, political, humanitarian and military indicators, the CEWS office collects and analyses country data and tracks situations in order to forestall the eruption of conflict (Cilliers and Sturman 2004). A Military Staff Committee (MSC) composed of the representatives of military top brass of countries of the PSC is also established under the PSC, whose function is to advise the PSC on issues of security.

Third, the Constitutive Act vested substantial powers in the Assembly of Heads of States and Government (HSG) which the latter did not previously enjoy under the defunct and discredited OAU. For example, article 23(1–2) grants the Assembly power to impose sanctions on member countries which fail to honour their obligations to, or comply with decisions of, the AU. These sanctions may take various forms, including 'denial of the right to speak at meetings, to vote, to present candidates for any position or post within the Union or to benefit from any activity or commitments therefrom'. Sanctions can also take the form of economic embargos and denial of transport and communication links with members states. This provision is significant in the AU's conflict resolution arsenal for compelling errant states, which persist in acts that can either provoke or escalate conflict or impede its resolution, to change course. Commenting on its invigoration with the expanded powers of the AU Assembly, Mwanasali (2008, 45) optimistically notes that '[the] organisation is no longer regarded by its members with the same defiance or outright contempt as its predecessor. There is a growing sense in the UN and the international community at large that the AU is a serious and legitimate partner in the maintenance of regional peace and security in Africa.'

If the creation of the PSC and the establishment of the ASF were a response to the proliferation of regional conflicts, the end of the Cold War generated an even greater imperative for the AU to assume a more proactive posture on conflict resolution. A key feature of the post-cold war era has been Africa's marginalization. This is reflected in a trend of disinvestment in Africa, declining ODA and Africa's dwindling share of world markets (Harsch 2003, 12–13). Importantly, the ending of the Cold War and the consequent erosion of Africa's strategic importance was accompanied by a reduced interest by Western governments to lead or be involved in peacekeeping efforts in Africa (Adebajo and Landsberg 2000). During the Cold War, for example, American support for Samuel Doe in times of rebellion against his regime was always guaranteed. However, when his regime faced internal rebellion in 1989, Doe could not count on his old and familiar patron. Similarly, Mobutu Sese Seko could not call on France, his traditional ally, when his beleaguered regime was besieged by rebels in 1997. Generally, while happy to assist in Africa's peacekeeping efforts, Western governments were prepared to contribute resources except personnel, requiring Africa to take the initiative in managing its conflicts. By providing resources other than personnel, Western governments were abdicating their traditional peacekeeping responsibilities in Africa. The Western retreat has, in the meantime, led to the AU embracing the 'African solutions to African problems' (ASAP) concept, albeit reluctantly. The AU has recorded some successes but also failures in conflict resolution – an issue to which we now turn.

## Conflict resolution in Africa: the AU's efforts so far

While the AU has attempted to use diplomacy and negotiation, intervention and peacekeeping have become the most popular of its methods of conflict resolution. The ubiquity of military intervention and peacekeeping has resulted mainly from the deficiency in the AU early warning systems, incapacitating the organization from forestalling the eruption of armed conflicts. In its peacekeeping efforts, the AU has sought to work in conjunction with its subregional organizations. ECOMOG has, for example, led peace-keeping efforts in the subregion both on behalf and at the behest of the AU. While in general the AU's peacekeeping operations continue to be marked by weaknesses, the organization can be credited for ending some conflicts and assisting in post-conflict reconstruction. The interventions in the Burundi and Ivory Coast conflicts are notable examples of the AU's successful conflict resolution initiatives.

### Burundi

Since gaining independence on 1 July 1962 from UN trusteeship under Belgian adminis-tration, Burundi has seen recurring conflict between its majority Hutu and minority Tutsi communities. This resulted in the death of hundreds of Burundians as well as prolonged political instability. Continuous violence and, in particular, the death of some 300,000 people and the displacement of further hundreds of thousands after the national elections of 1993 drew international attention to the conflict. In October 1993 soldiers from the Tutsi-dominated government assassinated the elected Hutu president, Melchoir Ndadaye, after just one hundred days in office. Cyprien Ntaryarmira, also a Hutu, elected by par-liament as a replacement died when the plane carrying him and the Rwandan president was shot down. Ntaryarmira had been in office for just two months. These developments sparked a decade-long conflict between Hutus and Tutsis. Prospects for ending the con-flict diminished considerably by January 2003 as breaches of a December 2002 ceasefire agreement in Arusha between forces of the transitional government and rebels continued. The conflict ended in 2005 as a result of the intervention of an AU peacekeeping force – the AU Mission in Burundi (AMIB) – dating back to 2003.

AMIB was approved at the HSG summit in February 2003 and was composed of soldiers from Ethiopia, Mozambique and South Africa. A force of 3,500, AMIB was dominated by South African soldiers. Its mandate included ensuring the holding of the ceasefire between government forces and the Conseil National pour la Défense de la Démocratie–Forces de la Démocratie (CNDD–FDD); disarming, demobilizing rebel groups and helping integrate them into society; and overseeing Burundi's post-conflict transition to democracy. The force landed in Burundi in October 2003. South Africa initially assumed the entire cost of maintaining AMIB. Later, Ethiopia and Mozambique received support from the US and the UK to help cover their costs. The UN was initially reluctant to deploy a force into Burundi until a ceasefire between the protagonists had been achieved. Eager to hand over responsibilities to the UN, the South African-led AMIB worked hard to ensure that hostilities ceased. Successful elections to the 100-member National Assembly and the 54-seat Senate were held on 4 and 29 July 2005, respectively, under the surveillance of AMIB. The polls also returned Pierre Nkurunziza, the former rebel leader, as president of Burundi. The 2005 elections brought peace, albeit temporarily and fragile, to Burundi and paved the way for AMIB to hand peacekeeping responsibilities over to the UN, which had already by June 2004 sent a contingent of peacekeepers, including 5,650 military personnel, 120 civilian police and 1,000 interna-tional civilian personnel, into the country (Howard 2008).

However, in haste to hand over peacekeeping responsibilities to the UN and leave Burundi, AMIB failed to see to the implementation of certain critical aspects of the

Arusha agreement. In particular, the provision calling for perpetrators of violence to be brought to justice was never implemented. The failure to implement this part of the ceasefire agreement left a deep sense of anger and injustice among communities which had become victims of violence. Burundi's fragile peace could potentially be undermined if victims become vengeful in the future as the country's history had shown. Similarly, neither AMIB nor the UN peacekeepers were bold enough to ensure the granting of provisional immunity to the Forces for National Liberation (FNL), the last remaining armed group (Human Rights Watch 2008). The FNL disagreed with the government over certain aspects of the peace agreement, including disarmament, and the release of political prisoners. Having engaged in various forms of atrocities, the FNL requested for provisional immunity from arrest, as such immunity had been granted to other former rebels. In spite of many challenges, the AU has been commended for successfully assisting in restoring stability to Burundi in the face of a dithering UN (Murithi 2008, 75).

### Ivory Coast

The AU's intervention in the Ivory Coast represents another bold, if not entirely successful, attempt at conflict resolution. Ivory Coast's thirty-nine years of post-independence stability lasted up to December 1999 when it was ruptured by a military coup. Led by General Robert Guéï, the coup toppled the government of Henri Konam Bedie, the successor of Félix Houphouët-Boigny. This plunged Ivory Coast, once the epitome of stability, economic development and prosperity in West Africa, into considerable uncertainty. The root causes of the conflict are many, principal among them the privileging of certain Ivorian communities by Houphouët-Boigny, the manipulation of the concept of Ivorian citizenship – *Ivoirité* – by post- Houphouët-Boigny political elites, and severe strains in the once strong Ivorian economy (Adebajo 2004b, 299). By 2002 the Ivorian conflict had deepened and had divided the country between the North and South. While the government of Laurent Gbagbo controlled the south, the north remained firmly under the control of the Patriotic Movement of the Ivory Coast (MPCI), the main rebel group. Two additional rebel movements – the Movement for Justice and Peace (MJP) and the Popular Movement of Ivory Coast's Far West (MPIGO) – emerged in late November 2002 both in western Ivory Coast (Akokpari 2008a). Subsequently, the MPCI was replaced by the New Force (NF) as the main coalition of rebels. Its leader, Guillaume Soro, was named Prime Minister under a political agreement signed in Ouagadougou on 4 March 2007.

The peace process in Ivory Coast had been tortuous. Mediation efforts under the auspices of ECOWAS in Accra and Lomé, although initially unsuccessful, eventually got the warring factions to sign an accord at Linas-Marcoussis on 24 January 2003. The Linas-Marcoussis accord called for the cessation of hostilities, the inclusion of rebels in a unity government, and the disarming, demobilization and integration of rebel fighters into the national army, the revision of the constitution and the eventual conduct of elections, among other things (Adebajo 2004b, 299). However, disagreements soon emerged over the interpretation and implementation of the Linas-Marcoussis agreement. While the government demanded the disarming and demobilization of rebels as a condition for constitutional reforms and the formation of a unity government, the rebels demanded constitutional changes, which would remove the controversial and discriminatory citizenship clause from the constitution as a condition for disarmament and demobilization. Suspicion and, sometimes, skirmishes between government and rebel forces became common and delayed the implementation of the Linas-Marcoussis accord.

Initially, France deployed a force of 4,000 troops from its permanent military base in Ivory Coast to monitor the ceasefire brokered under the 2003 Linas Marcoussis agreement, but by April the same year, an ECOWAS Peace Force for Côte d'Ivoire (ECOFORCE) was assembled and deployed in the country. ECOFORCE, numbering 1,288 personnel, was composed of soldiers from Benin, Ghana, Niger, Senegal and Togo. Its main mandate was to keep the warring factions apart. ECOFORCE was renamed the Forces of ECOWAS and had by November 2003 increased to 1,383. Earlier in May 2003, the UN Security Council established the UN Mission in Côte d'Ivoire (MINUCI). The council also undertook to deploy military officers to work with the French and the forces of ECOWAS (Adebajo 2004b, 300). In the meantime, key provisions of Linas-Marcoussis remained unimplemented. In July 2004 ECOWAS, OAU and leaders of Ivorian factions met in Accra, Ghana, and produced what came to be known as the Accra III Accord. The objective of this accord was to encourage the factions to implement the Linas-Marcoussis agreement. This yielded few results. Similarly, a peace deal between President Laurent Gbagbo and rebel NF leader, Guillaume Soro, in Ouagadougou, Burkina Faso, in March 2007 made little difference in the full implementation of Linas-Marcoussis. That peace in Ivory Coast remains tenuous is reflected in the January 2010 dissolution of the Independent Electoral Commission (IEC) by the president on allegations of fraud. Laurent Gbagbo also dissolved the government. Elections, which were key to peace in Ivory Coast and originally scheduled for October 2005, were postponed to 29 November 2010. This, too, was postponed indefinitely in March 2010 on account of inauspicious electoral conditions. Laurent Gbagbo, the interim leader, remains president although his term officially ended in 2005. These developments notwithstanding, relative, albeit uneasy, peace has returned to Ivory Coast. This is clearly to the credit of ECOWAS which, acting on behalf of the AU, boldly intervened in what threatened to become a protracted conflict. Elections were eventually held in November 2010, which returned Alassane Ouattara as president.

## Somalia

The interventions in Burundi and Ivory Coast are examples of the AU's relatively more successful efforts in conflict resolution. However, in Somalia and Darfur attempts of the AU in resolving the conflict have, until now, been anything but successful. Somalia has remained without a government since the overthrow of the twenty-two-year old autocratic regime of Mohamed Siyad Barre in 1991 (Saxena 2004). This had two serious implications for the integrity of the Somali state. First, it led to the secession of northern clans in May 1991 to form Somaliland, an enclave yet to receive international recognition as a sovereign state. Second, and more important, Somalia descended into anarchy as rival militias battled for control over Mogadishu. The absence of a central government coupled with a drought in the country spread hunger, disease and violence across Somalia. In December 1992 the US led a UN humanitarian initiative aimed at bringing relief supplies to Somalia. However, Washington withdrew after eight American soldiers were killed by Somali gunmen. American public opinion rose against Washington's Somalia mission after television screens showed the bodies of the dead Americans being dragged through the streets of Mogadishu (Wheeler and Bellamy 2001, 480). Earlier in April 1992 the UN had established an operation for Somalia – UNISOM I. A force comprising 50 military observers, 350 security personnel and up to 719 military support staff, its mandate was to monitor a ceasefire in Mogadishu. This mandate was expanded under an augmented UNISOM II of 28,000 military and police personnel in March 1993 to secure the environment for dispensing humanitarian assistance throughout Somalia. However, by 1995, UNISOM II had collapsed after suffering massive casualties.

The first African initiative to resolve the Somali crisis was undertaken by the Djibouti-based Intergovernmental Authority on Development (IGAD), which helped conclude a two-year peace process in October 2004. A Transitional Federal Government (TFG) of Somalia was set up and was led by Abdullahi Yusuf Ahmed. The TFG oversaw the election of a 275-member parliamentary body – the transitional federal assembly (TFA) which was based in Nairobi. Following a self-destructive policy of favouring members of his own clan, Ahmed failed to unite Somalia's warring factions. Consequently, he resigned in December 2004, plunging Somalia deeper into uncertainty (Gentleman 2008, A8). Rivalry between the TFG and the Alliance for the Re-Liberation of Somalia (ARS) continued as UN-led initiatives to reconcile them failed. However, in January 2009 a unity government was formed between TFG and ARS, which led to the addition of 200 ARS members and 75 civil society members to the TFA. However, before the authority of the TFA–ARS government could be consolidated, Mogadishu was overrun by the Islamic Courts Union (ICU), an opposition Islamist organization, previously controlling much of southern Somalia.

By mid-2006 the ICU had established firm control over Mogadishu, governing by sharia law and spreading its authority in all directions of the country. The ascendency of the ICU sent waves of discomfort to the West and especially the US, which had perceived Somalia as a haven for terrorists and the ICU as proxy of al-Qaeda (Baregu 2008). At the behest of the US, which also provided aerial and logistical support, Ethiopian troops entered Somalia in support of the beleaguered TFG. The AU scored an own goal when it endorsed the Ethiopian operation to dislodge a regime, albeit Islamist and radical, which was gradually bringing some semblance of order to an otherwise chaotic country. The historical hostility between Ethiopia and Somalia meant the former had ventured into a hostile territory; Ethiopian soldiers became targets of warlords and militia attacks. Nevertheless, by the end of December 2006, the Ethiopians had evicted ICU from Mogadishu and other commercial areas. The AU made another attempt at resolving the conflict in January 2007 with the PSC's establishment of a peacekeeping African Union Mission in Somalia (AMISOM). This was mandated to support the TFG, implement a security plan and secure a safe environment for the delivery of humanitarian aid. This mandate was approved by the UN Security Council which repeatedly extended it beyond the initial six months. One of AMISOM's challenges was getting African states to pledge and contribute troops. AMISOM currently has just over 5,000 of the 7,650 combat forces (besides support personnel) originally earmarked for the operation.[2] The AU's inability to secure additional troops, coupled with a weak, ill-equipped and poorly trained Somali force has left AMISOM and the TFG in jeopardy. In spite of UN support and many agreements between the TFG and various Islamist groups, little progress had been made by mid-2010 towards resolving the conflict. Ending the crisis and establishing a stable central government in Somalia remains a major headache for the AU.

### Darfur

The intervention in Darfur represents yet another example of a failed conflict resolution initiative by the AU. A deeply fractured society along regional, religious and racial lines, conflicts have not been new to Sudan. In 2003 two rebel groups – the Sudan Liberation Movement Army (SLM/A) and the Justice and Equality Movement (JEM) – based in the Darfur region rose in arms against the Arab-dominated Sudanese government. SLM/A and JEM accused Khartoum of oppression and marginalization of non-Arab populations in the region. Fighting alongside the Sudanese government was the Janjaweed, a militia group drawn largely from camel-herding Arab nomads. The conflict has claimed 200,000 lives and displaced more than 1.2 million people as combined government and Janjaweed onslaughts attempted to annihilate the SLM/A and JEM (UN News Center 12 June 2007). The conflict and its attendant population displacements caught international attention when in a report to the Senate Foreign Relations Committee on 9 September 2004, former US Secretary of State, Colin Powell, described Khartoum and Janjaweed atrocities, including widespread killings, torture and rape, against black populations in Darfur as amounting to genocide (Kessler and Lynch 2004, A01). With memories of mass atrocities and acts of genocide in Bosnia and Herzegovina and Rwanda still fresh, the international community had to act to prevent a repeat of Rwanda, or something similar, from happening. Having declared an intention in the Constitutive Act to intervene in a country on grounds of genocide, the AU was morally compelled to end the conflict through some form of intervention.

The continent's response to the Darfur conflict was the establishment of the AU Mission in Sudan (AMIS), a peacekeeping force in 2004. By mid-2005, the number of troops under AMIS had grown to 7,000 with a budget of $450 million. Its mandate was to ensure the integrity of the humanitarian ceasefire agreement signed on 8 April 2004 among the warring factions, to protect civilians, secure a safe environment for the delivery of relief supplies and help return internally displaced persons (IDPs) (Boshoff 2005). By October 2007, AMIS had increased to 9,000. Despite the increase in troop numbers, AMIS remained, for a large part, too small, poorly equipped and under-resourced to cover the entire Darfur region, an area the size of Texas or Spain. Initial attempts by the UN to augment AMIS with extra-African peacekeepers were thwarted by the Sudanese government. Khartoum opposed the AMIS expansion plan presumably on the basis that fears of such a force would not only weaken its authority in Darfur, but would also, given American accusation of it as a sponsor of international terrorism, aim at regime change in the country. However, after satisfying itself with clarifications on the mandate, size and nature of its deployment, in particular assurances that Sudan's sovereignty would not be compromised, Khartoum agreed on 12 June 2007 to accept the proposal for the deployment of a hybrid AU–UN force – UNAMID (United Nations 2007).

The establishment of UNAMID was approved by UN Security Council Resolution 1769 on 3 July 2007. It was to have an initial mandate of twelve months and was to ensure the safe delivery of humanitarian assistance. UNAMID was to run on a monthly budget of $106 million and was to be a force of 26,000 made up of military personnel, police units and civilian support staff.[3] UNAMID was expected to be in place by December 2007. At the end of April 2010, 21,993 of the projected 26,000 forces were in place in Darfur.[4] UNAMID presence made some difference in Darfur. A joint statement by concerned NGOs regarding the operation of UNAMID in July 2009 acknowledged an improvement in the security situation in Darfur. The NGOs applauded UNAMID's expeditious response to fighting between Janjaweed and SLM/A–JEM, the greater measure of protection enjoyed by civilians and the ease with which aid could be dispensed in refugee camps and in communities. The NGO report, however, noted that UNAMID could still do more. The Khartoum government systematically targeted humanitarian organizations. On 4 March 2009, Khartoum callously expelled thirteen international aid organizations and shut down three locally based human rights agencies, women centres and gender-based violence programmes.[5] The Darfur conflict remains far from being resolved. The 11 April 2010 national elections thought to mark the beginning of a new chapter in Darfur were boycotted by Sudan's leading opposition party candidate, Yasir Arman, over concerns of voter fraud and insecurity in Darfur (Baldauf 2010). The opposition boycott and questionable legitimacy of the post-election Khartoum government are certain to prolong the uncertainties in Darfur.

Moreover, the indictment of al-Bashir by the Hague-based International Criminal Court (ICC) on war crimes and crimes against humanity and the addition on 12 July 2010 of genocide to the charges may impact negatively on the AU's and its efforts in resolving the Darfur conflict. So far, the thirty AU signatories to the ICC are sharply divided over the indictment. On the one hand, one camp comprising Libya, Zimbabwe, along with former South African President, Thabo Mbeki, has remained sympathetic towards Bashir. Prioritizing political expediency over justice, Mbeki, the AU's appointed chairperson of the Committee of Eminent Persons to resolve the Darfur conflict, tried without success in 2009 to persuade the UN Security Council to drop Bashir's charges for a year. Mbeki argued that attempts at arresting the Sudanese leader would jeopardize AU's efforts in resolving the conflict. On the other hand majority of the AU members have either remained silent or like Jacob Zuma of South Africa and Yuweri Museveni of Uganda, have been openly critical of Bashir's alleged atrocities in Darfur and supportive of the ICC indictment. Museveni has, in fact, indicated his willingness to deliver Bashir to the ICC if given the chance (Pateno 2008). The polarization of the AU over Bashir's indictment deprives the organization of the required unity of purpose needed to address the Darfur crisis. Mr Bashir's reluctance to engineer a quick resolution of the Darfur conflict by cramping down on the Janjaweed militia and withdrawing government troops from the region is, perhaps, his hope of using it to extract concessions from the ICC and the international community which is getting increasingly frustrated by the persistence of the conflict. If this is the case, then the insistence of the ICC to press ahead with charges against the Sudanese leader is certain to make the AU's efforts in the Darfur crisis more difficult.

## Challenges facing AU conflict resolution initiatives

The difficulty of speedily resolving the conflicts in Somalia and Darfur is indicative of the many structural challenges facing the AU and in particular its conflict resolution efforts. A visible challenge is the lack of adequate finances and logistics. In 2004, the budget of the AU stood at $158 million, with $95.2 million devoted to peacekeeping and security operations. In that year the AU suffered a shortfall, and when the budget was reduced to $54 million, in 2007, with $35.7 million expected from external sources, a shortfall still occurred (Adekeye 2008, 135–6). Essentially, the lack of funds has resulted from member states' failure to pay their financial contributions to the AU and its Peace Fund. During the Burundi operation, the AU relied on countries contributing troops to fund their soldiers for one year. This placed the entire financial cost of AMIB on South Africa. The yearly budget for the operation was estimated at $165 million (Boshoff 2003). Inadequate financing severely compromised the AU's PKOs. The UN Secretary-General was quoted as warning in his report on AMIB that 'the financial and logistical constraints under which AMIB operate[d] prevent[ed] the force from fully implementing its mandate'

(Svensson 2008, 16). Both AMISOM I (Somalia) and AMIS (Darfur) were hampered by poor funding and inadequate logistics. Robert Feldman, a major in the US Foreign Military office, bemoaned AMIS's lack of equipment:

> The AMIS has no combat aircraft. Its fleet is mainly transport helicopters and a few Antonov AN-24 turboprops that are not equipped to serve as bombers. Compounding AMIS difficulties are Sudanese restrictions that often prevent its helicopters from flying, and allow only civilian pilots to fly the aircrafts.
>
> (Feldman 2008, 269)

Feldman lamented AMIS's lack of combat readiness and inferior firepower to the Sudanese military and the Janjaweed. The inability of the AU to equip peacekeepers sufficiently has disinclined states to commit troops, fearing that the lack of adequate combat equipment places them at risk.

The AU has in recent years relied on funding and logistics from external actors to execute its conflict resolution plans (Saxena 2004, 186). However, heavy dependence on external actors in conflict resolution has implications. Among others, it incapacitates the AU from timeously addressing a conflict. Additionally, it vitiates the AU's efforts to craft African solutions and compromises the independence of the AU as an actor in conflict resolution. The latter effect was amply revealed when at the behest of the US, Ethiopian forces evicted ICU, which was more or less restoring some order in Somalia, on grounds of its Islamist, radical and anti-American stance. During the brief period of ICU rule (from July to December 2006), Mogadishu which had been a scene of intense and bloody war between warring Islamist factions enjoyed a period of relative calm. The demise of the ICU at the hands of Ethiopian forces returned Somalia into chaos which AMISOM has struggled to mitigate. Somalia's political landscape has, since the withdrawal of Ethiopian troops in January 2009, been dominated by another radical Islamist group, Al-Shabaab. While attempting to consolidate its authority by fighting rival groups, Al-Shabaab also targets AMISOM troops both in Somalia and in their home countries. The latest of these attacks was the double bombing of Kampala which killed over sixty civilians who were part of a crowd watching a World Cup football game on 11 July 2010 (Khalif 2010).

The inability of the AU to translate key principles into action represents another challenge in its conflict resolution efforts. The principle of interference guaranteed by Article 4(h) of the Constitutive Act calling on the organization to intervene in a country in cases of gross human right abuses, has remained largely rhetorical. The AU has not shown sufficient will to chastise leaders who violate human rights. The AU did not, for example, consider the situation in Darfur grave enough to authorize action. It was only when the US Congress voted to rank the situation as genocide, did the AU take action. Even then the AU declined to label the atrocities visited by the Sudanese government forces and the Janjaweed on the local black population as genocide, preferring to see it as a normal domestic conflict. And when the ICC issued an arrest warrant for the Sudanese leader to be tried for genocide, the AU under the chairmanship of Colonel Gaddafi of Libya, passed a resolution to suspend its cooperation with the court. Also, in a typical AU style, the organization endorsed the 11 April 2010 Sudanese election as free and fair when international observers depicted it otherwise. Similarly, the AU has failed to prevail on Robert Mugabe to force reforms in Zimbabwe and, in fact, congratulated Nigerian leader, Umaru Yar Adua and Togolese leader, Faure Eyadéma who came to power through fraudulent elections and who as a result brought their respective countries on the brink of conflict. As well, Andry Rajoelina of Madagascar remained defiant after the AU imposed sanctions on his regime for failing to form a unity government with Marc Ravalomanana, whose elected government he violently deposed in March 2009. The AU lacks credible instruments of compulsion and does not seem able or willing to take any further action beyond the sanctions imposed.

The vagueness of Article 4(h) has not helped either. Article 4(h) lacks details and clarity on how intervention is to be carried out. Presumably this will be left to the PSC assisted by its auxiliary institutions – the Council of the Wise, the MSC and the CEWS – to make the call. However, as Cilliers and Sturman (2004) argue, the internal politics among countries constituting the PSC may undermine speedy consensus on when genocide, war crimes or crimes against humanity are deemed to have occurred.

Equally problematic is the AU's heavy reliance on military intervention as the dominant tool of conflict resolution. Military interventions have critical budgetary implications. According to the Washington-based Carnegie Commission on Preventing Deadly Conflict (CCPDC), the international community spent $200 billion on conflict management in the 1990s on seven major interventions – Bosnia and Herzegovina, Somalia, Rwanda, Haiti, the Persian Gulf, Cambodia and El Salvador. It noted further that $130 billion could have been saved through more effective pre-conflict approaches (CCPDC 2007). Yet, there are also human costs associated with military interventions. Reports indicate that by the close of 2009, AMISOM (Somalia) and AMIS (Darfur) lost fifty-one and thirty-three peacekeepers respectively. These statistics excluded civilian casualties and wounded peacekeepers. Humanitarian interventions and PKOs require a great deal of preparation and logistics. In Ivory Coast, Darfur and Somalia, the AU relied on logistical support from external partners. An organization in desperate need of funds and logistics, the AU needs to strengthen its CEWS and other preventive mechanisms to avoid the costly pressures of interventions.

Related to the reliance on military solutions is the added consequence of failing to address the root causes of conflicts. In general conflicts are symptomatic of deep seated structural, political and economic causes. Ending a conflict by intervention and getting warring factions to sign ceasefire agreements amount only to addressing a symptom, leaving unresolved the causes beneath. The failure to address structural problems has seen over 50 per cent of post-conflict countries relapse into war (Huggins and Clover 2005). Often, elections are hastily organized in the hope that a new democratic dispensation would self-correct the causes of conflict and ensure stability. In some cases, such elections are designed to provide an exit strategy for the intervening force. In reality, elections have frequently failed to guarantee post-conflict stability either because they were flawed or because elected governments failed to address the root causes of the conflict. In July 1997 ECOMOG supervised post-conflict elections in Liberia, which returned rebel leader, Charles Taylor, as president. The successful elections enabled ECOMOG, which had helped to end violence, to leave. However, by 2000, Liberia had relapsed into full-scale war. Similarly, the 29 March 2008 Zimbabwean elections hardly abated the country's protracted political crisis. In both Liberia and Zimbabwe, the root causes of the crisis were never addressed. In cases where conflicts have resulted from disputed elections the AU has resorted to the formation of inclusive power-sharing governments. The record of Africa's unity governments (UGs) in ensuring post-conflict and post-election stability, however, remains dubious. Besides being a union of enemies, UGs are marriages of convenience where there is everything but love. Artificial and unnatural, therefore, parties in a UG have looked on each other with suspicion and mistrust as shown by the fragility of the 2008 and 2009 unity governments in Kenya and Zimbabwe respectively.[6]

## Conclusion: the future of the AU in conflict resolution

The AU has excited hopes of succeeding where the OAU failed; in particular of being more robust in resolving Africa's conflicts. In principle, commitment to conflict resolution has been demonstrated by the Constitutive Act of the AU. Among other things the Act provided for the intervention of the AU in countries where genocide, crimes against humanity and war crimes are taking place. This was a groundbreaking innovation given that the OAU remained conservative and stuck to the old and partially discredited principle of non-interference in the internal affairs of states. The Constitutive Act also established a 15-member PSC that would exercise overall powers over issues of peace and security. In turn, the protocol on the PSC provided for the establishment of an African standby force (ASF) that would be composed of the subregional standby forces from the five regions of Africa: northern, southern, eastern, western and central. Other subsidiary structures under the PSC were the Council of the Wise and the MSC.

The AU's peace and security architecture has had some success as reflected in the largely successful interventions in the conflicts in Ivory Coast and Burundi. In these cases the AU was able to mitigate the conflict through the conclusion of peace agreements among the warring factions, and in the case of Burundi, supervised elections jointly with the UN. In Ivory Coast, elections have been postponed at least twice due to unfavourable electoral conditions, leaving the country in an uneasy peace. Yet, the AU's record at conflict resolution has been marred by its failure to end the conflicts in Darfur and Somalia. The conflict in Somalia remains unresolved notwithstanding the intervention of AMISOM.

Yet, the difficulty in ending the Somali and Darfur conflicts underscores fundamental challenges facing the AU's conflict resolution mechanism. The challenges also inform the prospects for the AU to become a credible actor in conflict resolution in the future. In addition to the challenges noted, external factors will continue to shape the AU's conflict resolution agenda especially if this is to be done through military intervention. A notable factor is the growing global disdain for regimes undermining human rights, human security and the rule of law and the consequent adoption of the responsibility to protect. This has informed the new AU thrust to intervene in states.

The US-led global war on terror will also shape the AU's conflict resolution efforts. Already at the behest of the US, the AU has encouraged its member states to commit to the war by passing anti-terrorism legislations (Akokpari 2008b, 81–2). Kenya and Ethiopia, for example, have not only passed anti-terror laws, but have also become strategic regional allies of the US because of the threat of terror from East Africa and the Horn. It was under this strategic partnership that Ethiopia intervened in Somalia to evict the radical Islamist ICU. However, the compulsion for intervention generated by terrorism may make the AU to be selective, intervening only in countries which guarantee American support. A potential danger of being influenced by external developments is that the waxing AU's conflict resolution momentum may wane if new global developments emerge to displace and replace current issues in importance.

In the final analysis the AU's conflict resolution credentials will remain paltry until it addresses the perennial financial problems facing it, reduces its reliance on military approaches to conflict resolution and on external actors, increases its will-power to translate rhetoric into reality, and focuses on addressing the root causes of conflicts rather than just ending them with the signing of peace agreements. We look forward to the day the AU becomes a truly credible actor in conflict resolution.

## Notes

1 The Panel of the Wise was appointed in December 2007 and is to serve a three-year term. Members of the panel include Salim Ahmed Salim, former Secretary-General of the Organization of African Unity; Elisabeth Pognon, President of the Constitutional Court in Benin; Ahmed Ben Bella, former President of Algeria; Miguel Trovoada, former President of Sao Tome and Principe; and Brigalia Bam, Head of South Africa's Independent Electoral Commission.
2 The initial plan was to have 9 battalions each with an 850-combat force (available online at: www.africa-union.org/root/AU/AUC/Departments/PSC/AMISOM/amisom.htm; accessed 20 March 2010).
3 UNAMID force of 26,000 was composed as follows: 19,555 military personnel; 3,772 police and a further 19 police units of 140 personnel each. See United Nations Security Council Resolution 1769 S-RES-1769(2007) page 3 on 31 July 2007 (retrieved 18 August 2008).
4 See United Nations Department of Public information (available online at: www.un.org/en/peacekeeping/missions/unamid/facts.shtml; accessed 20 March 2010).
5 See 'Building a Better UNAMID: A Joint NGO Statement' (available online at: www.darfurconsortium.org/member_publications/2009/July/ST.BuildingaBetterUNAMID.093109.pdf; accessed 20 March 2010).
6 Conceptually, the issue of unity (or power-sharing) governments is treated, from different perspectives, in this volume by Wolff (Chapter 1), Reilly (Chapter 2) and Roeder (Chapter 3).

## References

Adebajo, A. 2004a 'Introduction', in A. Adebajo and I. Rashid (eds.), *West Africa Security Challenges*. Boulder, CO: Lynne Rienner.
—— 2004b 'Pax West Africana? Regional Security Mechanisms', in A. Adebajo and I. Rashid (eds.), *West Africa Security Challenges*. Boulder, CO: Lynne Rienner.
—— 2008 'The Peacekeeping Travails of the AU', in J. Akokpari, T. Murithi and A. Ndinga-Mvumba (eds.), *The African Union and Its Institutions*. Johannesburg: Jacana Press.
Adebajo, A. and Landsberg, C. 2000 'Back to the Future: UN Peacekeeping in Africa', *International Peacekeeping* 7(4): 161–88
African Union 2000 *Constitutive Act of the African Union*. Addis Ababa: African Union.
Akokpari, J. 1999 'Changing with the Tide: The Shifting orientations of Foreign Policies in sub-Saharan Africa', *Nordic Journal of African Studies* 8(1): 22–38
—— 2008a 'You don't belong here: citizenship and Africa's conflicts – reflections on Ivory Coast', in A. Nhema and P. Zeleza (eds.), *Roots of African Conflicts: The Causes and Costs*. Oxford: James Currey.
—— 2008b 'Human Rights and Human Security in Post-9/11 Africa', in J. Akokpari and D. Zimbler (eds.), *Africa's Evolving Human Rights Architecture*. Johannesburg: Jacana Press.
Baldauf, S. 2010 'President Bashir's chief rival boycotts Sudan election', *Christian Science Monitor* 1 April.
Baregu, M. 2008 'The United States "Global War of Terror", Human Rights and the Responsibility to Protect in Africa', in J. Akokpari and D. Zimbler (eds.), *Africa's Evolving Human Rights Architecture*. Johannesburg: Jacana Press.
Boshoff, H. 2003 'Burundi: The Africa Union's First Mission', African Security Analysis Programme, Situational Report, 10 June 2003 (available online at: www.iss.co.za/uploads/burundi1june03.pdf; accessed 26 March 2010).
—— 2005 'The African Union Mission in Sudan: Technical and operational dimensions', *African Security Review* 14(3): 57–60.

Carnegie Commission on Preventing Deadly Conflict – CCPDC 1997 *Preventing Deadly Conflict-Final Report*, Washington, DC (available online at: www.wilsoncenter.org/subsites/ccpdc/pubs/rept97/finfr.htm; accessed 4 April 2010).

Cilliers, J. and Sturman, K. 2004 'Challenges Facing the AU's Peace and Security Council', *African Security Review* 13(1): 97–104.

Dersso, S. 2009 'The Role and Place of the African Standby Force within the African Peace and Security Architecture', Institute for Security Studies, ISS Paper.

Feldman, R. L. 2008 'Problems Plaguing the African Union Peacekeeping Forces', *Defense and Security Analysis* 24(3): 267–97.

Foltz, W. 1991 'The Organisation of African Unity and the resolution of Africa's conflicts', in F. M. Dengand and W. Zartman (eds.), *Conflict Resolution in Africa*. Washington, DC: Brookings Institute.

Gentleman, J. 2008 'Somalia's Fate Still Unclear After Leader Quits', *New York Times* 30 December.

Harsch, E. 2003 'Foreign Investment on Africa's Agenda', *Africa Recovery* 17(2): 12–13.

Howard, L. M. 2008 *UN Peacekeeping in Civil Wars*. New York: Cambridge University Press.

Huggins, C. and Clover, J. 2005 *From the Ground Up: Land Rights, Conflict and Peace in Sub-Saharan Africa*. Pretoria: Institute for Security Studies.

Human Rights Watch 2008 'Burundi: Release Civilians Detained without Charge' (available online at: www.hrw.org/english/docs/2008/05/29/burund18974.htm; accessed 4 March 2010).

Jonah, J. O. C. 1994 'The OAU: Peacekeeping and Conflict Resolution', in Y. El-Ayouty (ed.), *The Organisation of African Unity After Thirty Years*. Westport, CT: Praeger.

Khalif, A. 2010 'Al-Shabaab attack in Kampala not entirely unexpected', *Daily Nation* (Nairobi), 14 July.

Kessler, G. and Lynch, C. 2004 'US Calls Killings in Sudan Genocide', *Washington Post* 10 September (available online at: www.washingtonpost.com/wp-dyn/articles/A8364–2004Sep9.html; accessed 1 April 2010).

Mathews, K. 2008 'Renaissance of Pan-Africanism: The AU and the New Pan-Africanists', in J. Akokpari, T. Murithi and A. Ndinga-Mvumba (eds.), *The African Union and Its Institutions*, Johannesburg: Jacana Press.

Murithi, T. 2005 *The African Union: Pan-Africanism, Peacebuilding and Development*, Burlington: Ashgate.

—— 2008 'The African Union's Evolving Role in Peace Operations: The African Union Mission in Burundi, the African Union Mission in Sudan and the African Union Mission in Somalia', *African Security Review* 17(1): 70–82

Mwanasali, M. 2008 'From Non-Interference to Non-Indifference: The Emerging Doctrine of Conflict Prevention in Africa', in J. Akokpari, T. Murithi and A. Ndinga-Mvumba (eds.), *The African Union and Its Institutions*. Johannesburg: Jacana Press.

Okoth, G. 1987 'The OAU and the Uganda-Tanzania War, 1978–89', *Journal of African Studies* 14(3): 151–62.

—— 2008 'Conflict Resolution in Africa: The Role of the OAU and the AU', in A. Nhema and P. Zeleza (eds.), *The Resolution of African Conflicts: The Management of Post Conflict Reconstruction*. Oxford: James Currey.

Organisation of African Unity – OAU 1963 *Charter of the Organization of African Unity*. Addis Ababa: OAU.

Pateno, S. 2008 'Omar al-Bashir indictment taking toll', *Sudan Tribune* 7 August (available online at: www.sudantribune.com/spip.php?article28181; accessed 14 July 2010).

Potgieter, J. 2009 'Peacekeeping Forces for Peace Support Operations in Africa' (available online at: www.apsta-africa.org/news/article040809.php; accessed 1 April 2010).

Sarkin, J. 2008 'Humanitarian intervention and the Responsibility to Protect in Africa', in J. Akokpari and D. Zimbler (eds.), *Africa's Evolving Human Rights Architecture*. Johannesburg: Jacana Press.

Saxena, S. C. 2004 'The African Union: African Giant Step Towards Continental Unity', in J. M. Mbaku (ed.), *Africa at the Cross Roads: Between Regionalism and Globalisation*. Wesport, CT: Praeger.

Sesay, A. 1982 'The OAU and Continental Order', in T. Shaw and S. Ojo (eds.), *Africa and the International Political System*. Washington, DC: University Press of America.

Svensson, E. 2008 'The African Union Mission in Burundi: Lessons Learned from the African Union's first Peace Operation' (available online at: www.foi.se/upload/projects/Africa/FOI2561_AMIB.pdf; accessed 15 March 2010).

United Nations 2007 'Sudan accepts hybrid United Nations-African Union peacekeeping force in Darfur' (available online at: www.un.org/apps/news/story.asp?NewsID=22881; accessed 2 April 2010).

Weiss, T. G., Evans G. J, Hubert, D. and Sahnoun, M. 2001 *The Responsibility to Protect: Research, Bibliography, Background: Supplementary volume to the Report of the International Commission on Intervention and State Sovereignty*. Ottawa: International Development Research Centre.

Wheeler, N. and Bellamy, A. 2001 'Humanitarian Intervention and World Politics', in J. Baylis and S. Smith (eds.), *The Globalisation of World Politics*, 2nd edn. Oxford: Oxford University Press.

# 9 Political engagement, mediation and the non-governmental sector

*Katia Papagianni*

## Introduction

Mediation and peacemaking have traditionally been the preserve of diplomats, governments and intergovernmental organizations. Settling internal disputes and designing institutional arrangements that convince belligerents to give up their arms and to compete through the political process are high-powered political activities. They can influence the way power is shared and exercised within a country in the long term. This chapter defines mediation loosely as political engagement by a third party aiming to assist the resolution of political disputes among parties to a conflict. It is the kind of engagement that aims to open up dialogue among adversaries, strengthen political processes and create the political space within which parties can discuss long-term reconstruction, development, constitutional and reconciliation issues. This chapter discusses the role of international non-governmental actors in such national-level political engagement. Non-governmental organizations (NGOs) are prominent actors in a number of international policy fields, including human rights, humanitarian affairs and environmental affairs. Their influence and independent contribution to political outcomes has been well documents by scholars (Keck and Sikkink 1999; Risse *et al.* 1999). This chapter asks whether, and if so why, non-governmental actors have also gained access to mediation activities that go to the core of state sovereignty and power. Recognizing that the contribution of the non-governmental sector to conflict management is extremely varied and specialized, the chapter will not discuss the extensive work of NGOs at the community and grass-roots level. It will, rather, focus on their work on national-level political processes.

In the past twenty years, a variety of actors have entered the mediation and conflict management field in an effort to assist conflict parties give up violent confrontation and engage in political processes. The incidence of mediation activities and the number of negotiated agreements signed with the assistance of third parties have increased dramatically (Human Security Centre 2006). The United Nations (UN) remains a major actor,[1] while regional organizations such as the African Union (AU) and the Economic Community of West African States (ECOWAS) are becoming increasingly active in their respective regions.[2] Also, individual governments continue being engaged in mediation efforts. The examples of Norway's engagement in Sri Lanka for most of the last decade, Malaysia's contribution to the peace process between the government of the Philippines and the Moro Islamic Liberation Front (MILF), and Turkey's involvement in the Middle East are three among many. Furthermore, eminent personalities sometimes work as mediators as for example Kofi Annan in Kenya in early 2008 and George Mitchell in Northern Ireland. In addition to the above, development actors make important

contributions: the development arms of governments and intergovernmental organizations such as the UN and the European Union (EU) and civil society organizations carry
out development projects as well as reconciliation, dialogue and community level conflict
resolution projects. The roles of and relationships among these actors differ depending
on whether a clearly identified mediation process and mediation team are in place and on
whether a coordination mechanism is in place. Competition and disagreements are not
uncommon among them, especially in the many cases where the parties have not agreed
on a mediator.

Each of the above mediation actors face limitations in terms of the situations in which
they can engage and the methods and tools they can utilize. NGOs tend to contribute to
conflict resolution efforts mostly in intrastate conflicts. Their niche derives from the
limitations of other actors and from their ability to fill in the gaps in international mediation capacity. The types of organizations the chapter includes in its reference group are
international NGOs such as the Atlanta-based Carter Center, the Geneva-based Centre
for Humanitarian Dialogue (HD Centre), the London-based Conciliation Resources (CR),
the Hague-based Kreddha, the Helsinki-based Conflict Management Initiative (CMI),
the lay Catholic community of Sant'Egidio, the Berlin-based Berghof Foundation for
Peace Support, the South Africa-based African Centre for the Constructive Resolution
of Disputes (ACCORD) and other organizations which have engaged in national-level
political processes with the goal of facilitating the resolution of disputes.[3]

NGOs carry out a variety of activities. First, they initiate contact with armed groups,
explore their positions and their interest in negotiations, and maintain communication
with them while the fighting continues. Second, they facilitate confidential communication and the exchange of messages between governments and armed oppositions, often
while the fighting continues. Third, NGOs facilitate confidential face-to-face talks
between governments and armed opposition groups at the early stages of a conflict resolution process aiming to reach agreements on formal talks as well as on confidence
building measures such as ceasefires or exchange of prisoners. Fourth, NGOs support
peace processes led by governmental or intergovernmental actors by offering various
forms of technical assistance. Fifth, less frequently, NGOs may manage a public peace
process leading to a peace agreement. This list of NGO activities is of course not
exhaustive. As mentioned above, the chapter does not address the myriad of reconciliation and peacebuilding activities NGOs routinely carry out which contribute significantly
to conflict resolution efforts. Given the fact that many of the above activities are often
confidential, research faces difficulties in quantifying them and evaluating them. The
number of public mediation efforts at any given moment is limited. However, activities
such as the ones listed above which explore the potential or prepare for mediation are
widespread. The fact that practitioners work with varying levels of discretion contributes
to the difficulty in developing data to track its incidence.

The chapter makes four arguments. First, NGOs contribute to conflict management by
engaging in activities that states and international organizations cannot as easily engage
in, including assisting dialogue efforts in intrastate conflicts, maintaining contact and
discussions with armed groups, including groups which are proscribed by powerful
states. Second, NGOs tend to encourage national ownership of the peace process and
inclusion of as many national actors as possible in the process. They tend to advocate
against solutions imposed by international actors and in favour of nationally generated
solutions. This is often in contrast to the approach of states and intergovernmental
organizations, which are guided by their interests and tend to influence, or at least try to

influence, the content of agreements. Third, the chapter argues that the non-governmental sector has a solid track record when it comes to facilitating early contact among belligerents and preparing the ground for negotiations leading to peace agreements. Private mediation actors have not yet succeeded as much to occupy the ground of high-level diplomacy where they convene parties to the negotiating table for formal peace talks leading to the signing of agreements. Related to the above, the fourth argument the chapter makes is that often NGOs are effective in their work when they work closely with states which not only fund them and therefore make their work possible, but also support them politically. NGOs aiming to participate in national level conflict resolution efforts, therefore, try to strike a delicate balance between being independent from state power in the eyes of the parties, but being able to bring the resources and leverage of state power when needed.

The chapter begins with a discussion of the various factors that enable private mediators to become engaged in conflict management efforts as well as the limitations facing their work. It continues with a discussion of the contribution of NGOs to settlements. It concludes by arguing that the practice of mediation currently encompasses a number of diverse activities which do not always fit the traditional understanding of the term, namely that of a third party assisting conflict parties to overcome their differences through a clearly identified negotiation process. Many of the activities private mediators as well as intergovernmental organizations and governments engage in explore the ground for mediation, facilitate contacts among parties and enable dialogue, often in informal settings (Griffiths and Whitfield 2010). This wide variety of activities, ranging from preliminary contacts and preparations for talks to formal negotiation processes, means that engagement is a long-term process and that mediation actors more and more need to collaborate and support each other's efforts.

## Why is there a role for NGOs and what are its limitations?

One of the key contributions of NGOs to conflict resolution is that they are able to carry out activities that governments and intergovernmental organizations cannot as easily undertake.[4] The Carter Centre, for example, 'conceives itself as a useful alternative channel, available when formal restrictions or pragmatic policy considerations preclude actions by IGOs [intergovernmental organizations] and governments. Many conflicts fall outside purview of the legal mandate of IGOs, such as the United Nations, or fall into areas where official negotiations by the United States would be contrary to established policy and practice, but not contrary to US interests' (Taulbee and Creekmore 2003, 157).

There are several factors creating this niche for private mediation actors. First, as William Zartman writes in this volume (Chapter 4), in the post-Cold War period, the majority of conflicts have been civil wars as opposed to interstate conflicts. This has opened up possibilities of NGO involvement due to governments' concerns about sovereignty, confidentiality and impartiality of the third party. Governments, especially governments of strong states facing armed oppositions, tend to refuse the interference of prominent outsiders in their internal affairs and may prefer the assistance of quiet, private third parties who can ensure confidentiality and do not bring their own interests to the peace process.[5] A related concern of governments is to avoid bestowing legitimacy to the armed group by engaging them in a formal negotiation process led by a prominent international actor. Governments and international organizations 'may be constrained from acting effectively as they may be wary of conveying status and legitimacy on "rebels"' (Hottinger 2005). NGOs, on the other hand, do not bestow legitimacy to rebels in the same way the UN or another state would.

State concerns about sovereignty, confidentiality and the impartiality of the third party are linked.[6] Confidentiality is of paramount importance especially when talks are taking place while the fighting continues.[7] A state or an intergovernmental third party, such as the UN, inevitably attracts public and media attention in a way that NGOs do not.[8] Private mediation actors can more easily work under the radar and quietly facilitate communications between governments and armed opposition. Related to this is the fact that private mediation actors, most of the time, do not have a political agenda in a particular conflict and therefore do not have an interest to leak information in order to influence the negotiations one way or another. Griffiths emphasizes that this is a crucial characteristic of private mediation actors: 'The HD Centre has no political personality. No interests. If we started having interests, we would lose our raison d'etre.'[9] Hottinger makes a similar argument: 'lacking geopolitical interests and stakes in the conflict, [NGOs] may be more impartial, forming relationships with a wider variety of actors in the conflict, and hearing things officials actors do not' (Hottinger 2005, 2). Fabienne Hara also points out the limitations of official mediators when she writes that, in Burundi, 'all official mediators have been suspect of partiality' (Hara 1999, 144).

Importantly and related to the confidentiality concern, NGO activity is 'deniable': a government can easily disassociate from it without damaging bilateral or multilateral relations. Agreeing to the assistance of a non-governmental third party, allows governments to retain the ability to control the negotiations and to back out from negotiations with a relatively small political price apart of course from the price of potential retaliation by the armed opposition. This makes private mediators particularly vulnerable third parties. They are 'tolerated [by governments] as long as they remain useful'.[10] Governments could of course use their own intelligence services to build communication channels with an insurgency and they frequently do. However, when intelligence services are involved, it is not always easy to deny engagement in talks, should the information become public. Furthermore, governments may not trust their intelligence services because, for example, they may leak the fact of talks to opposition parties or the media out of political motivations. All these concerns strengthen the logic of conflict parties, and especially governments, seeking the assistance of a private and discreet mediation actor.

The example of Indonesia is apt here. Indonesia accepted the HD Centre and the Conflict Management Initiative as third parties in Aceh, but not the UN, ASEAN or another state. Similarly, the Carter Center's effort to restore relations between Uganda and Sudan in 1999, which involved talks with the two governments as well as with the armed groups in south Sudan (SPLA) and northern Uganda (Lord's Resistance Army), were kept quiet in order to ensure the participation of all four sides (Neu 2002). The HD Centre's confidential multi-year mediation work in European and Asian conflicts has entailed different phases of engagement, including exploring both sides' interest in talks, passing messages between the governments and armed groups, and eventually bringing to the negotiating table high-level representatives of both sides. In these cases, official governmental mediators would have been unacceptable for reasons of both sovereignty and confidentiality. It would have been extremely bruising for the governments concerned, if their contacts with the armed groups were to become public, especially in the context of electoral politics. The potential explosiveness of the fact that the governments even contemplated discussions with these groups meant that confidentiality was of paramount importance (*The Economist* 2008).

A second factor creating the political space for private mediation actors in internal conflicts, besides state concerns about sovereignty and confidentiality, is that governments are often unwilling to become involved as third-party mediators in a conflict, if such work risks jeopardizing bilateral relations. Certain tasks, such as engaging in sustained contact and communication with armed groups, are politically sensitive and run the real risk of damaging bilateral relations. Mediation processes are unpredictable, lengthy and often bruising for the third party. The example of Norway's efforts in Sri Lanka is instructive. As Whitfield writes, the Norwegian special envoy managed to build the LTTE's trust in Norway after numerous discussions, which led to a ceasefire in 2002. However, once progress stalled, 'the Norwegians came under increasing criticism for what was perceived as their partiality toward the Tigers. Over time they lost the confidence of the Sri Lankan government. Norway regretted that other international actors were reluctant to engage with the LTTE because of the opportunity lost to develop mutual understanding' (Whitfield 2010). Whitfield continues that:

> mediators who work to develop the trust of armed groups risk being perceived as, or actually becoming, partial to their cause. This is in part a structural issue, in that mediators who assume the role of a channel to the armed group are likely to develop a nuanced understanding of its grievances and demands. They may be called upon to explain them to official actors who do not engage with the armed groups themselves and can therefore risk appearing as their spokespersons.
>
> (Whitfield 2010)

The potential costs, then, for governments' engagement in dialogue and mediation efforts are considerable. Many governments prefer not to find themselves in this role, especially in conflicts where major national interests are not at stake. This is especially so in the context of electoral politics where governments are required to explain the reasons for engagement and report progress in the effectiveness of such engagement.

NGOs, on the other hand, do not need recognition of their work the way governments do. 'The beauty of [organizations such as the HD Centre] is that their mandate is to do what is best for the process. They are free from pressure. They are not required to report progress when there is no progress to report.'[11] Especially NGOs which have established a solid relationship with their donors, do not need to seek quick and frequent successes in their work. This is essential in a business where success is rare and difficult to define. NGOs:

> because [they] do not have constituents that demand success on each involvement, are less reluctant than principal mediators to become engaged. The Carter Center consciously targets difficult conflicts for its mediation efforts and avoid involvement where others seem ready and able to assume the asks.
>
> (Taulbee and Creekmore 2003, 158)

Therefore:

> the Carter Center and other well-established NGOs can afford to try and fail ... A failure does not necessarily undermine their reputations or erode support of relevant

constituencies to the degree that it might for governments ... As long as the Center enjoys the reputation as a useful channel and can maintain the support of its principal funding sources, it does not have to keep a scorecard that measures its efforts solely in terms of short-term outcomes.

(Taulbee and Creekmore 2003, 168)

This means that private mediation actors often have the political space to work in conflicts where governments are not interested in engaging in or situations too difficult and sensitive for governments to engage in. In discussing Sant'Edigio's role in the Mozambique peace process, Bartoli points out 'no single powerful actor had a sufficiently compelling interest in Mozambique to force itself into the negotiations' and that 'Mozambique did not fall under the international spotlight'. As a result, the Mozambique negotiations, 'provided the perfect opportunity to experiment in a very original way with innovative conflict resolution methods ... ' (Bartoli 1999, 260). The corollary of this, however, is that in conflicts where states have a stake and interest in the role of private mediation actors tends to be less pronounced or more controlled by states. Griffiths and Whitfield write that 'independent mediators generally have more access to conflicts of lower strategic priority', although they may 'find openings in high-priority cases ... through partnership or collaboration with official mediators' (Griffiths and Whitfield 2010, 12). This may also influence the relationship between private mediators and donor governments. Griffiths, for example, emphasizes that, in cases where donor governments do not have a core interest at stake, they encourage the HD Centre to become engaged and do not interfere in the day-to-day management of its engagement. However, in cases which are 'closer to their interests, they try to exercise greater control over HD's work'.[12]

A third reason creating the space for private mediation actors in conflict resolution is the fact that non-governmental actors are free to engage with and talk to all conflict parties, even proscribed groups, and to do so in a sustained manner. They of course need to carefully manage their relationships with their donors and the governments in the countries they are active in terms of sharing information with them about such contacts. It is a sensitive question for NGOs when and how to inform their host and donor governments about their contacts with armed groups, and how much information to share while preserving their independence and the trust of the armed groups. However, they are not constrained by domestic politics and the demands of electoral constituencies. In many cases, governments discreetly support the work of private mediators by providing an enabling security environment for such talks to take place. Part of this work entails complicated logistics, meetings and accommodation for parties which profoundly mistrust each other. This often requires security arrangements private actors cannot on their own provide. It also requires visas and travel documents, which only governments can provide. Friendly governments which can facilitate travel and host such meetings are invaluable assets for this work.

Although governments are also able to occasionally meet and discuss with representatives of armed groups active in other countries, even proscribed groups, without NGOs acting as intermediaries, they usually cannot as easily embark on a sustained, long-term engagement or organize regular meetings with such groups. Such engagement is too risky for a government and rarely remains confidential. Furthermore, in some cases, armed groups may not be willing to engage a state as a third party out of a concern that states may have preconceptions about them and be biased towards the state party to the conflict. Thus, the usefulness of private actors: they prepare discreet meetings with difficult groups, try to understand their positions and explore their interest in talks. In certain situations, government representatives may attend, often in their personal capacity. An example of such work is an organization called Conflicts Forum, which attempts to serve as an interlocutor between militant Islamist groups, such as Hamas and Hezbollah, and the West. Similarly, the HD Centre is engaged in confidential projects which enable senior diplomats from Western European states to meet informally with politically problematic groups in third countries. Direct and formal contact with these groups would jeopardize relations with the governments in these third countries. However, such contact is useful in shaping the understanding of politics in these countries and of the positions of these groups by Western officials. This work requires NGOs to strike a balance between being independent from yet close to individual governments. On one hand, a close relationship with certain governments might be seen as an asset by armed groups which are eager to present their case to these governments. On the other hand, it could be a liability in cases where the independence of private actors is compromised in the eyes of these groups.

The niche of NGOs in engaging with armed opposition groups has been strengthened by the increasing complexity of armed groups in the post-Cold War era which requires sustained engagement with them in order to understand them well. This is a phenomenon also identified by Zartman in this volume (Chapter 4). And, indeed, understanding the internal working and motivations of armed groups is crucial to mediators. As Hottinger points out, building a solid understanding of an armed group can take many years. One of the tasks of the mediator is 'to understand [an armed group's] intentions, reasoning, strategy and evolution in such a way as to be in a position to help prevent the situation from deteriorating, or occasionally to help set the venue and agenda within pre-negotiations' (Hottinger 2005, 2). Furthermore, keeping open the channels of communication with armed groups is important in:

> preventing armed groups from falling into total isolation, to the extent that they bury themselves in their own logic, making any form of contact more difficult. It is slow but essential work. An armed group's confidence in a political dialogue cannot be built overnight. It demands a significant investment of time and energy and constant follow-up. It is also complicated, especially as changes in leadership can be relatively common due to internal struggles or military defeats.
>
> (Hottinger 2005, 2)

Private actors are well suited for this work. They can remain engaged in the long term and do not face the political constraints that other mediation actors like governments of intergovernmental organizations face. As a senior adviser to the HD Centre emphasizes: 'an important role for NGOs is to remind the parties of the importance of not letting the thread of communication and talking break. Most conflicts cannot be resolved militarily and therefore, even when violence is taking place, the parties need to be reminded of the underlying logic of keeping a process in place.'[13] In Burundi, for example, 'a number of NGOs sustained contact with the Forces for the Defense of Democracy–National Council for the Defense of Democracy (FDD–CNDD), while discussing issues with them, organizing seminars and trying to help them build a political agenda solid enough to deal with the Burundian government. The FDD–CNDD eventually decided to negotiate in 2000' (Hottinger 2005, 2).

The ability of private actors to engage with proscribed groups is particularly important and useful in the conflict resolution field in the post 9/11 world. NGOs can maintain paths of communication with these groups and build an understanding of their positions, internal workings and their interest, or not, in negotiations. The UN's ability to work in certain conflicts, although still significant, has been curtailed due to the fact that some parties to conflicts have been designated as 'terrorist organizations' by powerful states. This has confronted the UN with a major political and operational challenge, as for example in the case of Palestine.[14] Many believe that the UN secretary-general or at least his envoys should be able to talk to any actor and that the UN plays a most useful role when it talks to actors that more powerful actors cannot talk to. On the other hand, the UN has trodden carefully about engaging groups that are not recognized by concerned powers as legitimate interlocutors (Jones 2007, 44). Thus, the constraints faced by governments and intergovernmental organizations such as the UN to engage with armed groups, especially proscribed groups, often creates a niche for private actors.

A fourth key factor allowing NGOs to play a role in national-level political processes is that states and intergovernmental organizations are willing to fund them, support them politically and incorporate them in their work. This is part of the trend identified by Zartman (Chapter 4 in this volume) of contemporary states defining their interests widely to include conflict management around the world and to therefore justify supporting NGOs working in conflict management. The influence of NGOs and their ability to access decision makers relies greatly on their networks in official circles both in the target countries where they work and in the capitals of states with interest and influence in a particular conflict. The Carter Center for example 'deals regularly with the leaders of countries and of insurgency groups rather than with people who have influence on such persons. Carter gives the Center direct access to publicity, heads of state, corporate executives, religious leaders, and top personnel in intergovernmental organizations and foundations' (Taulbee and Creekmore 2003, 156). Thus, 'the Center's approach, because it relies upon high-level dialogue, depends upon the access and clout provided by an eminent person' (Taulbee and Creekmore 2003, 157). NGOs aiming to participate in national-level conflict resolution efforts, therefore, try to strike a delicate balance between being independent from state power in the eyes of the parties, but being able to bring the resources and leverage of state power when needed. CMI enjoys similar benefits from its association with former Finnish President Martti Ahtisaari. The HD Centre brings into its work persons who in the recent past held high-level positions in governments or intergovernmental organizations. Also, it co-hosts with the Norwegian government annual gatherings of experienced mediators, including persons who work or have worked for governments and intergovernmental bodies, to share experiences and network with each other. This enables the HD Centre to develop its network of experienced senior practitioners and to learn from their work.[15]

As 'weak mediators', independent peacemakers must borrow leverage from others (Griffiths and Whitfield 2010). NGO 'weakness' is in many cases an advantage: 'while they lack the ability to promise or met out physical inducements, NGOs may be attractive to participants because they lack the means of coercing the principals into a settlement that one or the other side would find unacceptable' (Taulbee and Creekmore 2003, 167). However, in cases when talks progress beyond the initial stages of exploratory discussions and confidence building measures, leverage and resources become increasingly important. As Griffiths and Whitfield write, 'the early stages of a privately led mediation can proceed with a degree of confidentiality; if such mediation is to advance, however, it will eventually require the support and cooperation of official actors to reach a lasting agreement' (Griffiths and Whitfield 2010). Others agree: 'long-term success in mediation depends upon approval or follow-up action by governments or IGOs ... The attributes that make NGOs attractive mediators also mean they lack the resources to directly support the activities necessary to carry out agreements' (Taulbee and Creekmore 2003, 168). As Kittikhoun and Weiss point out, 'the UN experience in post-war reconstruction, peacebuilding and statebuilding is a very important strength' (see Chapter 6, in this volume). Hottinger also writes that 'without track one political pressure, help and backing, professional mediators or facilitators would be lost. Armed groups are in need of reassurance that the international community and its official representatives will back the peace process and help implement and guarantee the results' (Hottinger 2005, 3). Sant'Egidio agrees with this analysis:

> Sant'Egidio would prefer to speak of a synergy of efforts among all levels: institutional and non-institutional, official and from civil society ... The synergic approach to the peace process is essential in order to answer one of the great questions which are posed in every negotiation: the issue of guarantees.
>
> (Sant'Egidio, 24 April 2010)

Private mediation actors have in the past managed to bring the necessary leverage and resources to peace processes. Sant'Egidio's work in Mozambique is interesting in this regard. The Sant'Egidio mediation team kept the United States informed throughout the process and the US decided early on to indirectly support the process. Similarly, the mediation team communicated regularly with the United Nations and UN representatives were present during the final stage of the negotiations in 1992 (Bartoli 1999, 259). Bartoli writes that the peace process benefited enormously from US and Italian support since 'Sant'Egidio did not have the expertise to properly address all military, legal, economic, and institutional problems emerging from the peace process' (Bartoli 1999, 261). Finally, at the final stages of the negotiations, four observer countries – France, Portugal, the United Kingdom and the United States – supported Sant'Egidio's efforts. These four countries plus Germany remained engaged in the post-agreement period and supported the UN operation in Mozambique to implement the peace agreement signed in 1992 (Whitfield 2007).

Similarly, during its work in Aceh, the HD Centre brought leverage and gravitas to the process through the 'Wise Men', a group of prominent individuals with strong links to their governments, including the former Thai foreign minister, a retired US marine general who was at the time the US envoy to the Middle East peace process, and a former Swedish diplomat. The Wise Men participated as observers in the talks and, in early 2002, met with the parties bilaterally. Furthermore, as the talks progressed, the HD Centre secured financial support from the US and Japan, and unarmed military observers from Thailand and the Philippines to assist in the implementation of the ceasefire. Later on, when President Ahtisaari became engaged in Aceh, he did so as chairman of CMI. However, as Whitfield writes, 'his standing in Europe helped secure support of the process by powerful allies and the prompt establishment of a monitoring operation jointly undertaken by the European Union and regional states in the latter part of 2005' (Whitfield 2007, 308–9).

There are important limitations in the work of NGOs. First, and very importantly, NGOs tend to be vulnerable third parties. They can be pushed and manipulated by the parties more easily than official mediators such as states or intergovernmental organizations would. They can come under intense pressure and not have the resources to stick to their ground or to propose alternative ways of structuring a mediation process to the parties. In one of its projects which involved facilitating confidential talks between a government and an armed group, the HD Centre was told by both parties to 'stay in its box' and to not venture to engage in certain issues. This meant that the HD Centre did not 'loosen the shackles'[16] the parties imposed on it in a timely manner and missed opportunities to steer the process in a productive way. This reality brings into question NGOs' ability to be effective mediators if they are not able to assist the parties progress in their talks due to the restrictions the parties themselves impose on them. Undoubtedly, official mediators often face similar restrictions from the parties. However, they may not be as intense as those faced by NGOs.

A second criticism of the work of NGOs is that they crowd already crowded mediation processes. The past two decades have seen a multiplicity of actors entering the mediation field. This is positive, as already discussed, as different actors can complement each other's strengths and weaknesses. However, the multiplicity of actors can also be counter-productive and exploited by conflict parties who engage in 'mediator shopping', give different messages to the different potential mediators and may play them against each other. Hara argues that, 'in the case of Burundi, at least until the July 1996 coup, the various interpretations of the country's problem produced a fragmented and inconsistent international response ... The initiatives of private agents have contributed to the harmful cacophony of competing, incompatible messages' (Hara 1999, 148). The problem of multiple and often competing mediators is one frequently discussed and lamented in the mediation field. However, the problem is not limited to the role of NGOs. Certain conflicts are recipients of envoys and special representatives of dozens of countries and intergovernmental organizations, who indeed often present a fragmented image of the international community to the parties. Afghanistan, for example, is the recipient of special envoys from twenty-seven different countries. Also, before Kofi Annan consolidated the talks following the post-election violence in Kenya, several high-level persons arrived in Nairobi in early January 2008 to offer their assistance, including Desmond Tutu, Jendayi Frazier, the US assistant secretary of state for African affairs, four former heads of state, and the AU Chairman and Ghanaian President, John Kufuor (Gowan and Jones 2010, 23).

Undoubtedly, NGOs are part of this problem, especially because they are often over-eager to get 'their foot in the door'. This eagerness may lead to opportunistic and self-interested behaviour that does not result from an honest and accurate evaluation of whether they can actually contribute to a given peace process. At the same time, NGOs are willing to assist the efforts of a 'lead' mediator, if asked. For example, the HD Centre seconded staff and offered technical assistance to Kofi Annan's efforts in Kenya, while Conciliation Resources and the HD Centre currently participate in the International Contact Group established in late 2009 to support the Malaysia-led MILF peace process in the Philippines. An additional example is Berghof Peace Support, which at the request of the Norwegian facilitator in Sri Lanka was involved in strengthening the capacity of the major conflict stakeholders (Whitfield 2010).

Indeed, it is more and more frequently observed that official and nonofficial actors collaborate and share tasks in a peace process. In the Great Lakes, for example, 'in many cases, parallel diplomacy has worked alongside official mediators and complemented state diplomacy' (Hara 1999, 145). Some high level official representatives, 'realized they could capitalize on NGO creativity, flexibility, and skill, [and] have fostered partnerships and a synergy of unparalleled strength between government and the private sector. The UN secretary general's special envoy for Burundi, Ahmedou Ould-Abdallah, sought to ensure that most of the mediation activities being undertaken in Burundi by NGOs complemented his own efforts, and he apportioned the diplomatic workload according to his own strategy' (Hara 1999, 145). However, such collaboration is not always smooth. Ould-Abdallah realized that 'NGOs had their own agenda related to questions of visibility and fundraising, and consequently would exaggerate Burundi's problems with a destabilizing effect on his own work' (Whitfield 2007, 310).

A third weakness of private mediation actors is that they may work in certain situations in the absence of adequate analysis and rigor underpinning their approach and strategy. This tends to result both from the fact that NGOs inevitably work with limited resources, especially when compared to governments or intergovernmental organizations, and from the fact that they may choose to engage in a particular process out of self-interested motivations. Although resources are scarce throughout the conflict management field, NGOs in particular may often be unable to put in place comprehensive teams and to conduct adequate background research to support their work.

A fourth limitation of private mediation actors is that they have not yet succeeded as much to occupy the ground of high-level diplomacy where they convene parties to the negotiating table for formal peace talks leading to the signing of agreements. NGOs have a solid track record when it comes to facilitating early contact among belligerents and preparing the ground for negotiations leading to peace agreements. This has happened in a few cases as in the examples of Sant'Egidio's work in Mozambique, the HD Centre's work leading to the Cessation of Hostilities Agreement between the Acehnese armed group GAM and the Indonesian government in late 2002 (Huber 2004; Aspinall and Couch 2003), and the Carter Center's negotiation in 1995 of a ceasefire between the south Sudanese SPLA's John Garang and Sudan's president Omar al-Bashir (Neu 2002). But, these are rare examples and, as a result, the empirical evidence about the effectiveness of NGOs in carrying out such negotiations is thin. It is therefore not possible to reach strong conclusions about their effectiveness in such a role. However, it is possible to say that when found in a position of assisting parties to negotiate peace agreements, NGOs need to bring the leverage and resources of states and intergovernmental organizations to the peace process in order to prepare for the challenges of implementation and to put in place the security guarantees that the parties usually demand before laying down their arms. This issue will be discussed in the next section.

## NGO contribution to settlements

This section examines three issues regarding the contribution of NGOs to negotiated settlements: the question of whether NGOs can broker deals among conflict parties leading to peace agreements and whether they can do so effectively; the contribution of NGOs in setting the foundations of political processes in divided societies; and the question of how NGOs tend to approach the content of the eventual deal between conflict parties.

Scholars have written extensively about the fact that solving civil conflicts is particularly challenging given the intensity of the security dilemma facing belligerents once they put down their arms (Snyder and Jervis 1999). They have also argued that external actors make a crucial contribution to settling disputes by offering credible guarantees to the parties that they will not be victims of exploitation once they disarm (Walter 1999). Furthermore, Hartzell argues that the security dilemma persists not only in the immediate post-conflict phase of demilitarization and demobilization of combatants, but also later on in the phase of constructing state institutions. Therefore, she argues, negotiated settlements which incorporate institutions dividing political, military and economic power proportionally among groups may reduce the intensity of the security dilemma faced by adversaries (Hartzell 1999). The division of power within state institutions provides guarantees that one group will not seize control of the state and use its power against the others (Hartzell *et al.* 2001; Hartzell and Hoddie 2003).

The importance of guarantees in war termination brings into serious question the ability of private actors to contribute to the final settlement of disputes. Hara, for example, writes:

> Breaking the vicious cycle of fear requires the restoration of state authority ... To implement these reforms, will require a commitment that outstrips the capabilities of private agents. Violence can be deterred only when all parties feel the potential threat of a coercive power. For this reason, parallel diplomacy can help to initiate a negotiation or facilitate a political process, but it cannot be a substitute for state diplomacy when it comes to obtaining concessions from warring factions ... The political independence and the flexibility enjoyed by agents of parallel diplomacy are their strengths but also their Achilles' heel.
>
> (Hara 1999, 150–1)

Huber makes a similar argument:

> States have a significant advantage as mediators because of the overt leverage available to a global or regional power or a well-resourced donor country. Not only are they better able to muster additional political pressure and greater material benefits to induce parties to reach an agreement, but states have direct access to intergovernmental bodies like the UN or regional organizations that can organize peacekeeping operations and ensure sustained political support for the all-important phase of implementing an accord. They also have greater internal capacities for the planning, staffing, and material support that a sustained dialogue effort necessitates.
>
> (Huber 2004, 8)[17]

As mentioned earlier, private actors are aware of the importance of bringing leverage and resources to a peace process. They therefore routinely seek the support of states and intergovernmental institutions in their work. The question, however, arises about the credibility of commitments made by states and intergovernmental institutions to a peace process led by an NGO. Do the parties doubt these commitments more than commitments made to processes led by formal mediators? Does the fact that a 'weak' mediator leads a peace process signal to the parties lack of commitment by great powers and the international community in general? Hara points out to this risk when she writes that:

> having private agents become de facto representatives of the international response presents a grave danger of eroding the responsibility of states to intervene ... For states, the recent upsurge in private conflict prevention and resolution activities is welcome because it reduces the costs of intervention that states would otherwise have

to undertake. By selling off or subcontracting the diplomatic function, states avoid the domestic political risks associated with, say, the dispatch of a peacekeeping force.

(Hara 1999, 150–1)[18]

She adds that 'NGOs that are specialized in mediation and conflict resolution have the potential to play a positive role that official actors seem incapable of playing – but only if that role is undertaken within the framework of a coherent and coordinated official strategy' (Hara 1999, 152).

It is not possible to answer this question of the effectiveness of private mediators in brokering deals and crafting agreements with the parties given the limited track record of private mediators who have helped parties negotiate agreements. Also, it is important to remember that 'credibility' and 'guarantees' are not easily defined concepts. For example, is the threat or promise of substantial military deployment by a great power a more credible guarantee than the actual deployment of a much smaller force?[19] The answer to the question of NGO effectiveness is probably an unsatisfying 'it depends'. Bartoli argues, contrary to Hara, that in Mozambique 'the paradox in utilizing synergies was that, in all probability, they were possible because no single powerful actor had a sufficiently compelling interest in Mozambique to force itself into the negotiations' (Bartoli 1999, 260). It seems that, in the case of Mozambique, the interest of the international community was strong enough to support the efforts of Sant'Egidio, but not too strong to interfere with its mediation efforts.

The second contribution of private actors to settlements is in building a political process. Their early and lengthy engagement with parties, and their work in assisting parties to build trust, to understand each other's positions and to habituate themselves to making compromises, are important in efforts to build sustainable peace. The relationships parties build over years of engagement are crucial as they learn to interact with each other in politics. Also, NGOs tend to encourage national ownership of the peace process and inclusion of as many national actors as possible in the process. They tend to advocate against solutions imposed by international actors and in favour of nationally generated solutions. This is the result both of ideology and of strategy: NGOs rarely find themselves in the position of shaping a final settlement and most of the times are involved in efforts of getting the parties to the negotiating table through building trust and exploring each other's positions. As a result, NGOs tend to emphasize the importance of the process of talking and negotiating as opposed to the final content of a settlement. This is in contrast to the approach of states and intergovernmental organizations, which are guided by their interests and tend to keep an eye towards the content of the final settlement. For example, the African Union's engagement in the Comoros in the past decade has been predicated on the fact that secession is unacceptable and cannot appear as an option at the negotiating table. Similarly, international engagement in Somalia has been predicated on the assumption of a unified Somali state, and in Georgia, the European Union supports the territorial integrity of the Georgian state. Finally, in Kosovo, external parties supported Kosovo's independent statehood and contributed to that very outcome being reached.

Given that the ultimate aim of peacemakers and peacebuilders is to assist societies to resolve disputes through the political process as opposed to violence, the contribution of NGOs to the creation or strengthening of political processes is significant.[20] As Hara points out, official mediators often do not stay in the country long enough, in some cases may rarely visit the country, and when they do limit their interactions with the political elite. As a result, 'official mediators [may] find that their work has not been backed by intermediaries working diligently to build mutual trust among warring factions' (Hara 1999, 144). NGOs, on the other hand, 'through their partnership with civil society and the communities, bring a unique element to international response, one that most state-led diplomatic initiatives ignore' (Hara 1999, 145).

Related to the above contribution of NGOs to the building of a political process is the question of their contribution to the content of political settlements. As discussed earlier, as a result of their comparative advantage in working with armed groups, their lack of political interest in the conflicts they engage in, and the fact of their 'weakness' as a mediation actor, NGOs tend to emphasize the importance of the process of arriving at agreements, of the ownership of this process by national actors, and of the inclusiveness of that process. They cannot be heavy-handed and impose solutions or even strongly direct the parties towards an outcome. Bartoli writes the following about Sant'Egidio's work in Mozambique:

> the weaknesses of the negotiation team reduced the possibility of imposing outside solutions (through coercive diplomacy, military threat, and so forth), which forced the parties to negotiate for themselves. Because the mediation team lacked an authoritative stance, the two parties had to engage themselves in an effective, prolonged process that transformed not only positions but also the actors themselves. The paradox is that, positioned weakly, the mediation team established a strong and effective direct negotiation almost by default.
>
> (Bartoli 1999, 249)

Griffiths similarly says that 'the HD Centre cares that the parties reach a sustainable agreement, not about the content of the agreement. The HD Centre seeks to influence power-sharing and other parts of negotiated settlements through the parties themselves. We try to help them through the process of arriving at an agreement, but are agnostic about the type of power-sharing they will finally agree on.'[21]

The emphasis on process and long-term engagement with the parties is an important contribution of NGOs and one that is more and more being recognized as crucial for all mediation actors. This recognition stems at least partly from the fact that peace agreements tend to be fragile and imperfect, often keep in power criminal elites or result in governments that are unable to deliver upon the commitments they had entered into (Papagianni 2011). Given this reality, focusing on strengthening political processes is a crucial and realistic approach. Gowan and Jones write that the UN should also focus on the importance of political processes in its crisis diplomacy. They argue that there is a 'need to recognize that the UN and its international partners are rarely, if ever, able to create comprehensive peace. Instead, the goal is to design and implement political processes that act as credible alternatives to violence' (Gowan and Jones 2010, 9). They add that 'in the Middle East and Somalia, for example, the UN cannot impose or ensure peace, but it can keep open space for talking about peace' (Gowan and Jones 2010, 21).

## Conclusion

Private mediators work in a field that has significantly expanded in terms of its participants and activities in the past twenty years. It is also a field that more and more recognizes the importance of partnerships and coordination, but which is still struggling to devise norms to guide such partnerships. Mediation currently encompasses a wide array of activities ranging from early contacts with conflict parties and exploration of interest to talk, to facilitating formal peace processes, and to assisting parties to overcome their multiple disagreements while implementing peace agreements. This usually means that no one actor has the needed resources to engage in all aspects and all stages of a peacemaking effort. Also, very few, if any, mediation actors have the stamina and will to engage in the long term at all stages of mediation. Especially great powers are usually unable to keep their attention on one conflict for a long period of time given competing priorities (Griffiths and Whitfield 2010, 13). As a result, 'in many conflicts, no one actor can claim to have the necessary combination of leverage, legitimacy and technical expertise required to mount an effective mediation process' (Gowan and Jones 2010, 5).

The above creates opportunities for NGOs to engage in conflict management efforts and for different kinds of mediation actors to partner and collaborate with each other. There is, for example, a trend towards 'hybrid' mediation efforts meaning efforts led by more than one mediation actors as for example the joint AU–UN mediation effort in Darfur, the AU–SADC–UN–Organisation de la Francophonie effort in Madagascar, and Kofi Annan's team in Kenya which include the AU, the UN and the HD Centre, as already discussed in this chapter (Griffiths and Whitfield 2010, 10). There is also the trend, discussed earlier in the chapter, of NGOs supporting 'lead' mediators in their work. Gowan and Jones also recommend that 'the UN should embrace cooperation with other political actors and be prepared to act in a supporting or convening role in dealing with many conflicts, rather than trying to take the lead' (Gowan and Jones 2010, 3). The challenge for private mediators in the coming years will be to devise in partnership with formal mediation actors, such as governments and intergovernmental organizations, ways of collaborating and coordinating without compromising their independence.

## Notes

1 On the UN, see Kittikhoun and Weiss in this volume (Chapter 6).
2 On the AU and its various regional sub-organisations, see Akokpari in this volume (Chapter 8).
3 For a survey of 'private diplomacy' organizations, see Herrberg and Kumpulainen (2008) (available online at: at www.cmi.org).
4 For a similar view, see Taulbee and Creekmore (2003).
5 The concept of 'quite diplomacy' is explored by Collins and Packer in this volume (Chapter 5).
6 Interviewee #3, Swiss Ministry of Foreign Affairs, Berne, 11 February 2010.
7 Discussion with former senior British official, 17 February 2010.
8 For a similar argument see Hottinger (2005, 1).
9 Interview with Martin Griffiths, Director, Centre for Humanitarian Dialogue, 6 May 2010, Geneva, Switzerland.
10 Discussion with former senior British official, 17 February 2010.
11 Discussion with former senior UN official, HD Centre, Geneva, 16 February 2010.
12 Griffiths, interview, 6 May 2010, Geneva.
13 Discussion with former senior UN official and senior adviser to the HD Centre, HD Centre, Geneva, 16 February 2010.
14 For detailed account on the limitations of the UN's engagement in the Middle East peace process, see McCarthy and Williams (2007a, 2007b). See also End of Mission Report, Alvaro de Soto, UN Special Coordinator for the Middle East Peace Process and Personal Representative of the Secretary General to the PLO and the Palestinian Authority, May 2007 (available online at: www.guardian.co.uk; accessed 15 March 2010).
15 For more information on these gatherings of mediators, see: www.osloforum.org
16 Martin Griffiths, Discussion in Geneva, Switzerland, 17 February 2010.
17 Huber (2004, 8).

18 Hara (1999, 150–1).
19 See analysis on the weaknesses of these concepts in Stedman (2002, 5–8).
20 On the importance of strengthening political processes and the contribution of mediation in doing so, see Papagianni (2010).
21 Griffiths, 6 May 2010.

## References

Aspinall, E. and Couch, H. 2003 *The Aceh Peace Process: Why it Failed*, Policy Studies 1, East–West Center, Washington.

Bartoli, A. 1999 'Mediating Peace in Mozambique; The Role of the Community of Sant'Egidio', in Crocker, C. A., Hampson, F. O., and Aall, P. (eds.), *Herding Cats; Multiparty Mediation in a Complex World*. Washington, DC: United States Institute of Peace Press.

De Soto, A. 2007 End of Mission Report, Álvaro de Soto, UN Special Coordinator for the Middle East Peace Process and Personal Representative of the Secretary Genera to the Palestine Liberation Organization and the Palestinian Authority, May 2007 (available at: www.guardian.co.uk; accessed on 15 March 2010).

*The Economist*, 'The discreet charms of the international go-between', July 3, 2008.

Gowan, R. and Jones, B. D. with Batmanglich, S. and Hart, A. 2010 'Back to Basics: The UN and crisis diplomacy in an age of strategic Uncertainty', New York University, Center on International Cooperation.

Griffiths, M. and Whitfield, T. 2010 'Mediation Ten Years on: Challenges and Opportunities for Peacemaking', *Centre for Humanitarian Dialogue*.

Hara, F. 1999 'Burundi; A Case of Parallel Diplomacy', in Crocker, C. A., Hampson, F. O., and Aall, P. (eds.), *Herding Cats; Multiparty Mediation in a Complex World*. Washington, DC: United States Institute of Peace Press.

Hartzell, C. 1999 'Explaining the Stability of Negotiated Settlements to Intrastate Wars', *Journal of Conflict Resolution*, 43: 3–22.

Hartzell, C. and Hoddie, M. 2003 'Institutionalizing Peace: Power Sharing and Post-Civil War Conflict Management', *American Journal of Political Science*, 47: 318–32.

Hartzell, C., Hoddie, M. and Rothchild, D. 2001 'Stabilizing the Peace After Civil War: An Investigation of Some Key Variables', *International Organization*, 55: 183–208.

Herrberg, A. and Kumpulainen, H. (eds.) 2008 'The Private Diplomacy Survey 2008; Mapping of 14 Private Diplomacy Actors in Europe and America', Conflict Management Initiative and Initiative for Peacebuilding (available at www.cmi.org).

Hottinger, J. 2005 'The Relationship Between Track One and Track Two Diplomacy', in Ricigliano, R. (ed.), 'Choosing to Engage Armed Groups and Peace Processes', *Accord, A publication of Conciliation Resources*.

Huber, K. 2004 *The HDC in Aceh: Promises and Pitfalls of NGO Mediation and Implementation*, Policy Studies 9, East–West Center, Washington.

Human Security Centre 2006 *Human Security Brief 2006*, University of British Columbia, Canada.

Jones, B. D. 2007 'The UN's political role in a transitional international moment', Background Paper, Oslo Forum 2007, Centre for Humanitarian Dialogue.

Keck, M. and Sikkink, K. 1999 *Activists Beyond Borders. Transnational Activist Networks in International Politics*, Ithaca, NY: Cornell University Press.

McCarthy, R. and Williams, I. 2007a 'The UN was pummelled into submission says outgoing Middle East Special envoy', *The Guardian*, June 13.

—— 2007b 'Secret UN report condemns US for Middle Eastern failures; Envoy's damning verdict revealed as violence takes Gaza closer to civil war', *The Guardian*, June 13.

Neu, J. 2002 'Restoring relations between Uganda and Sudan: The Carter Center process', *Accord, A Publication of Conciliation Resources*.

Papagianni, K. 2010 'Mediation, Political Engagement and Peacebuildling', *Global Governance*, 10: 243–63.

—— 2011 'Can mediation transform societies?', Centre for Humanitarian Dialogue.

Risse, T., Ropp, S. C. and Sikkink, K. 1999 *The Power of Human Rights. International Norms and Domestic Change*. Cambridge: Cambridge University Press.

Sant'Egidio, website, accessed on 24 April 2010 (at: www.santegidio.org/en/pace/pace4.htm).

Snyder, J. and Jervis, R. 1999 'Civil War and the Security Dilemma', in Walter, B. F. and Snyder, J. (eds.), *Civil Wars, Insecurity, and Intervention*. New York, NY: Columbia University Press.

Stedman, S. J. 2002 'Introduction', in Stedman, S. J., Rothchild, D. andCousens, E. M. (eds.), *Ending Civil Wars. The Implementation of Peace Agreements*. Boulder, CO: Lynne Rienner.

Taulbee, J. L. and Creekmore, M. V. Jr. 2003 'NGO Mediation: The Carter Center', *International Peacekeeping*, 10: 156–71.

Walter, B. 1999 'Designing Transitions from Civil War', *International Security*, 24: 127–55.

Whitfield, T. 2007 *Friends Indeed? The United Nations, Groups of Friends, and the Resolution of Conflict*. Washington, DC: United States Institute of Peace Press.

—— 2010 'Engaging with Armed Groups: Challenges and Options for Mediators', *Mediation Practice Series*, second issue (forthcoming), Centre for Humanitarian Dialogue.

# Part III
# Case studies

# 10 Between theory and practice

## Rwanda

*Janine Natalya Clark*

The 1994 genocide in Rwanda has spawned a vast literature, as scholars and policy-makers alike try to explain and to make sense of what happened. What has tended to receive less attention, however, is the complex and multilayered conflict management process that preceded the genocide. It is this process – which culminated in the signing of the Arusha Accords on 4 August 1993 – that forms the focus of this chapter. For a book about the theory and practice of conflict management, Rwanda is a particularly important case study, as it highlights a critical gap between the two. In short, the Arusha peace process can be described as 'an extraordinary story of a sophisticated conflict resolution process gone disastrously wrong' (Jones 2001, 69). The purpose of this chapter, therefore, is to explain why it went so wrong.

## The context of the conflict in Rwanda

Civil war began in Rwanda on 1 October 1990 when the Rwandan Patriotic Front (RPF), formed in neighbouring Uganda in 1987, attacked northern Rwanda from its base in southern Uganda. The members of the RPF were the children of those Tutsis who had been forced to flee Rwanda in 1959. Up until that point, the colonial powers – first Germany and later Belgium – had always favoured Rwanda's minority Tutsis over the majority Hutus, regarding the former as Hamites and thus naturally superior to the Hutus (and the Twa). In 1959, however, the Belgians switched allegiance to the Hutus. This ignited an explosion of anti-Tutsi violence, driven by the deep-seated grievances and anger that the colonialists' discriminatory policies had created and fuelled among the Hutus. These grievances, in turn, were to play a significant role in the 1994 genocide, as Hutu extremists tapped into and exploited Hutu fears of once again being made subordinate to the Tutsis.

Following its attack on Rwanda in 1990, the RPF, which had close links to Uganda and President Yoweri Museveni, became engaged in a three-year conflict with the Rwandan army (FAR). According to Hutu extremists within President Juvénal Habyarimana's regime, however, it was not only the RPF who posed a fundamental threat. Rather, all Tutsis, by extension, were the enemy. The message that began to circulate, therefore, propagated in particular by the radio station Radio Télévision Libre des Mille Collines (RTML), was that the Tutsi '*inyenzi*', or cockroaches needed to be exterminated (Bowen 2004, 45; Dallaire 2004, 142; Rucyahana 2007, 34).[1] As the situation continued to deteriorate, moreover, two significant moments of crisis occurred. The first was the assassination, on 21 October 1993, of Melchoir Ndadaye, the first democratically elected Hutu president of neighbouring Burundi. For Hutu extremists in Rwanda, the murder of Ndadaye served to further underscore the insidious menace posed by the Tutsis. To cite Hintjens, 'By an unhappy coincidence, the killing of Ndadaye coincided with the RPF's second invasion of Rwanda, giving apparent plausibility to the notion of a Bahima (pan-Tutsi) conspiracy to re-conquer the entire region and re-impose the old feudal order in Rwanda' (1999, 278).

The second and more fundamental crisis moment occurred on 6 April 1994. As President Habyarimana was returning to Rwanda from Tanzania, his airplane was struck by two missiles and everyone on board was killed. To this day, it remains unclear who fired these missiles. While some commentators point the finger at the RPF and its leader, Paul Kagame (see, for example, Lemarchand 2006, 6), others maintain that the most likely culprits were Hutu extremists and members of Habyarimana's own political party, the Mouvement Révolutionnaire National pour le Développement (MRND), since they had the most to lose from the nascent peace process (see, for example, Prunier 1997, 221; Clapham 1998, 204; Cochrane 2008, 120). Regardless of who killed Habyarimana, the genocide began almost as soon as his airplane was shot down, thus underscoring the fact that it was highly planned and organized. Over the next three months, between 500,000 and one million Tutsis and 'moderate' Hutus were killed, a faster rate of slaughter than the Holocaust.

The causes of the conflict and genocide in Rwanda are heavily debated, and one particular issue that has received considerable attention is the part that ethnicity played in these events. The conflict was ethnic to the extent that it involved Hutu extremists – such as the Comité pour la Défense de la République and members of Habyarimana's *akazu* (literally 'little house') or inner circle – inciting hatred against Tutsis (but also against Hutu moderates and members of the opposition). Yet to describe the conflict as being solely or primarily about ethnicity is far too simplistic, for at least three main reasons. Firstly, prior to the arrival of the colonial powers, the labels 'Hutu' and 'Tutsi' denoted social, rather than ethnic, differences related to status, wealth and way of life (Fujii 2009, 60). These categories were also very fluid. A Hutu, for example, could become a Tutsi through ownership of cattle. It was the colonialists' policies, not least the introduction during the 1930s of identity cards, that transformed 'Hutu' and 'Tutsi' into fixed ethnic identities.

Second, while there was an important ethnic dimension to the conflict and genocide in Rwanda, ethnicity per se was not the cause of those events (Hintjens 1999, 248). Rather, what was critical was the manipulation and abuse of ethnicity, as extremists sought 'to make ethnicity the sole lens through which people viewed the country's current problems and the sole determinant for crafting possible solutions' (Fujii 2004, 102). Of course, such an instrumentalist view of ethnicity cannot explain why this elite manipulation of the masses was successful. To understand this, it is also necessary to consider the country's colonial history, the grievances that it engendered and the specific circumstances of the early 1990s, including the civil war between the FAR and the RPF, the uncertainties and fears that it generated and the impact of the economic crisis, fuelled by a fall in world coffee prices in 1989. To emphasize elite manipulation of ethnicity, however, is to highlight one of the key features of the genocide, namely its top-down dynamic. In essence, 'the episode's central feature was a deliberate, systematic, state-led campaign to eliminate a racially defined social group' (Straus 2006, 1). Elites, in other words, were the main drivers.

Third, to over-focus on ethnicity is to neglect other important cleavages that contributed to the violence in Rwanda. There was, for example, a very significant political dimension to the conflict, pitting moderates committed to multiparty democracy against those opposed to it. There was also a critical north–south dimension. In contrast to his predecessor Grégoire Kayibanda, who came from Gitarama in the south, President Habyarimana was from Gisenyi in north-west Rwanda and always favoured the minority northern Hutus. Under Habyarimana's rule, northern Hutu elites thereby gained substantial power and privileges that they were intent upon preserving. From their perspective, therefore, it was not only Tutsis who posed a threat to their positions but also Hutu opposition parties from southern Rwanda. These political and regional aspects of the conflict were closely linked to democracy-building in Rwanda.

In response to strong pressure from France and the conclusion of a Franco-African summit at La Baule in July 1990, Habyarimana announced the introduction of a multiparty system in Rwanda. Thus, by March 1992, five main opposition parties existed – the Mouvement Démocratique Républicain (MDR), the Parti Social Démocrate (PSD), the Parti Libéral (PL), the Parti Démocratique Chrétien (PDC) and the Comité pour la Défense de la République (CDR). In April 1992, Habyarimana further agreed to the creation of a coalition government with the opposition parties, headed by Dismas Nsengiyaremye from the MDR. In other words, 'There seemed to be genuine progress towards change' (Melvern 2006, 34). What is more, by agreeing to formal peace talks aimed at ending Rwanda's civil war, the new government played a key role in facilitating the conflict management process.

## Actors in the conflict management process

### The local conflict parties

Owing to the significant number of actors involved, the conflict management process in Rwanda was highly inclusive. The key actors in this process were of course the parties themselves, namely the RPF and the Rwandan government, both of which sent delegations to the Arusha negotiations. The RPF delegation – which included Dr Patrick Mazimpaka and Dr Théoneste Rudasingwa, the RPF vice-president and general secretary respectively – was united, organized and disciplined. It was thereby able to secure a strong position in the negotiation process. The government delegation, in contrast, was much weaker and far less effective. Headed initially by Foreign Minister Boniface Ngulinzira from the MRD, and subsequently by James Gasana from the MRND, the fundamental problem was that the government delegation was critically divided, comprising as it did 'at least three different tendencies, each responding to a separate centre of power' (Mamdani 2001, 210).

While Habyarimana's MRND had been the only political party in existence in Rwanda since 1973, the aforementioned moves towards political pluralism meant that during the Arusha talks, the government team consisted of opposition parties, who looked to the prime minister for direction; Habyarimana's men, who took their lead from the President himself; and Hutu extremists, represented by the CDR, who were guided by their leader Colonel Théoneste Bagosora. Not only was the government delegation thus extremely fragmented, but the hard-liners exploited the situation to portray the negotiations 'as talks between the internal opposition and the RPF, that is, between the RPF and its internal Hutu accomplices' (Mamdani 2001, 210).

*Primary mediators*

Beyond the RPF and the Rwandan government, there were a wide range of regional and international actors involved in Rwanda's conflict management process from the outset. Indeed, according to one commentator, 'Rwanda became a laboratory wherein sub-regional and regional inter-state organizations tested their capacity to engage in conflict management' (Jones 2001, 54). In the early stages of the process, it was Zaire that assumed a leading role. It was, for example, President Mobutu Sese Seku who organized the first regional summit, held on 26 October 1990 in Gbadolite, Zaire. It was also due to Mobutu's efforts that a ceasefire agreement between the FAR and the RPF was signed in N'Sele, Zaire, on 29 March 1991. Zaire thus played a vital role in laying the groundwork for the Arusha negotiations.

By the time that these negotiations began in July 1992, however, the initiative had shifted from Zaire to another of Rwanda's neighbours, namely Tanzania. This was a very positive development since Tanzania was regarded as far more neutral[2] than Zaire, the latter having supported President Habyarimana during the RPF attack on 1 October 1990. Although the Arusha negotiations were officially held under the authority of the Organization for Africa Unity (OAU), it was Tanzania that acted as mediator. In addition, Burundi, Nigeria, Senegal, Uganda, Zaire, Zimbabwe, the OAU, the United Nations (UN), as well as Belgium, France, Germany and the United States, were all involved in the negotiations as observers.

That so many actors were engaged in the process may be viewed as evidence of a genuine and widespread regional and international commitment to resolving the conflict in Rwanda. Two key points, however, should be noted. The first is that there are questions regarding certain actors' reasons for participating in the conflict management process. France, for example, viewed the English-speaking RPF as a threat to its interests in francophone Africa. According to one commentator, therefore, 'The Quai d'Orsay was, in short, pro-Arusha, not out of humanitarian concerns … but because Arusha was the best solution in terms of French interests' (Jones 2001, 77). During the negotiations, moreover, rather than assuming the role of a neutral observer, France strongly championed the position of the Rwandan government. A mutual mistrust accordingly developed between France and the RPF, which in turn extended to France's relations with Uganda, due to the latter's support for the RPF. That such negative relations existed between some of the central actors was not conducive to the management of the Rwandan conflict. Indeed, it might be argued that, 'the structure of international rivalries helped to exacerbate rather than moderate the conflict' (Clapham 1998, 199).

The second key point is that the involvement of so many actors encouraged the belief that the international community was sincerely committed not just to resolving the conflict but also to implementing any peace agreement reached (Khadiagala 2002, 471). Yet this belief ultimately proved to be ill-founded (Kuperman 1996), as highlighted in particular by the lack of international support and commitment to the ill-fated United Nations Assistance Mission in Rwanda (UNAMIR), created in 1993 to oversee the implementation of the Arusha Accords.

Turning to the mediators themselves, the main mediator in the Arusha talks was Rwanda's eastern neighbour, Tanzania. While President Ali Hassan Mwinyi was the official facilitator to the negotiations, he largely delegated this position to Ambassador Ami Mpungwe. As primary mediator, Mpungwe thereby played a vital role in the negotiations by, *inter alia*, setting the agenda for the Arusha talks, designing their structure, engaging in backroom diplomacy and threatening to withdraw Tanzanian mediation when the two sides failed to reach an agreement. Through its mediation efforts Tanzania was thus 'judged to have played an honest broker role' in the peace process (Jones 2001, 78).

It should be noted that the very propitious circumstances present at the time gave the mediators significant leverage. Mediation efforts, it has been suggested, should await the development of a 'mutually hurting stalemate' (Zartman 2008), a concept based on the idea that, 'when the parties find themselves locked in a conflict from which they cannot escalate to victory and this deadlock is painful to both of them (although not necessarily in equal degree or for the same reasons), they seek an alternative policy or Way Out (WO)' (Zartman 2008, 22). Some level of mutually hurting stalemate arguably existed in Rwanda in 1993. The significant military gains secured by the RPF in February 1993 – when it advanced to within 23 kilometres of Kigali – demonstrated to the Rwandan government that it faced a very formidable opponent. Similarly, the situation was also 'hurting' the RPF, owing to the creation, on 12 March 1993, of the UN Observer Mission Uganda-Rwanda (UNOMUR). Set up to monitor the border between Rwanda and Uganda, UNOMUR's presence was thus obstructing the RPF's supply lines from Uganda. At the same time, the US and various international donors were threatening to halt economic aid to Rwanda, in order to bring Habyarimana to the negotiating table and to keep him there. This, moreover, was no idle threat. When, for example, in 1993, the Rwandan government failed to comply with the conditions laid down by the US for continued economic aid – including reduced violence and respect for human rights – the latter responded by capping its aid at $6 million.

While such international economic and other pressure undoubtedly facilitated the negotiations, whether or not it ultimately proved effective is open to debate. According to Lemarchand, 'not only were the negotiations conducted under tremendous external pressures, but, partly for this reason, the concessions made to the FPR [RPF] were seen by Hutu hard-liners as a sell-out imposed by outsiders' (1994, 591–2). What is more, the pressure put on the parties to reach an agreement was incongruent with the lack of international support for the implementation of that agreement; 'it was clear to all and sundry that the international community had little will and less staying power to see the agreement implemented effectively' (Cochrane 2008, 121).

The main reason for this lack of international will was straightforward *realpolitik*. Quite simply, the international community had no strategic interests in landlocked Rwanda, a country dwarfed by its much larger neighbours. To cite Lieutenant General Roméo Dallaire, UNAMIR'S Canadian commander, 'It was clear to me that the mission was still considered a sideshow to the main event, which was always going on somewhere else far more important, such as Bosnia or Haiti or Somalia or Mozambique, just about anywhere other than the tiny central African country that most people would be hard-pressed to locate on a map' (2004, 55). That the early 1990s were a very turbulent and dramatic period internationally – as highlighted particularly by the US debacle in Somalia, the war in Bosnia and the elections in South Africa – further helped to distract the international community's attention from Rwanda (see, for example, Williams 2008, 60); while the UN's disastrous intervention in Somalia meant that there was little international appetite for a costly peacekeeping operation to oversee the implementation of the Arusha Accords. The result was that once the Arusha Accords had been signed, 'UN diplomats no longer saw Rwanda as a priority' (Neuffer 2003, 101).

Mediation in the Rwandan conflict was effective to the extent that it brought the parties to a very comprehensive peace agreement. Certainly, without mediation, it is highly unlikely that the Arusha Accords would have been signed. Yet, as will be discussed, both the process leading up to those Accords and the peace agreement itself contained fundamental flaws, part of the responsibility for which necessarily lies with the mediators themselves. Critically, they arguably failed to appreciate just how much Rwanda's northern Hutu elite had to lose under the terms of the Arusha Accords, which in the latter's eyes represented a victor's deal. Ultimately, therefore, mediation never actually resolved the conflict in Rwanda. Rather, 'A conflict which three and a half years of international mediation had failed to settle was resolved instead by military force in an equivalent number of months' (Clapham 1998: 207).

## The structure of the conflict management process

Almost as soon as the RPF attacked Rwanda on 1 October 1990, a flurry of diplomatic activity began. In mid-October, for example, on the initiative of Belgium, a series of regional talks took place, and on 17 October, a regional summit was held in Mwanza, Tanzania. This resulted in the Mwanza Communiqué, which, *inter alia*, provided a basis for further negotiations to take place and formalized the role of Rwanda's neighbours in the nascent peace process. A series of subsequent agreements, such as the Dar es Salaam Declaration on the Rwandese Refugees Problem (19 February 1991), ceasefires and pre-negotiations all paved the way for the Arusha talks to begin. That there were always very significant regional and international elements to the conflict management process in Rwanda made the structure of that process very complex and multilayered, involving a host of different actors and organizations with individual interests and priorities.

Yet it was precisely the inclusion of these diverse regional and international players that gave the process its dynamic character and helped to create the necessary momentum for the negotiations to move forward. In addition to these formal, so-called track-I international and regional diplomatic efforts, moreover, the process also involved unofficial, track-II initiatives by such actors as OXFAM-Rwanda and the Rwandan Catholic Church. The latter, for example, supported by the Vatican, put pressure on Habyarimana to negotiate; and in May 1992, secret talks took place between the Church and the RPF in Bujumbura, Burundi. It was this successful combination of official and unofficial diplomacy that made the Arusha talks possible.

On the issue of structure, three particular points stand out vis-à-vis the Arusha negotiations. The first is that their structure closely reflected the beliefs and principles of the man who led the process, primary mediator Ambassador Mpungwe. He was seeking not merely conflict management or conflict settlement but conflict resolution. With this in mind, Mpungwe heavily designed the process around communication, as the vehicle for allowing the parties to dialogically resolve their issues, to change their perceptions of each other and to reach an agreement acceptable to them both. According to Jones, therefore, 'the design of the Arusha process certainly conforms more closely to the conceptions of peace processes found in conflict resolution literature than in the more traditional negotiation/mediation literature' (2001, 71). If the structure of the process was thus too 'academic', this may help to explain why it ultimately failed. Perhaps a more obvious problem, however, is that the dialogue and communication that took place between the government and the RPF were always very uneven, owing to the parties' unequal bargaining positions.

Before coming to this issue, however, a second important point relating to the structure of the Arusha talks must be noted. In some peace processes, particularly contentious issues are postponed for resolution at a later date. The Dayton Peace Accords, for example, which ended the war in Bosnia-Herzegovina, left unresolved the heavily disputed status of Brčko District, instead submitting the matter to binding international arbitration; and the 1993 Declaration of Principles (DOP), signed by Israel and the Palestinian Liberation Organization (PLO), deferred negotiations concerning the most difficult questions, such as Jerusalem, final borders and security. By contrast, in the Arusha negotiations nothing was postponed.

However, the process was structured in such a way that the least controversial issues were dealt with first. Hence, during the first two stages of the negotiations, in July and August 1992 respectively, the focus was on issues pertaining to the rule of law and on the creation of a new ceasefire. This goal was successfully achieved on 14 July 1992, based on the previous N'sele ceasefire agreement negotiated by Mobutu in March 1991. The third stage of the negotiations dealt with power-sharing and political cooperation. Agreements were reached and initialled, but they were not actually signed, due to lack of support from President Habyarimana. The difficult issue of power sharing was further addressed during the fourth stage of the negotiations, in October 1992, when the parties agreed upon the creation of a multiparty transitional government, a shift from a presidential to a parliamentary system and, as a corollary, a significant reduction in the president's powers. The two most sensitive and contested issues, namely the composition of the transitional authorities that the parties had agreed to create and the integration of the FAR and the RPF, were reserved until the final stages of the negotiation process. What is interesting is that on both of these latter issues, it was the RPF who prevailed, bringing us to the third key point concerning the structure of the Arusha talks.

On 30 October 1992 and 9 January 1993, the parties signed Protocols of Agreement on Power-Sharing. The RPF, however, insisted that the extremist CDR should be excluded from the new transitional government. While the government delegation, backed by France and the US, was equally adamant that the CDR must be included, it ultimately conceded to the RPF's demands. As a consequence, Habyarimana and the CDR rejected the power-sharing Protocols and organized demonstrations against the Arusha talks, notably in the two Habyarimana strongholds of Gisenyi and Ruhengeri. The ensuing violence against Tutsis and moderate Hutus led the RPF, in turn, to end its ceasefire in February 1993. Yet this may have been a tactical move, designed to strengthen the RPF's bargaining position in the forthcoming negotiations on the issue of the armed forces (Jones 2001, 83).

Following a high level summit in Dar es Salaam on 7 March, organized by Tanzania, and the conclusion of a new ceasefire agreement, negotiations recommenced in March 1993. The government initially proposed only a 15 per cent share for the RPF in the armed forces, yet subsequently consented to the RPF's demand for a 50 per cent share. Thus, the final agreement was that there would be a 50:50 split in terms of command positions and a 60:40 split in favour of the FAR for all other positions. It is clear, therefore, that because the RPF delegation represented a very strong and united force, in contrast to the government delegation,[3] it was in a position to extract significant concessions and to secure its objectives. What this meant in terms of the structure of the Arusha talks, however, is that they were rather one-sided, 'a lop-sided negotiation dance' (Scourgie 2004, 69) which, in turn, produced a 'somewhat lopsided deal' (Jones 2001, 95).

## Settlement design

On 4 August 1993, 13 months after the Arusha negotiations began, President Habyarimana and Alexis Kanyarengwe, the chairman of the RPF, signed the Arusha Accords. These consisted of five main elements. First, all those refugees who had been forced to flee Rwanda as a result of the violence that began in 1959 would be free to return to Rwanda.[4] Second, the formerly warring factions would be integrated into a new army of 19,000 troops, of which the FAR would constitute 60 per cent and the RPF would represent 40 per cent.

Third, in keeping with the aforementioned Protocols of Agreement on Power-Sharing – which became an integral part of the Arusha Accords – a broad-based transitional government (BBTG) would be set up within 37 days of the signing of the Accords. This BBTG would include a 70-member Transitional National Assembly (TNA), in which the MRND, RPF, MDR, PL and PSD would each have 11 seats, the PDC would have four and the other registered parties would have one seat each (Article 62 of the 1993 Protocol).[5] The BBTG would also include a new cabinet, consisting of twenty-one ministers. Of these, five ministers would be members of Habyarimana's MRND; five would belong to the RPF; four would represent the MDR; three would come from the PSD; three would be members of the PL and one would be from the PDC (Article 55 of the 1993 Protocol). Regarding the top portfolios, the position of prime minister would go to Faustin Twagiramungu from the MDR, the job of minister of defence would fall to the MRND, and the position of minister of the interior would be accorded to the RPF (Article 56 of the 1993 Protocol).

Aside from the exclusion of the CDR, which will be discussed below, there were two particular problems with these power-sharing arrangements. The first was that the distribution of seats in the TNA and the cabinet meant that Habyarimana's party would now struggle to command a majority in parliament. In effect, 'The MRND had gone from an oligarchic party in control of the state to a minority party that wouldn't be able to win a vote' (Jones 2001, 93). It was therefore inevitable that hardliners within the Party would staunchly oppose the Accords. The second problem was that according to Article 21 of the 1992 Protocol, all cabinet decisions would require a two-thirds majority (and a complete consensus in particular cases, such as defence and security matters). Yet as one commentator notes, this decision-making process 'required an exceptional level of cooperation and good will from bitterly conflicting adversaries among whom these qualities had been evidently lacking' (Clapham 1998, 203). In-fighting and disagreements would be particularly serious, moreover, given that power now resided in the cabinet and prime minister rather than in President Habyarimana (Article 18 of the 1992 Protocol).[6] Questions inevitably arise, therefore, as to how this BBTG might have worked in practice. In the words of Lemarchand, 'In few other states has a power-sharing experiment been conducted under less auspicious auguries' (2006, 6).

Since these arrangements were only temporary, the fourth element of the Arusha Accords was that democratic elections would take place in 1995. Finally, all of the above developments were to be overseen by a neutral international force. To this end, the UN Security Council created UNAMIR, a peacekeeping force whose 2,548 members fell significantly short of the 5,500-strong force requested by UNAMIR's commander, Lieutenant General Dallaire. Furthermore, UNAMIR was not established until 5 October 1993, even though part of its mandate was to oversee the creation of the BBTG which should have been formed by 10 September 1993. From the outset, therefore, the very ambitious timetable laid out in the Arusha Accords began to slip.

The Accords stipulated that all of the aforementioned elements were to be realized within a twenty-two-month timetable. Yet just eight months after they were signed, nobody in Rwanda was thinking about their implementation. On 6 April 1994, genocide began. The relentless slaughter lasted for 100 days, by the end of which 80 per cent of Rwanda's Tutsi population had been killed. The Arusha Accords were therefore a spectacular failure. More than that, however, it can be argued that they were a major contributing factor to the genocide (Kuperman 1996, 230; Clapham 1998, 204; Stettenheim 2000, 213). To cite Paris, 'The evidence suggests that the mass killing of Tutsis was a last-ditch effort to block implementation of the Arusha Accords' (2004, 74). This thereby raises two critical questions: why did the Accords fail and why did Hutu extremists want to prevent their implementation?

According to Darby, 'a peace process must include five criteria. The protagonists must be willing to negotiate in good faith; the key actors must be included in the process; the negotiations must address the central issues in the dispute; force must not be used to achieve objectives; and the negotiators must be committed to a sustained process' (2001, 11). These criteria were largely absent in the case of Rwanda. First of all, there are questions as to whether the parties were actually negotiating in good faith. For example, there is evidence that both the government side and the RPF were continuing to arm themselves as the Arusha negotiations were taking place (Waugh 2005, 610; Melvern 2006, 39; Straus 2006, 31; Kinzer 2008, 115). Regarding Habyarimana himself, whose support for the process was essential, he never attended the Arusha talks; on 30 November 1992, he denounced the power-sharing protocols that preceded the Arusha Accords as 'mere pieces of paper'; and one month after the signing of the Accords, to which he was 'a reluctant signatory' (Khadiagala 2002, 476), a member of his family set up RTLM, the vitriolic anti-Tutsi radio station that played a crucial role in inciting people to kill. Prunier's assessment is therefore that Habyarimana signed the Accords 'not as a genuine gesture marking the turning-over of a new leaf and the beginning of democratisation in Rwanda, but as a tactical move calculated to buy time, shore up the contradictions of the various sections of the opposition and look good in the eyes of foreign donors' (1997, 194–5).

Regarding the second criterion, although the extremist CDR was included in the Arusha negotiations, the party was excluded from the new transitional government, as demanded by the RPF. For one commentator, therefore, the fact that the Arusha Accords failed to deal with the CDR means that they were 'signed stillborn' (Mamdani 2001, 211). The CDR and its leader, Bagosora, can be regarded as a classic example of 'spoilers', as defined by Stedman (1997). More specifically, they can be viewed as 'total spoilers' – as individuals who 'pursue total power and exclusive recognition of authority and hold immutable preferences' (Stedman 1997, 10). This thereby raises critical questions as to whether excluding the CDR was the correct approach. For some commentators it clearly was, as engaging with the extremists was simply not an option (see, for example, Clapham 1998, 206). For Stedman himself, however, the fact that the Accords contained no strategy for dealing with the CDR means that they were necessarily critically flawed. He suggests that a strong peacekeeping force, combined with credible threats against the use of violence by extremists, might have prevented the genocide (Stedman 1997, 25). The problem was that there was no international commitment to create such a force, and UNAMIR itself was in no position to threaten the extremists. What existed was to a large extent a no-win situation: 'Bringing the CDR into the new government would have doomed that government. Keeping it out had the same effect' (Kinzer 2008, 108–9). Yet had some attempt been made to actually deal with the CDR, this would perhaps have alienated and antagonized its members far less than their total exclusion from the process.

Turning to Darby's third criterion, the Arusha Accords did address the central issues in the dispute. Due, however, to the aforementioned divisions within the Hutu delegation and its relative weakness vis-à-vis the RPF delegation, the Accords did so in a way that largely favoured the latter. From the perspective of the Hutu camp, therefore, the Accords were a victory deal for the RPF (Stettenheim 2000, 224). Linked to this, although force was not used to achieve objectives, according to Darby's fourth criterion, the fact that one negotiating party was much stronger than the other meant that the two sides were not evenly matched. Hence, while one side was largely able to secure its goals, the other was consistently obliged to make major concessions. It was precisely because of everything that the northern Hutu elite stood to lose under the terms of the Arusha Accords, not only to the RPF but also to the Hutu opposition – from seats in parliament to control of the army – that the extremists were never going to accept these Accords. In short, 'the final result proved to be a recipe for disaster because it pushed well beyond what was acceptable in key sectors in Kigali on distribution of command posts and the distribution of seats in the BBTG' (Jones 2001, 95). As to the final criterion, neither the parties themselves nor the international community were committed to a sustained peace process. As previously noted, both sides continued to arm and various elements within the Hutu camp were 'venomously opposed' to the Accords (Barnett 2002, 62), for the reasons outlined above. What is more, international commitment to achieving a peace agreement in Rwanda appeared to largely dissolve when it came to actually implementing that agreement (Khadiagala 2002, 463). Most strikingly, as Dallaire petitioned the UN for additional troops to halt the unfolding genocide, the UN Security Council took the decision to reduce UNAMIR from 2,548 to just 270 troops.[7]

## The current status of conflict management in Rwanda

Rwanda's genocide ended on 18 July 1994, when the RPF took control of the country. A new government was formed the following day, and what is interesting is that it was in keeping with the provisions of the Arusha Accords. Thus, this power-sharing government was headed by Faustin Twagiramungu, from the MDR, and the twenty-one cabinet ministries were shared among the RPF, the MDR, the PSD, the PL and the PDC (the MRND and the CDR were excluded). It can be argued, therefore, that, 'The government that was inaugurated on July 19, 1994, was a genuine government of national unity. It was fully in the spirit of the Arusha Peace Agreements of August 1993' (Prunier 2009, 7). These very positive developments, however, were short-lived. In 1995, both Prime Minister Twagiramungu and Interior Minister Seth Sendashonga resigned, followed two years later by Justice Minister Alphonse Nkubito. As the wave of resignations continued, Twagiramungu's successor, Pierre-Celestin Rwigema, together with the Speaker of the National Assembly, Joseph Sebarenzi, and the Rwandan President, Pasteur Bizimungu, all resigned within a three-month period in 2000. All of them accused the RPF of, *inter alia*, abusing its power, of discriminating against Tutsi and Hutu survivors of the genocide and of committing human rights violations, such as the massacre at the Kibeho camp in April 1995.[8]

Since the collapse of this power-sharing government, the RPF regime and President Paul Kagame, the former RPF commander, have become increasingly authoritarian. In the words of Reyntjens, the victim has become a bully (2004, 197). During local elections in March 2001, for example, political parties were prohibited from campaigning and voters were required to put their thumbprint – effectively equivalent to a signature – next to the name and picture of their chosen candidate. During the 2003 elections, moreover, the strongest opposition parties were banned, including the MDR, which was accused of 'divisionism'; and Kagame, who had unofficially been Rwandan President since April 2000, 'was elected by a massive 95 percent of the vote after a campaign marked by arrests, "disappearances" and intimidation' (Reyntjens 2004, 186). At the same time, the regime has demonstrated a marked intolerance of critical voices and of anyone viewed as a potential threat to its power. In May 2001, for example, when former President Pasteur Bizimungu announced the creation of his own political party, the Parti Démocratique pour le Rénouveau–Ubuyanja, he was arrested in Kigali. In other words, just as the RPF manipulated the Arusha negotiations to its advantage, it is now manipulating the current political situation for its own ends.

The genocide is over, victims and perpetrators are living side by side in the 'land of a thousand hills' and the wheels of justice – in the form of national courts, *gacaca* courts and the International Criminal Tribunal for Rwanda (ICTR) – are in motion. Yet no real solution has been implemented in Rwanda. The government has adopted a comprehensive policy of national unity and reconciliation, epitomized by the creation in 1999 of a National Unity and Reconciliation Commission (NURC). This policy, however, is fundamentally flawed, seeking as it does to forge such unity and reconciliation through the suppression of ethnicity.[9] In Rwanda, ethnicity 'is crucial for addressing the roots of the injuries suffered by each community' (Lemarchand 2008: 69). Its denial, therefore, means that notwithstanding the holding of criminal and *gacaca* trials, post-genocide Rwanda is not fully confronting and addressing the past (Clark 2010). While there is of course much debate among scholars as to whether and how post-conflict societies should in fact deal with the past, the key point vis-à-vis Rwanda is that the official negation of ethnicity is in reality helping to obscure what is really happening, namely the political manipulation of ethnicity.

This manipulation can be seen in two main ways. First, it can be seen in what Reyntjens calls the 'Tutsization' and 'RPF-ization' of power (2004, 188). In a country where ethnicity supposedly does not matter, by 2000, 'out of a total of 169 of the most important office-holders, 135 (or about 80 percent) were RPF/RPA [Rwandan Patriotic Army] and 119 (or roughly 70 percent) were Tutsi'. Given that the Hutus constitute the overwhelming majority in Rwanda, it can be argued that these figures reveal 'a strong ethnic bias in favour of a small Tutsi elite' (Reyntjens 2004, 188). Second, the political manipulation of ethnicity is apparent in the Rwandan regime's refusal to cooperate with the Arusha-based ICTR, as a result of which no RPF crimes have been prosecuted at the Tribunal.[10] The fact that only one side is being held to account for its crimes serves to reinforce the notion, extremely useful to the RPF, that Tutsis were exclusively victims during the genocide.

Essentially, despite the efforts invested in Rwanda's conflict management process, the conflict was never in fact resolved. If Hutu extremists sought to exterminate the Tutsis, in order to preserve their power and to prevent the imposition of a new Batutsi autocracy, they ultimately failed. While hundreds of thousands of Tutsis were massacred, similar numbers returned to Rwanda from neighbouring countries, in keeping with the

Arusha Accords. The result is that, 'post-genocide Rwanda is not just a Tutsi state; it is a state largely controlled by the returnees, with the "Ugandans" holding the top jobs in the government, the economy and the army' (Lemarchand and Niwese 2007, 182). In other words, the genocide helped to create the very situation that the Hutu extremists had sought to avoid. Not only does the conflict thus remain unresolved but the Kagame regime is arguably sowing the seeds of further conflict, through its combined strategy of suppressing and abusing ethnicity.

## Conclusion

Based on conflict management theory, Rwanda in many respects should have been a success story. The Arusha talks were inclusive, the parties had expressed their commitment to the negotiating process, there was strong regional and international support for the process and a mutually hurting stalemate existed. In practice, however, Rwanda presented enormous challenges for conflict management theory. Theories on how to deal with spoilers, for example, meant little in a situation where Hutu extremists were implacably opposed to, and fixated upon, destroying and burying a peace agreement that represented a fundamental threat to their power. Similarly, while a mutually hurting stalemate may have encouraged the parties to sign the Arusha Accords, such a stalemate cannot lead to a peaceful resolution of conflict if, as in Rwanda, the final agreement benefits one side while significantly 'hurting' the other. Perhaps the key lesson to be drawn from this chapter, therefore, is that an overly theoretical approach to conflict management is too limited and should thus be avoided. For a fusion, rather than fissure, of theory and practice, conflict management theory should be combined with empirical insights and case study analysis.

## Notes

1 Fujii notes that 'Through a mixture of music, banter, jokes and editorials, the station [RTLM] reinforced the genocidal message over and over again' (2004, 104).
2 Jones observes that, 'It has been suggested that the Tanzanian government supported the RPF, and although this may well be true in the sense of sympathy, it does not appear to have been true in the sense of taking sides' (2001, 100 n. 23).
3 For Jones, 'This strength/weakness distinction can be seen as a critical variable in explaining the Arusha process, both for understanding the agreements reached and for understanding what would follow the signing of the Arusha peace deal' (2001, 73–4).
4 During the 1980s, the Hutu government in Kigali had 'declared that Rwanda was too over-populated to accept the repatriation of the approximately 600,000 Tutsis in exile' (Peskin 2008, 156).
5 Both the 1992 and the 1993 Protocols of Agreement on Power-Sharing are available online at: www.incore.ulst.ac.uk/services/cds/agreements/pdf/rwan1.pdf
6 According to the Protocol signed on 30 October 1992, Habyarimana was to remain as president during the transition period but his role was to be largely symbolic.
7 Dallaire maintains that he could have stopped the unfolding slaughter in Rwanda, had the UN Security Council granted his request for extra troops (2004, 374).
8 For a discussion of this massacre, see Prunier (2009, 38–42).
9 According to Straus, the banning of references to ethnicity stems from the RPF government's erroneous conclusion that, 'participation in the genocide was massive and that participation stemmed from widespread ethnic commitment and racist indoctrination' (2008, 168).
10 On this issue, see Del Ponte (2008).

# References

Barnett, M. 2002 *Eyewitness to a Genocide: The United Nations and Rwanda*, Ithaca, NY: Cornell University Press.

Bowen, R.W. 2004 'Genocide in Rwanda 1994 – An Anglican perspective', in C. Rittner, J. K. Roth and W. Whitworth (eds.), *Genocide in Rwanda: Complicity of the Churches?*, St Paul, MN: Paragon House

Clapham, C. 1998 'Rwanda: The Perils of Peacemaking', *Journal of Peace Research*, 35: 193–210.

Clark, J. N. 2010 'National Unity and Reconciliation in Rwanda: A Flawed Approach?', *Journal of Contemporary African Studies*, 28: 137–54.

Cochrane, F. 2008 *Ending Wars*, Cambridge, UK: Polity.

Dallaire, R. 2004 *Shake Hands with the Devil: The Failure of Humanity in Rwanda*, London: Arrow Books.

Darby, J. 2001 *The Effects of Violence on Peace Processes*, Washington, DC: United States Institute of Peace Press.

Del Ponte, C. 2008 *Madame Prosecutor: Confrontations with Humanity's Worst Criminals and the Culture of Impunity*, New York, NY: Other Press.

Fujii, L. A. 2004 'Transforming the Moral Landscape: The Diffusion of a Genocidal Norm in Rwanda', *Journal of Genocide Research*, 6: 99–114.

—— 2009 *Killing Neighbors: Webs of Violence in Rwanda*, Ithaca, NY: Cornell University Press.

Hintjens, H. 1999 'Explaining the 1994 genocide in Rwanda', *Journal of Modern African Studies*, 37: 241–86.

Jones, B. D. 2001 *Peacemaking in Rwanda: The Dynamics of Failure*, Boulder, CO: Lynne Rienner.

Khadiagala, G. M. 2002 'Implementing the Arusha Peace Agreement on Rwanda', in S. J. Stedman, D. Rothchild and E. M. Cousens (eds.), *Ending Civil Wars: The Implementation of Peace Agreements*, London: Lynne Rienner.

Kinzer, S. 2008 *A Thousand Hills: Rwanda's Rebirth and the Man who Dreamed It*, Hoboken, NJ: John Wiley & Sons, Inc.

Kuperman, A. J. 1996 'The Other Lesson of Rwanda: Mediators Sometimes Do More Damage than Good', *SAIS Review*, 16: 221–40.

Lemarchand, R. 1994 'Managing Transition Anarchies: Rwanda, Burundi and South Africa in Comparative Perspective', *Journal of Modern African Studies*, 32: 581–604.

—— 2006 'Consociationalism and Power Sharing in Africa: Rwanda, Burundi and the Democratic Republic of Congo', *African Affairs*, 106: 1–20.

—— 2008 'The Politics of Memory in Post-Genocide Rwanda', in P. Clark and Z. D. Kaufman (eds.), *After Genocide: Transitional Justice, Post-Conflict Reconstruction and Reconciliation in Rwanda and Beyond*, London: Hurst & Co.

Lemarchand, R. and Niwese, M. 2007 'Mass Murder, the Politics of Memory and Post-Genocide Reconstruction: The Cases of Rwanda and Burundi', in B. Pouligny, S. Chesterman and A. Schnabel (eds.), *After Mass Crimes: Rebuilding States and Communities*, Tokyo: United Nations University Press.

Mamdani, M. 2001 *When Victims Become Killers: Colonialism, Nativism and the Genocide in Rwanda*, Kampala: Fountain Publishers.

Melvern, L. 2006 *Conspiracy to Murder: The Rwandan Genocide*, London: Verso.

Neuffer, E. 2003 *The Key to My Neighbour's House: Seeking Justice in Bosnia and Rwanda*, London: Bloomsbury.

Paris, R. 2004 *At War's End: Building Peace After Civil Conflict*, Cambridge: Cambridge University Press.

Peskin, V. 2008 *International Justice in Rwanda and the Balkans: Virtual Trials and the Struggle for State Cooperation*, New York, NY: Cambridge University Press.

Prunier, G. 1997 *The Rwanda Crisis: History of a Genocide*, London: Hurst & Co.

—— 2009 *From Genocide to Continental War: The 'Congolese' Conflict and the Crisis of Contemporary Africa*, London: Hurst & Co.

Reyntjens, F. 2004 'Rwanda Ten Years on: From Genocide to Dictatorship', *African Affairs* 103: 177–210.

Rucyahana, J. 2007 *The Bishop of Rwanda: Finding Forgiveness Amidst a Pile of Bones*, Nashville, TN: Thomas Nelson Inc.

Scourgie, L. 2004 'Rwanda's Arusha Accords: A Missed Opportunity', *Undercurrent*, 1: 66–76.

Stedman, S. J. 1997 'Spoiler Problems in Peace Processes', *International Security*, 22: 5–53.

Stettenheim, J. 2000 'The Arusha Accords and the Failure of International Intervention in Rwanda', in M. Greenberg, J. H. Barton and M. E. McGuiness (eds.), *Words over War: Mediation and Arbitration to Prevent Deadly Conflict*, Lanham, MD: Rowman & Littlefield.

Straus, S. 2006 *The Order of Genocide: Race, Power and War in Rwanda*, Ithaca, NY: Cornell University Press.

—— 2008 'Rwanda's Security Trap and Participation in the 1994 Genocide', in J. P. Chrétien and R. Banégas (eds.), *The Recurring Great Lakes Crisis: Identity, Violence and Power*, London: Hurst & Co.

Waugh, C. 2005 *Paul Kagame and Rwanda: Power, Genocide and the Rwandan Patriotic Front*, London: McFarland & Co.

Williams, P. D. 2008 'The Peacekeeping System, Britain and the 1994 Rwandan Genocide', in P. Clark and Z. D. Kaufman (eds.), *After Genocide: Transitional Justice, Post-Conflict Reconstruction and Reconciliation in Rwanda and Beyond*, London: Hurst & Co.

Zartman, I. W. 2008 'The Timing of Peace Initiatives: Hurting Stalemates and Ripe Moments', in J. Darby and R. MacGinty (eds.), *Contemporary Peacemaking: Conflict, Peace Processes and Post-War Reconstruction*, 2nd edn, Hampshire: Palgrave Macmillan.

# 11 The challenges of implementation
## Guatemala

*Virginie Ladisch*

## Introduction

The signing of the Comprehensive Peace Accords on 29 December 1996 marked the end of over three decades of civil war in Guatemala. Outside the National Palace, thousands gathered in the plaza to celebrate 'one of those rare moments in deeply polarized Guatemala when national reconciliation seemed a real possibility' (Jonas 2000a, 9). Seeing the military commander side by side with the leader of the Unidad Revolucionaria Nacional Guatemalteca (Guatemalan National Revolutionary Unity, URNG), a sight unthinkable for so long, filled bystanders with a sense of hope for a stable democracy based on equality for all its citizens and respect for human rights. Over a decade has passed since that historic moment, yet Guatemala remains one of the most unequal societies, with increasing levels of violence and targeted attacks against human rights defenders.

With so much international attention and resources dedicated to supporting the peace process, one may ask what went wrong and why the vision of peace put forward in the Accords still eludes Guatemala today. The answer, in part, lies in the discrepancy between the broad vision for change set out in the accords and minimal detail on design. The accords failed to specify mechanisms for implementation and compliance, thus leaving too much up to future political negotiations without factoring in the lack of political will or fierce opposition those reforms would face.

## Context of the conflict in Guatemala

The longest and bloodiest in the Western Hemisphere, Guatemala's thirty-six-year long civil war (1960 to 1996) claimed over 200,000 civilian lives. Guatemala's indigenous Maya were disproportionately targeted in the civil war, making up 83 per cent of all victims (while constituting about half of the total population) and leading the Comisión de Esclarecimiento Histórico (Historical Clarification Commission, CEH) report to declare genocide took place against the Maya (Guatemala Memory of Silence 1999, 85). However, to categorize the civil war as an ethnic conflict would be an over-simplification that would obscure the root causes of the war and ongoing violence in Guatemala.

The underlying struggle in Guatemala revolves around unequal access to land and resources dating back to independence from Spain in 1821 and the establishment of an export-focused economy, centred largely on coffee (Paris 2004, 129). This created a system of land concentrated in the hands of the so-called agro-elite, who in turn had significant influence on politics through their connections to military-backed authoritarian regimes. In an effort to break this pattern of unequal distribution of wealth, during what is called Guatemala's 'democratic spring', presidents Juan José Arévalo (1945–50) and Jacobo Arbenz (1951–4), implemented a series of reforms including abolishing forced labour, establishing a minimum wage, and, most significantly, extensive agrarian reform (in 1952) which redistributed land to over 100,000 peasants (Jonas 2000a, 18). Part of the agrarian reform led to the expropriation of unused land from the US-based United Fruit Company. In the context of the Cold War, these reforms were seen as part of Soviet Expansion and a threat to US interests. Economic interests of the oligarchy combined with US Cold War interests culminated in a CIA-led coup in 1954. The newly installed US-backed military regime immediately repealed all reforms and quelled any dissent by force and intimidation.

In response to the new military regime's increasingly repressive techniques, and inspired by the Cuban revolution, the first insurgent group formed in 1960 and launched its first military strike in 1962. Initially, the guerrilla forces were primarily Ladino[1] and concentrated in the Eastern part of the country. After suffering significant military setbacks, the insurgency regrouped and broadened their base. Over the next two decades, a number of different guerrilla groups emerged, and in 1982 four of them united to form the URNG. Posing a much more serious challenge to the government, the military intensified its counter-insurgency campaign. Purposefully exaggerating the links between Mayan communities and the guerrillas, indiscriminate attacks on civilians, including women and children, became part of the counter-insurgency strategy. From 1981 to 1983 alone, 440 villages were razed to the ground and as many as 150,000 civilians were killed or disappeared. In addition, Mayan leaders were specifically targeted in an attempt to destroy the cohesion of the indigenous community (Guatemala Memory of Silence 1999, 23). While, from the military's perspective this was a highly effective strategy, leading them to declare victory in the civil war by 1983, the insurgents were far from having been comprehensively defeated. To the contrary, with poverty and inequality in Guatemala further increasing throughout the first half of the 1980s, social unrest spread and protests against the state continued. Their claim of victory increasingly hollow, the military initiated a controlled transition to civilian rule in 1984, but retained de facto power after the election of civilian president Vinicio Cerezo in 1985. While the new government was too weak to establish any real civilian control over the military, it managed to begin setting the stage for eventual peace negotiations with the guerrilla forces.

With the return to civilian rule, the URNG continued its military activities, but began shifting some of its focus to the political process and repeatedly and publicly requested political negotiations. Maintaining that it had defeated the insurgency, the government rejected any suggestion of dialogue with the URNG. This only began to change with the end of the Cold War. The Guatemalan military could no longer rely on US backing on the basis of its own anti-communist policies and instead began to face increasing pressure to conform with human rights standards. By 1990, a mix of international pressure, domestic economic crisis and continuing social unrest made it clear to the military that they could not bring the war to an end with arms. Thus, support for a political solution gained traction and laid the ground for peace negotiations to begin.

One of the first major breakthroughs was achieved at a secret meeting in Oslo, Norway in March 1990. The culmination of months of shuttle diplomacy, a URNG delegation met with a delegation from the Guatemalan government in a chalet outside Oslo. After several days, they signed the Basic Agreement for the Search for Peace by Political Means, agreeing to 'initiate a serious process which will culminate in the attainment of peace and the enhancement of functional and participatory democracy in Guatemala'. While the 'Oslo process' did not lead directly to a peace agreement, the issues identified and discussed as part of this process were incorporated in the official negotiating agenda. It thus created a framework for the UN-led negotiation process, which ultimately resulted in the signing of the peace agreement. In addition, the consultations 'helped to bring about a transformation in public opinion in favor of a negotiated process to end the armed confrontation – even amongst those who had been most staunchly opposed to recognizing the URNG' (Alvarez 2002a).

## Actors in the conflict management process

At the negotiating table, in addition to the two key parties – the URNG and the Guatemalan state – elements from civil society and the international community played a significant role. A brief analysis of each key actor helps explain how the process unfolded and also holds the key to understanding the continuing challenges faced in the implementation phase.

### *The local conflict parties*

The National Advancement Party (PAN) led the negotiations on behalf of the Guatemalan government. Following years of military rule in Guatemala, political parties, the PAN included, remained particularly weak and lacked a broad base of support. The PAN assumed a majority in Congress in the 1995 elections with 42 out of 80 seats, while its leader, Álvaro Arzú, came to power with a margin of less than 2 per cent in the presidential run-off election of January 1996. Despite his narrow victory, Arzú took office on a strong note bolstered by his party's majority in Congress. He was thus able to push ahead with the peace negotiations, but that leverage did not last long enough to help in the implementation phase since in the 1999 Congressional elections the PAN lost its majority in Congress. Meanwhile, the military retained significant political influence. As in the past, there was a constant threat of yet another military coup. Given the dire economic situation, the government also suffered from a very weak fiscal base. As a consequence, the government was in no position to credibly negotiate real and substantial reforms, but rather largely motivated by its desire to improve its image internationally in the hopes of securing financial aid and development assistance.

Thus, it was crucial to have the military's support for the peace process. Initially, many within its ranks were opposed to negotiating directly with what they perceived as a militarily defeated URNG. Eventually, as a result of factional splits within the military, more moderate officers who saw potential benefits in peace took the lead. They wanted to prioritize the long-term stability of the country and restore the integrity of the military as an institution, which had suffered badly after decades of brutal counterinsurgency and increasing levels of criminal activity. Thus, in order to regain legitimacy, both at home and abroad, the military agreed to go along with the negotiations and give up its role in internal security (Stanley and Holiday 2002, 431). However, its ongoing influence behind the scenes meant that military elites were able to control the transition, and most importantly avoid external vetting of military forces.

On the other side of the table, the URNG faced two serious limitations that affected its leverage. The first was that it did not pose a serious military threat and therefore was not in a very strong bargaining position. This in turn influenced the way the government viewed the negotiations; almost as a ruse to get the guerrillas to finally put down their arms without having to make any significant concessions. Furthermore, just as the PAN had a weak civilian base, the URNG could not claim to represent the indigenous populations. Even though many Mayans did support and participate in the insurgency, its leadership was exclusively Ladino. Many within the Mayan community viewed the URNG with suspicion, in part because the guerrillas were not able to protect the civilian population effectively against the military. At the political level, the URNG and Mayan communities did not see eye to eye either, with the former angling for political power and the latter striving for the recognition, respect and protection of their rights.

As a result of the intense lobbying by civil society in the previous phase of negotiations (primarily in the early 1990s in the 'Oslo process'), the key parties realized that civil society could not be shut out. Civil society gained a space at the table in the form of Asamblea de la Sociedad Civil (Civil Society Assembly, ASC), established in 1994 as part of the 'Framework Accord for the Renewal of the Negotiating Process between the Government of Guatemala and the URNG'. This was a unique innovation of the Guatemalan peace process, through the effectiveness of civil society representatives was undermined by the ASC's limited mandate which gave it a seat but no vote in the negotiations.

By creating the ASC, the negotiating parties hoped they would be able to give civil society a voice but little influence. As its appointed leader, Catholic Bishop Quezada Toruno[2] stated: 'sometimes I think that the new Assembly could have been a consolation prize for the "Oslo sectors" which had participated in the various meetings after the Oslo accords with the URNG, since [the parties] refused in principle to allow civil society to be present at the negotiating table. Perhaps they even thought that the Assembly was never going to be threatening or have any success' (in Krznaric 1999, 5).

Composed of ten 'sectors' – religious, trade union, popular organizations, the Atlixico conglomeration of political parties, the Mayan sector, women's organizations, NGOs, research centres, human rights organizations and the press – ASC represented over 100 organizations. The ASC was tasked with creating consensus documents on the key issues in the negotiations, presenting these documents to the URNG and government and endorsing the final accords. Its consensus documents were non-binding and it was not given a direct seat at the negotiating table. Despite its limitations, in the process of preparing the key documents, the ASC was able to generate discussion, debate and finally some level of consensus within civil society on the key issues included in the peace negotiations. This was an important step in beginning to revitalize civil society after three decades of civil war and extended periods of military rule. Even though its documents were non-binding, several of its proposals were included in the accords, most notably in the Accord on Identity and Indigenous Rights (1995). In the area of land reform, however, the efforts of the ASC were overshadowed by the Chamber of Agricultural, Commercial, Industrial and Financial Associations (CACIF) and its lobbying on this crucial area of the negotiations.

Originally part of the ASC, CACIF is the umbrella organization of private sector organizations in Guatemala. It withdrew from ASC in 1994 on the grounds that the latter also included illegal and unrepresentative groups and created the so-called Business Peace Commission (CEPAZ) to serve as its liaison to the negotiations. Business leaders realized that the peace process might help end their international isolation and create a climate for greater international investment and trade. At the same time, they had an interest in limiting the types of reforms passed and maintaining the economic status quo. While CEPAZ played a key role in guaranteeing business interests, it also worked to assuage the fears of certain elements of CACIF who were staunchly opposed to peace negotiations (Krznaric 1999, 12).

One key domestic group was left out of the formal peace process: the victims. Through the ASC, some Mayan leaders were able to help shape the proposals submitted to the negotiating parties, but overall there was very little space given to the indigenous population. They suffered the majority of violations in the conflict, but did not get anything close to proportional representation at the negotiating table. This dynamic whereby Ladinos claim to represent indigenous victims or speak on their behalf, continues in Guatemala and remains a source of ongoing tension (Isaacs 2010a, 120).

Initially Mayan activists lobbied for direct representation at the negotiating table to discuss the issue of indigenous rights. Despite support from the URNG, the government rejected this proposal, leaving them with the ASC as their only avenue to influence the peace accords. While several indigenous activists opposed the characterization that 60 per cent of the population was treated as one 'sector' of society along with other special interest groups, they had to resign themselves to use the ASC as a vehicle to table their demands. 'Although many remained dissatisfied with this perceived under-representation, an early success of indigenous participation in the Assembly was the recognition of indigenous peoples within that forum as "peoples" rather than "groups".' Given the rights attached to 'peoples' by international law, it legitimized and framed a new way of conceiving and talking about national reform (Alvarez 2002b). Despite their lack of representation at the table, many indigenous leaders were very supportive of the peace accords and continue to refer to them as a basis in their calls for justice and respect for human rights.

*Primary mediators*

The international community focused a significant amount of attention and resources on the peace process. The 'Group of Friends' (Mexico, Spain, Norway, the US, and to a lesser extent, Venezuela and Colombia) supported the UN in the process of bringing the parties to the negotiating table and lent significant diplomatic support to the process. Perhaps even more important was the financial element and the leverage of the international financial institutions (IFIs). Taking a lesson from El Salvador, where IFIs negotiated a deal with the government that was in tension with the UN-negotiated terms of the peace, in Guatemala the IFIs coordinated their efforts with the UN. They were united in their support for the accords and used elements of conditionality to help pressure the government (Jonas 2000a, 167). In a break from their usual rhetoric, 'the financial institutions now argued that lasting peace would not be possible without a reduction in Guatemala's sharp social and economic inequities and regarded the country as a test case for a new approach to post-conflict sustainable development in war-shattered states' (Paris 2004, 130–1).

At a crucial juncture within the peace negotiations – when various factors threatened the course of the negotiations, the Consultative Group of Donor Countries (primarily US and Europe and IFIs) met in Paris in June 1995 and decided to withhold major funding for Guatemala until a final peace accord was signed and tax reform was implemented.

This clear message helped shift interest back to the peace negotiations, especially by key pro-business groups like CACIF, who saw that the signing of the peace would be in their interest, as long as they could limit the level of substantial reforms (as they did very successfully) (Jonas 2000a, 46).

In contrast to the negotiations in El Salvador involving a trio of actors (the ARENA government, the FMLN and the UN), the variety of actors in Guatemala evokes the image of an orchestra. With the government/military, URNG, UN, ASC, IFIs and Group of Friends, the challenge was to create a harmonious tune. The multiplicity of voices gave a richness and breadth to the accords, but to the detriment of depth and feasibility.

## Capacity/leverage of the primary mediator

Following the breakdown of internally led talks in 1993, both the government and URNG saw merit in having an international presence oversee the peace process (despite historically strong resistance to UN involvement by successive Guatemalan governments). In the 1994 Framework Agreement to restart negotiations, both parties agreed to have the UN 'serve as moderator of the bilateral negotiations between the Government and the URNG', and 'to verify all agreements both in their substantive and operational aspects'. The UN's role was thus elevated from an observer to taking the lead in the negotiations, with Jean Arnault as the 'moderator' (understood to mean mediator). Using shuttle diplomacy combined with direct talks, Arnault successfully gained both parties' trust and played a key role in translating the URNG's demands into something the government could accept (Stanley and Holiday 2002, 429). At this time, the ASC also took an active role in presenting proposals to the negotiating team on each of the key issues.

Under this new arrangement, significant progress was made in 1994, with both parties signing the Comprehensive Agreement on Human Rights in March 1994. This agreement asserted both parties' commitment to respect human rights and fulfil their obligations under international humanitarian law in the conduct of war, and called on the government to respect and protect the autonomy of the judiciary, disband illegal security forces, professionalize the security sector and uphold the right of freedom of association. Immediately upon signature, this agreement went into force. Another groundbreaking element of this agreement was that it invited the UN to send a verification mission to the country before the official ceasefire agreement. The UN General Assembly thus established a Mission for the Verification of Human Rights and of Compliance with the Commitments of the Comprehensive Agreement on Human Rights (MINUGUA) in Guatemala in September 1994 and deployed it in November 1994. This underlined the international support for the peace process and enhanced its credibility. Even though human rights violations persisted, MINUGUA's public reports put the spotlight on the government serving as a reminder that the world was watching. This continued international presence in the country also provided a safe space for victims to give their testimony and report violations of the Human Rights Accord.

At the request of the government and the URNG, the UN also took on a role in verifying the December 1996 Oslo ceasefire agreement between the parties. By resolution of the Security Council, it attached a peacekeeping mission the United Nations Verification Mission in Guatemala to the existing civilian mission (MINUGUA) established three years earlier to monitor the implementation of the Human Rights Accord of 1994. This sent an important signal regarding the international community's continued commitment to the peace process.

After the completion of the peacekeeping mission within MINUGUA in May 1997, MINUGUA's role evolved into something much broader: verifying the implementation of the peace accords, including initial steps in the area of institutional reform. Yet, while MINUGUA was initially given strong international backing after the peace accords were signed, it soon became clear that the UN mission lacked the leverage needed to ensure parties' compliance during the implementation phase in the face of strong resistance, for example to tax reform. Operating on the basis of a General Assembly resolution, it lacked the credibility that would have come with a Security Council resolution. As a result, 'Guatemalan parties expected the UN to be hand-holders rather than hard-nosed verifiers' (Stanley and Holiday 2002,424) and opponents of the peace accords continued to challenge the UN presence and sought to intimidate its representatives. MINUGUA constantly had to find a balance between criticizing the government for lack of compliance without creating a backlash. Ascribed both a verification and good offices role, without a formal mechanism for addressing non compliance, it was difficult for MINUGUA to harshly denounce the lack of implementation of the accords.

## The structure of the conflict management process

Following the return to civilian rule in Guatemala, Central American presidents gathered in Esquipulas, Guatemala in 1986 to discuss regional peace issues. They met again in 1987 to adopt a regional peace plan, which put forward the principle of democratization as a prerequisite for conflict resolution.

In the face of continued resistance to negotiations from the military and private sector interest groups, the Catholic Church played a key role in facilitating a broader public debate on the issue. As a result, the government established the National Reconciliation Commission (CNR) and convened a National Dialogue in 1989. This was the first opportunity for civil society to discuss a pathway to negotiations and served to place the process of ending the civil war in a political rather than purely military framework (Alvarez and Prado 2002). The CNR held direct talks with the URNG and signed the Oslo Accord in 1990, which committed the parties to a political solution. Following consultations between the URNG and key sectors of civil society, the government and URNG held direct talks, under the mediation of Catholic Bishop, Quezada Toruno. The result was the Initial Framework Agreement, signed in Mexico in April 1991, which identified the eleven issues to be negotiated.

A key turning point in negotiations came in 1993, when then president Serrano attempted to seize complete power by dissolving Congress and suspending the constitution, fuelling protest and demand for democracy from both the business sector and civil society. Although motivated by very different reasons, the near crisis served to generate a consensus regarding the need to stabilize the political situation and to negotiate an end to the civil war. The business sector regarded a stable government as necessary for attracting foreign investment, while for civil society, a stable democracy was seen as crucial to protecting human rights and establishing a more just society.

As a result, in 1994, bilateral talks between the URNG and government of Guatemala resumed under the auspices of the UN with the support of the Group of Friends. This transition from an internally to an internationally moderated negotiation process was marked by the 1994 Framework Agreement, which in addition to calling for UN mediation, also gave a formal space for civil society to engage in the peace process through the ASC. 'Structurally, the accord created a mechanism for articulation between ethnically, culturally, and politically diverse world of Guatemala and the larger world of the international community. To build on the plurality of forces in Guatemalan civil society was an often under recognized innovation' (Jonas 2000a, 57).

Shortly after the talks resumed, the Comprehensive Accord on Human Rights was signed in March 1994 and went into effect immediately. This was seen as a crucial confidence building measure. It called for the UN to set up a verification mission to monitor this accord thus bringing further international attention directly inside Guatemala to serve as a watchdog and also to signal international commitment to peace. A few months after the breakthrough on the human rights accord, two more accords were finalized in June 1994: the Agreement on the Resettlement of the Populations Groups Uprooted by Armed Conflict, and the Agreement on the Establishment of the Commission to clarify past human rights violations and acts of violence that have caused Guatemalan population to suffer (known as the CEH agreement based on the name of the 'truth commission' it established). The CEH accord satisfied almost no one: the URNG was pushing for a truth commission modelled off the one in El Salvador, while the government was staunchly opposed to any form of investigative commission. International pressure broke the impasse with the proposal to have a historical clarification commission that would investigate human rights violations but not name individual perpetrators. This compromise was reviled by both sides: some far-right elements threatened a coup while pro-peace sectors of civil society accused the URNG of caving under pressure and betraying its commitment to pursue justice for victims. The political backlash that ensued caused a nine-month delay in the negotiations. Finally with the arrival of the UN Verification Mission in the fall of 1994 talks resumed, although in a very tense atmosphere. The next accord on Identity and Rights of Indigenous peoples was not signed until March 1995. Then an international scandal involving revelation of CIA involvement in Guatemala's civil war further stalled the progress of the talks compounded by the fact that nationally attention turned to the 1995 electoral campaign.

Shortly after taking office in 1996, the narrowly elected President Álvaro Arzú of the PAN declared his commitment to restart negotiations. From that point onwards, the negotiations moved at a very rapid pace, in stark contrast to the previous year. This shift resulted from political calculations by both the URNG and Arzú's administration. The URNG saw Arzú as an honest broker with whom they could negotiate, especially in contrast to the Frente Republicano Guatemalteco (FRG) party (far-right anti-peace party led by former military dictator Rios Montt), which lost the election by a margin of less than 2 per cent (Stanley and Holiday 2002, 436). Arzú, in turn, realized that international aid was conditional on brokering a settlement, and therefore took steps to show his commitment to peace by making some reforms to the military and police. For Arzú's administration the peace accords provided the opportunity to make some needed changes to modernize the state under the cover of the peace accords. At the same time 'the implementation processes agreed to were so complex and involved so many different actors that the government could easily allow individual reforms to languish if opposition proved too strong' (Stanley and Holiday 2002, 430).

With the signing of the Civil–Military Accord in September 1996, many viewed the peace process as irreversible. However, the peace process was almost derailed by a scandal in 1996, when a high-ranking leader of the Organización del Pueblo en Armas (ORPA), one of the guerrilla groups integrated into the URNG, kidnapped Olga de Novella, a member of Guatemala's richest families and close friend of Arzú. This event, and the subsequent suspected cover-up by the UN, delegitimized both the URNG and the UN, and provided those who opposed the peace process with ammunition against the negotiating parties. Surviving this fiasco, in large part due to international pressure and the guidance of the UN Secretary-General's Special Representative, Jean Arnault, the negotiations resumed and moved into the next phase of operational themes. The Group of Friends, especially the Europeans, stepped in to help support the drafting of the operational accords, culminating in the signing of the comprehensive accords in 1996.[3]

## Settlement design

The vision put forward in the 11 peace accords that constitute the settlement of the civil war in Guatemala went far beyond calling for a cessation of hostilities. It strived to present a blueprint for transforming Guatemala into a politically, socially, economically and culturally more inclusive state. Its goal was broad – to look at the causes and consequences of the violence, and ways to address them (Alvarado 2006). This vision is emphasized throughout the accords, as in the Civil–Military Accord which reiterates that, 'All the Guatemalan peace agreements posit that a firm and lasting peace must be based on respect for human rights and for the multi-ethnic, multicultural and multilingual character of the Guatemalan nation; national economic development with social justice; social participation; the conciliation of interest; and democratic institution building'. While the goals of the peace accords were far-reaching, it lacked detail proposals for how to design the new democratic order. This lack of clarity is one of the key reasons for the delay in implementation.

The eleven accords of the settlement include six substantive and five operational[4] ones on human rights, a truth commission, the resettlement of refugees and displaced people, identity and rights of indigenous people, the socio-economic and agrarian situation, strengthening civilian power and the role of the armed forces, and reform of the constitution and electoral system. In all, there were 119 commitments to be implemented in four years (2000–4), among them 66 in relation to socio-economic development and the agrarian situation, 23 on strengthening civilian power and the role of the armed forces, and 18 stemming from the accord on identity and rights of indigenous people (Salvesen 2002, 9). Fundamental to accomplishing all the necessary changes was to improve the government's fiscal basis, providing it with the financial means to fund a vast range of social and economic projects and policies. It was widely recognized within Guatemala and among the international supporters of the peace process that this would only be possible following a revision of the tax code, but it took significant international pressure before CACIF dropped its resistance and the parties were finally able to agree to include a provision in the accords calling on the government to raise taxes (which was subsequently blocked in the implementation phase).

One of the key operational accords, the accord on Constitutional Reform and the Electoral Regime, compiles the various amendments to the Constitution called for in the substantive accords. As stated in the accord, these reforms 'constitute a substantive, fundamental basis for the reconciliation of Guatemalan society within the framework of the rule of law, democratic coexistence, full observance of and strict respect for human rights, an end to impunity and, at the national level, the institutionalization of a culture of peace based upon mutual tolerance and respect, shared interests and the broadest possible public participation in all structures of power'. Among some of the key reforms, it called on the government to sponsor amendments to the constitution that would:

- Grant constitutional recognition of the identity of the Maya, Garifuna and Xinca peoples, within the unity of the Guatemalan nation.
- Stipulate that the state recognizes, respects and protects the various forms of spirituality practised by the Maya, Garifuna and Xinca peoples.
- Define and characterize the Guatemalan nation as being one of national unity and multi-ethnic, multicultural and multilingual in nature.
- Provide guarantees of the administration of justice and, as such, include: (a) free access to the administration of justice in the person's own language; (b) respect for the multi-ethnic, multicultural and multilingual nature of Guatemala; (c) defence counsel for those who cannot afford it; (d) impartiality and independence of judges; (e) reasonable and prompt resolution of social conflicts; and (f) provision of alternative conflict-resolution mechanisms. In addition, the present content of Article 203 should be reproduced in summarized form in a separate paragraph.
- Professionalize the Career Judicial Service.
- Define the functions and main characteristics of the National Civil Police as follows: 'The National Civil Police is a professional and hierarchical institution. It is the only armed police force with national jurisdiction and its function is to protect and safeguard the exercise of the rights and freedoms of individuals; to prevent, investigate and combat crime; and to maintain public order and internal security. It shall be under the control of civilian authorities and shall show strict respect for human rights in carrying out its functions.'
- Define the role of the armed forces as: 'The Guatemalan armed forces are a permanent institution in the service of the nation. They are unique and indivisible, essentially professional, apolitical, obedient and non-deliberative. Their function is to defend the sovereignty of the State and the integrity of its territory. They consist of land, sea and air forces. Their organization is hierarchical and is based on the principles of discipline and obedience.'
- Establish the president as: 'The Commander-in-Chief of the Armed Forces [who] shall issue his orders through the Minister of National Defence, whether the Minister is a civilian or a member of the armed forces.'

It also called for the creation of an electoral reform commission that would 'consolidate a pluralistic representative democracy in Guatemala', by taking steps to ensure transparency, facilitate broader access and participation in elections (by for example creating a single identity document as a way of overcoming problems with documentation), and reform campaign financing.

In order to facilitate the integration of the URNG into political life, the accords included an amnesty clause that exempted URNG members from prosecution for taking arms up against the state. However, in addition to that, there was another clause, which could broadly be interpreted to cover crimes committed by the counterinsurgency.[5] This infuriated civil society, which already was angry that the CEH could not name perpetrators. Civil society actors fought hard and mobilized effectively to pass the National Reconciliation Law (1996), in which the crimes of genocide, torture and forced disappearance would not be covered by the general amnesty for political crimes (Isaacs 2010b, 258). However, in Guatemala impunity continues until today and in many respects is one of the greatest impediments to the implementation of the peace accords and poses a formidable obstacle to fulfilling the vision of a democratic state based on the rule of law and respect for human rights.

## Implementation challenges

While the content of the accords was far-reaching, the operational provisions for implementation and verification were rather vague. A reflection of the limited political leverage of the URNG and PAN, the accords were only able to provide a framework for discussion on key issues for the transformation of the state and failed to provide specific measures for their implementation (Holiday 2000, 79). The responsibility for implementation was spread out to a variety of actors, in a way that dilutes the responsibility of any one actor, and thus causes significant problems of accountability and enforcement (Stanley and Holiday 2002, 423).

The UN was assigned an overall monitoring role (which ended in 2004) but it had limited leverage to enforce compliance. On the national level, the Comision de Accompaniento (Follow-up Commission) was created to interpret the letter and spirit of the accords and facilitate their implementation, yet it had no enforcement powers. In addition to the Follow-up Commission, a number of further special commissions were set up to discuss and make recommendations on key issues, including judicial reform, education and multilingualism and multiculturalism. These commissions were a positive step in that they provided a space for civil society, including indigenous representatives, to take part in political deliberations, a stark contrast to their previous exclusion. However, the impact of these commissions is mixed: some fell apart, some could not come to agreement and for those that did produce reports, their recommendations were not implemented by the government (Stanley and Holiday 2002, 424). Once again, these commissions did not have any enforcement or decision-making powers. The flip side of opening the process to civil society was that the responsibility for implementation became further diluted. With so many actors part of the implementation process, it was difficult to identify any particular body with responsibility for implementation and apply targeted pressure on it. In this context of diffuse (and deliberately confused) responsibility, a weak state with very few resources at its disposal and ongoing impunity, the political wrangling between the main parties to the peace process set the stage for the most significant setback for the implementation of the reforms: the rejection of the government's reform proposals in the 1999 referendum.

Arzú's enthusiasm for the peace accords began to wane in 1998, as his government backed off from commitment to pass new tax legislation. By June 1998, the approach of presidential elections in 1999 began to overshadow the implementation of the peace accords with the focus shifting on how to win the elections rather than the referendum.

The Accord on Constitutional Reforms and the Electoral Regime listed the specific constitutional reforms the government was required to sponsor within sixty days of the signing of the peace. The constitutional amendments were necessary to give the government the legal basis to reform the army and judiciary and to implement several aspects of the indigenous rights accord. It called upon the Congress to draft or amend any necessary legislation to comply with the accords, and also 'to agree to any other constitutional or legal amendments that may be required to maintain consistency and compatibility with the reforms proposed by the Parties'. This clause is what in part led to the defeat of the referendum.

The government first tried the easiest route by getting Congress to vote only on the provisions specifically listed in the accord. However, since the other political parties had not been part of the negotiation, they resisted passing reforms without first having input. Since the Constitution requires two-thirds majority from Congress, Arzú had to make concessions in order to get the amendments passed. He also argued that it was important to reach a level of consensus with opposition parties (FRG in particular) in order to prevent them from blocking the reforms at the implementation stage. The government thus created the Instancia Multipartidaria (Multiparty Body) in 1997 as a forum, outside Congress, to discuss and draft reforms beyond those specifically agreed in the Accord on Constitutional Reforms and the Electoral Regime. This Body, however, collapsed in 1998, in large part due to FRG's efforts to push through a provision that would have allowed former dictator Rios Montt to run for President (Stanley and Holiday 2002, 439). The debate went back to Congress, where each political party and a few key civil society organizations lobbied to get their own agendas included in the reform package. After two and a half years of political debate and legal setbacks, the result was an unwieldy package of about fifty reforms, up from the twelve required by the peace accords.

In 1999, this package was put to the population in a referendum. The government failed to carry out a comprehensive outreach campaign in support of the referendum, and the limited UN effort, overshadowed by the very effective 'no' campaign mounted by business elites and parties opposed to the reform in the final weeks before the referendum, was unable to compensate for the government's failure. This reflects the fact that neither the URNG nor the PAN had enough political leverage beyond the core of their supporters to push through the implementation of the accords. It also highlights the tension between the accords' 'participatory rhetoric and elitist origins' (Stanley and Holiday 2002, 438). Moreover, the PAN government did not work to get broad political support or buy in for the peace accords. Instead of presenting the accords as a long-term national project in which everyone had a stake, it tried to link any positive developments made in the area as PAN initiatives (Holiday 2000, 80). The PAN thus appropriated ownership of the accords hoping to gain electoral support, but this strategy backfired: only 17 per cent of the registered voters cast their ballots, and of those 55 per cent voted against the referendum. With such low turnout, 'the main winner of this vote was abstention, and the main loser was the peace process itself' (Jonas 2000b, 31). Without the constitutional amendments, there was no legal basis upon which to enact the reforms called for as part of the peace negotiations. In the defeat of the 1999 referendum, the peace process lost momentum and a window of opportunity to turn accords into reality was closed. It was a win for the traditional elites who were intent on preserving the status quo and unwilling to give up their hold on power, to the detriment of a real peace in Guatemala.

## The current status of conflict management in Guatemala

The failed efforts to pass constitutional amendments in 1999 were a setback in the implementation of the accords from which Guatemala has still not recovered. On the positive side, operational measures, including the definitive ceasefire, demobilization of URNG and return of refugees were successfully completed. Another important achievement was the establishment of the Historical Clarification Commission, whose final report attributed 93 per cent of violations to the army and 3 per cent to URNG, and declared that from 1980 to 1983 the actions and policies of the army were genocidal.

This was a crucial acknowledgment of the magnitude of the violations and provided human rights and indigenous activists the basis for further mobilization in demand of justice.[6]

On the whole, however, the peace accords have failed to bring about the vision for an inclusive and rights respecting democracy. They remain plans on paper that have not been turned into real reforms. Political and socio-economic divisions continue to be primarily drawn along ethnic lines as the indigenous population remains largely excluded from economic, social and political life (Isaacs 2010c, 1). Making up about half of the country's population, indigenous Mayans account for close to three-quarters of Guatemalans who live in poverty or extreme poverty (Isaacs 2010c, 9).

As in earlier decades, there is a clear link between rising inequality and the increase in violence that Guatemala has experienced of late. According to a report by the Human Rights Ombudsman, in 2009, there were 6,498 violent deaths, up from 5,781 in 2007. These rising levels of violence are attributed in large part to illegal armed groups and clandestine security organizations that have their roots in the civil war. These groups are not common criminals; their ranks count retired and active members of the security forces, military and intelligence service, as well as members of the economic elite. As part of the peace accords, these groups were supposed to be dismantled, but they were never fully demobilized. Rather, they adapted their former counter-insurgency tactics to the new post-war context, with the aim of protecting their hold on power and personal gain. They have transposed techniques used to fight the insurgency and apply them to intimidate and threaten those activists fighting for the implementation of the peace accords, in the area of land reform for example. Several provisions of the peace accords were aimed at eliminating clandestine security forces and professionalizing the police, judiciary and military. These measures were seen as essential to guaranteeing respect for human rights. However, with the failure of the 1999 referendum, these reforms were not implemented. The illegal armed groups target those who are demanding an end to impunity, both for crimes of the past, and current corruption. The driving force behind these illicit groups are those who opposed the peace process, largely those who control the power and wealth of the country and have a lot to lose if the accords are in fact implemented. Thus while the peace is signed, and outright hostilities ended in 1996, the battle for real reform in Guatemala continues to play out on a stage where impunity reigns.

What accounts for this failure and what lessons might be extracted that could be applied in further peace negotiations? The causes of this failed implementation are numerous, complex and interrelated. However, we can extract two elements worth highlighting: the first is the structure of the accords itself and the second is the lack of political will for implementation.

In order to achieve democracy and greater equality, the accords called for ambitious and comprehensive political, institutional, social and economic reforms. While the vision was very comprehensive, the Accords failed to propose a specific design. The actual structural changes needed to sustain peace were left for later discussion and constitutional reform. Furthermore, the peace accords presented lofty goals for a new state, but did not reflect any broad consensus. They also failed to detail mechanisms for implementation, including, crucially, identifying those responsible for implementation and structures within which they could be held accountable and compliance be enforced. Put bluntly, 'in the end, the Guatemalan accords are little more than an undemocratic elite pact, without the efficiency and decisiveness that elite-based arrangements sometimes bring' (Stanley and Holiday 2002, 457). This is one lesson to extract from Guatemala: to be wary of overly vague accords that do not include a firm implementation schedule and verification structure. Second, there was a lack of political will to implement these accords. The scope and level of ambition set out in the accords would have required significant political will as well as the resources to implement them (Alvarado 2006). To date, however, the government has only established ad hoc efforts rather than adopting a long term strategy for implementation.

While international financial institutions played a key role in providing pressures and incentives for signing of the Peace Accords, in the implementation phase very few were willing to condition ongoing aid on the compliance with accords, and even fewer were willing to fully cut off aid until the Accords were implemented (Gavigan 2009, 70). Some of these international actors failed to call the bluff of the domestic parties, especially the government, and assumed that the government had signed up to the accords in good faith (Jonas 2000a, 171). Even if the government was committed to the peace accords, it lacked the necessary leverage, broad support and resources to implement the reforms. Another part of the problem was that the IFIs and the government did not see eye to eye on a cornerstone of the entire reform process: ideologically, the IFIs were not committed to the progressive taxation approach, and pushed more for increasing indirect taxes, rather than insisting on taxing business elite and landowners who had historically refused to pay taxes. This combination of inadequate political analysis of the government's willingness and ability to implement the accords and an ideological position hesitant to support progressive taxation resulted in IFIs not using the full potential of their leverage to ensure that genuine socio-economic reforms were implemented.

The lack of political will and ability on the part of those tasked with implementing the peace was further exacerbated by a very strong and well-organized opposition to the Peace Accords. Economic elites in particular, proved to be a very influential 'uncivil actor' during the negotiation phase and in the post-accord period, effectively managing to block any real reform (Krznaric 1999, 13). Through its strong influence on the government (especially the Arzú administration) and its ability to forge a broad coalition against some of the key changes envisaged by the Peace Accords, CACIF was able to block any significant reform of the socio-economic sector. In the 'Accord on Socioeconomic Aspects and the Agrarian Situation', CACIF made sure there were no measures calling for substantial land reform and in the implementation phase, it managed to block major changes to the taxation system.[7] It further protected its interests by producing a document that was sufficiently vague so as not to tie down future governments to specific reforms (Krznaric 1999, 13). The latest evidence of this was the degree of resistance from the economic elites and their affiliated political parties to President Colom's proposal for a modest tax increase to about 10 per cent of GDP, still under the 12 per cent called for in 1996 (Isaacs 2010a, 112). Without higher taxes, the government does not have access to the funds necessary to invest in developing social infrastructure. The wealthy maintain their hold on a disproportionate amount of the resources while the poor become increasingly destitute. Meanwhile, the sectors of civil society supportive of the peace accords, failed to effectively mobilize in the implementation phase. In the post-accord phase, there was a complete lack of any institutional structure to allow various civil society organizations to continue participating in the peace process on an equal footing (Alvarez and Palencia Prado 2002, 4). In this model, popular participation took place in a context where structural exclusion has not been addressed, so while marginalized groups participate to some degree, they do not have the political leverage need to convert their voices into concrete changes (Stanley and Holiday 2002, 458).

## Conclusion

As stated in the Agreement on Constitutional reform, 'the aim [of the accords] is not to propose case-by-case measures, but to reformulate the whole conception of State organs and institutions with a view to strengthening democracy in line with present-day constitutional trends'. This statement highlights one of the main pitfalls in the design of the Guatemalan peace agreement. The accords were too comprehensive on the one hand – in terms of the complete revamping of the nation they were proposing – yet not comprehensive enough when it came to specific policies, and most importantly, a strategy for implementation and verification. In a context where the forces for the status quo have proven stronger than the forces for change, the military and economic structures of Guatemala remain untouched.

Peace negotiations represent a struggle to balance the immediate concern of reaching a lasting ceasefire with long-term considerations of prevention by addressing the root causes of conflict. In Guatemala, some of the key actors did try to put forward a long-term, forward-looking approach but were not able to support that vision with realistic and implementable measures. With the failure of the 1999 constitutional referendum, which would have provided a legal basis for that vision, structural causes of conflict remain largely unchanged and the clandestine forces that protect the status quo continue to operate. In a state where 98 per cent of attacks against human rights defenders go unpunished, impunity remains one of the greatest obstacles to the fulfilment of the accords. It is important not to minimize the achievements that have been made since 1996, however, if one evaluates the degree to which the underlying roots of the conflict were addressed by the peace agreements, there is still a long way to go before reaching positive peace in Guatemala.

## Notes

1 Ethnically identified as descendents of Spanish colonizers.
2 Who previously served as the 'conciliator' for the negotiations in the early 1990s.
3 At the request of the negotiating parties, the Group of Friends would respond to needs or help to resolve impasses. Mexico was the convener and had close ties to both sides which it used at key moments to apply pressure. Norway did a lot of informal diplomacy to help to resolve impasses such as the crises at the end of 1996 (ORPA kidnapping). Spain was the link to Western Europe. The US used its ties with the army to pressure it to accept civilian control.
4 For copies of all the accords, see: www.usip.org/resources/peace-agreements-guatemala
5 See clause 23, Agreement on the Basis for the Legal Integration of the Unidad Revolucionaria Nacional Guatemalteca.
6 For a comprehensive analysis of the CEH and its effect on democracy building, see Isaacs (2010b).
7 Legislation to increase taxes was passed early in 1998, but quickly repealed after widespread protests.

## References

Agreement on Constitutional Reforms and the Electoral Regime 1996 (available online at: www.usip.org/files/file/resources/collections/peace_agreements/guat_961207.pdf; accessed 4 October 2010).

Agreement of the Strengthening of Civilian Power and on the Role of the Armed Forces in a Democratic Society 1996 (available online at: www.usip.org/resources/peace-agreements-guatemala; accessed 4 October 2010).

Alvarado 2006 'Desarrollo humano e inclusión en tiempos de paz', Guatemala: el Procurador.

Alvarez, E. 2002a 'The Grand National Dialogue and the Oslo consultations: creating a peace agenda', London: ACCORD (available online at: www.c-r.org/our-work/accord/public-participation/guatemala-national-dialogue.php; accessed 4 October 2010).

—— 2002b 'The Civil Society Assembly: Shaping Agreement', London: ACCORD (available online at: www.c-r.org/our-work/accord/public-participation/guatemala-civil-society-assembly.php; accessed 4 October 2010).

Alvarez, E. and Palencia Prado, T. 2002 'Guatemala's Peace Process: Context, Analysis and Evaluation', London: ACCORD (available online at: www.c-r.org/our-work/accord/public-participation/guatemalas-peace-process.php; accessed 4 October 2010).

Basic Agreement for the Search for Peace by Political Means (Oslo Agreement) 1990 (available online at: www.c-r.org/our-work/accord/public-participation/guatemala-basic-agreement.php; accessed 4 October 2010).

Framework Agreement for the Resumption of the Negotiating Process between the Government of Guatemala and the UNIDAD Revolucionaria Nacional Guatemalteca 1994 (available online at: www.usip.org/files/file/resources/collections/peace_agreements/guat_940110.pdf; accessed 4 October 2010).

Gavigan, P. 2009 'Organized Crimes, Illicit Power Structures and Guatemala's Threatened Peace Process', *International Peacekeeping*, 16: 62–76.

Guatemala Memory of Silence 1999 Report of the Commission for Historical Clarifications, Conclusions and Recommendations.

Holiday, D. 2000 'Guatemala's Precarious Peace', Current History (available online at: http://davidholiday.com/publications/Guatemalas_Precarious_Peace.pdf; accessed 4 October 2010).

Jonas, S. 2000a *Of Centaurs and Doves: Guatemala's Peace Process*, Boulder, CO: Westview Press.

—— 2000b 'Democratization through Peace: The Difficult Case of Guatemala', *Journal of Interamerican Studies and World Affairs*, 42: v–38.

Isaacs, A. 2010a 'Guatemala on the Brink', *Journal of Democracy*, 21: 108–22.

—— 2010b 'At War with the Past? The Politics of Truth Seeking in Guatemala', *International Journal of Transitional Justice*, 4(2): 251–74.

—— 2010c 'Guatemala, Countries at the Crossroads', Washington, DC: Freedom House (available online at: www.freedomhouse.org/uploads/ccr/country-7832-9.pdf; accessed 4 October 2010).

Krznaric, R. 1999 'Civil and Uncivil Actors in the Guatemalan Peace Process', *Bulletin of Latin American Research*, 18:1–16.

Paris, R. 2004 *At War's End: Building Peace After Civil Conflict*, Cambridge: Cambridge University Press.

Salvesen, H. 2002 'Guatemala: Five Years After the Peace Accords: The Challenges of Implementing Peace', Oslo: PRIO (available online at: www.prio.no/files/file44990_guatemala_report_salvesen.pdf).

Stanley, W. and Holiday, D. 2002 'Broad Participation, Diffuse Responsibility: Peace Implementation in Guatemala', in Stedman, S. (ed.), *Ending Civil Wars: The Implementation of Peace Agreements*, Boulder, CO: Lynne Rienner.

UN News Service 2008 'Human Rights Defenders at Grave Risk in Guatemala, UN Expert Finds' (available online at: www.unhcr.org/refworld/docid/47bd63141a.html; accessed 4 October 2010).

WOLA 2007 'The Captive State: Organized Crime and Human Rights in Latin America' (available online at: www.wola.org/media/WOLA-rpt-OrganizedCrimeFinal.pdf; accessed 4 October 2010).

# 12   The failure of prevention

## Kosovo

*Marc Weller*

The Kosovo conflict was perhaps the most predicted one in modern history. For years, Kosovo had been referred to as the 'powder keg of the Balkans'. The inability of the international community to address it effectively serves as something of an indictment of the modern system of international conflict settlement, both globally and within Europe. However, the Kosovo conflict, along with the other challenges posed by the violent dissolution of the former Yugoslavia, also served to advance and shape some of the institutions, mechanisms and doctrines associated with conflict management in the wider Europe.

The period of high tension and eventual hostilities in Kosovo extended over exactly twenty years, although the issue is as yet far from concluded. It started when the resurgence of nationalist politics manifested itself in Serbia's campaign to modify the constitutional basis of Tito's Yugoslavia in 1988 and provisionally terminated with Kosovo's declaration of independence on 17 February 2008.

The complexity of this episode is commensurate with its duration. Its multifaceted nature is not only derived from the background factors of the conflict and its long prehistory, or from the twists and turns of events as the crisis progressed. Instead, Kosovo was such a complex situation because it touched on a number of important structural aspects of international order – and this at the very moment when the world, and especially Europe, was still searching for the principles of operation of the post-Cold War international order. Hence, when considering the succession of peaceable and forcible international interventions in relation to the former Yugoslavia, a number of structural tensions are revealed which proved too great for the international system to overcome. These relate both to the legal and institutional underpinnings of international action, and to the actual practice of international politics.

In terms of rules and institutions, the first factor inhibiting action was the principle of non-intervention. Non-intervention would preclude international action in relation to matters essentially within the domestic sphere of a state. Traditionally, governments have shown great deference to this principle, which was particularly relevant during the Cold War – a period marked by violent ideological confrontation over the issue of internal governance. While much effort was spent, especially in Europe, on developing international mechanisms aiming to prevent conflict between states, the principle of non-intervention in internal affairs retained its relevance. This classical rule of international law and international relations isolated developments in and around Kosovo from international involvement until it was too late for useful conflict prevention activities.

Second, there was the doctrine of territorial unity, which purports to protect existing states from challenges to their territorial integrity from within. Given the potentially secessionist dimension of the Kosovo issue, there was even greater hesitancy to become involved. And, at the time there was no institutional mechanism in Europe that could overcome these hesitations and administer collective action in the face of the growing crisis. The OSCE was reconfiguring itself from an instrument administrating the Cold War to a pan-European security organization. NATO was considering its own identity and a shift from collective self-defence to the exercise of some collective security functions. The Western European Union was abolished at the time. And the EU was still developing its foreign and security policy identity. Nevertheless, the principal Western European leaders saw in the various emanations of the Yugoslav conflict a proving ground for an imagined new European security identity that did not yet exist. The result was catastrophic failure.

While these factors are well known, the emergence of significant obstacles to action in terms of practical international politics was perhaps somewhat more surprising. First, it turned out that the organized international community was only able to focus on one major European conflict at any one time. After initial engagement with the conflict in Croatia, this turned out to be the conflagration in Bosnia and Herzegovina, which broke out with full force in spring 1992. It was clear by then that the situation in Kosovo was steadily deteriorating. But there was great hesitation to detract from any progress that was being made in relation to the settlement of that admittedly very dramatic conflict.

Second, there was reversion to interest-based politics on the part of the (former) great European powers. While the roots of the Balkan conflicts were claimed to lie in a resurgence of ethnic identity issues and ethnoterritorial claims that had been left unaddressed since Versailles, it emerged that some of the European states too appeared to revert to the mindset of that era. Calculations of national interests on the part of certain key states involved outweighed the need to achieve coherence in the collective crisis management attempts. The UK and France were reluctant to act against their old war-time ally Serbia. Italy was reputed to have gained strong commercial interests in Serbia, including lucrative communications licences for its company. Germany and Austria were seen to favour Slovenia and Croatia, two former elements of the Austro-Hungarian Empire. Hence, even when the EU had gained the institutional capacity to engage with a crisis of this kind, its members were unable to act jointly. Instead, it was left to the US to do the heavy lifting at key points in the development of the crisis, backed at times by the transatlantic alliance, NATO, and on other occasions the UN Security Council. During the Cold War transition, both institutions were heavily dominated by the US.

## The context of the conflict in Kosovo

The former Socialist Federal Republic of Yugoslavia was an edifice dedicated to the doctrine of brotherhood and unity. According to this Titoist maxim, ethnic conflict and strife of the past had lost its relevance in the new, socialist workers' republic that had been created after the Second World War. In fact, during the Tito years, multiethnic life did appear to function in ethnically mixed areas, in particular in Bosnia and Herzegovina, where the population consisted of three roughly equal ethnic Serb, ethnic Croat and ethnic (mainly Muslim) Bosniaks. In other parts, the respective titular ethnic groups tended to dominate public life in the six republics and the two autonomous territories (Serbia, Montenegro, Slovenia, Croatia, Macedonia and Bosnia and Herzegovina, along with Kosovo and Vojvodina). In some areas, this design resulted in a gradual waning of influence by previously dominant groups. In Kosovo, for instance, the number of ethnic Serbs dwindled, while the political influence of the majority ethnic Albanians increased.

Under Tito's constitution of 1974, the power of the republics and autonomous territories was carefully balanced. There was a rotating presidency and wide-ranging self-governance assigned to the eight constituent units. The two autonomous territories, Kosovo and Vojvodina, shared in these powers, although they were also subordinated to one of the republics – Serbia.

The carefully crafted constitutional balance was upset when nationalism under Slobodan Milošević gripped Serbia. While a number of other societies in Eastern Europe embraced a peaceful post-Cold War transition to democracy, Yugoslavia was soon in the grip of a major constitutional crisis. The largest constituent unit, Serbia, appeared to seek the ascendency in the federation, in part by establishing direct rule in Vojvodina and in particular in Kosovo. Moreover, Belgrade established centralized control over the armed forces. Croatia and Slovenia sought to counter this threat by proposing a looser, confederal-type constitutional settlement.

Belgrade had little incentive to agree to a reduction in the very powers it was just about to acquire. It appeared clear that Slovenia and Croatia could not revise the constitution unilaterally, without Serbia's assent. There was also little or no precedent for a successful unilateral secession that might have offered an alternative to the two republics. Indeed, during spring and early summer of 1991, European leaders and the US government expended considerable effort in seeking to make this latter point to the leaders of both entities.

The unilateral declaration of independence of Slovenia and Croatia of 25 June 1991 resulted in an armed confrontation with the Yugoslav National Army. While conflict with Slovenia ceased within ten days, significant fighting spread in Croatia. Under the Brioni agreement, achieved through intercession of an EC troika, a three-month suspension of implementing the declarations of independence was agreed in order to generate space for a settlement. The EC/EU, acting through its troika mechanism, and later the EC and the international conference on Yugoslavia, sought to lead the resolution of the conflict from this point onwards.

The EC conference on the former Yugoslavia chaired by Lord Carrington proceeded from the assumption that secession would be possible for those states in favour. Others might form a looser confederal-type association. The terms of the secession were to be agreed through the conference. In this way, it was hoped, Serbia's professed concern for its ethnic kin, who now found themselves in the newly independent republics, could be addressed. Accordingly, there were provisions for territorial autonomy of majority-ethnic Serb areas in Croatia, for instance. There was also a general commitment to minority rights and other tools that had been routinely applied in Western Europe to address ethnic diversity.

However, this approach overlooked the fact that Serbia was not genuinely interested in the fate of ethnic Serb populations. Instead, Belgrade sought to implement territorial ambitions under the colour of ethnopolitical demands. Belgrade argued that history had shown that ethnic Serbs could only safely live within Serbia. Hence, the areas mainly inhabited by ethnic Serbs should be joined to Serbia. Only then would the republics (minus the affected territories) be allowed to achieve independence.

While the other republics agreed to the EC peace proposal, Serbia alone refused it. Faced with this blockage in the settlement process, it was agreed that Serbia's consent would be circumvented. The EC declared its willingness to recognize those republics that unilaterally committed themselves to the key principles established in its settlement plan, including in particular minority rights and territorial autonomy for minority areas. In this way, the essence of the plan would be implemented, even if Serbia continued to refuse to adopt it. After all, its key elements concerning the protection of non-dominant groups were thought to address Serbia's concerns and would benefit ethnic Serbs, whether or not Serbia participated in the agreement.

This approach led to the recognition, at different points, of Croatia, Slovenia, Macedonia and Bosnia and Herzegovina as independent states, following the advice of the EC Badinter Arbitration Commission attached to the peace conference. By this time, armed conflict in Croatia had continued, leading to the armed occupation of around one-third of its territory. Ethnic Serbs had generally been the majority population in these areas, but there were others that were also incorporated into the territory. Those areas brought under control from Belgrade were subjected to a brutal policy of what subsequently became known as 'ethnic cleansing'. Non-Serb populations were terrorized and forced to leave their homes.

The United Nations had by this time established a peacekeeping operation which extended to the ironically named 'UN Protected Areas' in Croatia, i.e., areas under Serb control. Ethnic cleansing however continued in these areas.

The independence of Bosnia and Herzegovina in spring 1992 was greeted with an armed offensive of ethnic Serb militias, and the regular Yugoslav army deployed there. While the regular forces gradually diminished their direct involvement in the ensuing conflict, Belgrade remained closely intertwined with the authorities in 'Republika Srkpsa' led by Radovan Karadžić and Ratko Mladić – an entity that occupied roughly half of Bosnia and Herzegovina's territory and claimed to be an independent state. Ethnic Croats had also established their entity within Bosnia and Herzegovina with the support from Croatia.

The UN continued to persist in its peacekeeping mission administered through UNPROFOR, the UN Protection Force. This operation was designed to address basic humanitarian needs while peace negotiations continued. Moreover, key states sought to isolate the rest of Europe from the conflict through the maintenance in place of an arms embargo covering the region, including the embattled authorities of Bosnia and Herzegovina.

However, various international attempts to negotiate peace were frustrated, in the main by Serbia. Serbia used the veneer of international discussions to cover its campaign of continued ethnic cleansing in Bosnia and Herzegovina, and the consolidation of territorial control exercised by ethnic Serb authorities. It is estimated that roughly 100,000 non-Serbs (mainly Bosniaks) were killed in consequence of this policy, with about half of the population of Bosnia and Herzegovina being forcibly displaced.

By 1994, the United States started to take a more active role in attempts to conclude the conflict. An alliance between Croatia and the Bosnian government was shaped. In Operation Storm of 1995, Croatia recaptured much of its territory occupied by ethnic Serb forces, creating a further wave of displacement – this time of ethnic Serbs. Bosniak forces in Bosnia and Herzegovina made military advances for the first time. And the weak international peacekeeping force was gradually replaced by a far more robust intervention force. This development was triggered by the taking of the mainly Muslim enclave of Srebrenica by ethnic Serb forces, followed by the execution of some 7,000 Bosniak males. Srebrenica, along with other enclaves, had been declared a UN safe area, but the UN command failed to make good its pledge to use NATO air power in order to deter attacks or incursions against them.

In September 1995, NATO used limited force against ethnic Serb military and communications targets in Bosnia. The Dayton peace settlement ensued, providing for the continued legal personality of Bosnia and Herzegovina as one state. However, within the state, a complex territorial structure was established, allowing for the continued existence of Republika Srpska and, to an extent, its Croat counterpart, within Bosnia.

Throughout this period, the situation in Kosovo had remained very tense, but relatively calm. The Kosovo leadership under Ibrahim Rugova, elected President in an 'unofficial' poll, had declared independence of the territory and requested recognition along with the republics. This plea had been internationally ignored. Instead, Kosovo was placed under ever more stringent direct rule from Belgrade. Ethnic Albanians were excluded from public positions – a dramatic factor in a largely state-run economy as it then was. Ethnic Serbs were encouraged to settle in Kosovo to address the population balance. At that point, Kosovo was believed to be less than 10 per cent ethnic Serb, with ethnic Albanians making up nearly 90 per cent, along with small minority communities.

In view of the horrors unfolding in Bosnia and Herzegovina, the ethnic Albanian leadership resisted calls from within the territory, and also from Bosnia, to open a 'third front'. In addition to Bosnia and Croatia this would have involved launching a military campaign against the Belgrade authorities in Kosovo, thus dividing its forces further. Instead, a peaceful resistance campaign was built up, which sought to challenge Serb rule by establishing parallel state institutions, in particular schools, from which ethnic Albanians had been excluded.

However, international settlement attempts were principally focused on the conflict in Bosnia and Herzegovina. It was only when a violent movement, the Kosovo Liberation Army (KLA) became active in Kosovo, that the issue became more prominent on the international agenda.

## Actors in the conflict management process

### The local conflict parties

The key actors directly involved were the government of the rump Yugoslavia and the Republic of Serbia on the one side. They controlled most of the former Yugoslav national army, and the entire state security apparatus. On the other side, in Kosovo, the LDK party under Ibrahim Rugova dominated, until its influence was partially displaced by the KLA and the political parties that emerged from it from 1996 onwards. The position of Kosovo was made more complicated by a very active diaspora movement that was committed in part to support to the LDK parallel government under Prime Minister Bujar Bukoshi and President Rugova. However, more radical elements within the diaspora soon lent support to the KLA, pressing at times for positions that were more hard-line than those represented by the Kosovars in the region.

### International actors

On the international scene, the EC/EU sought to establish itself as a credible actor. Later, the EC Conference was replaced by the International Conference on Yugoslavia, co-chaired with the United Nations, which was already running the ill-fated UNPROFOR mission in Croatia and Bosnia and Herzegovina. This was backed by the so-called

Contact Group, consisting of the US, UK, France, Germany, Italy and Russia. The Organization for Security and Cooperation in Europe (OSCE) was also deployed, although its effectiveness was diminished due to the operation of the principle of consensus decision making. Its long-term mission in relation to Kosovo and the region was suspended when Serbia withdrew consent for its operation. At a later stage, the OSCE took charge of the so-called Kosovo Verification Mission that emanated from the Hoolbroke agreement of the autumn of 1998. The verification mission had been established to monitor compliance by all parties in Kosovo with UN Security Council Resolution 1199, especially with the ceasefire provisions. That venture was ill-conceived and ended in failure, ultimately leading to the outbreak of hostilities with NATO in 1999.

The EC/EU's attempt to play a strong role as a conflict management agency was inhibited by the failure of its members to agree clear policies, and by the fact that several of its members were seeking a more individual role. For instance, the EC/EU was represented in the Rambouillet talks through one 'EU' mediator among the trio of three international representatives. However, this involvement was somewhat symptomatic of the unclear identity of the EU as a foreign affairs player over the relevant period. The Rambouillet conference was in fact chaired by the foreign ministers of the UK and France, leaving the EU mediator in a subordinate position. The chairs, in turn, reported to the Contact Group, consisting, as was noted above, of the UK, France, Germany and Italy, on the European side, instead of the EU as a unitary actor.

At the global level, the UN Security Council only became more strongly engaged on the Kosovo issue when actual conflict in the territory intensified in 1998. The Council acted in close coordination with the Contact Group, which essentially served as a mechanism to (attempt to) bind the Russian Federation into a consensus of how to proceed. Involvement of the UN Security Council also brought China into play, in its role as a permanent member of the Security Council. China was traditionally hostile to UN involvement in the internal affairs of states.

Hence, rather than resulting in 'joined-up global governance' ranging from the mediation effort on the ground to the EC/EU, the Contact Group and the Security Council, friction emerged at all levels, including the global level. Russia, in particular, became increasingly keen to be recognized and treated as a Great Power once again, having been somewhat displaced from its Cold War status of a 'superpower'. While Russia tolerated action in the Contact Group, including even the threat of the use of force against Yugoslavia/Serbia in order to achieve a political settlement, it strongly objected to the actual implementation of this threat. After the use of force by NATO, the Contact Group was unable to operate for a considerable period. Moscow even took unilateral action by introducing its armed forces into Kosovo at the point of the withdrawal of Belgrade's security forces.

For some time, the Contact Group acted as the so-called 'quint', without the participation of Russia. However, Russia rejoined when it came to the final status settlement for Kosovo. But Moscow was frustrated once more when the status talks failed to result in an agreed settlement. Kosovo's unilateral declaration of independence, with the support of the US and many EU states, was seen by Russia as a further provocation.

### Capacity of the primary mediator

The role of primary mediator shifted over time, as will be related below. Initially, the EC Conference on the former Yugoslavia addressed the Kosovo issue peripherally.

The subsequent international conference effort, resulting in the Geneva follow-on talks, fared little better. When conflict broke out, by 1998, the US launched a mediation effort led by Ambassador Chris Hill, who engaged in shuttle diplomacy in relation to both sides. He was eclipsed, at times, by Ambassador Richard Holbrooke, who was seen to enjoy better contacts with Slobodan Milošević. During the period of Rambouillet, US Secretary of State Madeleine Albright in turn sought to eclipse him, taking on a direct role inside and outside of the negotiations. The weight of the US effort was crucial in persuading the Kosovo Albanian side that it would have to settle for an interim agreement. However, no corresponding influence was brought to bear on Yugoslavia/Serbia. The Milošević government remained impervious to US threats at whatever level they were made. Russia did not deploy its full weight in favour of the settlement that was on offer, joining instead with Serbia in objecting to the deployment of the NATO-led peacekeeping force in Kosovo foreseen at Rambouillet. Russia also opted out of the Contact Group consensus during the later phase of the Ahtisaari negotiations on Kosovo's final status. Its position offered reassurance to Belgrade that no settlement would in the end be imposed upon it by the Security Council if it refused a compromise offered by the UN special envoy.

The team of the UN special envoy, who had taken up residence in Vienna for the negotiations, was composed of representatives drawn from the UN, but also drafted in from key Contact Group states, or their trusted allies. While the standing of the UN Special Envoy, Marti Ahtisaari, was considerable, his credibility was undermined by the eventual failure of the Contact Group to agree on the outcome of his mission, illustrated especially by Russia's opting out of the Contact Group consensus (detailed above). The attempt to replay these negotiations through a troika composed of a senior Russian, US and German emissary was in turn undermined by the realization that the US remained committed to the Ahtisaari final status package, which foresaw internationally supervised independence for Kosovo.

## The structure of the conflict management process

In the 1990s, Kosovo did not feature much in the initial attempts to address the Yugoslav conflicts. It was not considered eligible for statehood. Hence, it was principally excluded from the initial EC conference. Kosovo was only permitted to attend at the fringes of several subsequent settlement conferences, including the major London conference of the summer of 1992. By then, the conflict in Bosnia and Herzegovina dominated the international agenda. It was thought that opening the Kosovo issue might provoke the rump Yugoslavia/Serbia to leave the conference process altogether. Instead, the Kosovo issue was supposed to be addressed through a follow-on mechanism – a working group convened in Geneva. However, that process never blossomed into a substantive negotiation. Instead, it gave the misleading impression that the Kosovo issue was being addressed somewhere else, when this was not in fact the case.

The Dayton settlement is widely credited with providing the starting gun for the armed confrontation in Kosovo that was to develop over 1996 and the subsequent years. The Rugova leadership in Kosovo had been sustained by a pledge offered by the international mediators that the Yugoslav conflict would not be considered terminated until all aspects, including Kosovo, had been addressed. However, Dayton covered only Bosnia and Herzegovina. It resulted in a partial rehabilitation of the rump Yugoslavia and the Serb republic, including the lifting of some international sanctions. More radical elements in

Kosovo saw this as confirmation of their view that Kosovo would only attract international interest if it launched its own armed campaign.

The insurgency in Kosovo was initially conducted on a small scale. However, it resulted in a round of further repression in the territory which, in turn, swelled the ranks of the KLA. Heavy-handed counter-insurgency tactics, which in part resembled elements of the ethnic cleansing campaigns that had been observed in Bosnia and Herzegovina, resulted in the exodus of significant number of ethnic Albanians. By early 1998, around 300,000 had been displaced or turned into refugees flooding into neighbouring states.

It was really only at this very late stage that a significant international effort was mounted to engage the Kosovo conflict – at the very point when it had already largely spun out of control. The UN Security Council called, in mandatory Chapter VII resolutions, for a halt of violence on both sides, and a withdrawal or cantonment of Yugoslav/Serb forces, and for rapid progress towards a political settlement. With the support of the Contact Group, US Ambassador Hill led a process of indirect negotiations between Belgrade and the LDK leaders in Kosovo. This process sought to arrest developments through an interim agreement which would provide for the return to substantial self-administration for Kosovo. However, neither side was willing to commit to the quite detailed proposals that were emerging from the Hill team.

In view of the looming humanitarian crisis, NATO threatened the use of force late in September 1998, demanding a cessation of hostilities, withdrawal of forces and the rapid achievement of a political settlement in accordance with the requirements set by the Security Council. An air strike was averted through a last-minute settlement negotiated by US interlocutor Richard Holbrooke. However, the agreement was in fact fragmentary. Moreover, it had only been concluded with one side to the conflict – Slobodan Milošević in Belgrade. It only generated a short period of calm on the ground, which both sides used to regroup their forces. By the end of the year, a full-scale armed confrontation had broken out again. This time, hundreds of thousands of displaced were exposed to the harsh conditions of the Balkan winter. Moreover, the so-called Račak massacre, where some forty-five ethnic Albanian villagers had been killed execution style, led to a last-ditch attempt to achieve a negotiated settlement.

The Contact Group (including Russia) summoned the parties to an international conference where a settlement was to be achieved in a matter of weeks. Whichever side failed to accept an agreement was subjected to a threat of the use of force to be administered by NATO.

The meeting was held at Château Rambouillet near Paris. It was guided by the Contact Group and formally chaired by the UK and French Governments at Foreign Minister level, with three principal mediators supposedly acting together (Chris Hill (US), Wolfgang Petritsch (EC/EU), Boris Mayorski (Russia)). The mediation team was supported by lead lawyer James O'Brian and his junior John Lewitzki, who conducted many of the actual technical discussion with the parties. The Contact Group members and relevant international organizations were also represented in the Château with significant delegations, although they mainly exercised a watching brief.

The format of the discussion was mainly that of proximity talks. This, it was thought, would avoid a confrontation among the two delegations likely to lead to a walkout. Each delegation inhabited a separate meeting chamber. Contact was possible over meals, where separate rooms were served from buffets offering the same fare. In accordance with the precedent of Dayton, the delegations were meant to be strictly isolated within the confines of the Château until an agreement was forthcoming – a concept that turned out to be somewhat naïve in the age of mobile communications.

The Contact Group offered a short listing of non-negotiable principles. The parties were considered to have accepted these by virtue of their attendance at the talks. These principles, including a commitment to the territorial integrity of the rump Yugoslavia, and an undertaking that the agreement, once reached, could not be altered by either side alone, appeared to be based on undertakings given to Belgrade at the time of the Holbrook discussions. This approach was not really consistent with the pledge that any agreement would be considered as merely interim t, committing both sides to an autonomy deal for a limited period – a fact that would only be brought out once the negotiations progressed.

In addition to the non-negotiable principles, the parties received a draft for a framework agreement and, successively, annexes regulating the proposed constitutional settlement, human rights, community rights, economic issues and military matters. Each party was expected to offer detailed comments on each provision put forward by the mediators. The Kosovo side engaged in this process, while Belgrade initially failed to engage. It was only after a visit by the UN mediator to Slobodan Milošević in Belgrade that Yugoslavia/ Serbia appeared to offer substantive contributions.

While much effort had been expended in persuading Belgrade to engage, little attention had been paid to the Kosovo side. The Kosovo delegation was dominated by the KLA, and by parties affiliated with it. The LDK under Ibrahim Rugova found itself in the minority. Moreover, to prevent a split, the delegation had agreed to take decisions only by consensus. This meant that any one member could inhibit signature to the agreement at the end of the day.

Kosovo was busily offering amendments to the technical provisions of the agreement that had been put forward. However, there was a unified view that any agreement reached would indeed merely be an interim one, after which the people would be free to determine the future of the territory. A draft that had emerged after the Hill visit to Belgrade appeared to favour the opposite view, offering an interim agreement that would, for all intents and purposes, also be a permanent one.

This issue led to a split in the Contact Group and among the mediators. The US, at times represented by US Secretary of State Madeleine Albright, was willing to concede, at least in a side letter, that the will of the people would indeed be assessed through a referendum after the expiry of the interim period. The final text of the actual agreement called for a meeting to consider the mechanism for a final settlement to be set up in view, *inter alia*, of the performance by the parties to the agreement, the Helsinki Final Act (often read as code for the principle of territorial integrity) and the will of the people.

By the end of the negotiations, both parties were in fact fairly close to a possible agreement on the terms of political settlement for the interim period. Whether that constitutional settlement could have worked in practice has been questioned at times, given its complexity and the very wide range of separate rights accorded to the ethnic Serb community in Kosovo as such. But the question of whether the agreement was genuinely an interim agreement, and what would occur after the proposed interim of three years, remained divisive within the Kosovo delegation. Its leader, Hashim Thaçi, later Prime Minister of independent Kosovo, alone opposed signature. This would have led to a collapse of the pressure meant to be brought to bear on Serbia to accept through the threat of NATO force. In the end, Kosovo managed to offer language that left it somewhat obscure whether it had accepted the text, or whether it would do so after a review by constituencies (essentially KLA field commanders) at home.

A further meeting was called at the Kleber Conference Centre in Paris, in the hope to obtain the definite consent of the parties after having addressed the issue of implementation. According to Annex B to the agreement, NATO would exercise a leading role in military implementation. In view of the failure of the essentially unarmed OSCE 'verification' mission that had been meant to help implement the Holbrooke agreement of the previous year, Western delegations in the Contact Group regarded this requirement as non-negotiable, as did Kosovo. This view was also shaped by the dramatic failure of UN peacekeeping in other parts of the region. However, Russia did not feel bound into the Contact Group consensus on this issue, and argued, along with Yugoslavia/Serbia, that at most there should be a UN peacekeeping operation. In any event, by the time of the Kleber follow-on meeting, Belgrade had evidently concluded that it would rather ride out a military campaign by NATO than sign onto the Rambouillet project, engaging in a campaign of frustrating dialogue during the final days of the conference.

While Russia had in fact supported the forcible summons to the Rambouillet Conference in the Contact Group, it vigorously opposed the use of force by NATO after the failure of the negotiations. Through the mechanism of the G-8 and other means, it became possible however to involve the Russian Federation in the efforts to terminate hostilities in June 1999. Security Council Resolution 1244 (1999) provided for an (effectively) total withdrawal of Serb forces from Kosovo, the establishment of a United Nations interim administration and substantial autonomy for Kosovo, to be followed by a final status process.

## Proposed settlement design

The Rambouillet draft is a complex document indeed. It offers wide-ranging autonomy for Kosovo during the interim period. However, the FRY retained jurisdiction in relation to territorial integrity, maintaining a common market, monetary policy, defence, foreign policy, customs, federal taxation and federal elections. Kosovo's competences were established indirectly, through an assignment of powers to the individual Kosovo institutions. Kosovo itself was not clearly designated as an entity. Instead, residual powers were to be exercised at communal level. Indeed, much emphasis was placed on local self-government, as one way of ensuring that the ethnic Serb community would benefit from autonomy within autonomy. In addition, the communes would have been able to develop relationships among themselves – that is to say, an ethnic Serb entity might have been formed from among the majority-ethnic Serb communities.

There was guaranteed representation for non-dominant groups, particularly the ethnic Serb community, at all levels, including the Kosovo Assembly. Community members in the Assembly would have had the right to exempt their constituents from legislation which, in their view, would adversely affect their fundamental constitutional rights or vital interests. In addition, national communities would be able to establish institutions for non-territorial, functional autonomy. Moreover, minority rights and full protection of human rights was guaranteed.

The Rambouillet settlement therefore went out of its way to deny a distinct legal personality to Kosovo, while maintaining FRY (and to a significantly lesser extent, Serb) jurisdiction over key areas. Moreover, the ethnic Serb community would enjoy its own regional and local territorial autonomy, functional autonomy, consociational power-sharing mechanisms (guaranteed representations, at least soft vetoes), and minority rights additional to the already highly advanced catalogue of human rights rendered applicable in the territory.

This multilayered system of protection, mainly for the benefit of the ethnic Serb population, may have been rather too complex to allow Kosovo to function as a polity. The Kosovo side was of course much preoccupied by the need to figure out how the system could actually work in practice. From the perspective of the Contact Group, the issue looked different. The rump Yugoslavia/Serbia was to be given every reassurance in relation to the fate of ethnic Serbs during the interim period. Hence, generating a settlement that might be acceptable to Belgrade was the principal objective – making peace prevailed over the attempt to achieve a workable constitutional design. In the end, Kosovo's hesitations about the workability of that design gave way to wider considerations. From Kosovo's perspective, obtaining the presence of NATO on its territory, and achieving an undertaking relating to the exercise of the will of the people at the conclusion of the interim period, were the most important elements. Moreover, there was strong pressure not to undermine the threat of the use of force against the side opposing a compromise by refusing the draft, however deficient it appeared from Kosovo's perspective.

This latter issue raises the fundamental problem evidenced in the Rambouillet process, along with all subsequent settlement efforts. Belgrade was principally only willing to deal on the basis of an undertaking that what appeared to be an interim agreement would permanently guarantee its territorial integrity. Kosovo was only willing to accept an interim agreement if it was clear that it would only apply for a period of three years, to be followed by a mechanism for a final settlement that did at least not preclude a referendum on independence. Both positions were essentially irreconcilable. The mediation instead focused on making autonomy attractive to the rump Yugoslavia/Serbia, but offering very wide-ranging concessions on the rights of ethnic Serbs in Kosovo and their continued affiliation with Serbia which was, in fact, not a contested issue. Kosovo was happy to offer wide-ranging concessions on that point, provided its principal aim was not frustrated.

Kosovo in the end accepted the Rambouillet package, while Serbia refused to sign. At this point, Russia sharply distanced itself from the Contact Group position, arguing that the annex on military implementation had not been collectively agreed. Moreover, when NATO actually used force in accordance with the threat that had been previously supported, at least implicitly, by the Contact Group and the Security Council, international opinion was sharply divided.

The Security Council reasserted itself when it came to the conclusion of hostilities. In Resolution 1244 (1999), adopted under mandatory Chapter VII of the UN Charter, the Council confirmed that the rump Yugoslavia/Serbia would withdraw from Kosovo (with some minor exceptions). The territory would instead be placed under United Nations administration. That administration would help to develop institutions of self-government in Kosovo which would progressively assume the functions of public authority in the territory during the interim period. Once that aim had been achieved, there would follow a final status process.

The UN administration (UNMIK) assigned to itself in its very first regulation full powers of government in the territory. By the end of 1999 it devised a Joint Interim Administrative Structure. This generated a system of co-governance between local ministers (representing majority and minority communities) and UN administrators.

This was followed by the promulgation of an interim Constitutional Framework. According to this document, more and more powers were transferred to local actors. Again, there were provisions for power sharing in guaranteeing representation for non-dominant groups, in particular the ethnic Serb community. However, in consequence of the experiences with excessive consociationalism under the Dayton Accord for Bosnia and Herzegovina, there were no hard vetoes or blocking powers. Instead, the special representative of the UN secretary-general reserved key powers relating to security and justice for the UN administration. Moreover, he continued to exercise the right to overrule local decisions if they were, in his view, incompatible with the Constitutional Framework.

The ethnic Serb community remained to some extent aloof from the offer of soft power sharing contained in the Framework Constitution. Belgrade retained a significant element of control, especially in relation to northern Kosovo (Mitrovica) that had remained under ethnic-Serb dominance. A parallel system of government funded from Belgrade was maintained there, and in some other areas. Members of the ethnic Serb community also dissociated themselves by boycotting elections and other public functions for certain periods.

The system of governance was also prone to difficulties within the ethnic Albanian community. The significant number of seats reserved for the Serb ethnic community and others meant that it was difficult for any one party to obtain an clear majority. Moreover, there was international pressure to generate inclusive governance, assigning power and posts to all the principal parties. On the other hand, personal animosities among the leaders of the major parties dating back to the period of armed struggle rendered coalition politics problematic.

## The current status of conflict management in Kosovo

The Rambouillet accords had foreseen a mechanism to determine a final status process within three years. The UN administration offered a policy entitled 'Standards before Status', holding out the prospect of status talks once the provisional institutions of self-government had proven themselves according to a set of benchmarks. What started out as a set of concise criteria was developed by the UN into a catalogue of standards ranging in the end over some 120 pages. Kosovo attempted to develop a complex matrix to try and track and advance its own performance. Progress, however, was hesitant. Nevertheless, the so-called March riots of 2004 generated a sense that status discussions could not be put off for much longer. After an alleged assault on ethnic Albanian children by ethnic Serbs on the dividing line with northern Kosovo, elements of the majority population attacked ethnic Serbs, their property and their religious and cultural heritage.

By 2005, the UN started to prepare for the launch of the final status process. That process was to be led by UN Special Envoy Martti Ahtisaari. He was supported by a deputy, Albert Rohan, and a team of legal and other experts (UNOSEK). The experts appeared to have chosen roughly to represent the principal Contact Group states and other interested parties. The mediation was based in Vienna. Initial rounds of discussions were held in various palais around the town, and later moved to the more austere building housing the UN institutions and offices in Vienna.

Whereas Rambouillet followed a proximity format, this time both sides faced one another across the conference table. The proceedings were conducted by the mediators. Meetings here held in thematic working groups, forcing the parties to address specific, technical issues. This procedure had apparently been agreed with the Serb side – a fact it later came to regret. As was the case in Rambouillet, the parties therefore did not really engage on the major underlying clash of interest – continued association with Serbia or independence. Instead, particular issues such as power sharing and community rights, decentralization, protection of cultural objects, etc., were addressed.

The mediators invited the parties to present positions on these issue areas, at times prompted by questionnaires or lists of issues handed to the parties. They would then refine these into compromise papers on each of the major issue areas under discussion. Often, the claim of the mediators that these represented an emerging agreement of the parties was disputed by both sides. Nevertheless, a series of specific proposal emerged as a result of this working group process. Belgrade then changed tack and requested top-level discussions on the issue of status. However, given the divergent attitude of both sides, these produced no common ground.

The conference process had generated a dynamic that represented high risks for both parties. The Contact Group had declared at the outset of the final status process that once negotiations had commenced, no side would be allowed to block a final settlement. It also envisaged endorsement of a deal by the UN Security Council. This opened up two alternative scenarios. The work-group method might generate the substance of a settle-ment on most issues that would need addressing other than status. The Security Council might then impose this settlement on the parties. It might do so with a determination that Kosovo would be entitled to hold a referendum on independence. Or it might confirm the continued territorial unity of Serbia, while holding Kosovo to the compromises it had made in the negotiations, thinking that it was trading concessions on internal governance for the status it was seeking.

The Ahtisaari package that was put forward to the Council did not address the issue of status directly. However, in terms of competences and institutions, it offered to Kosovo everything it needed to act as a state. On the other hand, there remained impor-tant requirements relating to decentralization, community (minority) rights, cultural heritage and other issues. Moreover, the proposal provided for continued international involvement in the governance of Kosovo.

The proposal was accompanied by a separate document, containing the recommenda-tion of the special envoy on status. He argued that the political situation made a return of Kosovo to the jurisdiction of Serbia impossible. Instead, the only viable solution would be what he termed supervised independence. While Kosovo would achieve statehood, the concerns of communities, including especially the Serb community, would remain subject to international supervision for a period.

The UN secretary-general endorsed this proposal, but it did not attract endorsement from the Security Council. Instead, the Council attempted to engage directly with the parties in order to find a compromise solution. A further mediation effort was undertaken by a Troika under the leadership of Wolfgang Ischinger, again without result. In the end, on 17 February 2008, Kosovo declared itself independent.

While this decision is often considered an act of unilateral secession, this view is not entirely correct. While independence was not obtained in agreement with Belgrade, it was nevertheless the result of an exhausting final status process administered by the United Nations. Moreover, Kosovo accepted the Ahtisaari package in its entirely, and enshrined its provisions in its own constitution. Hence, Kosovo unilaterally accepted the outcome of the mediation effort and kept in place the whole range of concessions it had made in the expectation of an agreed secession.

Serbia, backed by the Russian Federation, continued to challenge Kosovo's status. It persuaded the UN General Assembly to request an advisory opinion from the International Court of Justice (ICJ) on whether or not the unilateral declaration of independence by the Provisional Institutions of Self-government in Kosovo was in accordance with international law.

Both parties came under increasing international pressure to address practical issues of this kind, rather than focusing on further discussions of status, after the ICJ delivered its opinion on the lawfulness or otherwise of Kosovo's declaration of independence in July 2010, expecting the ICJ to hold that the Provisional Authorities of Self-government in Kosovo had not enjoyed legal authority to declare independence. Hence, Kosovo's declaration of independence would be *ultra vires*, or in violation of mandatory Security Council Resolution 1244 (1999) which, in Serbia's view, memorialized the commitment of the organized international community to the continued territorial integrity of Serbia. However, the ICJ found that the declaration of independence had not been adopted in violation of general international law, or in conflict with the more specific legal requirements flowing from the UN Security Council's decisions relating to Kosovo. This finding, while non-binding, severely undermined Serbia's campaign to seek a reopening of the status issue – a campaign that would not have promised a great deal of success, given that Kosovo had already been recognized as a state by sixty-nine governments at that time.

The EU, which had been unable to agree on a unanimous position in favour of the recognition of Kosovo, reasserted itself as a mediator at this point. In the context of discussions with the parties about their future relations with the Union, it obtained initial agreement to launch a new round of talks. These would focus on practical coexistence of Serbia and Kosovo, irrespective of the disagreement on status between the two sides. However, the collapse of the governing coalition in Kosovo, and the resulting need to hold fresh elections in December 2010, delayed progress.

## Conclusion

The Kosovo episode highlights a number of significant failings in the international architecture for the management of ethnic or secessionist conflict. First, it confirms that traditionally significant international involvement in conflict settlement attempts will generally only be triggered by actual violence. While violence was widely predicted, decisive international action was only launched when it had started to occur. Of course, by then, the positions of the parties tend to be deeply entrenched. Their constituencies, affected by the violent contestation, will have coalesced around maximalist demands made by the more radical leadership on both sides. It is far more difficult to walk the parties back to a position of balanced, reasonable compromise once that point has been reached.

Happily, since then, a stronger emphasis is being placed in international practice on early, or preventative, involvement in conflict management. Moreover, at least in Europe, the institutional furniture for addressing conflicts has been improved, and will be improved further, as the EU Lisbon Treaty is being implemented. However, providing the EU with a diplomatic service and a stronger crisis management capacity will not in itself resolve many of the issues that obstructed effective action throughout the Kosovo episode. The difficulty of shaping a policy consensus among the EU member states will remain.

The attempt to achieve integrated conflict management, joining the regional layer with the UN system through the medium of the Contact Group (and therefore the inclusion of Russia), was a further source of disappointment in this episode. In critical phases of the crisis, the Contract Group consensus broke down, rendering this mechanism, as well as the UN Security Council, inoperative. It is unlikely that there will be a significant number of further conflicts of this kind at the heart of Europe. Instead, other instances that have arisen (south Ossetia and Abkhazia), that are awaiting settlement (Nagorno-Karabakh, Transnistria), or that may arise (Ukraine), fall into the area of Russia's so-called near abroad. It is unlikely that the mechanisms ultimately employed to settle the Kosovo issue, relying heavily on US leadership and even NATO military involvement, can be employed in that context. Instead, Russia on the one hand, the EU on the other, and the OSCE binding them together and bringing in the US in a more tempered way, will tend to offer more likely avenues for progress.

In terms of substantive approaches to ethnopolitical conflict settlements, developments in Kosovo reflect both the changing realities on the ground, as well as the changing fashions among international conflict settlement professionals. The initial Hill proposals, and the Rambouillet agreement, offered strongly corporate consociational structures to the ethnic Serb population in Kosovo, in exchange for a restoration of Kosovo's autonomy at least for an interim period. During the period of UNMIK administration, the Constitutional Framework still offered consociational elements. However, given that these concerned a polity that was now actually being administered internationally (and without Serbia's involvement), their effect was significantly tempered. They offered opportunities for co-governance to non-dominant communities, without risking deadlock in the political system should that offer not be taken up.

The Ahtisaari settlement, which was in the end fully adopted in Kosovo's independence constitution, contained a complex mixture of tools of ethnopolitical conflict settlement. The constitutional design offered some modest, albeit still predominantly corporate consociational elements, as far as guaranteed community (minority) representation was concerned. However, rather than emphasising this power-sharing dimension, community interests in the main were to be guaranteed through decentralization and local self-governance, coupled with a very strongly entrenched and broad set of minority rights. This constitutional design was meant to be supported, during an interim phase, through international involvement by way of so-called 'supervised independence'. While that latter element did not formally emerge, given the deadlock in the UN Security Council over Kosovo's final status, international involvement in the Kosovo constitutional administration nevertheless persisted in an informal way.

# References

### Dissolution of Yugoslavia

Judah, T. 2009 *The Serbs: History, Myth and the Destruction of Yugoslavia*, 3rd edn. New Haven, CT: Yale University Press.

Petritsch, Wolfgang, Robert Pichler and Martin Prochaszka 2005 *Kosovo-Kosova: Der Lange Weg zum Frieden. Mit einem Beitrag von Martin Prochaszka*. Wieser Verlag.

Trbovich, Ana S. 2008 *A Legal Geography of Yugoslavia's Disintegration*. Oxford: Oxford University Press.

Weller, M. 2011 *Twenty Years of Crisis: The Violent Dissolution of Yugoslavia*. Oxford: Oxford University Press.

### Kosovo negotiations

Judah,T. 2008 *Kosovo: What Everyone Needs to Know.* Oxford: Oxford University Press.
Ker-Lindsay, J. 2009 *Kosovo: The Path to Contested Statehood in the Balkans.* London: Tauris & Co. Ltd.
Perritt, Henry H., Jr. 2009 *The Road to Independence for Kosovo: A Chronicle of the Ahtisaari Plan.* Cambridge: Cambridge University Press.
Weller, Marc 2008 *Peace Lost: The Failure of Conflict Prevention in Kosovo.* Leiden and Boston, MA: Martinus Nijhoff.
—— 2009 *Contested Statehood: Kosovo's Struggle for Independence.* Oxford: Oxford University Press.


### Collected documents

Bethlehem, Daniel and Marc Weller 1997 *The Yugoslav Crisis in International Law: General Issues Part 1.* Cambridge: Cambridge University Press.
Krieger, Heike 2001 *The Kosovo Conflict and International Law: An Analytical Documentation 1974–1999.* Cambridge: Cambridge University Press.
Ramcharan, Bertrand G. 1997 *The International Conference on the Former Yugoslavia: Volume 1: Official Papers.* The Hague: Kluwer Law International.
—— 1997 *The International Conference on the Former Yugoslavia: Volume 2: Official Papers.* The Hague: Kluwer Law International.
Trifunovska, Snezana 1994 *Former Yugoslavia Through Documents: From its Creation to Its Dissolution, Part 1.* The Hague: Kluwer Academic Publishers.
—— 1999 *Former Yugoslavia Through Documents: From its Dissolution to the Peace Settlement, Part 2.* Boston, MA: Brill.
Weller, Marc 1999 *The Crisis in Kosovo, 1989–1999.* Cambridge: Documents and Analysis Publishing.

# 13 A never-ending story
## Cyprus

*Christalla Yakinthou*

The Cyprus conflict is one that has evaded a clear resolution for more than three decades. From the outside, it is something of a bizarre enigma; stemming in part from the straightforward image it deceptively portrays. After the war of 1974 and the resultant forced population separation to create an ethnically Turkish 'north' and an ethnically Greek 'south', open conflict between Greek and Turkish Cypriots has been limited. Each community lived completely separated from the other for twenty-nine years, until checkpoints opened in 2003 enabling people to cross between the sides, and they have done so more or less peacefully since then. Open conflict is extremely rare, and diplomacy continues to be the means through which the war is conducted. There is no communication between political elites, except during negotiations, and neither recognizes the legitimacy of the other. Since 1983, when the Turkish Cypriots unilaterally declared independence, a cold war over recognition has been conducted between the communities, where the Turkish Cypriot side has made significant efforts to garner international support for its breakaway status, and the Greek Cypriot side has made equally significant efforts to block that recognition. While the Turkish Cypriots have superior military force in their favour, the Greek Cypriots have legal recognition; the Republic of Cyprus *de jure* represents the whole island.

The lack of violence and steady calls over forty years by many Greek and Turkish Cypriots for the island's reunification have encouraged a long procession of high-level peacemakers, track-two conflict resolution experts, NGOs and international organizations to try their hand at bringing peace to Cyprus. Thus, the country provides rich material for the study of conflict management in divided societies. This chapter will examine the most recent resolution efforts, with an eye to understanding why existing approaches to conflict management appear thus far unable to 'solve' the problem of Cyprus.

## The context of the conflict in Cyprus

While primarily characterized as an ethnic conflict, Cyprus also contains the strands of fierce ideological battles, and the legacy of multiple colonizations. Its geography has been important; situated in the Mediterranean Basin, the Mediterranean Sea separates it from North Africa, Southern Turkey, Syria, Lebanon and Israel. Thus, while the conflict is currently perceived to be a dispute between Greek Cypriots, Turkish Cypriots, and Turkey, it has also developed out of regional and global power struggles over a geo-strategically valuable island in the post-Empire and Cold War periods.

An Ottoman province between 1571 and 1878, the island's administration was turned over to Britain at the Congress of Berlin, in exchange for British protection of Ottoman borders from the expanding Russian Empire. In the 1923 Treaty of Lausanne, Turkey officially recognized British rule over Cyprus, and two years later Cyprus was declared a British Crown Colony. It remained so until 1960, when it became an independent republic.

That republic was created as a rigid consociational structure, where power was shared between Greek and Turkish Cypriots under a presidential system of government with strong vice-presidential veto powers. The structure, as it was originally designed, broke down in 1964 as a result of political discord between the groups in government. The discord led to a constitutional crisis, which in turn led to the withdrawal of the Turkish Cypriot representatives from government, and of the Turkish Cypriots into enclaves to protect themselves from the violence that intensified subsequently.

Yet violence in Cyprus did not begin only in 1964. As is true of many conflict societies, history in Cyprus is bent to legitimize each community's identity and its struggle to meet its goals. In the official Greek Cypriot narrative, Cyprus is gloriously Greek, and Cypriots are the descendants of Mycenaean ancestors who colonized the island in the fourteenth century BC. The development of Greek nationalism on the Greek mainland and islands was carried to Cyprus early in the twentieth century, and in the interwar period a movement began first among the intellectual elite and then among the villages that aimed to free Cyprus from British rule and unite it with 'Motherland Greece' (Katsiaounis 1996). At the same time, Turkish nationalism was developing among Turkish Cypriot intellectuals alongside the evolution of the Young Turk movement in early twentieth century Turkey (Nevzat 2005). Cyprus was seen as a land steeped in the blood of Turkish martyrs; so legitimately Turkish. These developing counter-nationalisms were beginning to define themselves against the other, and to close out the space for shared identity or peaceful coexistence (Bryant 2004).

By 1955, the pro-Greek movement had evolved into an armed guerrilla group called EOKA,[1] which sought to end British colonial rule and unite the island with Greece (*enosis*). Seen by many Greek Cypriots as a liberation army, EOKA was viewed by Turkish Cypriots as a terrorist organization which attempted to ethnically cleanse the island. A counter-group called TMT[2] was formed in 1957 by the Turkish Cypriot community whose main goal was *taksim* – the partition of the island between Greece and Turkey. Both groups were armed, trained, and supported by their respective kin-states. As instruments of nationalism, the groups were also closely allied to the Greek and Turkish political far-right, and took the opportunity created by their power and political support to kill democrats, leftists and supporters of intercommunal cooperation (Milios 2007; Hitchens 1997, 53).

As the violence increased, Britain, Greece and Turkey negotiated one unsatisfactory proposal for the island's future after another. Under considerable pressure, Greco-Turkish negotiators came up with a plan for the country's independence. Thus was created the 1960 Republic of Cyprus (RoC); a compromise that was accepted by Cypriot political leaders for strategic reasons, but to which few were committed. However, the violence settled down, and for four years the groups worked reluctantly together. After the 1964 constitutional crisis, tensions once again increased as the Greek Cypriot community strengthened its hold on government institutions and Greek Cypriot paramilitary groups increased their persecution of the Turkish Cypriot community (Patrick 1976). Economic blockades and paramilitary persecution were to continue until 1967 (Patrick 1976; Mirbagheri 1998, 44), despite the deployment of UN peacekeepers in 1964 and UN-led efforts to negotiate a settlement between the parties. The decade of negotiations between 1964 and 1974 were focused on reaching a compromise that would reconcile the Turkish Cypriot desire to stick to the 1960 Constitution with the Greek Cypriot wish to renegotiate one of the core provisions of this constitution and reach a new agreement where each side's institutional political power was more reflective of its actual share in the population.

In July 1974 Greece's military junta, along with members of the Greek Cypriot political and military elite, undertook a failed *coup d'état* which aimed to overthrow the government of the Republic of Cyprus under President Archbishop Makarios and annex Cyprus to Greece. The coup provoked a military intervention from Turkey under the terms of the 1960 Treaty of Guarantee (after the British government of the day refused to become involved). Turkey took control of the northern third of the island, stretching from Morphou/Guzelyurt in the west to Famagusta in the east. The resulting occupation forced a population redistribution. Turkish Cypriots were moved to the newly controlled Turkish north of Cyprus, and Greek Cypriots were moved to what was left of the territory in the island's south. People were relocated into houses and villages abandoned by the other community. Each with very different understandings and memories of the conflict, and very different goals for the future, the sides began the process of reconstructing their lives.

After the de facto partition of the island in 1974, the Greek Cypriot community focused on rebuilding its economy and reconstructing the social fabric. The war had caused the displacement of some one-third of the Greek Cypriot population, and close to one-half of the Turkish Cypriot population. The Greek Cypriot economy had been devastated by the loss of extensive agricultural resources and tourism revenue; its main sources of wealth. The Republic has continued to function as a democratic state, though it does so under conditions of exceptionality (Constantinou 2008). In 2004 it became a full member of the European Union (EU).

The post-1974 development of the Turkish Cypriot community took a different path. During the period between the collapse of the 1960 settlement in 1964 and the Turkish intervention and partition of Cyprus, Turkish Cypriots had created an (initially) temporary administrative structure, the so-called Provisional Cypriot Turkish Administration (PCTA); (Patrick 1976). Anxious to add legitimacy to their newly expanded territory in 1975, the Turkish Federated State of Cyprus (TFSC) was declared. In 1983 the community declared its breakaway state, the Turkish Republic of Northern Cyprus (TRNC). The state has remained internationally unrecognized by all but Turkey. Since then, Turkish Cypriots focused on building a self-sustaining liberal state to reinforce their independence from the RoC and the Greek Cypriot community. Without access to the economic or political benefits of international recognition, it is heavily dependent on Turkish economic, political, and military support.

Closely tied with the Republic's EU accession was the first complete peace plan offered to the Cypriot people. In April 2004, after two intense years of negotiation, bilateral talks, and, eventually, working committees, the UN presented a complete design for a new Cypriot State. Dubbed the Annan Plan[3] after then-UN Secretary-General Kofi Annan, the plan was supported by the Turkish Cypriot leadership, as well as by Greece and Turkey, but rejected by the Greek Cypriot government alliance. The plan needed the support of the majority of the Greek and Turkish Cypriot electorates to be accepted, and as such, was put to referendum, where it failed to gain a majority of Greek Cypriot votes.[4] The following month, the RoC acceded to the EU as a still-divided country. A number of NGOs and civil society organizations in both north and south Cyprus maintain that there is a serious democratic deficit which affects policies and approaches in both communities to migration, human rights and people trafficking. This has been linked to the rapid post-war modernization both societies had to undergo (Varnavas and Yakinthou 2010).

## Actors in the conflict management process

### *The local conflict parties*

Elites in Cyprus have not been conflict breakers, so much as ethnic entrepreneurs, perpetuating the conflict in order to protect their personal power bases, each blaming the other for intransigence. Earlier in this volume (Chapter 4), Zartman argued that conflicts tend to resemble a prisoners' dilemma game, where a result which is favourable to the opponent is worse than continued conflict. Cyprus is an exemplar of this argument. Indeed, the Greek Cypriot response to the Annan plan that 'something which gives so much to the enemy cannot be good for us' is highly illustrative of the depth of the dilemma. Conflict management in Cyprus is also characterized by personality politics, and many of the actors historically involved in the resolution process have defined their lives by the conflict, and built their careers on it.

In the north, one of the founding members of the TMT, Rauf Denktaş, served four consecutive five-year terms as president of the TRNC, albeit in a number of governing alliances with parties from across the ideological spectrum. As the founder of the Turkish Cypriot state, and a key figure in the anti-*enosis*[5] struggles between 1955 and 1974, Denktaş has been an important figure to both Greek and Turkish Cypriots. For many years, he formed a link between Turkey and Cyprus, always ensuring that Turkish policy on Cyprus safeguarded his state. He was also a protective figure to the Turkish Cypriot community, against the memory of Greek Cypriot threats. He, along with figures like Greek Cypriot leaders Glafkos Clerides and Tassos Papadopoulos represent an institutional memory of the modern Cyprus conflict. With a famed aversion to re-unification of Cyprus, Denktaş led a group of political elites who saw very few incentives for compromise and cooperation with the Greek Cypriots (Yakinthou 2009b, 97–100). Known for walking out in the middle of negotiations, his withdrawal was a predictable safety net for Greek Cypriots, who could rely on Turkish Cypriot withdrawal from intercommunal talks without losing face themselves.

However, his monopoly on the moral and political leadership of the Turkish Cypriot community was broken in January 2004, when socialist party CTP[6] was elected to government, and its leader Mehmet Ali Talat became prime minister. When Talat was elected president in 2005, Denktaş withdrew from politics.

In the south, hard-line Greek Cypriot elites with a history of involvement in the Cyprus problem have generally been elected president,[7] indicating Greek Cypriot willingness to defer to traditional authorities on matters relating to the Cyprus conflict. By and large, they seem to have been elected on two grounds: first, they 'understood' the Cyprus conflict because of their long involvement; and second, they were considered strong negotiators who would bring the Greek Cypriot community back to a position of advantage. However, as we will see below, this trend changed in 2008.

Archbishop Makarios of the Cypriot Orthodox Church was first president of the RoC. Considered the political and spiritual figurehead of the Greek Cypriot community, he was a key player in the anti-colonial movement. He remained president of the wholly Greek

Cypriot republic for seventeen years, until his death. His most significant successor was former EOKA lawyer Glafkos Clerides. Clerides and Denktaş best embody the nature of the principal actors involved in the Cyprus conflict, an area densely populated by lawyers. In 1950s colonial Cyprus, Clerides defended EOKA fighters caught by the British, while Denktaş prosecuted them on behalf of the crown. In the 1960s, both men became advisers for their respective leaderships; Denktaş for vice-president Kuçuk, and Clerides for president Makarios. In 1975, Clerides and Denktaş negotiated the post-war population exchange. In the post-partition 1970s, Clerides was part of the Greek Cypriot advisory team when the peace talks commenced, while Denktaş led the talks for the Turkish Cypriot community.[8] In 1993, Clerides was elected president of the RoC, a post he held until 2003. In the on-again off-again peace talks, Clerides' opposite number was always Denktaş. Greek Cypriot presidential elections took place during a particularly intense period of the Annan Plan negotiations, and Clerides, who campaigned to be given the mandate to complete the negotiations and then retire, was defeated by hardliner Tassos Papadopoulos. Papadopoulos was another of the EOKA lawyers and a central figure in the pre-independence *enosis* movement. His election can be seen partly as a reaction by the Greek Cypriot electorate against Clerides' support of the peace plan (BBC 2003; Ker-Lindsay and Webb 2004; Martin 2006, 42).

In light of the above, the 2005 Turkish Cypriot election of socialist party CTP's Mehmet Ali Talat to the TRNC's presidency, and the 2008 Greek Cypriot election of communist party AKEL's[9] Demetris Christofias as RoC president appeared significant. For the first time in the conflict's history, the current political leadership on both sides were relatively 'clean slates', with no direct relationship with either EOKA or TMT, or with the Turkish and Greek nationalist movements. The election of these two left-wing party leaders initially signalled a break with the stagnant negotiating policies of previous leaderships. However, as time and new negotiations wore on, the leaders became hemmed in by the cultures of nationalism and patriotic rhetoric which have had free reign for the last half-century. As a result, in early 2010 Talat was voted out of office by well-known anti-solution centre-right candidate Dervis Eroglu. Since his elections, talks between the two sides have progressed extremely slowly.

But when CTP and AKEL finally found themselves in power at the same time, they also realized that they were actors entrapped within the nationalist, zero-sum environment to which they had both contributed and been opposed. Christofias, as president of the RoC, found himself unable to step too far outside the established negotiation boundaries. He was president of a state with an occupying army at borders he did not recognize, and having to negotiate with his old comrade – now leader of a non-recognized state. As Turkish Cypriots watched Greek Cypriots prosper as an EU country, and perceived that none of the Union's promises to their community were being fulfilled, Talat faced an anti-EU and anti-Greek Cypriot public backlash. He was consequently voted out of power by a candidate who ran on a decidedly populist and nationalist agenda. To much of the voting public on each side, the other was, and still is, the enemy. Every move that each man made was cross-examined in the media and in the public for its impact on the national cause. And critics, on both sides, are vociferous. In both communities, alliances are important to maintain power, for few parties win outright majorities. On the Greek Cypriot side, the only alliance AKEL is not willing to make is with DISY,[10] the one party that can guarantee them a super-majority in government and strong support to negotiate and stand by a peace plan. However, DISY was founded to represent EOKA fighters, and housed a number of people accused of killing both Turkish Cypriots and Greek Cypriot AKEL members during the late 1960s and early 1970s (Papadakis 2003, 256; Coufoudakis 1983). Since the early 2000s, DISY has made a deep change in its approach to the Cyprus conflict, going from staunchly supporting the concept of a Hellenic Cyprus, to being the only major party which openly campaigned in support of the Annan Plan in 2004. It is now the most pro-reconciliation Greek Cypriot party, and has publicly supported Christofias' continued commitment to the negotiations in times when all other parties called for his withdrawal. An AKEL–DISY alliance is necessary for any proposal to gain public support, but remains one which AKEL is unwilling to make (Drousiotis 2009). The past appears to be too large an obstacle.

Like many of the other conflicts examined in this book, the Cyprus conflict is bedevilled by internal rivalries. Any cross-community cooperation between the leaders or efforts at showing understanding is demonized by rival parties as weakening the national cause. Indeed, it seems that the most remarkable aspect of the Cyprus conflict is its ability to absorb all change into the status quo.

Maximalist political rhetoric on all sides regarding solution of the conflict, electoral pressure, and a thirty-year-long negotiating process have significantly inhibited the ability of political leaders to forge alliances. On the whole, cooperation has been conceptualized by elites as contingent upon a solution, rather than a factor upon which a solution is contingent. As a result of this perception, the political and public environment has tended to inhibit the behaviour of the few elites who have tried to build alliances, or to cooperate.

### The 'external' conflict parties

At the international level, the most relevant actors are Turkey, Greece, Britain, the European Union, and the United States. Turkey and Greece are the core international players, as kin-states to the two Cypriot communities. Both have played the roles of protector and antagonist in the conflict, and both continue to have complicated relationships with both Greek and Turkish Cypriots. They are actors with formal stakes in the conflict and its management and resolution, and partners in the negotiating process. Their relationship with one another as NATO partners affects, and has been strained by, the conflict in Cyprus. Especially during the Cold War period, the international focus was on controlling intercommunal tension so as not to spark a Greek/Turkish war, which would have damaged the south-east wing of NATO, affecting the balance of power.

The United Kingdom is the next most significant actor and formal stakeholder on the island, with continued guarantor veto power over changes to the 1960 constitution (a power held together with Greece and Turkey), military bases on the island, and relations with Greece, Turkey and both Cypriot communities to balance. The UK's role is further complicated, to some extent, by incompletely overlapping memberships in the EU (with Greece and the RoC) and NATO (with Greece and Turkey). Moreover, the UK also views Cyprus within its strategic perspective on the Middle East and North Africa. The United States, too, considers Cyprus within a broader context of NATO and of its own Middle East–North Africa–Mediterranean strategic context, in which it has generally supported resolution of the conflict. Finally, the EU has moved from catalyst for resolution of the conflict to the conflict's manager since the RoC's accession in 2004. It continues to play the role of supporting actor to the UN in the settlement negotiations, and tries to effect change in Cyprus through the various development and reconciliation-focused programmes it has instigated on the island. Nonetheless, for the EU the Cyprus conflict remains one of the factors standing between Turkey and its accession to the Union.

## Capacity of the primary mediator

The UN has been the primary mediator in the Cyprus conflict, with the exception of a single wavering moment immediately post-2004, when it appeared that the EU would be given the mantle. Established under Resolution 186 (1964),[11] the UN operation in Cyprus 'tried to provide a comprehensive peacekeeping, peacemaking and peacebuilding structure' (Richmond 2001, 102). It twinned the goals of controlling an outbreak of war and finding a constitutional settlement. The years 1999–2004 mark the UN's most robust post-war attempt to resolve the conflict.

The UN's capacity to persuade the Cypriot parties to accept a solution has been limited and undermined significantly by the parties' selective, strategic interpretations of the UN's mandate (Mirbagheri 1998, 79–80). In this, the UN was handicapped from the beginning. Additionally, the lack of protracted violent conflict, and the absence of a mutually hurting stalemate have dulled incentives for Cypriot elites to compromise, thus giving the UN less scope for negotiation.

The international community's fear of condoning a contested secession after 1974 contributed to its endorsement of the Greek Cypriot community's *de facto* control of the internationally recognized RoC. This had two important consequences: the first was that the only legitimacy Turkish Cypriot leaders would receive was at the negotiating table; providing an incentive to perpetuate the negotiations (Richmond 1998, 215–18). The second was that this sole representation of the government enhanced the Greek Cypriots' moral authority to speak as the only legitimate Cypriot voice in the UN and in other forums (James 2002, 99).[12] This established a pattern which allowed them to blur the line between 'Cypriot' and 'Greek Cypriot' interests; a major factor producing intransigence in the Greek Cypriot community, culminating in their rejection of a compromise solution in April 2004. According to Richmond, the UN thus became a 'victim of the conflict itself' (Richmond 2001, 105).

UN interests have shifted over time, affecting its peacemaking capacity in Cyprus. Despite the above, the UN had a strong early involvement in Cyprus, shaping proposed solutions to the conflict. In the immediate post-breakdown period, it attempted dynamic forms of direct intervention that combined both peacekeeping and peacemaking. In early 1964, former Ecuadorian President Galo Plaza was appointed by the UN Secretary General as Mediator on Cyprus. The report he subsequently produced (Plaza 1965) attempted to create inroads towards a solution to the problem, but instead significantly increased tension (Mirbagheri 1998, 43). Plaza subsequently resigned after Turkish Cypriot claims of bias. His resignation precipitated a self-protective move by the UN, and catalyzed the watering down of subsequent UN peacemaking attempts. Post-Plaza, the secretary-general's mission of good offices centred on protecting the integrity of UN peacemaking by not alienating either community. Subsequently, the UN's oscillating efforts in Cyprus have reflected internal UN, Cypriot and international pressures.[13] The UN has over the years been trapped by regional instability and power shifts between Greece and Turkey (Bahcheli 1990).

Agreements have been few and far between. The first, post-1974, was the 1977 Framework Agreements between Makarios and Denktaş which set the framework for all subsequent negotiations. The 1979 Kyprianou–Denktaş Communiqué (10 Point Agreement), and the 1992 Boutros Boutros-Ghali Set of Ideas, were a brief respite from the tradition of disagreement. Boutros-Ghali wove the role of mediation into the framework of good offices by holding the threat of the UNFICYP's withdrawal over the heads of the interlocutors to pressure them to negotiate in good faith (Richmond 1998, 200). However, the dynamism Boutros-Ghali represented was short-lived, and by 1996 the UN had again fallen into what Richmond has described as a 'sterile and apathetic' role (Richmond 2001, 119).

The period between the 1994 collapse of Boutros-Ghali's 'Confidence Building Measures' and the appointment of Kofi Annan to the position of UN Secretary-General in 1998 was marked by high levels of tension, elevated by a number of domestic and regional crises.[14] The atmosphere again darkened in December 1997 at the EU Luxemburg Summit when accession negotiations were opened with the RoC, while the EU remained silent regarding Turkey's candidacy. In 1998 as a direct result of the Luxemburg decision, Turkey and the Turkish Cypriot government moved their bottom line negotiating basis from federalism to confederalism (Hannay 2005). The move was a significant signal that negotiations would not progress, because Greek Cypriot negotiators had long been clear that confederation was unacceptable (Pfirter 2006). After two years of stalemate, Kofi Annan began to signal that work would again begin on Cyprus. That work culminated in the 2004 Annan Plan.

Ker-Lindsay has argued that the failure of traditional mediation in drawn-out disputes like Cyprus has changed the UN's approach to peacemaking, evolving from traditional mediator into a hybrid and more assertive role (Ker-Lindsay 2009). Indeed, the UN's approach during its 2004 efforts in Cyprus more closely resembled the resolution of labour disputes than international political conflicts. Ker-Lindsay argued that this approach was ultimately damaging to the peace process, and seemed 'to be less about trying to help the parties to reach a settlement that the parties can accept and more about trying to avoid or end the frustration associated with managing long term peace processes' (Ker-Lindsay 2009, 231–2).

## The structure of the conflict management process

In the 2002–4 negotiations, the process was shaped by the conflict's many years of atrophy, together with Cyprus' impending EU accession, scheduled for May 2004. Cyprus' EU accession was a window of opportunity for external actors to create incentives for Cypriot elites to resolve the conflict. EU accession was to be used as a lever to encourage political compromise, so as to admit a reunified Cyprus into the Union.[15] The regional context was favourable: Washington, Ankara, Athens, the EU, the British, were all brought on board, and the Russians were 'at least acquiescent' (Hannay 2005, 63–4). The process was based on the UN's perception that without firm deadlines, the interlocutors would remain indefinitely at the pre-negotiation stage.[16]

Mindful of the conflict's history of procrastination, the UN began to work internally on the outline of a comprehensive solution to the Cyprus conflict in 2000. This first set of 'Preliminary Thoughts' was followed by a second document which advanced the negotiations by suggesting that a single text should be the basis of further negotiations. The negotiations were then terminated for a year by the Turkish Cypriot interlocutor. Trying to interlink with the December 2002 EU Copenhagen summit, the UN submitted the first proper negotiating text (Annan I) to the Cypriot leaders in November that year.

They submitted the second revised plan one month later. Annan III was presented in February 2003; the same month that presidential elections in the RoC brought hard-line DIKO leader Papadopoulos to power. Annan IV was submitted in March 2004, and by this time parliamentary elections had seen a significant swing to the left in the TRNC, with Talat becoming prime minister, and taking over the negotiations.

The UN's task was Herculean. There were considerable periods during the negotiations where one or both sides were not cooperating with the mediators. '[Sometimes] the team of the Secretary-General simply were hearing views on various subjects and they tried to visualize what would have been an acceptable compromise between sides that were not really talking to each other with a view to settle' (Markides 2004). As a result, 'the UN team under de Soto was driven *faute de mieux* to draw up the first Annan Plan based on drafts and concepts that had been in circulation for years and in some instances for decades' (Kyle 2004, 17). A core member of the UN negotiating team maintained that there was 'very little engagement in [the] negotiations' by either side, and that the interlocutors were 'more willing to discuss options' in one-on-one shuttle talks than they were during face-to-face negotiations.[17] This is reflected in the high number of proximity and shuttle talks as measured against face-to-face discussions. During the Annan negotiations, there were only 72 face-to-face meetings between the leaders, as compared to 150 bilateral meetings between then UN Special Representative to Cyprus Alvaro de Soto and each leader separately, and 54 meetings in the proximity phase.

Because the 1964 constitutional deadlock ran deep in both communities' historical memories, the UN had to create a highly detailed blueprint of institutional and political reunification which would leave no unanswered questions. Its goal was to address all contentious issues, and 'propose a crystal-clear solution' (Pfirter 2006). The complexity of this task was compounded by the situation's fragility: the architects of the Annan Plan had to reconstruct reality for mutually suspicious communities that had lived entirely without each other – refusing to acknowledge even the existence of the other as a political entity – for a generation. To avoid clashing interpretations of its provisions, the Annan Plan was remarkably thorough in its detail. This was underlined by de Soto: 'if you look around in the last few years, at the different peace agreements that have been signed, a lot of them are very jerry-built essentially and have raised enormous questions that create for somewhat chaotic situations. Whereas here it is all spelled out' (de Soto 2004). By the fifth plan:

> The one hundred and ten laws became one hundred and forty laws, and those draft laws were to be in operation from the very first day, that is to say that the federation would have a taxation law, a budget, everything in place from the very first day. There was a provision that if by reason of the complexity of the system you fail to amend a particular law, it continues as it is, unless amended.
>
> (Markides 2004)

This vast task involved 300 Cypriots and some 50 UN experts working in 14 technical committees. It was labelled by one UN team member as an almost 'super-human' effort by those involved.[18] The resulting plan in its entirety ran to some 9,000 pages.

## Settlement design

Various forms of power sharing have been suggested for Cyprus over the course of the conflict. The 1977 High Level Agreements settled on a 'bicommunal, federal republic'

(High Level Agreement, pt. 1), and while Turkish Cypriot negotiators have considered in the past a heavily devolved confederation to be their ideal, and Greek Cypriots a majoritarian democracy, no credible proposals have deviated from some form of ethno-territorial federation.

Both the 2004 Annan Plan, and the current negotiations propose a federal consociation, with some version of a rotating presidency and the devolution of most communal matters to the constituent entities. Because current negotiations are insufficiently progressed to make any useful commentary, this section will instead examine the 2004 Annan Plan, as the most recent complete proposal.

The Annan Plan was inspired by the Swiss and Belgian systems (Yakinthou 2009b, 75–7). The United Cyprus Republic (UCR) was designed as a federal, liberal consociational state. It was devised to be an indissoluble partnership between the federal government and two equal constituent states, called the Greek Cypriot Constituent State and the Turkish Cypriot Constituent State. The constitution specified the powers and functions vested in the federal government, devolving the bulk of powers (including the day-to-day functioning of the states) to the constituent states.

The federal state envisaged in the Annan Plan was comprised of an executive (which included a Presidential Council, a Federal Administration and Federal Police), a legislature (Senate and Chamber of Deputies), a judiciary (the Supreme Court), and independent institutions (Central Bank; Office of the Attorney-General; Office of the Auditor-General). There was to be no hierarchy between federal and constituent state laws. The powers of the federal legislature included the approval of international treaties for ratification; the election of the Presidential Council; the adoption of the federal budget; and, by special majority, the referral of serious crimes by members of the Presidential Council and the independent institutions to the Supreme Court.

The Senate was to be composed of twenty-four senators from each constituent state, elected 'on a proportional basis by the citizens of Cyprus, voting separately as Greek Cypriots and Turkish Cypriots' (UCR Constitution, Article 22/3). Ordinary decisions were to be taken by a simple majority of its members, which included one quarter of present and voting senators from each constituent state. For the approval of the federal budget, Presidential Council elections, and matters deemed as being of critical interest to the constituent states, a special majority would be needed to pass decisions. This would require at least two-fifths of sitting senators from each constituent state (ten) to support the bill (UCR Constitution, Article 25(2)).

The Chamber of Deputies was to be composed proportionally, according to the population of each constituent state,[19] and the number of people holding citizenship in each constituent state. A maximum of 75 per cent of the deputies were to hold the internal citizenship of the Greek Cypriot state and a minimum of 25 per cent that of the Turkish Cypriot State. Deputies were to be elected for five years on the basis of proportional representation (PR), and all decisions were to be taken by a simple majority of members present and voting.

The Presidential Council, the executive, was to contain nine members elected from a single list with the endorsement of a clear majority (a minimum of 40 per cent) of senators from each constituent state. The Council's composition was intended to reflect the country's population ratio; however at least two members were required to come from each constituent state. Were the plan to come into force over the next few years, while relative populations remain as at present, it was required that six members would come from the Greek Cypriot state and three from the Turkish Cypriot state.[20] The President of the Council was to represent the country as both the head of state and the head of government. The offices of president and vice-president of the Council would rotate on a twenty-month basis from a member of the Greek Cypriot state to a member of the Turkish Cypriot state (Annan 2004, para. 44). The president and vice-president were required to come from different constituent states, and the president was to be deputized by the vice-president.

Presidential Council members were each to head a department, as decided by the Council. The Presidential Council would also appoint members of the judiciary and independent offices. Decisions were to be taken by consensus, or by simple majority of voting members. A minimum of one voting member from each constituent state would need to have voted in favour of a decision in order for it to be passed, and neither the president nor the vice-president was to have a deciding vote (UCR Constitution, art. 42).

The federal administration and judiciary specified in the Annan Plan also followed consociational principles: staffing of the public service was to be in accordance with the relative populations of the constituent states.[21] The federal police was to be composed of an equal number of staff from each constituent state, and the head and deputy head of the federal police would not be permitted to come from the same constituent state.

The Supreme Court was to be comprised of an equal number of judges from each constituent state and three non-Cypriot judges (UCR Constitution, Article 6(2)). All Supreme Court judges[22] were to be appointed by the Presidential Council. Decisions were to be taken by consensus, or by simple majority of the Cypriot judges. If there were no majority among the Cypriot judges,[23] the non-Cypriot judges would participate in the decision of the court to cast a single vote (UCR Constitution, Article 36(2)). The Supreme Court was to have jurisdiction over the resolution of deadlocks in federal institutions if the deadlock was retarding decision making (UCR Constitution, Article 36(6)).

The Annan Plan also provided detailed procedural guidance on all aspects of the country's reunification. Reunification would involve extensive reshuffling of populations with the settlement of disputed territory claims,[24] and the reshaping of the geographical boundary of each constituent state according to negotiated agreements between the sides. Citizenship, similarly, has double relevance as individuals would, in the Plan, be identified both as members of the UCR and of the constituent state upon which their ethnic identity is based. Internal constituent state citizenship would be important because the Plan envisaged limitations being placed on the freedom to establish permanent residence within the state in which the citizen does not hold constituent state citizenship. These limitations were to be removed upon Turkey's entry into the EU or upon agreement by representatives of both constituent states.

## Principal challenges to adoption

The primary challenges to the Annan Plan's adoption were sociopolitical. While the plan received the support of Turkish Cypriot political and community elites, it did not find similar endorsement among Greek Cypriot leaders. The then-president, his party, and the powerful Cypriot Orthodox church rejected the plan outright and forcefully. In his address to the country, Papadopoulos charged that the plan was a betrayal of Cypriot Hellenism (Papadopoulos 2004). The Bishop of Kyrenia condemned the plan's supporters to hell (Molyva 2004). Major coalition party AKEL – historically supportive of reconciliation – wavered until the last minute, and then opposed the plan. AKEL leader Christofias asked for the public to give a 'soft no' in order to cement a 'strong yes' at a later date. The only major party which supported the plan was ex-president Clerides' DISY. The referendum period was one of great crisis in Greek Cypriot politics, where, for the first time, the public was confronted with the reality of a post-war solution, and it was very different to the perception that had been shaped for them by political elites. In a state of extreme anxiety and tension unparalleled since the 1970s, the Greek Cypriot community split deeply down the middle. People who supported the plan were labelled traitors to the national honour, agents of foreign powers, or plain naïve fools. It has taken a number of years for the society to recover from this tear in the public consciousness. Sitting beneath this split is the society's complete unpreparedness for the compromises required by a resolution.

At the most obvious level, the principal challenge to resolution of the conflict over its many years has been elite support, both Greek and Turkish Cypriot. And while this remains a problem in both communities, it veils a deeper and much more problematic challenge: that of public readiness to end the war. More specifically, a major problem which continues to prop up the conflict is the complete lack of intercommunal trust, and willingness to see the other's trauma as legitimate. This means that the principal challenges to adoption of a solution are not only overcoming the usual zero-sum interlocutor mentality and coalescing international support, but also bringing the broader public on board.

Both communities came to believe over the years in the unshakable legitimacy of their cause. Turkish Cypriots believed that it was abundantly clear to the international community that the only means of protecting their survival as a community was with their own statehood. Thus, recognition of the TRNC was seen as something just. The Greek Cypriot land that was taken was simply the price of freedom. They highlighted the exchange: Turkish Cypriots had gained territory in the island's north, but had left property in the south. The Turkish army's presence was seen in the first two post-war decades as being necessary to protect the community's security. On the flip side, Greek Cypriots did not see what had happened in the 1960s as causing any kind of significant threat to the Turkish Cypriots as a community. Likewise, the 1974 Turkish invasion was not seen as contextual, but a brutal land-grab; the Turks taking advantage of the Greek coup attempt. The coup itself was perceived as an entirely internal matter, with Greek Cypriots being the primary victims. Thus the conflict was a straightforward case of invasion and occupation. Its solution, therefore, was a matter of the occupying army withdrawing, and territory being returned to its rightful owners. Many Greek Cypriots will argue that the Turkish army's continued presence on the island[25] undermines any possibility of negotiating in good faith. Turkish Cypriots will argue that they do not feel safe without the military presence. But both sides also know that the army is the Turkish Cypriots' king against the Greek Cypriot ace of international legitimacy.

The pressure of extended non-recognition, complete dependency on Turkey for political survival, and the RoC's impending EU accession leaving the Turkish Cypriot community even further behind caused a crack in the belief that the Turkish Cypriot community could continue as it was. Between 2002–4, the political opposition joined trade union and civil society leaders in explaining the concessions that would need to be made, and the benefits gained in exchange. Many in the community had a reaction which mirrored the later Greek Cypriot antipathy to the plan; however, two years of heavy debates paved the way for the 64 per cent vote in favour of the solution in the 2004 referendum. On the Greek Cypriot side, however, the domestic conditions were vastly different. EU membership was all but assured so long as they continued to support the negotiating *process*. Their international legitimacy was guaranteed, and the plan seemed to be fraught with a greater risk than was worth taking. Counting against the plan was also the shock, stemming from the first ever public admission by the community's political elites, that not all the land taken by Turkey would be returned, and not all displaced people would return to their homes. For a people who had for thirty years been raised with the absolute conviction that any negotiated solution would facilitate the return of all displaced people, this caused an almost violent cognitive dissonance. An entire political system had been built supporting a communal split in consciousness which simultaneously allowed people to live in a post-war situation surrounded by military symbols and signs of the conflict, and remain cocooned in a very bizarre reality which promoted the illusion that the war was a mere violent blip on the screen of reality, and that quotidian pre-conflict life would resume as it was pre-1974 as soon as a solution could be negotiated.

## The current status of conflict management in Cyprus

Since 1964 there have been a number of UN-led efforts to resolve the conflict. Over those years, many calls have been made by civil society groups and politicians for the international community to help bring peace, or justice, to the country. However, the crux of the conflict's irresolvable nature lies in these two loaded terms. Peace and justice are still being defined by each side's leaderships as a gain that will legitimize and justify an important loss to the other community. There are very few moves to explain why compromise is so important, or, indeed, valuable. The Christofias–Talat period demonstrated how even conciliatory elites can end up unable to move too far outside the cage created by the many years of nationalist extremism. They are hemmed in by unhappy publics that have been misled for many years, and left with broken promises by the international community. Underlying public pressure on the leadership is fear of the unknown, of a past that has been simultaneously suppressed and exploited for political gain and of a negotiating process that none of the elites are explaining clearly.

For too long, international focus has been fixated on bringing Greek and Turkish Cypriot leaders to the negotiating table to broker a political agreement. Not nearly enough attention has been paid to understanding and working to heal the psychosocial wounds of war and deconstructing poisonous attitudes about the other side. The UN's 2004 efforts in Cyprus made obvious the fact that no amount of elite-level international peacemaking will solve a conflict which continues to harbour deep-seated unresolved resentments which can be used by ethnic entrepreneurs to sway a vulnerable electorate.

The situation in Cyprus remains tense, especially as the leaders are again coming to a critical point in the new negotiation process. The status quo has outlasted almost forty years of post-war negotiations, and if it continues, it will cement the de facto partition. There is also a quiet belief among many Greek Cypriots, and a growing number of Turkish Cypriots, that some version of the current status quo may be the conflict's best solution. This perception rests upon the shaky premise that the 'known' is safer than the 'unknown'; that is, that the current uncertainty of division is preferable to the future uncertainty bought by any solution.

Though only whispered as an option, this would also constitute a solution to the conflict. However, to take forty years and still only to get back to square one raises a number of questions about the effectiveness of the entire game of international conflict management.

## Notes

1 National Organization of Cypriot Fighters, Ετνική Οργάνωσις Κυπρίων Αγωνιστών.
2 Turkish Resistance Organization, Türk Mukavemet Teşkilatı. TMT replaced a group called Volkan founded the year before, which was a more organic Turkish Cypriot underground group.
3 Formally titled 'Basis for a Comprehensive Settlement of the Cyprus Problem'.
4 The Greek Cypriot community voted against the plan with a 76 per cent majority. The Turkish Cypriot community voted in favour of the plan with a 64 per cent majority.
5 *Enosis* is the Greek work for union. It was used as the slogan for the union of Cyprus with Greece.
6 Cumhuriyetçi Türk Partisi, Republican Turkish Party.
7 With the single exception of George Vassiliou, who ran as an independent, and was in industry previous to his political life.
8 Denktaş was Turkish Cypriot chief negotiator from 1975 until 2004, when he was replaced by Talat.
9 Ανορθωτικό Κόμμα Εργαζόμενου Λαού, Progressive Party for the Working People.
10 Δημοκρατικός Συναγερμός, Democratic Rally.
11 Resolution of 4 March 1964, UN Document S/5575.
12 The Republic of Cyprus was initially recognized by the UN as the sovereign body for two key reasons: firstly, international dislike of secession; secondly, the UNFICYP needed to be invited by the sovereign body. So if the UN was to recognize two sovereign bodies, it would necessarily reduce the Greek Cypriots to the status of a 'community', which would not put them in a frame of mind conducive to signing the invitation; there was, and continues to be a general international predisposition to see the Republic of Cyprus as a legal political authority. That is, nation-states prefer to recognize other nation-states. The sovereign entity which the UN and the international community chose to work with was therefore the Republic of Cyprus under the control of the Greek Cypriot community. It must be made clear, however, that the UN Council did not create the authority of the Greek Cypriot regime. James maintains that 'rather, what it did, was to make an influential proclamation of a position which had already been adopted in very significant quarters. There was never much likelihood that the Council would do otherwise' (1995).
13 For an explanation of international pressures on the UN, see Hannay (2005), Richmond (1994) and Newman (2001).
14 The Imia–Kardak crisis in January 1996, three Greek Cypriot deaths on the island in the same year, and an averted missile crisis in 1997.
15 For a more thorough examination of the EU's role in the conflict, see Yakinthou (2009a), Tocci and Kovziridze (2004), Tocci (2004), Müftüler-Bac and Güney (2005), Yakinthou (2009b).
16 Member of UN core negotiating team in Cyprus. Confidential interview with author (2006).
17 Member of UN core negotiating team in Cyprus. Confidential interview with author (2006).
18 Member of UN core negotiating team in Cyprus. Confidential interview with author (2006).
19 Proposed Constitution of the United Cyprus Republic, Article 5(1)a.
20 Only four of the six Greek Cypriot members and two of the three Turkish Cypriot members will have full voting rights.
21 With the safeguard that at least one-third of every level of the public service must be staffed by members of each constituent state.
22 Both Cypriot and foreign.
23 This provision was added into the third version of the plan.
24 Population resettlement, and the issue of property are very important aspects of the Cypriot reunification juggernaut, but outside the scope of this chapter. There have been a number of recent publications on this issue. For an outline of the issue, see Gürel and Özersay (2006).
25 Troop numbers are estimated at between 20,000 and 40,000, depending on the source.

## Primary sources

Annan, Kofi 2004 'Report of the Secretary-General on His Mission of Good Offices in Cyprus', United Nations Document, 28 May, UN doc. S/2004/437.

de Soto, Álvaro 2004 Opening Statement and Press Conference by Secretary-General's Special Advisor on Cyprus, Ledra Palace, Nicosia, 20 April.

Drousiotis, Makarios 2009 'Fragile Structure of AKEL–DIKO Coalition Crumbles', 22 March (available online at: www.makarios.eu/cgibin/hweb?-A=3365&-V = search accessed on 15 May 2010).

Markides, Alecos 2004 Former Attorney-General of Republic of Cyprus. Interview with author, 2 July.

Member of UN core negotiating team in Cyprus 2006 Confidential interview with author.

Molyva, Demetra 2004 'Synod calls for rejection', *Cyprus Weekly*, 23–9 April.

Papadopoulos, Tassos 2004 Address to the Nation by the President of the Republic of Cyprus, 7 April.

Pfirter, Didier 2006 Legal Adviser to the UN Secretary General's Special Assistant. Interview with author, 6 October.

Plaza, Galo 1965 'Report of the United Nations Mediator Galo Plaza to the Secretary-General', UN doc. S/6253-A/6017.

'Cyprus election threatens peace plan', *BBC News*, 17 February 2003.

## Secondary sources

Bahcheli, Tozun 1990 *Greek–Turkish Relations since 1955*, Boulder, CO: Westview Press.

Bryant, Rebecca 2004 *Imagining the Modern, the Cultures of Nationalism in Cyprus*, London: I.B. Tauris and Co.

Constantinou, Costas M. 2008 'On the Cypriot States of Exception', *International Political Sociology*, 2: 145–64.

Coufoudakis, Van 1983 'Cyprus', in McHale, V. (ed.), *Political Parties of Europe*, Westport. CO: Greenwood Press, 104–33.

Güney, Aylin and Kudret Özersay[m1] 2006 'The Politics of Property in Cyprus', PRIO Report 3. Nicosia: PRIO Cyprus Centre.

Hannay, David 2005 *Cyprus: The Search for a Solution*, London: I.B. Taurus and Co.

Hitchens, Christopher 1997 *Hostage to History: Cyprus from the Ottomans to Kissinger*, London: Verso.

James, Alan 2002 *Keeping the Peace in the Cyprus Crisis of 1963–64*, Hampshire: Palgrave.

Katsiaounis, Rolandos 1996 *Labor, Society and Politics in Cyprus During the Second Half of the Nineteenth Century*, Nicosia: Cyprus Research Centre.

Ker-Lindsay, James 2009 'The Emergence of "Meditration" in International Peacemaking', *Ethnopolitics*, 8(2): 223–33

Ker-Lindsay, James and Keith Webb 2004 'Cyprus', *European Journal of Political Research*, 43: 969–79.

Kyle, Keith 2004 'A British View of the Annan Plan', *Cyprus Review*, 16(1), spring, 13–28.

Martin, Harriet 2006 *Kings of Peace, Pawns of War*, London: Continuum.

Milios, John 2007 'The Greek Nation: An Inherently Totalitarian Concept. Concerns to Be Borne in Mind During the Reconciliation Process in Cyprus', *Cyprus Review*, 19(1) spring.

Mirbagheri, Farid 1998 *Cyprus and International Peacemaking*, London: Routledge.

Müftü ler-Bac, Meltern and Güney, Aylin 2005 'The European Union and the Cyprus Problem', *Middle Eastern Studies*, 41(2): 281–93.

Nevzat, Altay 2005 *Nationalism Amongst the Turks of Cyprus: The First Wave*, Oulu: Oulu University Press.

Newman, Edward 2001 'The Most Impossible Job in the World: The Secretary-General and Cyprus', in James Ker-Lindsay and Oliver Richmond (eds.), *The Work of the UN in Cyprus: Promoting Peace and Development*, Hampshire: Palgrave.

Papadakis, Yiannis 2003 'Nation, Narrative and Commemoration: Political Ritual in Divided Cyprus', *History and Anthropology*, 14(3): 253–70.

Patrick, Richard A. 1976 *Political Geography and the Cyprus Conflict: 1963–1971*, Ontario: University of Waterloo.

Richmond, Oliver P. 1994 'Peacekeeping and Peacemaking in Cyprus 1974–1994', *Cyprus Review*, 6(2): 7–42.

—— 1998 *Mediating in Cyprus: The Cypriot Communities and the United Nations*, London: Frank Cass Publishers.

—— 2001 'UN Mediation in Cyprus, 1964–65: Setting a Precedent for Peace-making?', in James Ker-Lindsay and Oliver Richmond (eds.), *The Work of the UN in Cyprus: Promoting Peace and Development*, Hampshire: Palgrave.

Tocci, Nathalie 2004 'Reflections on Post-Referendum Cyprus', *International Spectator*, 39(3), July–September.

Tocci, Nathalie and Kovziridze, Tamara 2004 'Cyprus', in Bruno Coppieters *et al.* (eds.), *Europeanization and Conflict Resolution: Case Studies from the European Periphery*, Ghent: Ghent Academia Press.

Varnava, Andrekos and Christalla Yakinthou 2010 'Cyprus: Political Modernity and the Structures of Democracy in a Divided Island', *Oxford Handbook of Subnational Democracy*, Oxford: Oxford University Press.

Yakinthou, Christalla 2009a 'The European Union's Management of the Cyprus Conflict: System Failure or Structural Metamorphosis?', *Ethnopolitics*, September.

—— 2009b *Political Settlements in Divided Societies: Cyprus and Consociationalism*, London: Routledge.

# 14 The potency of external conflict management

## Northern Ireland

*Adrian Guelke*

At the end of the dramatic month of January 2010, the political institutions created by the Belfast and St Andrews Agreements were hanging by a thread. The negotiations among the parties were at a difficult stage and it seemed likely that the British and Irish governments would have to put forward their own plan in the expectation that the parties would acquiesce in its implementation, as they had done in the case of the St Andrews Agreement of October 2006. But if that ploy failed, resignations and new elections seemed bound to follow. However, just a week later, on 5 February, a deal, the Hillsborough Agreement, had been reached between the parties, proof of the old adage that a week is a long time in politics (Agreement at Hillsborough Castle 2010). Excited reporters described the deal as completing the peace process, with the devolution of policing and justice powers characterized as the last piece in the jigsaw (Murray Brown 2010).

The deal set out a timetable to address the issues in dispute. In accordance with this timetable a cross-community vote in the Northern Ireland Assembly to authorize the transfer of policing and justice powers took place on 9 March, with the devolution of the powers following on 12 April. Before the vote on 9 March a working group with representatives of the Democratic Unionist Party (DUP) and Sinn Féin had reached an accord on proposals to provide a way forward on the regulation of parades. The DUP had insisted that as a price for its agreement to the devolution of policing and justice powers, progress should be made toward the establishment of a new mechanism for handling parades. However, this issue remains far from resolved. In early July the Orange Order had rejected the new legislative framework for the regulation of parades that the DUP and Sinn Féin had agreed to. And the potential for contentious parades to cause unrest was underlined by the violence that occurred in Belfast at the climax of the marching season around 12 July. This did much to dampen the euphoria that had arisen as a result of the successful devolution of policing and justice powers, underscoring the endless capacity of the peace process in Northern Ireland to confound successively both pessimists and optimists. Ironically, a consequence of the stance of the Orange Order was the extension of the mandate of the Parades Commission for another year.

The issue of the devolution of policing and justice powers had been unfinished business from the St Andrews Agreement. In terms of the timetable set out then by the British and Irish governments, this was supposed to happen by May 2008. The DUP was successful in delaying matters as long as they were able to argue credibly, first, that there were financial arrangements that needed to be put in place if the devolution of these powers were not to cause budgetary difficulties and, second, that public confidence in local control of security was lacking. But these reasons for delay lost most of their force during the course of 2009. The British government agreed in October 2009 to a generous financial package to support the transfer of powers and public confidence in local control of security forces soared in the wake of Martin McGuinness's strong stand against dissident Republicans following the deaths of two soldiers and a policeman in March 2009. In fact, the primary obstacle to a deal had ceased to be about the arrangements for the devolution of justice and policing powers as such. The tangential issue of parading, especially the DUP's demand that the Parades Commission be abolished as a quid pro quo for the party's agreeing to set a date for the devolution of policing and justice powers, became the principal bone of contention between the parties during the negotiations in January 2010.

At the time of the re-establishment of the devolved government in May 2007, it had appeared that the devolution of justice and policing powers was the last issue that might capsize institutions accepted by all of Northern Ireland's significant political parties and thereby prevent the development of normal or at least routine politics. However, by the time of the Hillsborough Agreement it was apparent that without a much better working relationship between the DUP and Sinn Féin the devolved government was likely to continue to be ineffective in a number of areas, including education. The British general election of May 2010 presented an early test of the new spirit of cooperation between the DUP and Sinn Féin after the accord on policing and justice.

In the general election, the DUP faced an electoral challenge from a new anti-Agreement party, the Traditional Unionist Voice (TUV), which had emerged as a potentially major force as a consequence of the success of its leader, Jim Allister, in the elections for the European Parliament in June 2009. Peter Robinson's grip on the leadership of the DUP remained in question as a result of the scandal involving his wife, Iris, despite his resumption of the position of First Minister after he had briefly stood down as First Minister at the height of the scandal (Enright 2010). Gerry Adams's continuing leadership of Sinn Féin was also in doubt as a result of questions that have arisen about his conduct in relation to child abuse allegations involving his brother.

In the event the outcome of the elections provided the peace process with a major boost. The TUV fared poorly as did the Ulster Unionist Party (UUP), which had voted against the devolution of policing and justice powers in the Northern Ireland Assembly. Its alliance with the Conservative Party lost the party its sole MP, who won re-election as an independent. However, while DUP candidates mostly polled strongly and confounded predictions that the party's commitment to power sharing with Sinn Féin would lose the party votes, Peter Robinson lost his own seat to a member of the cross-community Alliance Party. By contrast, Adams's vote was unaffected by the issue of the behaviour of his brother.

The change of government in the United Kingdom with the establishment of a Conservative–Liberal Democrat coalition under the leadership of David Cameron presents some potential difficulties for the future. In particular, there is a danger that the Conservative party's interventions in Northern Ireland politics prior to the general election will complicate the role of the government as a conflict manager. However, paradoxically, the complete failure of the Conservative alliance with the UUP has reduced this risk considerably. Consequently, it is the coalition's economic policies that may prove the larger problem for the province. During the British election campaign Cameron had indicated that far from his wishing to exempt the province from public expenditure cuts, he viewed the large size of the public sector in Northern Ireland as a reason why it should be a prime target for cuts. This prospect needs to be seen against the background of economic recession as a consequence of the global downturn, which has had an especially severe impact on the economy of the Republic of Ireland, with spillover effects on Northern Ireland. Unless the coalition's plans in respect of Northern Ireland are radically revised, a very sharp increase in the level of unemployment in the province seems inevitable (Gordon and Rutherford 2010).

The issue of unemployment is connected to another remaining challenge to the peace process, the activities of Republican dissidents in organizations such as the Real IRA and the Continuity IRA, groups that originated from splits with the Provisional IRA. The dissidents had received massive publicity locally, nationally and globally in March 2009 when they had killed two soldiers and a police officer. The coverage helped to give credibility to their campaign to overturn the peace process and this was reflected in a boost to recruitment by the dissidents as well as an increase in the number of attacks on the security forces.

When Ian Paisley took office as First Minister, with Martin McGuinness as Deputy First Minister in 2007, it had seemed possible the conclusion of the Northern Ireland peace process was within reach and the time might soon arrive when there would no longer be any need for the British and Irish governments to continue to play the role of conflict managers. What the crisis of January 2010 demonstrated was that Anglo-Irish cooperation to underwrite political stability in Northern Ireland remains important. Just as significantly, it once again underlined that the interpretation of the political settlement in Northern Ireland as a triumph of political accommodation achieved under the mechanism of consociationalism remains an inadequate reading of what has happened.

This is not to argue that the political institutions at the heart of the settlement are not consociational. However, they are not the product of political accommodation between political elites within Northern Ireland. What might be argued is that in Northern Ireland's case political accommodation may eventually follow the effective functioning of consociational institutions. The signs of that still remain mixed. But to understand what Northern Ireland has in common with other deeply divided societies in which devices such as power sharing have been employed to address intercommunal strife, the context of the Northern Ireland problem requires some explanation.

## The context of the Northern Ireland conflict

The roots of the conflict in Northern Ireland can be traced back to the circumstances of the foundation of Northern Ireland. The creation of Northern Ireland as a separate political entity within the United Kingdom dates back to the 1920 Government of Ireland Act, which unilaterally partitioned the island of Ireland. However, the partition of Ireland on the basis of a division of six and 26 counties had been foreshadowed by the negotiations that had taken place during the First World War between the British government, Unionists and representatives of the Irish Parliamentary Party, which favoured Home Rule. In this context, Home Rule meant the devolution of power to a parliament in Dublin. The Government of Ireland Act established a parliament in Belfast to rule over the six counties of Northern Ireland. It became known as Stormont after the parliament's relocation to the Stormont estate in East Belfast in 1932.

Most of the resistance to the British government's post-war blueprint for the future of Ireland came from the Southern counties. The Government of Ireland Act provided for the establishment of a devolved parliament for the Southern twenty-six counties. However, the radicalization of opinion among Catholics reflected in the triumph of

Sinn Féin candidates across Ireland in the general election of 1918 ensured that these provisions of the Act could not be applied to the South. Violent conflict between British security forces and Irish nationalists ultimately culminated in negotiations that resulted in a treaty between the British government and Irish nationalists. This established the Irish Free State with its own different set of political institutions. One further consequence was that the Council of Ireland envisaged under the Government of Ireland Act to encourage cooperation between the parliaments in Belfast and Dublin was not established.

The terms of the Anglo-Irish Treaty setting up the Irish Free State proved contentious and divided nationalist opinion. Civil war between the treaty's supporters and opponents ensued in which the pro-treaty forces emerged victorious. A common misunderstanding is that the civil war was fought over the issue of partition. In fact, partition was already a *fait accompli* by the time of the treaty. Opponents of the treaty were more exercised over the limits on the sovereignty of the new state than over partition. Another factor reducing the salience of partition during the civil war was the treaty's provision for the establishment of a Boundary Commission to determine what the border between Northern Ireland and the new entity should be. That raised nationalist expectations that areas contiguous to the border with the Irish Free State that had nationalist majorities would be transferred to Southern rule.

In the event, these hopes were dashed. The chairman of the Boundary Commission, Justice Richard Feetham, employed the argument of economic viability to propose only very modest changes on both sides of the existing boundary. So unsatisfactory were these proposals from a Southern perspective that the Irish government quickly agreed with the Northern Ireland government that the Commission's recommendations be set aside in favour of the status quo. Unionists commonly refer to this agreement of 1925 as constituting Southern acceptance of partition. They argue that the 1937 constitution that was enacted by de Valera broke this Southern commitment to accept the border through laying claim to Northern Ireland in Articles 2 and 3 of its provisions.

The question of partition remains at the heart of the conflict in Northern Ireland. Unionists wish Northern Ireland to remain part of the United Kingdom, while nationalists wish to see the (eventual) dissolution of Northern Ireland as a political entity and the creation of a united Ireland. What gives added force to this political division is its coincidence with the sectarian divide between Protestants and Catholics. Virtually all Protestants are Unionists and most Catholics are nationalists. Thus, in a 1990 survey of over 2,000 respondents in Northern Ireland, not a single individual describing him- or herself as a Protestant supported a nationalist party, while there was a solitary Catholic supporter of the more moderate of the two main Unionist parties (Stringer and Robinson 1992, 44). The primacy of the Unionist–nationalist divide means that all proposals for the governance of Northern Ireland tend to be viewed first and foremost from the perspective of whether they seem likely advance or retard the possibility of a united Ireland.

A difficulty for Unionists and for that matter for the British government is how partition tends to be viewed in the rest of the world. There is widespread sympathy for the view that Ireland should be a single political entity. A further difficulty is that even if the principle of partition is accepted on the basis that Catholics and Protestants had different national identities (Irish and British respectively), it is hard to justify the particular border that was imposed on Ireland. On the basis of a provincial opt-out, the whole of Ulster and its nine counties should have been excluded from the Southern entity, while an opt-out on a county-by-county basis would have resulted in a four-county Northern Ireland. But the controversial implementation of partition did not create the sectarian divisions in the north-east of Ireland. In particular, Belfast was the site of sectarian riots at regular intervals through the course of the nineteenth century (Boyd 1987). At the time of partition, Protestants outnumbered Catholics by roughly two to one within the borders of Northern Ireland.

From a Unionist perspective, maintaining Protestant unity appeared to represent the safest way of ensuring the continuance of the union with the rest of the United Kingdom and this was the strategy adopted by successive Unionist governments from 1921 until the early 1960s. The consequence was a further reinforcement of the divisions between Protestants and Catholics. During the period, 1921–63, the Unionist government defeated a succession of violent challenges to its rule by the Irish Republican Army (IRA) with local security forces. Another factor also helped to keep the Irish Question out of British politics. It was a constitutional convention that anything within the remit of the parliament in Northern Ireland should not be discussed in the House of Commons at Westminster. Consequently, issues such as discrimination against Catholics did not get an airing in London. The people of Northern Ireland elected twelve representatives to the House of Commons but throughout the first forty years of Northern Ireland's existence these for the most part formed a barely noticed addition to the Conservative benches and had little impact on national politics.

Change came in the 1960s with a reformist government in Northern Ireland that led to political divisions among Protestants and that raised, but failed to satisfy, Catholic expectations. The result was increasing Catholic mobilization behind a civil rights movement pressing for an end to discrimination in imitation of the civil rights movement in the United States. A Protestant backlash and violent clashes on the streets followed. This culminated in the onset of what is known in Northern Ireland as the troubles, the term used to describe a prolonged period of violent disturbances. The troubles are generally dated from 5 October 1968 when the banning of a civil rights march by the Stormont Minister of Home Affairs led to clashes in the city of Londonderry/Derry between the demonstrators and the police. This violent breakdown of the political system preceded the deployment of British troops in aid of the civil power which followed in August 1969. It also preceded the formation of what was to become the main Republican paramilitary organization in Northern Ireland, the Provisional IRA. This was formed in December 1969. The main Loyalist paramilitary organization, the Ulster Defence Association (UDA), was formed in September 1971.

The 1970s were the most violent years of the troubles. In the early years of the troubles, the British government sought to limit its involvement to reform of the security forces and to maintaining the Unionist government while pressing it to introduce reforms. This approach failed. It led to a radicalization of Catholics who were fearful that after the limited reforms, the situation in Northern Ireland would disappear from the international limelight and they would be left to face continuing Unionist domination of the political system. Following further violence in response to the introduction of internment without trial in August 1971, the British government introduced direct rule from London in March 1972. Ironically in the light of later attitudes, it was the Unionist government's resistance to the transfer of responsibility for security to Westminster that precipitated this step.

Direct rule paved the way for a major political initiative by the British government to reshape government in Northern Ireland. This culminated in the Sunningdale Agreement of December 1973. It led to the establishment of a power-sharing government in Northern Ireland, which took office in January 1974. The experiment in power sharing lasted only five months. The Executive was brought down by a general strike by Protestant workers. The Protestant community was especially angered by the Sunningdale Agreement's provision for the establishment of a Council of Ireland. This was widely represented by opponents of the deal as a slippery slope to a united Ireland. The collapse was caused by the resignation of the Executive's Unionist members, who were responding to clear indications that the Protestant community rejected power sharing, feared the Council of Ireland and preferred the alternative of direct rule from London, as the outcome of Westminster elections in February 1974 had underlined (Bardon 1992, 706). A prolonged period of direct rule followed.

A crisis in the prisons in the early 1980s polarized opinion and led to the intervention of Sinn Féin, the political wing of the Provisional IRA, in electoral politics. The British government's response to the rise of Sinn Féin was to seek to address Catholic alienation through involving the Irish government on a consultative basis in the governance of Northern Ireland. To the fury of Unionists, in November 1985 the British government signed the Anglo-Irish Agreement with the government of the Republic of Ireland that enshrined the basis of cooperation with the Republic in an international agreement. Protests on the streets of Northern Ireland failed to bring about the demise of the Anglo-Irish Agreement. This forced Unionists to contemplate negotiations with the Social Democratic and Labour Party (SDLP) to secure its removal and helped to create the basis for talks among the constitutional parties in the early 1990s.

The talks among the constitutional parties (i.e. those parties without paramilitary connections) failed to reach agreement, but, nonetheless, provided impetus for a broader peace process. By 1992 there were signs that the Republican movement was seeking an alternative to continuance of the Provisional IRA's 'long war'. Talks between the leader of the SDLP, John Hume, and the President of Sinn Féin, Gerry Adams, prompted the British and Irish governments to issue a joint declaration in December 1993. This promised that if the Provisional IRA brought its campaign of violence permanently to an end, the way would be opened for Sinn Féin participation in negotiations on a new political dispensation for Northern Ireland. The response from the Republican movement was to seek further clarification of the two governments' declaration, but finally at the end of August 1994 the Provisional IRA announced an indefinite cessation. This was followed by a ceasefire by the main Loyalist paramilitary organizations in October 1994.

However, the paramilitary ceasefires did not lead immediately to negotiations among the parties. Indeed, the delay was a factor in the Provisional IRA's abandonment of its ceasefire in February 1996. Elections for the purpose of establishing the parties to the negotiations were held at the end of May 1996. Despite the end of the IRA ceasefire, Sinn Féin fared well in the elections to the Forum, as it was termed, though the party remained excluded from the negotiations. However, in Sinn Féin's absence, negotiations among the remaining parties made little headway. Following the election of new governments in both the UK and in the Republic of Ireland, there was a resumption of the IRA ceasefire in July 1997. This paved the way to negotiations among the parties, including Sinn Féin, but excluding two Unionist parties that left the talks on Sinn Féin's entry into the process. Ultimately, these talks led to the achievement of the Belfast Agreement – also commonly referred to as the Good Friday Agreement – on 10 April 1998.

The Belfast Agreement was endorsed by large majorities in referenda in Northern Ireland and the Republic of Ireland. However, the size of the 'Yes' vote in Northern Ireland of over 70 per cent of those voting tended to mask the fact that whereas

Catholics had voted almost unanimously for the Agreement, Protestants were evenly divided between 'Yes' and 'No'. This became evident in the voting for the Northern Ireland Assembly in June, when pro-Agreement Unionists achieved only a narrow victory over anti-Agreement Unionists. The picture was complicated by the fact that the anti-Agreement forces contained within their ranks a number of members of the Ulster Unionist Party (UUP), the leading pro-Agreement party. Henceforth, these anti-Agreement members of the UUP waged a relentless campaign against the pro-Agreement leader of the party, David Trimble.

Disagreement over the interpretation of the Belfast Agreement in relation to the decommissioning of paramilitary weapons proved an obstacle to its implementation. A devolved power-sharing government eventually came into existence in December 1999, but lasted only to February 2000 after the IRA failed to begin decommissioning. After an IRA initiative to allow inspection of some of its arms dumps, the devolved government was re-established in June 2000, but the issue of decommissioning continued to cast a shadow over its existence. However, it was other activities by the IRA and not the issue of decommissioning as such that brought the power-sharing experiment to an end in October 2002. Thus, after allegations of spying by the IRA on government, the secretary of state suspended the institutions ahead of expected Unionist resignations from the Executive over the spying scandal (Gillespie 2008, 272–5). By this time, there had been two acts of decommissioning by the IRA.

A third act of decommissioning accompanied a major effort to re-establish devolution in October 2003. The breakdown of the choreographed steps towards restoration of the power-sharing Executive helped to ensure the victory of the two radical parties on either side of the sectarian divide in the Northern Ireland Assembly elections of November 2003. But the efforts of the two governments to revive the functioning of the Agreement continued. In December 2004 they narrowly failed to secure the acceptance of the DUP and Sinn Féin for their proposals. That initiative was followed by a profound crisis in the peace process as a result of a bank robbery later that month and a murder following an argument in a bar. There were accusations of the involvement of the Provisional IRA in both events. But, paradoxically, the crisis gave impetus to the peace process by ending the procrastination of the leaders of the Republican movement over the issue of decommissioning. After the complete decommissioning of IRA weapons in September 2005, as well as efforts by the Republican movement to distance its members from criminal activities, the path was cleared for the two governments to put pressure on the Unionists to agree once more to power sharing.

This culminated in the St Andrews Agreement of 13 October 2006. The description of the document as an agreement was somewhat misleading insofar as it implied that the DUP and Sinn Féin had signed up to its terms. In truth, it was not a deal but a set of proposals put forward by the two governments with a timetable for implementation. But it was carefully calculated to secure the acquiescence of the two parties and would not have survived if it had been repudiated by either of them. However, the parties were by no means irrevocably committed to follow the two governments' wishes. In fact, modifications were made to the terms to benefit the two radical parties, including the provision that the largest party in the Assembly would be able to nominate the First Minister, regardless of whether the party was in the largest designation. What is more, it was only on 26 March 2007, the last possible date for preventing the collapse of the whole process that the DUP finally committed itself to a specific date for power sharing with Sinn Féin. Crucially, this was after the holding of elections to the Northern Ireland Assembly.

*Table 14.1* European Parliament elections, main parties' percentage of first preferences, 1979–2009

| Party | 2009 | 2004 | 1999 | 1994 | 1989 | 1984 | 1979 |
|-------|------|------|------|------|------|------|------|
| Sinn Féin | 26.0 | 26.3 | 17.3 | 9.9 | 9.1 | 13.3 | |
| DUP | 18.2 | 32.0 | 28.4 | 29.2 | 29.9 | 33.6 | 29.8 |
| UUP | 17.1† | 16.6 | 17.6 | 23.8 | 22.2 | 21.5 | 21.9 |
| SDLP | 16.2 | 15.9 | 28.1 | 28.9 | 25.5 | 22.1 | 24.6 |
| TUV | 13.7 | | | | | | |
| Alliance | 5.5 | (6.6)* | 2.1 | 4.1 | 5.2 | 5.0 | 6.8 |

*Independent supported by Alliance and other small parties.
†The UUP candidate stood in this election under the banner of Ulster Conservative and Unionist New Force (UCUNF).
*Source*: Nicholas Whyte 2009

Thus, the first election in which the DUP could be described as a pro-Agreement party was the European elections of 2009. It was also the first European Parliament election since 1979 (and the holding of the first direct elections to the European Parliament) that the DUP candidate did not head the poll in Northern Ireland (see Table 14.1).

## Actors in the conflict management process

### The local conflict parties

Northern Ireland is commonly described as a deeply divided society. Indeed, the sharpness of its divisions makes it an exemplar of the category. Emphasizing the depth of its divisions, Donald Horowitz has described Northern Ireland as a severely divided society (Horowitz 2001). There remains more room for argument about the nature of the province's divisions. In the academic literature it is most commonly described as an ethnonational cleavage, reflecting, in part, the influence of the writings of McGarry and O'Leary on Northern Ireland (for example, McGarry and O'Leary 1995). But there are some difficulties with such a description, since while it is the case now that Protestants and Unionists commonly identify themselves as British (itself an overarching category that includes, for example, the English, Scots, Welsh and Cornish) and Catholics and nationalists commonly identify themselves as Irish, this is a relatively recent development. Political fashion has followed academic usage, with Loyalist murals, in particular, asserting that nationality is at the heart of the Northern Ireland conflict. However, before the start of the troubles in the late 1960s, it was perfectly possible to assert that one was Irish, Protestant and a Unionist, just as there is no contradiction in someone today asserting that he or she is both Scottish and a Unionist. The process whereby being Irish has become synonymous with being a nationalist, committed to the ideal of a united Ireland, has been a gradual one. Alongside the rise of Britishness as more than simply a political commitment to the preservation of Northern Ireland as part of the United Kingdom, the notion of the Celts as an overarching ethnic identity, bringing together the Irish, Scots, Welsh, Cornish and Bretons, has lost any political force.

An alternative to nationality is the description of the conflict as one between Protestants and Catholics. However, objections can also be made to the straightforward description of the conflict in Northern Ireland as a sectarian one. The most obvious is that the conflict has little to do with the different religious beliefs of Protestants and

Catholics. The even simpler description of the conflict as a communal one has the virtue that it transverses different time periods. It also gets to the heart of the matter, the existence of a deterrence relationship between two communities in the north-east of Ireland that pre-dated partition. Analysing the failure of efforts to achieve normalization of relations between Protestants and Catholics in Ulster in the 1850s, Frank Wright wrote the following: 'once violence became more reciprocal and less one sided, people were in danger of finding their identity determined by those whose violence they feared most' (Wright 1996, 242). And the separation of the communities in Northern Ireland remains underpinned by the fear of the violence of the other side. While the peace process has greatly reduced the level of intercommunal violence, there have continued to be sufficient episodes of such violence to ensure that the threat of violence has far from disappeared as a factor in people's identities or behaviour, including their assumptions about what places constitute safe areas. Twenty years ago, John Whyte presciently wrote that if the political parties by some miracle achieved an accommodation on the constitutional question, security issues were likely to loom large as a problem in the normalization of relations in the society (John Whyte 1990, 88). It is striking that it has been security issues that have caused most of the difficulties in the peace process, including the question of paramilitary disarmament, policing, criminality and parades.

There is a small minority of people living in Northern Ireland who do not consider themselves to be part of either of the province's two communities, but at the same time there has been a process of absorption into the two communities of immigrants who have not been either Protestants or Catholics in a religious sense. There are also some mixed residential areas in generally the most affluent parts of the province in which attachment to either of the two communities is slight, providing some space for political parties that cross the main communal fault-line. The most important of these for the last forty years has been the Alliance Party. However, as the figures for Assembly elections given in Table 14.2 underline, most of the electorate have voted either for one of the Unionist parties or for one of the nationalist parties, with political competition taking place within each community and not between them.

In this context, the role played by the two governments has been hugely significant. Indeed, in retrospect, the turning point in the Northern Ireland conflict was the Anglo-Irish Agreement of November 1985 that institutionalized cooperation over Northern Ireland between the British and Irish governments. It paved the way to their joint promotion of the peace process in the 1990s. But a downside of what might be called the

*Table 14.2* Assembly elections of 2007, 2003 and 1998: results for five main parties in terms of percentage of first-preference votes and seats*

| Party | Vote 2007 | Seats 2007 | Vote 2003 | Seats 2003 | Vote 1998 | Seats 1998 |
|---|---|---|---|---|---|---|
| DUP | 30.1 | 36 | 25.71 | 30 | 18.01 | 20 |
| Sinn Féin | 26.2 | 28 | 23.52 | 24 | 17.63 | 18 |
| UUP | 14.9 | 18 | 22.68 | 27 | 21.25 | 28 |
| SDLP | 15.2 | 16 | 16.99 | 18 | 21.96 | 24 |
| Alliance | 5.2 | 7 | 3.67 | 6 | 6.50 | 6 |

*Elections to the Northern Ireland Assembly took place in 18 six-member constituencies, with MLAs elected on the basis of the single transferable vote system of proportional representation.

*Source*: Nicholas Whyte 2009

two governments' coercive diplomacy has been a lack of commitment by the Unionist parties in Northern Ireland to the principles of deals they have accepted on the basis that rejection would have left them in a worse position.

A further reason why the role of the two governments has been so important is that there is more to the Northern Ireland problem than the province's internal divisions. The problem has a significant external dimension that stems from Northern Ireland's lack of international legitimacy as a political entity. The problematic nature of Northern Ireland's status as conditionally part of the United Kingdom explains why successive British governments have been more or less compelled to seek the support of the Irish government in their efforts to address the conflict. In short, underpinning the Irish dimension has been British acceptance of the proposition that a settlement without such an element would be unlikely to secure the support of the international community.

## Primary mediators

Prior to the troubles, the British and Irish governments appeared to be the main antagonists, so that the problem of Northern Ireland could be presented as caused by either British imperialism or Irish irredentism. But from a relatively early juncture during the troubles, the two governments cooperated to seek a resolution of the conflict within Northern Ireland and showed a willingness to adjust their own positions so as to facilitate the process. Thus, it is reasonable to regard the British and Irish governments as the primary mediators in the conflict. A factor that encouraged the cooperation of the two states was their common membership of the European Community from the beginning of 1973. From outside of Britain and Ireland and Europe, the other most important actors to contribute to the peace process were the governments of the United States and of South Africa. President Clinton and former Senator George Mitchell both played an important role in the negotiations that resulted in the Belfast Agreement (Mitchell 1999). However, it should be stressed that American involvement generally enjoyed the support of both the British and Irish governments, particularly after the changes of government in Britain and the Republic in 1997. What was dubbed the Mitchell draft in the negotiations on the Belfast Agreement was the handiwork of the two governments to the extent that they made it clear to him what could and could not be changed (O'Kane 2007, 152–3). But if Mitchell's role in writing the Belfast Agreement has been overstated, the importance of his review of the Agreement in 1999 has been undervalued.

Another instance in which American influence was exaggerated was in relation to the declaration of the first IRA ceasefire. It stemmed in part from the media's misinterpretation of the implications of the outcome of Sinn Féin's conference in July 1994 on the two governments' joint declaration of December 1993. The conference's rejection of the governments' terms was widely but wrongly viewed as ruling out a ceasefire. The consequence was that when an American delegation to the party revived speculation that there would be a ceasefire, it was mistakenly credited with changing the minds of the leadership. Nonetheless, Sinn Féin leaders clearly placed considerable weight on American support in the negotiations on the Belfast Agreement and subsequently on its implementation. A feature of American involvement in the peace process has been its consistency under three Presidents. It was the one aspect of Clinton's foreign policy that George W. Bush did not seek to change.

The South African government has also played a useful role in assisting the peace process. The prestige of the African National Congress (ANC) was used by Sinn Féin leaders to help sell the Belfast Agreement to the rank and file and most particularly to imprisoned members of the IRA. And South African mediation was even more significant in the crisis in 2000 when the institutions were suspended as a result of the failure of the IRA to embark upon decommissioning following Trimble's agreement the previous year to devolution (McDonald 2000). The Republican movement recovered from this debacle by agreeing to international inspection of a number of its arms dumps as a confidence-building measure. The South African role in this initiative was underscored by the choice of the ANC's Cyril Ramaphosa as one of the inspectors.

## The structure of the conflict management process

The Northern Irish peace process was launched by the joint declaration of the British and the Irish governments in December 1993 and then underwritten by the announcement of both Republican and Loyalist paramilitary ceasefires in 1994. It owed much to the spirit of the times. Particularly important were the examples of the South African transition culminating in the inauguration of Nelson Mandela as President of a non-racial South Africa and the Oslo peace process in the Middle East underscored by the handshake between Rabin and Arafat on the lawn of the White House. If violent conflicts as intractable as those in South Africa and Israel/Palestine could be resolved through negotiations, surely, so the argument went, the politicians in Britain and Ireland had a duty to initiate negotiations on the Irish Question.

Although Northern Ireland had not become an arena of superpower rivalries, it was still affected by post-Cold War political changes. This was because an assumption of the Provisional IRA – and a justification for its strategy of a 'long war' – was the belief that the British government was determined to maintain a presence in Ireland for strategic and economic reasons. The end of the Cold War made it possible both for the British government to declare that it had no selfish strategic or economic interest in Northern Ireland and for this to be accepted by the Republican movement. The priority given by the British government to sustaining the paramilitary ceasefires on both sides of the sectarian divide dictated an inclusive approach to negotiations at the outset of the peace process. This was most evident in the extraordinary lengths the government went to in devising rules for the election of the Northern Ireland Forum in 1996 that would secure the success of small Loyalist political parties linked to the major Loyalist paramilitary organizations. The strategy followed by the two governments was to be as inclusive as possible of the different shades of opinion in Northern Ireland and consequently, all-party or multiparty forums were the norm. However, the extent to which all the parties that wished to contribute had an input into the process varied from negotiation to negotiation and how far the governments paid attention to the views of the parties other than the major ones in each community remains a matter of considerable contention and dispute.

In the process that followed, the British and Irish governments played the leading role at all the critical stages of the negotiations. This was the case leading up to the Belfast Agreement and in the subsequent crises over its implementation, then in the putting together of the St Andrews Agreement and in the 2010 crisis over its implementation. While ideas that originated from the parties in Northern Ireland were certainly included in the settlement, progress was rarely achieved in the absence of high-level representation of the two governments. The single significant exception to this were the negotiations that took place in terms of George Mitchell's review of the operation of the Belfast Agreement in 1999 that persuaded Trimble to agree to devolution in advance of

IRA decommissioning. Nonetheless, the process structure is most accurately described as management by the two governments.

## Settlement design

The Northern Ireland political settlement is embodied in two documents, the Belfast Agreement of April 1998 (or less formally known as the Good Friday Agreement) and the St Andrews Agreement of October 2006. The Hillsborough Agreement of February 2009 might now be added to the earlier documents. However, much the most important of these documents is the Belfast Agreement and that is reflected in a jocular description of the St Andrews Agreement as 'the Good Friday Agreement in a kilt' (Wilford 2008, 67–8). But note also needs to be taken of the legislation implementing these agreements. Thus, in the case of the St Andrews Agreement the legislation introduced a new rule of very considerable political importance. It provided (though in a curiously roundabout manner) that the largest party in the Assembly would nominate the First Minister, regardless of whether the party belonged to the largest designation in the Assembly or not (Part 2, Section 16C [6] of Northern Ireland [St Andrews Agreement] Act 2006). This means that there might be a Sinn Féin First Minister if the Unionist vote is divided among three parties.

Two principles have underpinned the design of Northern Ireland's political institutions, proportionality and parallel consent. The first is reflected in the use of the d'Hondt mechanism for the choice of ministers in the Executive. There are eleven ministers in addition to the First Minister and the Deputy First Minister, who jointly occupy the Office of First Minister and Deputy First Minister (OFMDFM). The parties nominate to their choice of ministries in sequence according to their strength in the Assembly. However, this procedure did not apply to the initial choice of a justice minister in 2010 (the eleventh minister). This was on the basis of a cross-community vote. The second principle is embodied in the concept that important decisions of the devolved government should be acceptable to a majority of both communities as far as that is practicable, a notion that has underpinned the British government's approach to the governance of Northern Ireland since the early 1970s. The system of designation of members of the Northern Ireland Assembly as Unionist, nationalist or other provides the basis for the operationalization of parallel consent, though this is qualified slightly by the availability of an alternative procedure employing a weighted majority of 60 per cent of members of the Assembly present and voting (and requiring the support of at least 40 per cent of members in both the Unionist and nationalist designations). Further, important decisions include matters that may be deemed such by at least thirty members of the Assembly.

The devolved institutions form Strand One of a three-stranded settlement. The Irish dimension is enshrined in the settlement in the form of a North–South Ministerial Council overseeing functional cooperation between Northern Ireland and the Republic of Ireland in a number of areas. The Belfast Agreement did not lay down the areas in which there should be cross-border cooperation or which of the possible areas should be given priority. The Annex to the section on Strand Two simply stated that the areas 'may include the following' (Belfast Agreement 1998) and then listed twelve possible fields for such cooperation. A further set of negotiations took place in December 1998 to determine the details. It was agreed then that there would be six implementation bodies responsible for inland waterways, food safety, trade and business development, special European

Union programmes, the Irish and Ulster Scots languages, and aquacultural and marine matters. It was also agreed that the six areas of further cooperation would be transport, agriculture, education, health, environment and tourism. A safeguard for Unionists was that it was stated in the Belfast Agreement that the functioning of the North–South Ministerial Council would be mutually interdependent with that of the Northern Ireland Assembly.

Unionist fears that functional cooperation between Northern Ireland and the Republic of Ireland might be used to facilitate progress towards a united Ireland had once made this aspect of a negotiated political settlement highly controversial and problematic. But once Unionist fears that such cooperation might be used as a lever to ease Northern Ireland out of the United Kingdom had been allayed, their objections to such cooperation largely fell away. As a consequence, the operation of Strand Two, though affected by crises in the implementation of the Belfast Agreement, has hitherto not been a major source of disagreement among the parties and is no longer the centre of political attention. A further factor in reducing Unionist concerns about the consequences of North–South cooperation was the Agreement's encouragement of other ties under Strand Three. An innovative aspect of the Belfast Agreement was its establishment of East–West cooperation among the different governments across Britain and Ireland along the lines of the Nordic Council. A merit of the British Irish Council was that it was acceptable to nationalists while it helped to reassure Unionists that the effect of the Belfast Agreement would not be to distance them further from the rest of the United Kingdom.

## The current status of conflict management in Northern Ireland

There is a basic flaw in interpretations of the Northern Ireland peace process that treat the success of the process as grounded in consociationalism. Thus, the focus of the writings of McGarry and O'Leary has been on the consociational nature of the settlement, most notably in the volume edited by Rupert Taylor (McGarry and O'Leary 2009, 25). A weakness of this approach is simply this. Consociational institutions have functioned for a fraction of the period of the peace process and have rarely done so effectively for any significant period of time or in the absence of threats from one of the parties participating in them to bring them down. A more realistic view is that Northern Ireland's consociational institutions are the product of its peace process and, more particularly, of conflict management by the two governments that initiated and have sustained the peace process.

If Northern Ireland's settlement is best viewed through the prism of conflict management, this does not necessarily mean that what has been achieved in Northern Ireland has little relevance to the resolution of other conflicts or is insignificant. It has most relevance to conflicts taking place within particular regions, such as the long-running conflict in Kashmir. However, it might be argued that the increased propensity of the Western powers to involve themselves in the internal governance of at least nominally independent states has widened the number of situations to which mechanisms of the Northern Ireland peace process might be applied. Indeed, the point might be made that the consociational model is particularly attractive to external parties seeking to influence political developments, since its institutionalization of differences facilitates the management of these sorts of conflicts by external parties. And consociationalism can be regarded as a particularly potent tool of external conflict management. It is a somewhat ironic outcome for a system of government devised originally to embody the politics of accommodation in small states seeking to preserve their independence.

Northern Ireland's settlement provides interesting lessons for other divided societies, but these lessons require careful interpretation. The success of the province's peace process owes a great deal to cooperation between the British and Irish governments. They have sustained the process in often difficult circumstances when support for the political settlement they largely created has waned. At times, it seemed likely that the settlement would collapse altogether but their efforts prevented failure. It remains to be seen whether the political institutions, which no longer face any short-term threat to their survival, are able to enhance cooperation across Northern Ireland's communal divide and thereby promote political accommodation and ultimately reconciliation.

## References

*Agreement at Hillsborough Castle* 2010 (5 February), Belfast.

Bardon, Jonathan 1992 *A History of Ulster*, Belfast: Blackstaff Press.

Belfast Agreement 1998 (available at: www.nio.gov.uk/agreement.pdf); also reproduced with other relevant documents of the Irish peace process in Cox *et al.* (2006).

Boyd, Andrew 1987 *Holy War in Belfast*, 3rd edn. Belfast: Pretani Press.

Cox, Michael, Guelke, Adrian and Stephen, Fiona (eds.) 2006 *A Farewell to Arms? Beyond the Good Friday Agreement*, Manchester: Manchester University Press.

Enright, Anne 2010 'Diary', *London Review of Books*, 32(2), 28 January.

Gillespie, Gordon 2008 *Years of Darkness: The Troubles Remembered*, Dublin: Gill and Macmillan.

Good Friday Agreement, see Belfast Agreement.

Gordon, David and Rutherford, Adrian 2010 'Friendless Ulster has most to lose in cutbacks', *Belfast Telegraph*, 6 August.

Horowitz, Donald L. 2001 'The Northern Ireland Agreement: Clear, Consociational, and Risky', in John McGarry (ed.), *Northern Ireland and the Divided World: Post-Agreement Northern Ireland in Comparative Perspective*, Oxford: Oxford University Press, 89–108.

McDonald, Henry 2000 'ANC brokered IRA peace offer', *Observer*, 14 May.

McGarry, John and O'Leary, Brendan 1995 *Explaining Northern Ireland: Broken Images*, Oxford: Blackwell.

—— 2009 'Power Shared after the Deaths of Thousands', in Rupert Taylor (ed.), *Consociational Theory: McGarry and O'Leary and the Northern Ireland Conflict*, Routledge: London.

Mitchell, George J. 1999 *Making Peace*, London: W. Heinemann.

Murray Brown, John 2010 'Deal on policing hailed as last piece of jigsaw', *Financial Times*, 6/7 February.

Northern Ireland (St Andrews Agreement) Act 2006 (available online at: www.niassembly.gov.uk/transitional/info_office/Act.pdf).

O'Kane, Eamonn 2007 *Britain, Ireland and Northern Ireland since 1960: The Totality of Relationships*, Routledge: London.

St Andrews Agreement 2006 (available online at: www.nio.gov.uk/st_andrews_agreement.pdf).

Stringer, Peter and Robinson, Gillian (eds.) 1992 *Social Attitudes in Northern Ireland: The Second Report*, Belfast: Blackstaff Press.

Whyte, John 1990 *Interpreting Northern Ireland*, Oxford: Clarendon.

Whyte, Nicholas 2009 and ongoing *Elections Northern Ireland* (available at: www.ark.ac.uk/elections).

Wilford, Rick 2008 'Northern Ireland: St Andrews – the Long Good Friday Agreement', in Jonathan Bradbury (ed.), *Devolution, Regionalism and Regional Development: The UK Experience*, London: Routledge, 67–93.

Wright, Frank 1996 *Two Lands on One Soil: Ulster Politics before Home Rule*, Dublin: Gill and MacMillan.

# Index

Added to a page number 't' denotes a table and 'n' denotes a note.

CPSIA information can be obtained at www.ICGtesting.com
Printed in the USA
BVOW02s0240041214

377449BV00008B/17/P